Harvard Studies in East Asian Law 6

China's Practice of International Law: Some Case Studies

CHINA'S PRACTICE OF INTERNATIONAL LAW: SOME CASE STUDIES

Edited by Jerome Alan Cohen

With Contributions by

Philippe Ardant
Hungdah Chiu
Jerome Alan Cohen
G. I. A. D. Draper
George Ginsburgs
Gene T. Hsiao
James C. Hsiung
Ko Swan Sik
Shao-chuan Leng
Carl Pinkele
Gilbert P. Verbit
Byron S. J. Weng

Harvard University Press
Cambridge, Massachusetts
1972

Library of Congress Catalog Card Number 72–80656
SBN 674–11975–4
Printed in the United States of America

To the memory of
John M. H. Lindbeck
who did so much to help so
many undertake the study
of contemporary China

Acknowledgments

The panel on China and World Order of the American Society of International Law is grateful to the A.S.I.L. and to the Ford Foundation for their support of its work. We especially appreciate the wise counsel of Stephen Schwebel, Executive Director of the A.S.I.L., and the administrative assistance of Richard Edwards. We also wish to thank Lois Dougan Tretiak for her valuable aid in editing this volume for publication and Mrs. Bertha Ezell for her skillful typing of the manuscript.

Contents

Abbreviations

AJIL *American Journal of International Law*

ASIL American Society of International Law

JMJP *Jen-min jih-pao* (People's daily)

NCNA New China News Agency

NRC *Nieuwe Rotterdamse Courant*

PR *Peking Review*

SCMP *Survey of China Mainland Press.* United States Consulate General, Hong Kong

SDD *Sbornik deistvuyushchikh dogovorov, soglashenii i konventsii, zaklyuchennykh SSSR s inostrannymi gosudarstvami* (Collection of treaties, agreements, and conventions concluded by the USSR with foreign states and in force)

TYC *Chung-hua jen-min kung-ho-kuo t'iao-yüeh chi* (Collection of treaties of the People's Republic of China; Peking)

UNTS *United Nations Treaty Series*

WCC *Chung-hua jen-min kung-ho-kuo tui-wai kuan-hsi wen-chien chi* (Collection of documents relating to the foreign relations of the People's Republic of China; Peking)

Introduction

Jerome Alan Cohen

The People's Republic of China (PRC) was proclaimed on October 1, 1949. China's size and importance, the controversial nature of the revolutionary regime and the continuing existence of its rival and predecessor, the Republic of China (ROC), on the island refuge of Taiwan immediately confronted the PRC and the international system with a host of fascinating and difficult legal problems. The foreign ministries of the world eagerly awaited the new Communist elite's response to these problems.

What would be the PRC's attitude toward its recognition by other governments? Upon what terms would it agree to establish diplomatic relations? Would Peking respect the traditional privileges and immunities of diplomats? In the absence of diplomatic relations, would it permit trade and other contacts, and, if so, how were these unofficial relations to be structured? In concluding agreements, would Chinese Communist negotiators behave in a significantly different manner from their predecessors? Would Peking regard itself as bound by the treaty commitments of previous Chinese governments? How would it deal with the many boundary problems that had plagued its predecessors? Would the Communists prove to be more vigorous than their Nationalist rivals in seeking to protect the overseas Chinese? What position would the PRC adopt toward participation in international organizations, especially the United Nations?

Answers to these questions and others were soon forthcoming. The realities of existence compelled the People's Republic to begin to develop positions on virtually the entire spectrum of issues compendiously described as public international law. Yet, during the PRC's first two decades, this record was relatively neglected by American legal scholarship. Moreover, the references to Peking's views of international law that one found in the popular journals and press of this country were usually of a sweeping, ideological nature. Such crude generalizations were often based upon allegations made by the executive or legislative branches of the United States government, which continued to support the PRC's Nationalist rival in the Chinese civil war. These allegations were, of course, liberally supplemented by materials emanating from Nationalist China and from organizations in this country that disseminated its views.

In the 1960s, as the Sino-Soviet dispute became more public and vitriolic, Soviet propaganda agencies did their utmost to reinforce the image of a China that rejects all the rules of international society. And, during the Great Proletarian Cultural Revolution of 1966–1969, the PRC, by openly flouting long-accepted principles of international law —including principles that it had often observed in calmer days— seemed bent upon providing anti-Maoist propagandists with more than enough words and deeds to document their claims.

In February 1967, at the height of the Cultural Revolution, the American Society of International Law organized a study panel of legal scholars, social scientists, lawyers, and government officials to consider problems relating to "China and International Order." Although the time hardly seemed propitious, the belief that underlay organization of this group was that China would eventually emerge from its national paroxysm and again demonstrate serious interest in participating in the world community and that at that time it would be vital to have developed a sophisticated understanding of China's theory and practice of international law.

In view of the fact that introductory surveys of this subject had recently been launched,[1] the panel agreed that the next desirable step would be to carry out detailed studies of the PRC's position on many different aspects of international law. Several surveys of China's treaty practice were known to be under way;[2] it seemed essential to stimulate

1. See James C. Hsiung, *Law and Policy in China's Foreign Relations* (New York: Columbia University Press, 1972); and Jerome Alan Cohen and Hungdah Chiu, *People's China and International Law* (Cambridge, Mass.: Harvard University Press, forthcoming).

2. See Luke T. Lee, *China and International Agreements* (Leyden: A. W. Sijthoff, 1969); Douglas M. Johnston and Hungdah Chiu, *Agreements of the People's Republic of China, 1949–1967: A Calendar* (Cambridge, Mass.: Harvard University Press, 1968); Hungdah Chiu, *The People's Republic of China and the*

research on other important questions as well. Accordingly, the panel commissioned a series of modest case studies. Some of these were to analyze the PRC's use of international law in dealing with a particular country or international organization. Others were to focus on the PRC's treatment of specific legal problems in its relations with all countries. The object of both kinds of case study was to obtain new information, new insights, and a broader, more balanced and nuanced perception of Chinese practice than has previously been available in the polemical atmosphere of Sino-American relations.

This volume presents the fruit of this effort. Four of its essays deal with basic problems of Peking's international conduct: recognition and the establishment of diplomatic relations, the regulation of foreign diplomats serving in China, manipulation of the concept of "unequal treaties," and the PRC's conditions for participation in international organizations. The other six essays concern certain legal problems that have arisen in China's relations with a given country or international organization. All of these case studies contribute to our understanding of the extent to which China's new governing elite perceives and evaluates events in terms of international law, actually invokes international law, modifies accepted interpretations, and practices what it preaches.

It is neither necessary nor feasible to summarize the contents of these essays here. Yet it may prove useful to touch upon some of their highlights and to introduce the authors.

In a comprehensive analysis of twenty years of China's recognition practice, Professor James C. Hsiung of the Department of Politics of New York University distinguishes essentially two periods: the first decade after 1949, when Peking displayed a "self-oriented" perspective that regarded recognition questions almost exclusively from the point of view of its desire for recognition by other states; and the second decade, when Peking became increasingly preoccupied with developing an "outward-directed" perspective capable of coping with the problems of recognizing a host of newly independent states. Theory and practice forged during the first period had to be adapted to the needs of the second. During the earlier period, the PRC, like many other states, viewed recognition as a factual matter that acknowledged a

---

Law of Treaties (Cambridge, Mass.: Harvard University Press, 1972); and Douglas M. Johnston, *China's Treaty Practice* (Cambridge, Mass.: Harvard University Press, forthcoming).

government's effective control over the territory of a state and that did not imply approval of the way in which the new government came to power, of its sociopolitical system, or of its policies. Beginning in 1958, however, the PRC occasionally departed from these tenets; for example, it prematurely granted recognition to the Algerian provisional government three days after that revolutionary regime was formed in exile, and because of policy disapproval, it subsequently rejected recognition of the long-established regime in Israel.

Professor Hsiung makes a stimulating comparison between the evolution of the PRC's recognition policy and the similar but more gradual shift in American recognition policy from the Jeffersonian de factoism of our then still revolutionary government to the gradual adoption of Wilsonian criteria of political acceptability. Of great practical interest is this essay's discussion of the distinction that the PRC makes between the unilateral act of recognition and the subsequent bilateral process of negotiating the establishment of diplomatic relations, a process in which the PRC has insisted that the other state sever its relations with, and withdraw recognition from, "the Kuomintang (Nationalist) reactionary clique."

The first part of the study by Dr. Ko Swan Sik, head of the Department of Public International Law of the Inter-University Institute of International Law in the Hague, traces the course of Sino-Dutch negotiations concerning the establishment of diplomatic relations from the time of Dutch recognition in March 1950 until agreement was reached in November 1954. Like Professor Hsiung, Dr. Ko notes that it is unusual, but hardly inconsistent with international law, for a new government to seek to impose conditions upon the establishment of relations with the preexisting government of another state rather than vice versa. Yet the case of the Netherlands reveals that, although Peking long insisted that the Hague not only sever diplomatic relations with Taipei but also vote to seat Peking as the exclusive representative of China in the UN, Peking finally agreed to exchange permanent diplomatic representatives without winning a Dutch concession on the UN question. It should be noted, however, that Peking limited the level of bilateral diplomatic representation to that of chargé d'affaires and also restricted trade contacts on this ground. From the point of view of other states that may wish to move toward establishing relations with the PRC, perhaps the most potentially instructive aspect of this Dutch experience is the legal status and competence extended to the Dutch representative at the negotiations, who was permitted to reside in China for over four years as an ad hoc negotiator and who sometimes was allowed to take up matters that had no direct connection with his designated task.

The second part of Dr. Ko's essay analyzes the legal implications of a bizarre 1966 episode that began when a member of a Chincse delegation to an international welding conference in the Hague was found seriously injured outside his residence in the Chinese mission. He was taken to a hospital, but, with the apparent participation of a PRC diplomat, was then spirited back to the mission, where he soon died. This "abduction," Dr. Ko finds, did not reflect any general Chinese policy of attempting to enforce an extraterritorial jurisdiction over nationals but was, rather, an act of political expediency, one that violated the Netherlands' territorial sovereignty. Dr. Ko similarly characterizes the subsequent PRC refusal to permit Dutch judicial authorities to question the other members of the visiting delegation, who held service passports, about the circumstances of their colleague's death; although Peking at one point branded the investigation "illegal," it made no effort to justify this claim by arguing, for example, that it had given diplomatic asylum to the delegates. Finally, according to Dr. Ko, the PRC violated traditional standards of diplomatic immunity when, in retaliation for the Dutch refusal to permit the delegates to leave the country until they were questioned, it prohibited the Dutch chargé d'affaires in Peking from leaving China. Dr. Ko recognizes, however, that the refusal to issue an exit permit to the Dutch diplomat, when viewed together with later similar sanctions against certain other foreign diplomats, may suggest support for a novel view that authorizes reprisals against diplomats. Indeed, he points out, one cannot exclude the possibility that both China's effort to endow its nondiplomatic delegation with de facto diplomatic immunity and its treatment of the Dutch chargé as though he were a nondiplomatic officer suggest that the ideology and collectivist state structure of the new China favor the idea of indivisibility of state and individual and blur the distinction between diplomats and other state officials.

The comprehensive analysis of China's recent diplomatic practice by Professor Philippe Ardant of the Faculty of Law and Economics at Poitiers is far less tentative than the previous essay in asserting that the PRC has developed an original, coherent conception of diplomatic relations. According to Professor Ardant, the Chinese believe that their diplomacy is an instrument of world revolution and it therefore cannot conform to the same rules as Western or even Soviet diplomacy. To be sure, China has not formally renounced the traditional rules of the game and occasionally purports to measure its own conduct by those standards. But, Professor Ardant maintains, this is only lip service rendered when politically convenient, and a survey of practice verifies the impression that the PRC has no intention of submitting to the norms now embodied in the 1961 Vienna Convention on Diplomatic Relations. Nevertheless, he points out, Peking expects nonrevolutionary states to abide by those norms. Indeed, it has even articulated a theory to justify this position. In lieu of the customary bilateral reciprocity according to which state A treats the diplomats of state B in the same manner as state B treats the diplomats of state A, it claims that reciprocity need only be geographic—that is, state A must treat the diplomats of state B the same as it does other foreign diplomats within its territory, while state B is free to apply a different regimen to the diplomats of state A so long as it does not discriminate between them and other foreign diplomats within its territory. This theory permits PRC representatives abroad to enjoy the benefits of the traditional rules while their own government subjects foreign diplomats in China to a much more confining standard. Yet, Professor Ardant charges, in practice the PRC fails to adhere to its nondiscriminatory standard, and the degree of diplomatic protection enjoyed under China's rules actually varies with the degree of cordiality currently prevailing between the PRC and the government that a diplomat represents.

Professor Ardant concedes that his sharply etched portrait is importantly influenced by China's behavior during the Cultural Revolution, the earliest phase of which he was able to observe firsthand as a member of the French mission in Peking. But he maintains that the excesses of that period reflected only "a particularly vigorous formulation" of a revolutionary outlook that antedates the Cultural Revolution. In his view, the motivating force behind the conception that PRC diplomats are "proletarian fighters" is not only Chinese Communist ideology but also Chinese history. The imperial Chinese tradition offers the contemporary elite little past experience for the guidance of relations between equal states, and the century of semicolonial humiliation that preceded the founding of the PRC continues to fuel the exaggerated resentment and hypersensitivity that mark Peking's post-1949 conduct.

If states that have established diplomatic relations with the People's Republic sometimes experience extraordinary difficulties, the challenge is even greater for states that seek contacts with it in the absence of diplomatic relations. By focusing on the fourth Sino-Japanese trade agreement, the essay by Gene T. Hsiao, Professor of Government at Southern Illinois University (Edwardsville), illustrates the problems that Japan has encountered in devising mutually acceptable arrangements for doing business with the PRC while at the same time maintaining official relations with its rival on Taiwan. Most of these problems have derived from China's determination to shape the arrangements in such a way as to give them as much official coloration as possible. Thus Hsiao describes Peking's efforts to endow the agreement between ostensibly nongovernmental associations with treaty character and to confer most of the attributes of diplomatic immunity upon its trade representatives and its trade office. On the most controversial question that plagued the agreement, he concludes that international law fails to support the PRC's assertion of a "right" to fly its national flag from its trade office in Japan and to demand that the Japanese government accord the PRC flag the same degree of protection as the flags of recognized governments. Although one has to be cautious in drawing inferences about Peking's general attitude toward public international law on the basis of its commercial dealings, Hsiao's analysis of the combination of tactics it employed during both the negotiation and enforcement stages of the agreement—demonstrating generosity, offering temptations and applying pressures—plainly has broad implications.

In the contentious atmosphere of Sino-American relations and in the wake of the Cultural Revolution, it is all too easy to overlook the fact that not all states have had serious disputes with the PRC. Although minor frictions involving international legal questions occasionally crop up in every bilateral relationship, China's interaction with a number of states, such as Ceylon, Nepal, and Tanzania, by and large has demonstrated its ability to conduct the customary range of political and economic contacts within the accepted rules of the game. The significance of Gilbert P. Verbit's personal memoir about Tanzania's negotiation of a cultural exchange agreement with the People's Republic derives precisely from the fact that there was nothing significant about that experience. China's application of international law when concluding that agreement could not be distinguished from the customary behavior of many other states of various political persuasions. The agreement reached did not even contain the reference to "the five principles of peaceful coexistence" that was so often a hallmark of China's legal commitments of the early 1960s. Moreover, there was nothing unusual about the manner in which Peking carried out its obligations under the agreement, and Professor Verbit, of Boston University Law School, suggests that this happy experience encouraged Tanzania to enter into subsequent commitments with China.

By focusing on the Sino-Soviet border controversy, George Ginsburgs and Carl Pinkele of the Graduate Faculty of the New School for Social Research present quite a different view of the process by which the PRC negotiates international agreements and the role that international law plays in the settlement of disputes between the two great Communist powers. The authors trace the development of the border problem from the earliest days of Sino-Soviet relations through the lengthy, unsuccessful negotiations held in Peking in 1964. Their essay is a comprehensive effort to place China's invocation of international law in the dynamic political and ideological context in which it occurred. They find that, during the period studied, both parties belatedly, sparingly, and quietly resorted to international law, being reluctant both to diminish prospects for compromise by rigidifying their positions and to apply ideologically impure bourgeois legal strictures in lieu of the higher ethical principles that are supposed to prevail among "socialist" states.

Messrs. Ginsburgs and Pinkele shed light upon China's legal position regarding all of its borders and indicate the political factors that led the PRC to make boundary treaties with its less powerful neighbors but not with the USSR or India. They conclude that the border controversy was not a major cause of the Sino-Soviet rift, that the substantive territorial questions themselves were susceptible of settlement, and that the difficulties lay primarily at the ideological and psychological level. China demanded, as the prerequisite of an agreement, that there be formal renegotiation of the entire boundary rather than merely certain portions of it; that the existing boundary, while constituting the basis for settlement, be acknowledged as the product of the "unequal treaties" imposed by tzarist Russia upon China during the nineteenth century; and that the USSR withdraw from territory that the Chinese claim it occupies in violation of the "unequal treaties." By acceding to these conditions, the Soviet Union might well have obtained a favorable border settlement, but at the cost of what it regarded as an unacceptable loss of "face."

Hungdah Chiu's essay, which details the twentieth century Chinese development of the concept of unequal treaties, helps us to appreciate the PRC's determination to eradicate the remaining symbols of foreign domination of China by terminating all of the old boundary treaties and by substituting in their stead new treaties that are concluded on the basis of equality. His comparison of Nationalist and Communist views of unequal treaties points out the greater flexibility and breadth with which the PRC manipulates the concept, declaring treaties "unequal" according to political expediency without ascribing any definite content to the term. Moreover, Professor Chiu, a member of the Law Faculty of National Chengchi University in Taipei, emphasizes the difference in principle that exists between Nationalist and Communist Chinese writers concerning the legal implications of branding a treaty "unequal." The former have not regarded unequal treaties as void *ab initio* but as subject to abrogation or revision because of changed circumstances. The latter, on the other hand, have claimed that unequal treaties violate international law and are without legal validity. Yet Professor Chiu's essay reveals that this distinction has not always been observed in practice. For example, as the study of the Sino-Soviet border dispute also confirms, despite the PRC's claim that boundary treaties imposed during the nineteenth century were "unequal," its position has been to respect them pending peaceful renegotiation rather than to regard them as void.

How has the People's Republic dealt with treaties to which it has freely acceded? Professor Shao-chuan Leng of the University of Virginia and I have analyzed the PRC's treatment of the Geneva Convention Relative to the Protection of Civilian Persons in Time of War during the course of Peking's efforts to protect persons of Chinese descent who had been interned or detained in India as a consequence of the major hostilities that occurred in 1962 over the Sino-Indian border dispute. China protested vigorously that India's actions violated international law, but it did so in general terms that neither affirmatively invoked the Civilian Convention nor carefully articulated other bases of legal support for its charges. As is common in diplomatic practice, the task was left to its publicists. Although under the Convention, China's challenge to the mass internment of all persons of Chinese descent residing in certain strategic areas of India presents a close question during the period of hostilities, surely it is difficult to justify India's continuing internment of hundreds of Chinese years after hostilities had ceased. More dubious was the PRC's claim that, because diplomatic relations were maintained during the conflict, international law required India to permit Chinese diplomats the same degree of information about and access to confined nationals as they would enjoy in peacetime. Of course, just as the credibility of India's defense of internment weakened with the passage of time after hostilities ceased, so too did its justification of its refusal to permit China ordinary diplomatic protection of its nationals.

China's challenge to visits to the internment camp that the International Committee of the Red Cross (ICRC) conducted without China's consent reflects a misunderstanding of the important difference between the ICRC's traditional independent activities undertaken in behalf of humanity, as recognized by article 10 of the Convention, and the additional activities that the ICRC might undertake under article 11 as a substitute for a protecting power. It also rests upon a misinterpretation of the qualification, "subject to the consent of the Parties to the conflict concerned," that article 10 imposes upon the ICRC's independent activities. The PRC implicitly asserted, contrary to the Convention's preparatory work and long-standing practice, that this phrase includes all parties to the conflict, including the power of origin of protected persons, rather than merely those parties whose cooperation is necessary to carry out the contemplated humanitarian activity. In light of Peking's opposition to the right of "nonforcible repatriation" for prisoners of war upon which the United Nations insisted in Korea, it is interesting to note that, in the Indian case, probably because the provisions of the Civilian Convention differ from those of the Prisoner of War Convention, the PRC recognized the right of interned civilians to voluntary repatriation.

China sought to makes its policy toward Indian nationals in China appear consistent with its demands for protection of Chinese nationals in India. It repeatedly emphasized the fact that it had not interned or detained Indian civilians on account of the conflict. It claimed to allow India the customary peacetime rights to protect nationals detained on criminal charges, and it also claimed to allow Indian diplomats and Indian Red Cross representatives access to Indians who were being held as prisoners of war. In practice, however, Peking restricted New Delhi's access to a detained criminal accused, and it never permitted Indian representatives to visit the prisoners of war.

In seeking to protect persons of Chinese descent in India, China simply assumed that even those who had acquired Indian nationality were Chinese nationals, and its claims for protection made no distinction between dual nationals and persons who enjoyed only Chinese nationality.

The final two essays of the volume concern China's attitude toward international organizations. Byron Weng, of the Political Science Department of Wright State University in Dayton, Ohio, surveys the conditions that Peking attached to its participation in both intergovernmental and nongovernmental organizations during the first two decades of its existence. He notes four factors that the PRC generally took into account: the extent to which the ideological orientation of a given organization was deemed to be "correct," the nonparticipation in the organization of the Republic of China, the prevailing political climate within the organization, and the degree to which the organization provided institutional safeguards to protect the interests of minority states. Weng analyzes the extraordinary prerequisites for Peking's entry into the UN that were laid down by its then Foreign Minister, Ch'en Yi, in September 1965. He concludes that these extreme demands were not serious conditions but expressed the PRC's lack of interest in entering the UN at that time; when after the Cultural Revolution Peking began to display renewed interest in the UN, these demands were quietly abandoned and were forgotten by the time the General Assembly voted to replace Taipei's delegation with Peking's.

Colonel G. I. A. D. Draper, of the School of European Studies of the University of Sussex, nicely complements the previous essay by providing an in-depth study of the PRC and the International Red Cross. This is a lively account of Peking's participation in the 1952 and 1957 international conferences of the Red Cross and of the dramatic manner in which its delegates walked out of the latter conference after the nongovernmental international organization had bungled its handling of the delicate "two China" problem. Although this incident put an end to the PRC's attendance at major Red Cross conferences, the author notes its contribution to subsequent meetings of other Red Cross institutions. He also describes the frustrations that the International Committee of the Red Cross experienced in vainly seeking to persuade China—during the Korean war, the Tibetan revolt of 1958–1959, and the Sino-Indian conflict—to permit it to carry out humanitarian activities on Chinese territory. Also galling was Peking's refusal to agree to ICRC investigation of atrocity charges that Peking itself had made to the ICRC against United Nations forces in Korea. Colonel Draper attributes the ICRC's difficulties with China to a fundamental clash of principles, the PRC being committed to an ideology that refuses to believe in the impartiality and neutrality of any international organization. Yet he concedes the strength of Peking's argument against the ICRC's exclusively Swiss composition and suggests consideration of reforms that would more truly internationalize that institution while retaining as many advantages as possible of the existing situation.

This collection of essays merely samples contemporary China's practice of international law. Plainly, many other detailed studies must be completed before one can generalize with confidence. Yet the contributions to this volume do suggest certain tentative conclusions. At a minimum, it seems clear that the People's Republic has not overtly rejected the entire fabric of the international law that had developed as of the time when communism triumphed in China in 1949. Although usually reluctant to invoke international law, the PRC has often at least given lip service to its interpretation of customary and conventional norms when nonlegal techniques of persuasion and dispute resolution have proven inadequate. There have been many occasions when Peking has purported to perceive and evaluate events in terms of broadly accepted international legal principles. Moreover, the PRC has not only demanded that the elites of other states adhere to those principles in practice but has also frequently claimed that its own conduct conforms to them.

Nevertheless, these essays further suggest that, although the PRC has not articulated a comprehensive new theory of international law, it has explicitly or implicitly rejected or sought to modify accepted principles in important respects and has maintained an innovative, distinctive outlook. We should also note that, whether the views which it has expressed on any specific question be characterized as traditional, reformist, or revolutionary, Peking has in a number of instances failed to practice what it has preached.

None of these conclusions should startle students of law and politics. The evolution of Soviet attitudes toward international law had previously demonstrated that a vigorous challenger of the status quo often will find itself in a minority position and, despite initial hostility toward international law, will be tempted to resort to traditional doctrines in order to safeguard state sovereignty against the incursions of the majority. Moreover, no state can do without the cooperation of other states, and contacts such as trade and cultural exchange require some common institutional and legal framework. In addition, revolutionary governments, like other governments, strive for power and influence in the world community and therefore often make their claims in the manner that is most likely to be persuasive to other nation-states. This is especially true when, as in the PRC's case, the revolutionary government continues to be engaged in a contest for legitimacy with the government that it seeks to overthrow. Furthermore, because reciprocity is the basis of international law, no government can long expect its legal claims to be honored unless it demonstrates a corresponding willingness to honor the similar claims of its foreign counterparts. For these reasons it is not surprising that to a considerable extent the PRC's articulation of its foreign policies has taken account of, and claimed consistency with, basic principles of international law.

On the other hand, it would be surprising if the PRC did not make some distinctive impact upon international law in view of its Marxist-Leninist-Maoist ideology of struggle against imperialism; the fierce nationalism that derives from China's bitter heritage of foreign exploitation; the totalitarian order, "socialist transformation" of the economy, and Cultural Revolution that have been instituted internally; the continuing civil war with the Nationalist forces; and the PRC's long-standing exclusion from many international organizations and bilateral diplomatic relationships.

Finally, in light of the record of other nation-states, it would also be surprising if the People's Republic did not occasionally succumb to the pressures of political expediency and in practice ignore even the rules of the game as it ordinarily interprets them.

1 / China's Recognition Practice and Its Implications in International Law

James C. Hsiung

THE PROBLEM OF UNIVERSALITY

In view of the current ideological and cultural disunity of mankind, many questions concerning the "universality" of international law have been raised. For example, should a newcomer with a totally different ideological and cultural background be considered an "outlaw," as the Soviet Union was once viewed, because it is strange to the traditional (Europocentric) international society and its law?[1] Or, conversely, should the validity and desirability of the law that has grown out of the traditional Western value system be reviewed in light of the new demands and challenges inherent in the rapid changes caused by ideological and cultural diversification?[2] While these debates are still

1. The Soviet Union was characterized as an "outlaw state" by a leading Western authority. See Herbert W. Briggs, *The Law of Nations*, 2nd ed. (New York: Appleton-Century-Crofts, 1952), p. 870.

2. This question has been raised by several eminent scholars, e.g., Wolfgang Friedmann, *The Changing Structure of International Law* (New York: Columbia University Press, 1964); Rosalyn Higgins, *Conflict of Interests: International Law in a Divided World* (London: Bodley Head, 1965); Oliver J. Lissitzyn, *International Law Today and Tomorrow* (Dobbs Ferry, N.Y.: Oceana, 1966); B.V.A. Roling, *International Law in an Expanded World* (Amsterdam: Djambatan, 1960); and John N. Hazard, "A Pragmatic View of the New International Law," American Society of International Law *Proceedings* (1963), pp. 79–91. See also F.S.C. Northrop, "Naturalistic and Cultural Foundations for a More Effective International Law," *Yale Law Journal* 59:1430–1450 (1950) and *The Taming of Nations* (New York: Macmillan, 1952); J.J.G. Syatauw, *Some Newly Established Asian States and the Development of International Law* (The Hague: Nijhoff, 1961); Edward McWhinney, *Peaceful Coexistence and Soviet-Western International Law* (Leyden: A.W. Sijthoff, 1964); McWhinney, "The 'New' Countries and the 'New' International Law," *AJIL* 60:1–33 (1966); John N. Hazard, "Codifying Peaceful Coexistence," *AJIL* 55:109 (1961) and "New Personalities to Create New Law," *AJIL* 58:952 (1964); and Richard A. Falk, "Revolutionary Nations and the Quality

unsettled—and unsettling—the People's Republic of China (PRC) has often been cited as a potential challenger to established international law.[3] The PRC's attitudes toward and practice of international law have engaged the attention of a few scholars in the West, but any conclusive findings must await the availability of more empirical information.[4] The dilemma is that, until Communist China participates more widely in international life, evaluation of its attitudes and practice cannot be definitive; yet the uncertainty of the Chinese Communist position regarding international commitments, including those concerning the maintenance of world peace and security, has in large measure hampered the full absorption of the PRC into the international community.

---

of International Legal Order," in Morton A. Kaplan, ed., *The Revolution in World Politics* (New York: John Wiley, 1962), pp. 310–331.

3. Richard L. Walker, *The Continuing Struggle: Communist China and the Free World* (New York: Athene, 1958), p. 92; H. Arthur Steiner, "Communist China in the World Community," *International Conciliation* 533:394–399 (May 1961). India in 1963 accused the PRC of being "the first state which has defied all rules of international law and international behavior after the Second World War." The Indian Embassy in Peking, "Chinese Aggression and International Law," *India Calling*, April 1963, cited in a PRC note of protest to the Indian Embassy dated June 3, 1963, and reproduced in Indian Ministry of External Affairs, *White Paper, No. 9* (1963), p. 165. Similar charges were made in US Department of State, *The Conduct of Communist China*, prepared for the House Committee on Foreign Affairs, 88th Congress, 1st Session (Washington, D.C.: Government Printing Office, 1963) and Department of State, *US Policy on Non-Recognition of Communist China* (1958).

4. See, for instance, Jean Beauté, *La République populaire de Chine et le droit international* (Paris: Pedone, 1964); Hungdah Chiu, "Communist China's Attitude Toward International Law," *AJIL* 60:245 (1966); "Certain Legal Aspects of Communist China's Treaty Practice," ASIL *Proceedings* (1967), pp. 117–126; Jerome Alan Cohen, "Chinese Attitudes Toward International Law—and Our Own," ASIL *Proceedings* (1967), pp. 108–116; and R. Randle Edwards, "The Attitude of the People's Republic of China Toward International Law and the United Nations," *Papers on China* 17:235–271 (1963), (East Asian Research Center, Harvard University); Douglas M. Johnston, "Treaty Analysis and Communist China," ASIL *Proceedings* (1967), pp. 126–135; Shao-chuan Leng, "Communist China's Position on Nuclear Arms Control," *Virginia Journal of International Law* 7:101 (1966); Luke Lee, "Treaty Relations of the People's Republic of China: A Study of Compliance," *University of Pennsylvania Law Review* 116:244 (1967); and Tang Tsou, "Mao Tse-tung and Peaceful Coexistence," *Orbis* 8:36 (1964). See also Carl Q. Christol, "Communist China and International Law—Strategy and Tactics," *Western Political Quarterly* 21:456–467 (1968); George Ginsburgs and Carl Pinkele, "The Genesis of the Territorial Issue in the Sino-Soviet Dialogue," Chapter 6 of this volume; and James C. Hsiung, "Communist China's Conception of World Public Order: An Attitudinal and Pragmatic Analysis of Some Basic Issues of International Law" (Ph.D. dissertation, Columbia University, 1967), a revised and expanded version of which will be published in book form, entitled *Law and Policy in China's Foreign Relations*, under the auspices of the East Asian Institute, Columbia University, Spring 1972.

What is more frustrating in the current study of the PRC's international behavior as it bears on international law is that, caught uncomfortably between ideological commitment and pragmatic prudence, Chinese practice is at times conflicting. Perhaps for this reason Communist China's jurists hold different views on the universal applicability of international law.[5] The complexity of the problem cautions against bold conclusions drawn exclusively from studies of Peking's ideological militancy without regard to its more pragmatic actions. The Cultural Revolution further complicates an appraisal of Peking's thinking regarding international law. Logical assumptions from the Maoist militancy point in one direction, while the reported PRC feelers for concluding a "peaceful coexistence" agreement with the United States,[6] however propagandistic in nature, would counsel greater caution against premature conclusions.

In the face of all these uncertainties, complicated by the Chinese Communists' ambivalence on the matter, what one might do is to focus on a few selected areas where empirical data are available for analysis. If any general patterns of practice can be identified to support the assumption of a body of coherent attitudes in Peking's thinking on international law, the findings will provide at least a background against which future trends can be evaluated. In the present study, I have chosen Communist China's practice in diplomatic recognition over the past two decades. Before explaining my reasons for choosing this subject matter, I shall first dwell briefly on the nature of law in the rapidly and vastly changing international community.

It can hardly be denied that law is not a "body of rules," as it was once thought to be, but a process of decision-making involving the conveyance (or preclusion) of "consensus and expectations."[7] In a

5. Chiu, "Communist China's Attitude," pp. 251–257; Hsiung, "Communist China's Conception of World Public Order," chap. II.

6. *The New York Times* (Nov. 27, 1968), p. 1.

7. Lissitzyn, *International Law*, p. 36. Resting the ultimate basis of general international law upon "general consensus and expectations of states" is an expansion of the traditional precept of *opinio juris sive necessitatis*. The difficulties of ascertaining the existence of *opinio juris*, that is, the conviction that a conduct is required or permitted by international law, are patent in a fast-changing world in the nuclear age. The new precept is broader in its application and considers "custom" or "general practice" as but one form of evidence of "consensus and expectations." Whereas the traditional view considers that customary international law is created by uniformities in the *actual conduct* of many states accompanied by the presence of *opinio juris*, the new thesis makes it possible to accept norms created by other forms of communication. These include even the verbal form of communication among others, so long as they create expectations and, hence, reliance by other states. *Cf.* B. Cheng, "United Nations Resolutions on Outer Space: 'Instant' International Customary Law?" *Indian Journal of International Law* 5:23 (1965).

world facing rapid and kaleidoscopic changes in technology as well as ideological-cultural tensions, such conveyance of *opinio juris* (consensus and expectations) is the ultimate basis of general international law, if it is to continue to respond to new challenges and new demands. The importance of considering the practice of states is not that it in itself is the ultimate basis of international law, but that it is substantive evidence of a general consensus or expectation accepted or acceptable as law. Conversely, dissent or change of consensus is an indicator that a certain norm is not supported by universal consensus, although it would be impossible to measure precisely how strong a dissent must be (that is, supported by how many states) before an existing norm is changed, or precisely when a rejected norm ceases to exist. Another intricate question that cannot be answered with precision is: How does dissent or change of consensus, if supported by a growing number of states, bring about a new norm or a revision and do so without violating the existing law before the change becomes definitive? Nevertheless, the discovery of dissent or change of consensus at least indicates a possible trend toward change.

A meaningful study of PRC practice points to such questions as: In what specific ways and for what reasons does it give (or withhold) its share of consensus to certain "hard-core" norms of international law?[8] Does the People's Republic purposely acquiesce in certain norms or, conversely, indicate its rejection thereof? How does it espouse norms of its own advocacy (*de lege ferenda*)? How does its practice measure up to norms that it supports?

The present study will focus on PRC recognition practice and, in its course, have occasion to entertain at least some of the other questions.

Numerous studies have been done on whether or not the PRC should be recognized.[9] Yet, to the best of my knowledge, no serious study has been made on how the PRC treats recognition of it by other states,

8. For the idea of a "hard core" of widely applied norms, see Richard A. Falk, "The Adequacy of Contemporary Theories of International Law—Gaps in Legal Thinking," *Virginia Law Review* 50:240 (1964).

9. Robert Newman, *Recognition of Communist China* (New York: Macmillan, 1961); G. Fitzmaurice, "Chinese Representation in the U.N.," *Yearbook of World Affairs 1952* (London), pp. 36–55; Quincy Wright, "The Status of Communist China," *Journal of International Affairs* (Columbia University) 11:171–189 (1957); Herbert Briggs, "Chinese Recognition in the U.N.," *International Organization* 6:192–209 (1952); Charles G. Fenwick, "The Recognition of the Communist Government of China," *AJIL* 47:658–661 (1953); L. C. Green, "The Recognition of Communist China," *International Reporter* 3 (1952); D. P. O'Connell, "Status of Formosa and the Chinese Recognition Problem," *AJIL* 50:405–416 (1956); Pitman B. Potter, "Communist China," *AJIL* 50:417–418 (1956).

how it recognizes other states, what doctrine it espouses or can be inferred from its practice, and so forth. There is more information available on the PRC's recognition practice than on other questions. One can use not only Chinese Communist sources but also materials obtainable from states having relations or contacts with Peking. Though PRC sources reveal very little about Peking's juristic thinking, when properly analyzed they offer a relatively coherent picture of Chinese Communist recognition practice. Some doctrinal assumptions can also be deduced and corroborated or supplemented by outside sources.[10]

As my ultimate purpose is to ascertain the PRC's attitude, I have used the original Chinese sources as much as possible, so as to probe the true intent and thinking of PRC leaders, especially where subtle nuances are involved. It is, for example, from a careful examination of the original Chinese communications to foreign governments that I have discovered that PRC recognition practice has undergone three distinct stages heretofore unnoticed.

Recognition is usually a first step toward diplomatic relations and, in the present ideologically divided world, it may even lead to a modus vivendi with an entity having a totally different social system. From the granting or denial of recognition, the use of recognition for political purposes, and the peculiar meanings attached to recognition, one can infer much about a state's foreign policy outlook in a given stage. A study of PRC recognition practice could thus reveal something larger than the immediate issue at hand. Though it is, strictly speaking, not within the purview of the present essay to survey Peking's foreign policy or world view, such ultimate interest is not precluded.

No system of law can function efficiently if it is not clear who are recognized as its subjects, entitled to the rights, and bound by the obligations which it prescribes. Although an entity answering the general definition of a sovereign state (for instance, possessing a people, located in a defined territory, and effectively controlled by an independent authority) would appear entitled to acceptance by the world community as a sovereign state, it nevertheless cannot function effectively under international law in relation to states that do not recognize its existence or that of its government.

The discrepancy between a fact-in-itself and a fact-in-relation-to-others has given rise to conflicting theories of recognition: the declara-

10. See, for example, K. P. Misra, *India's Policy of Recognition of States and Governments* (Bombay: Allied, 1966), p. 35.

tory and the constitutive. Some jurists, such as Sir Hirsch Lauterpacht, have attempted to compromise the two theories by making recognition constitutive but stipulating that existing states are under a legal obligation to recognize an entity which answers the definition of a sovereign state.[11] The use of de jure and de facto recognition in state practices is a compromise intended to resolve the dilemma.

In historical development, recognition as a legal institution has gained increasing importance with the proliferation of states and advancement of modern technology, which have resulted in what one author has called the "horizontal" and "vertical" expansion of international law.[12] The question of diplomatic recognition did not receive much attention from the earlier writers on international law, such as Grotius and Pufendorf. Although Europe from as early as the seventeenth century more than once had faced the problem of new states and new governments, the founders of modern international law showed no more than tangential interest in the subject.[13] In the nineteenth century, with changes in the international personality of countries and the entry of a number of new states, including those in Latin America, international society became less homogeneous than the former Europocentric community. In 1856, for instance, Turkey was, by the Treaty of Paris, "admitted to the benefits of the public law and the concert of Europe." The admission of a number of non-Western states thrust to the fore the question of increasing diplomatic recognition. By the end of the nineteenth century, recognition had received so much attention as to prompt James Lorimer to call it "the basis of international law."[14]

Most of the states coming to maturity in the twentieth century have cultural and ideological backgrounds totally different from the "older" (Western) states. They pose a serious challenge to the original European-defined value system and the international law derived from it. In the second half of this century sharp differences have emerged over the recognition of Israel and the People's Republic of China. The latter's recognition by France in 1964 made the world's headlines. James Brierly's remark in 1951 that "recognition has probably been more dis-

11. Sir Hirsch Lauterpacht, *Recognition in International Law* (Cambridge, Eng.: Cambridge University Press, 1947).

12. Refer to Friedmann, *The Changing Structure,* for the idea of such expansion.

13. Refer to J. J. Lader-Lederer, "Recognition—a Historical Stocktaking," *Nordisk tidsskrift for international ret* 27:64–92, 117–142 (1957).

14. James Lorimer, "La Doctrine de la reconnaissance," *Revue de droit international* 16:333 (1884).

cussed among international lawyers in recent years than any other part of the international legal system,"[15] seems still valid today.

I must begin my analysis with a note of caution. With very few exceptions, PRC writers seldom explicitly discuss the *legal* implications of recognition. Besides, because of Peking's relatively limited contacts with foreign countries, there have not yet been enough occasions for contesting the legality of recognition or nonrecognition in the domestic tribunals of Communist China. Even when some suits involving foreign nations have come up, few scholars outside of China have known about them. Under these circumstances, one must speculate on the possible PRC position on certain questions, such as de jure and de facto recognition, and to focus more specifically on the *political* underpinnings of its practice. Silence does not mean that the problems do not exist.

In order not to lose sight of either the historical evolution of PRC recognition practice or the legal and political issues surrounding it, the following discussion is arranged first chronologically and then topically.

THE EVOLUTION OF PRC RECOGNITION PRACTICE

The Initial Period (1949–1955)

One of the first acts of the PRC upon assumption of power on October 1, 1949, was to announce its birth to foreign governments. As a revolutionary regime, its anxiety for diplomatic recognition can be easily understood. In a proclamation, Mao Tse-tung announced to the world that the new regime in Peking "[is] the *sole legal government* representing the entire [Chinese] nation . . . [and is] willing to establish diplomatic relations with the government of any country which is willing to abide by the principles of equality, mutual benefit, and mutual respect for territorial sovereignty."[16] (Emphasis added.) Chou En-lai, Premier and concurrently Foreign Minister, in a letter of transmittal to foreign countries, stressed the need for diplomatic ties.[17] From the wording in Chou's letter and the subsequent responses, it appears that at least each of the diplomatic missions accredited to

15. James Brierly's "Forward," in Ti-chiang Ch'en, *The International Law of Recognition* (London: Stevens, 1951), p. xi.

16. Text in *WCC 1949–1950*, vol. I (1957), p. 3. Unless the original sources are in English, or otherwise noted, all translations are mine.

17. *Ibid.*, p. 5.

the Nationalist government in Nanking received a copy of the notification.

Although recognition was obviously very much in the minds of the PRC leaders, the official note shunned the word altogether. Instead, it addressed itself to the desire for entry into diplomatic relations. A few questions immediately come to mind: Does this omission imply that the PRC leaders were unaware of recognition, or that they confused recognition with diplomatic relations? If the omission was deliberate, what were the reasons? From a study of Peking's official communications with foreign governments, I have reached the following findings:

1. The PRC did not seem to be unaware of recognition, although it was not explicitly mentioned in Peking's notification of October 1, 1949, or in subsequent outgoing communications until at least the end of 1955. One notable exception can be mentioned. The Soviet Union was the first to respond to the PRC message, but, like all other socialist states (except the Democratic Republic of Vietnam),[18] it did not *expressly* recognize the PRC but simply stated a desire to establish diplomatic relations. The Soviet note, dated October 2, 1949, reads in part:

> Having considered the request of the Central People's Government of China, the Soviet Government, prompted by the unswerving determination to maintain friendly relations with the Chinese people, and confident that the Central People's Government of China is the expression of the will of the overwhelming majority of the Chinese people, informs you that it *has decided to establish diplomatic relations* between the Soviet Union and the Chinese People's Republic and to exchange Ambassadors.[19] (Emphasis added.)

In his acknowledgment, Chou En-lai specifically thanked the Soviet government for being "the first friendly state to *recognize* the People's Republic of China."[20] (Emphasis added.) This was possibly the only instance in which an *implied* recognition was explicitly acknowledged by Peking, but I think it sufficient to indicate an awareness of the legal nature and implications of recognition. Under international law, as a

18. After its formation, the Democratic Republic of Vietnam on January 15, 1950, sent a note to the PRC, expressly extending "recognition" and requesting the establishment of diplomatic relations. See note 42 below.

19. *U.S.S.R. Foreign Policy, 1949* (Moscow: Gospolitizdat, 1953), p. 171, quoted in Academy of Sciences of the USSR, Institute of Law, *International Law* (Moscow, 1961), p. 119. The Chinese translation of the note is in *WCC 1949–1950*, vol. I (1957), p. 6.

20. Chou's reply to Gromyko, the Soviet Foreign Minister, *WCC 1949–1950*, vol. I (1957), pp. 5–6.

classic writer put it, "recognition is not necessarily express, it may be implied."[21] The prevailing view is that, while recognition cannot be accomplished by inference only,[22] it is essentially a matter of intention.[23] The Soviet desire for diplomatic relations and exchange of ambassadors clearly conveyed an intention to recognize the PRC. This was further supported by the Soviet acceptance of the PRC as the representative of the "will" of the "overwhelming majority of the Chinese people" (pending its complete takeover of the whole mainland). Premier Chou quite correctly inferred recognition from the Soviet actions. Unlike its official communications, PRC literature published for "internal" consumption, such as the *Jen-min shou-ts'e* (People's handbook), has always used the term "recognition" freely when listing countries that have recognized the PRC.

2. The PRC, nevertheless, did seem to play down recognition, at least in its official notes during 1949–1955. There may be a number of reasons for this deemphasis. First, it was not impossible that the experience of the "phantom Republic"[24] of 1912 was in the minds of Mao Tse-tung and other PRC leaders in 1949. Foreign powers had allegedly manipulated the promise of recognition to exact political concessions from the young republic. PRC literature is often acrimonious about this.[25] The three principles laid down by Mao on October 1, 1949—"equality, mutual benefit, and mutual respect for territorial sovereignty"—could reflect an apprehension that foreign powers might repeat the game of wringing political concessions out of recognition. This apprehension probably explained why Peking played down recognition and also insisted on the minimum conditions for entry into diplomatic relations.

Soviet influence may also have been responsible for Peking's lack of emphasis on recognition per se. In the Soviet view, recognition simply *declares* the existence of the government of a new state; its more sub-

21. John Bassett Moore, *A Digest of International Law* (Washington, D.C.: US Government Printing Office, 1906), vol. I, p. 73.

22. US Secretary of State Colby to the US Chargé d'Affaires in Mexico Summerlin, May 25, 1920, *Foreign Relations* 3:167 (1920), cited in Briggs, *The Law of Nations*, p. 126.

23. Green H. Hackworth, *A Digest of International Law* (Washington, D.C.: US Government Printing Office, 1940), vol. I, p. 166.

24. The term is borrowed from Lucian Pye, *The Spirit of Chinese Politics* (Cambridge, Mass.: M.I.T. Press, 1968), pp. 3 and 166.

25. K'ung Meng, "A Critique of the Bourgeois International Law Regarding 'Subjects of International Law' and Theories of Recognition by States," *Kuo-chi wen-t'i yen-chiu* (Studies in international problems) 2 (1960); English translation by JPRS, no. 3453:32–44 (June 27, 1960).

stantive meaning lies in the establishment of diplomatic relations. A Soviet textbook on international law makes the following characterization of diplomatic recognition:

> By recognition in International Law we mean a legal act by which one State or a group of States *declares* the character and scope of their relations with the government of a new State as an International Person. Such a declaration is customarily accompanied by an expression of the desire to establish diplomatic relations and exchange representatives. *It is in the establishment of diplomatic relations* which facilitate cooperation between States, *that the practical meaning of recognition above all consists.*[26] (Emphasis added.)

This "declaratory" view assigns less significance to recognition than would the "constitutive" school, but nevertheless accepts recognition as an institution of international law. The PRC seemed to follow this view except that during 1949–1955 it placed even greater emphasis on the establishment of diplomatic relations.

A potent reason for deemphasis of recognition was the "two Chinas" dilemma, which became increasingly obvious as time went on. Peking was obviously apprehensive that if it forced the issue many states might recognize both regimes, possibly one de jure and the other de facto. That situation would only petrify the "two Chinas" impasse. By skirting recognition per se and focusing on diplomatic relations, Peking could win more friends among the uncommitted nations both because it effectively ruled the mainland and because it could offer much in trade. This was probably the least dangerous way to function internationally, leaving the legal status of the "two Chinas" unsettled. And it is hardly contestable under international law that the maintenance of effective diplomatic relations is a semblance of de jure recognition. Peking was so preoccupied with diplomatic relations that it was not much interested in mere recognition by another state if it did not have a concommitant interest in establishing diplomatic relations. When Israel and Afghanistan on January 9 and 12, 1950, respectively, recognized the PRC without mention of any intention regarding diplomatic ties, Peking's response was lukewarm at best, though diplomatically adequate. It merely thanked the Israeli and Afghan governments for the "decision taken in regard of the government of the People's Republic of China."[27] (PRC attitudes toward Israel will be discussed in another context.)

In PRC parlance, entry into diplomatic relations had a peculiar twist.

26. Academy of Sciences of the USSR, *International Law,* p. 117.
27. *WCC 1949–1950,* vol. I (1957), pp. 22–24. Emphasis added.

First of all, it meant that the recognizing state must sever its diplomatic relations with the Republic of China on Taiwan or, if it maintained no such ties, promise never to do so. For example, Chou En-lai stated in his December 18, 1949, reply to a Burmese notification of recognition, which also proposed the exchange of diplomatic envoys:

The Central People's Government of the People's Republic of China is willing to establish diplomatic relations between the People's Republic of China and the Union of Burma and exchange diplomatic envoys, on the condition that your government *severs its relations with the remnants of the Kuomintang reactionary clique.*[28] (Emphasis added.)

From Peking's point of view, severance of diplomatic relations with the Nationalist government also meant the withdrawal of recognition from it. In a note on April 4, 1950, the PRC Foreign Ministry referred specifically to an oral assurance by the Netherlands government that, along with the latter's hope for establishing diplomatic relations with Peking, it would terminate its relations theretofore maintained with the Nationalist Chinese.[29] During the PRC–Pakistan negotiations on the establishment of diplomatic relations, the Pakistani government, on January 29, 1950, explicitly informed Peking that it had "formally withdrawn recognition from the Chinese Kuomintang government based on Taiwan."[30]

Besides, a foreign government having diplomatic relations with Peking was expected to support the PRC's exclusive right to represent China in the United Nations and in international relations at large. ("Exclusive" means, inter alia, the expulsion of the Nationalist Chinese representatives from all organs of the UN.) In the initial months of its existence, the Peking government was known to circulate a uniform questionnaire which asked governments that maintained diplomatic relations with it to comply with two cardinal conditions: severance of relations with the Nationalists and support of the PRC as the sole legitimate government of China.[31] To ensure that both this set of conditions and the triad of "equality, mutual benefit, and mutual respect for territorial sovereignty" would be respected, Peking entered into detailed negotiations with each recognizing state prior to the formal establish-

28. *Ibid.*, p. 17. The same condition was insisted upon by the PRC vis-à-vis Norway (p. 20), Sweden (p. 25), and Switzerland (p. 29).
29. *Ibid.*, p. 30.
30. *Ibid.*, p. 28.
31. Refer to Ko Swan Sik, "The Establishment of Diplomatic Relations and the Scope of Diplomatic Immunity: The Dutch Experience with China," chapter 2 of this volume.

ment of diplomatic relations.[32] Though we have no detailed information in all cases, we know at least that the reluctance of the Netherlands government to support Peking's claims to exclusive representation in the United Nations was responsible for a suspension of negotiations between 1950 and 1954. The subsequent PRC reluctance to expand diplomatic relations beyond the chargé d'affaires level was in part attributed by the Dutch Foreign Minister to this factor.[33]

What became clear is that the PRC during the years 1949–1955 reserved the right to accept or reject diplomatic relations with a recognizing state, depending upon the success or failure of the ad hoc negotiations. Such negotiations usually followed recognition by a foreign state; and the results were, as a rule, embodied in a "joint communiqué." The only exceptions were: (a) when the recognizing state was from the Communist bloc; (b) when a state merely recognized Peking but professed no interest in diplomatic relations;[34] and (c) possibly when a package negotiation (including both recognition and the terms for diplomatic ties) had preceded the announcement of a state's recognition of the PRC.[35] The practice of ad hoc negotiations has continued beyond 1960.[36] While a government is under no obligation in international law to accept diplomatic relations with a recognizing state or government,

32. In the cases of Britain, Norway, Switzerland, and the Netherlands, for example, when each had notified Peking that a chargé d'affaires had been appointed, the PRC did not accept him as such but as an ad hoc negotiator for the specific purpose of negotiating in Peking the terms for the establishment of diplomatic relations. The same applied in the cases of Norway and Pakistan after they had respectively appointed a minister and a special envoy. The appointees were in most cases already in Nanking, where they had been accredited to the Nationalist Chinese government until October 1, 1949. See *WCC 1949–1950*, vol. I (1957), pp. 19, 22, 26–27, 29, 30.

33. Ko Swan Sik, "The Dutch Experience with China."

34. As in the cases of Israel and Afghanistan. See *WCC 1949–1950*, vol. I (1957), pp. 22–24.

35. Although I presume this to be true, very few cases can be cited in this category. Most probably Indonesia, with which the PRC on March 28, 1950, decided to establish diplomatic relations, is one example in point. In a notification on that date, the PRC informed the new Indonesian government of its decision, presumably as a result of prior negotiations. No separate joint communiqué regarding the establishment of diplomatic relations, as is commonly found in most other instances, is known to exist. *WCC 1949–1950*, vol. I (1957), pp. 31–32.

36. For example, after recognizing (expressly) the Republic of Mali on October 17, 1960, the PRC entered into negotiations with its government on the establishment of diplomatic relations between them. On October 27, a joint communiqué, issued simultaneously in both capitals, announced that the two governments had decided to exchange ambassadors. In fact, the same procedure of ad hoc negotiations was followed in the establishment of diplomatic relations between the PRC and Cuba in 1960 (joint communiqué on September 28, 1960). *WCC 1960*, vol. VII (1962), pp. 294, 306, 253.

attaching conditions to the establishment of diplomatic relations with a recognizing state, as the PRC did and still does, is rather uncommon in the practice of other states. In the existing practice, if any conditions are attached at the time recognition is extended, they usually originate from the grantor state, rather than the reverse. This PRC practice might indicate the relative importance that its leaders place on recognition and diplomatic relations, which are closely related but nevertheless separate and different in nature and in significance.

Still another reason why Peking played down recognition in the initial years was probably its bitter reaction to the United States refusal to recognize it. Nonrecognition by the US obviously had such a serious impact upon the PRC's political claims and its full participation in international life that PRC writers denounced nonrecognition due to political motivations as an act tantamount to aggression under international law.[37] After the US–PRC ambassadorial talks began in August 1955, the question of recognition became further complicated. Under international law, such contacts could create a presumption of recognition unless rebutted by an explicit denial of intention. From the outset of the talks, the United States properly made such a denial. The rituals that subsequently developed also were so designed as to override a presumption of US recognition.[38]

Peking conceivably could have felt it necessary, during the course of the extensive talks, to discount recognition as a necessary amenity for establishing the status and rights of an international person, including the capacity to negotiate with a nonrecognizing state. (In the 1960s, after its policy had changed, the PRC used US nonrecognition as an excuse for not participating in such international undertakings as the disarmament talks that might result in undesirable restrictions on its freedom of action.[39]) In retrospect, the ambassadorial talks could have given the PRC the idea that the recognition impasse could be bypassed.

37. K'ung Meng, "A Critique of the Bourgeois International Law," p. 51. For a study of US policy of nonrecognition of the PRC, see Dorothy Rae Dodge, "Recognition of the Central People's Government of the People's Republic of China: Legal and Political Aspects" (Ph.D. dissertation; Ann Arbor, Mich.: University Microfilms, 1955); and A. Doak Barnett, *Communist China and Asia* (New York: Harper, 1960), pp. 430–458.

38. For an interesting account, and the only available one, see Kenneth Young, *Negotiating with the Chinese Communists* (New York: McGraw-Hill, 1968).

39. *JMJP* editorial (Apr. 3, 1962); English translation in *PR*, no. 14:5–7 (1962). See also O. Edmund Clubb and Eustace Seligman, *The International Position of Communist China* (Dobbs Ferry, N.Y.: Oceana, 1965), p. 31.

At least PRC attitudes toward the question have undergone some changes since 1955, when the talks began.

In any event, between October 1, 1949, and the end of 1955, the PRC was, according to its official registry, recognized by 24 of the world's preexisting states. On the other hand, it greeted the independence of three new states subsequent to its own establishment.[40] Thus, Peking's view on recognition during the period was almost exclusively determined by its own anxiety and experience with other states' recognition of itself (i.e., a self-oriented perspective). Except for its reply to the Soviet Union, Peking avoided the express use of the term "recognition" in its replies to recognition by other states. Instead, as the occasion arose, it merely conveyed a reciprocal willingness to see diplomatic and/or other relations materialize at an early date.

The decisions which Peking had to make regarding the recognition of newly independent states entailed a totally different perspective (that is, an outward-directed perspective). The first test came when the German Democratic Republic was formed on October 25, 1949. Sending his government's "hearty congratulations," Chou En-lai raised the prospects for diplomatic relations, but did not expressly mention recognition.[41] In another instance, the PRC stated that it "*considers* the government of the Democratic Republic of Vietnam (DRV) as the *legitimate government* representing the will of the Vietnamese people."[42] (Emphasis added.)

We need not go into the question of the distinction between de jure recognition and the recognition of a de jure authority ("legitimate government") at this point. But it is worthwhile to note that in the PRC notification to the Vietnamese government the word "recognize" was again absent. This is all the more interesting when the DRV, in a note

40. The PRC was recognized during 1949–1955 by these twenty-four states: the Soviet Union, October 3, 1949; Bulgaria, October 3; Rumania, October 3; Hungary, October 5; Korea, October 4; Czechoslovakia, October 5; Poland, October 5; Yugoslavia, October 5; Outer Mongolia, October 6; Albania, November 21; Burma, December 16; India, December 30; Britain, January 6, 1950; Ceylon, January 7; Norway, January 10; Denmark, January 9; Israel, January 9; Afghanistan, January 12; Finland, January 13; Sweden, January 14; Pakistan, January 5; Switzerland, January 17; the Netherlands, March 27; and Nepal, August 1, 1955. In contrast, the PRC recognized (without using the word) three newly independent states, the Democratic Republic of Vietnam, January 18, 1950; Indonesia, March 28, 1950; and the Democratic Republic of Germany, October 25, 1949. See *WCC*, I, II, and III.

41. *WCC 1949–1950*, vol. I (1957), pp. 14–15.

42. Message from Chou En-lai on behalf of the PRC government, January 18, 1950, *ibid.*, pp. 24–25.

dated January 15, 1950, had declared that it "*recognizes* the People's Government of China under the leadership of Chairman Mao Tse-tung." (Emphasis added.) Following the independence of Indonesia, Chou En-lai on March 28, 1950, informed his Indonesian counterpart, Mohammed Hatta, that the PRC was willing to establish diplomatic relations with the new government on the basis of "equality, mutual benefit, and mutual respect for territorial sovereignty." As before, the PRC statement skipped recognition per se.[43]

The Transitional Period (1956–1959)

The years 1956–1959 saw the emergence of a few newly independent states, including Sudan, Ghana, and Guinea, heralding an upsurge of the anticolonial tide soon to sweep across the African continent. During the same period, states like Egypt and Cambodia switched their recognition from the Nationalist Chinese government to Peking. The PRC now was impelled to face seriously the problem of recognizing these emergent states and to weigh the implications of recognition. In fact, it became less restrained in the express use of "recognition."

The first known occasion when the PRC *explicitly* extended its diplomatic recognition to a new state was on January 4, 1956, to the Republic of Sudan. In addition to "congratulating" Sudanese independence, the official message from Chou En-lai went further than on any previous occasion. "In pursuance of the wishes of the Chinese people," it stated, "the government of the People's Republic of China declares its *recognition* of Sudan as an independent state, and expresses its hope to enter into diplomatic relations with your government."[44] (Emphasis added.)

Although increasingly after 1960 the PRC came around to the practice of expressly granting recognition to new states, what it did in regard to Sudan was not immediately repeated. When Morocco and Tunisia became independent three months later, Chou sent each a message of congratulations on April 4, 1956, but made no mention of either recognition or diplomatic relations. There was only a vaguely phrased wish to "see the development of friendly and cooperative relations between our two countries."[45]

43. *Ibid.*, pp. 31–32. See also my note 34.
44. *WCC 1956–1957*, vol. IV (1958), p. 1.
45. *Ibid.*, pp. 55–56.

After Tunisia dissolved its monarchy and adopted a republican form of government in July 1957, Chou En-lai on August 2 expressly recognized the new Tunisian government.[46] But this act of recognition should not be construed as anticipating immediate diplomatic relations. It was not until January 1964 that the two governments reached an agreement to establish diplomatic relations, climaxing a visit to Tunis by Premier Chou and his Foreign Minister, Ch'en Yi.[47] In 1957, Peking was understood to be seeking a new base for continent-wide activities in Africa, including aid to the Algerian revolutionaries, for the usefulness of Cairo as a base was reduced by the increasing anti-Communist stand of Nasser. Peking even feared that Nasser might seek a reconciliation with the "imperialists."[48] While Morocco was willing, Tunisia was hesitant about establishing full diplomatic relations with Peking between July 1957 and the end of 1963. Most probably, Peking's express recognition—which in 1957 was quite unusual in view of its previous practice—was intended as a friendly gesture to win Tunisia's good will. It did not necessarily indicate an approval of Tunisia's turning to a republic.

The PRC was known to separate recognition from approval in many cases, including that of Morocco, which was a semiautocratic Islamic monarchy, though with a strong left-wing nationalist movement based on trade unions. Peking recognized Morocco in October 1958, possibly because of substantial trade interest and a common sympathy for the FLN movement in neighboring Algeria.[49] A joint PRC-Moroccan communiqué of November 1, 1958, announced that each would establish an embassy in the other's country.[50] It appears certain that practical interests, rather than approval of the domestic form of government in a given country, increasingly were guiding Peking's policy of recognition and diplomatic relations, at least so far as the nonaligned and the emergent states are concerned.

There were, nevertheless, some slight variations in Peking's responses to the independence of new Afro-Asian states. When Ghana became an autonomous dominion, Chou En-lai on March 5, 1957, congratulated Premier Kwame Nkrumah. Vice Premier Nieh Jung-chen was sent as

46. *Ibid.*, p. 363.
47. Sino-Tunisian joint communiqué of January 11, 1964. English text in *SCMP*, no. 3139:43 (Jan. 15, 1964).
48. Richard Lowenthal, "China," in Zbigniew Brzezinski, ed., *Africa and the Communist World* (Stanford: Stanford University Press, 1963), pp. 164–165.
49. *Ibid.* See also US Department of State, Research Memorandum, REA 23 (June 13, 1968), p. 4.
50. *WCC 1958*, vol. V (1959), p. 197.

Peking's special envoy to attend the celebrations at Accra. An intention to recognize Ghana can be said to have been conveyed through these acts, though the issue was not expressly raised.[51] On August 30, 1957, when Malaya achieved independence, Peking sent a message of congratulations from Mao Tse-tung in his capacity as the then President of the People's Republic. In a separate message, Premier Chou En-lai sent his congratulations and, furthermore, expressly recognized Malaya. Though he expressed a general wish that "friendly relations between our two countries will increasingly be strengthened and develop," Chou did not go beyond recognition to raise the question of diplomatic relations.[52] To this day, Malaysia has no diplomatic relations with Peking, while it maintains a consulate in Nationalist China on Taiwan. This case lends support to my previous contention that Peking's recognition of the Tunisian Republic in 1957 need not be viewed as anticipating forthcoming diplomatic relations. While its attention during 1949–1955 was focused more on diplomatic relations than recognition, Peking now was reconciled to recognition even without an immediate prospect for diplomatic intercourse.

The same pattern of response with which the PRC greeted the independence of Malaya was repeated when the United Arab Republic was formed on February 23, 1958. In addition to a congratulatory message from Mao Tse-tung, Chou En-lai sent one of his own extending express recognition.[53] After Kassem overthrew the Iraqi royal house in a palace coup, his new republican government, on July 16, 1958, received express PRC recognition, which was extended by Foreign Minister Ch'en Yi.[54]

The PRC reacted rather exuberantly to the proclamation of the Algerian provisional government (GPRA) on September 19, 1958. In a personal letter, Premier Abbas Ferhat expressed the hope that Peking would be "among the first" to recognize the GPRA. As if not to fail him, Peking, on September 22, sent three separate cables to GPRA. The first came from Mao himself, offering congratulations and wishing it "even more glorious and greater victory in the brave Algerian people's fight for national independence and against colonialism."[55] The second

51. *WCC 1956–1957*, vol. IV (1958), p. 304. See also discussion accompanying note 74.
52. *Ibid.*, pp. 364 and 365.
53. *WCC 1958*, vol. V (1959), p. 71.
54. *Ibid.*, p. 131.
55. *Ibid.*, p. 185.

message, sent by Premier Chou, repeated the felicitations, had more praise for the "irresistible tides of anticolonialism," and offered assurances that "the Chinese people will, as in the past, stand resolutely on the side of the brave and dauntless Algerian people."[56] And the third, signed by Foreign Minister Ch'en Yi, explicitly extended Peking's recognition and also expressed the hope that "the friendship between the Chinese and Algerian peoples will further develop and will be strengthened."[57] The lack of mention of "diplomatic" relations was not surprising in view of the fact that the GPRA was in fact a "government-in-exile" fighting an underground revolutionary war against French colonial rule. Nevertheless, the PRC recognition heralded the stationing in Peking of an Algerian mission with full diplomatic status.[58]

Another occasion on which Peking acted with similar exuberance was the independence of Guinea. In a letter to Mao Tse-tung, dated October 4, Premier Sékou Touré announced the formation of the Guinean Republic and requested the establishment of diplomatic relations. Mao and Chou, in two separate messages on October 7, offered their felicitations. In another message, Ch'en Yi expressly agreed to recognize the Guinean Republic and stated his government's readiness to *negotiate* with Guinea on the establishment of diplomatic relations and the exchange of envoys.[59]

The general relaxation in attitude reflected a PRC attempt to circumvent the impact of US nonrecognition by cultivating friendship with as many states in the "third world" as possible. Although similar attempts had been made before, as in Peking's "unofficial" trade relations with Japan,[60] the 1956–1959 period saw a more self-assured PRC extending its contacts from the immediate surrounding regions to the Middle East and other parts of the world. Chou En-lai's approaches at the Bandung Conference of 1955 had paved the way for this expansion. In a few cases, trade and other informal relations eventually led to recognition and the establishment of formal diplomatic relations.[61]

56. *Ibid.*, p. 187.
57. *Ibid.*, p. 188.
58. See discussion of this below.
59. *WCC 1958*, vol. V (1959), pp. 195–197.
60. Alexander Eckstein, *Communist China's Economic Growth and Foreign Trade* (New York: McGraw-Hill, 1966), pp. 202–212.
61. Egypt is a good example, see Lowenthal, "China," p. 153; and Eckstein, *Communist China's Economic Growth*, pp. 192, 194, 234. More significantly, PRC writers openly admitted the usefulness of trade as a first step to diplomatic recognition. "Under international custom," wrote Wang Yao-t'ien, "trade treaties and agree-

It is evident that Peking was consciously exploiting the subdiplomatic ties, technically bypassing the recognition question. This can be seen for example in a report which Chang Han-fu, Vice Foreign Minister, made to the Fourth Session of the First National People's Congress on July 15, 1957. Despite US "obstruction," Chang stated that the PRC had by then established diplomatic relations with 27 countries, "semidiplomatic" relations with 2, trade relations with 68 (including nongovernmental trade), and "friendly contacts" with a total of 101 countries. He characterized ties short of express recognition as a "new form of diplomatic relations, that of the people's diplomacy."[62]

As Peking began this more subtle maneuver, a number of states that had continued to recognize Nationalist China beyond October 1, 1949, began to switch their recognition to the PRC. Among the first to do so during this period was Egypt. The decision reached on May 16, 1956, by the new Cabinet of the Egyptian Republic under Nasser was promptly communicated to Premier Chou both through the PRC commercial attaché in Cairo and the Egyptian commercial attaché in Peking. Simultaneously Cairo announced that it was withdrawing its recognition of the Nationalist Chinese government. In its acknowledgment, the PRC expressly acknowledged Cairo's *recognition* and indicated a warm desire to establish diplomatic relations and to exchange diplomatic representatives.[63] In three other similar cases during this period, when it was recognized by Syria (July 3, 1956),[64] Yemen (August 21, 1956),[65] and Cambodia (July 18, 1958),[66] the PRC responded in the same way as it had to the recognition by Egypt. This *express* acknowledgment of another country's recognition reversed Peking's earlier practice, which deliberately skirted the term "recognition" and simply addressed itself to the question of diplomatic or subdiplomatic relations where the other party was so willing. Both this reversal and the practice of gradually taking the initiative to accord express

---

ments can be concluded between two states which have not yet established diplomatic relations. Therefore, concluding trade treaties and agreements can lay the foundation for the establishment of diplomatic relations. *China's* [diplomatic] *relations with Ceylon and Egypt were developed in this way.*" [Emphasis added.] Wang Yao-t'ien, *Kuo-chi mao-i t'iao-yüeh ho hsieh-ting* (International trade treaties and agreements: Peking: Ts'ai-cheng ching-chi ch'u-pan-she, 1958), p. 116.

62. Text in *WCC 1956–1957*, vol. IV (1958), pp. 348–354.
63. *Ibid.*, pp. 59–60; and note 1 on p. 60.
64. *Ibid.*, p. 93.
65. *Ibid.*, p. 101.
66. *WCC 1958*, vol. V (1959), p. 142.

recognition to nonaligned and emergent states indicate that Peking was groping for a more flexible recognition policy between 1956 and 1959.

The Most Recent Period (since 1960)

A clear pattern has emerged in PRC practice since 1960, as vast numbers of new Afro-Asian states have gained independence from former colonial rule. On each occasion, Premier Chou En-lai offered the PRC's congratulations, and in a separate message Foreign Minister Ch'en Yi extended diplomatic recognition on behalf of the PRC government.[67] As a rule, Premier Chou's message hailed the independence of a former colony as a "great victory" of the native population against "imperialism and colonialism." An example is Chou's congratulations to President Qahtan Al Sha'abi of the People's Republic of Southern Yemen, on November 30, 1967, although Chou's wording may be a little bit more exuberant than in some other cases:

> On the occasion of the proclamation of the independence of the People's Republic of Southern Yemen, I wish to express, on behalf of the government of the People's Republic of China and the Chinese people, warm congratulations to Your Excellency and the government and people of the People's Republic of Southern Yemen.
>
> The independence of Southern Yemen is a great *victory of the national liberation movement* of Southern Yemen and, in particular, a great victory of the armed struggle over the last four years; it is the result of the *prolonged struggle against imperialism and colonialism* waged by the people of Southern Yemen.
>
> The Chinese government and people have always sympathized with and supported the struggle of the people of Southern Yemen. We wish the people of Southern Yemen, who have a glorious anti-imperialist tradition, *new successes after independence in opposing imperialism, colonialism and neo-colonialism* and safeguarding national independence.[68] (Emphasis added.)

Ch'en Yi's messages were usually more matter-of-fact, terse, and to the point, granting his government's recognition and, with varying degrees of warmth, expressing a wish for the betterment of relations between the two countries. To use the example of Southern Yemen, Ch'en Yi's message, addressed to his counterpart in Aden, merely stated:

67. See, for example, *SCMP*, no. 2249:54 (May 3, 1960), in regard to Togo (Apr. 27, 1960); no. 2284:32 (June 24, 1960), for Mali Federation (June 19, 1960); no. 2288:49 (June 30, 1960), for Malagasy (June 25, 1960); no. 2288:50, for Somaliland (June 25, 1960), etc. In most recognition cases in the 1960s, there was hardly any exception to this formula.

68. NCNA, Peking, Nov. 30, 1967; also in *SCMP*, no. 4072:46 (Dec. 4, 1967).

On the occasion of the proclamation of the independence of the People's Republic of Southern Yemen, I wish to express, on behalf of the government of the People's Republic of China, warm congratulations to the government of the People's Republic of Southern Yemen. I have the honor to inform Your Excellency that the government of the People's Republic of China has decided to *recognize* the People's Republic of Southern Yemen. I do hope that friendly relations and cooperation between our two countries will develop.[69] (Emphasis added.)

Occasionally, Liu Shao-ch'i as the head of state also sent his own congratulatory messages, as on the independence of the Congo (Leopoldville), June 26, 1960,[70] the establishment of the Republic of Ghana, July 1, 1960,[71] and the independence of Zambia (former Northern Rhodesia).[72]

The PRC merely sent warm greetings without reference to recognition when the Republic of Ghana was formally established on July 1, 1960,[73] but the case need not be viewed as an exception to Peking's standard practice since 1960. It should be recalled that Ghana had first become an autonomous dominion within the British Commonwealth in 1957. On that occasion the PRC not only offered felicitations but even sent a special envoy to Accra to observe its celebrations.[74] The event took place during the transitional period (1956–1959) when the PRC still resorted to *tacit* recognition. To the extent that the PRC felt that it had recognized Ghana back in 1957, there was no need for doing so again in 1960, when the same African nation gained the new status of a republic under the same head of state, Kwame Nkrumah.

Generally, the practice of extending *express* recognition to newly independent states has been consistently followed in the post-1960 period. One known exception is the case of Kuwait, which has not been expressly recognized by Peking to date, though on its independence day, June 29, 1961, Chou En-lai offered his government's congratulations.[75] If the latter was meant to be a tacit recognition, it would not amount to much today, as Kuwait has established diplomatic relations with the Nationalist Chinese government. One writer has suggested that Peking's abstention from expressly recognizing Kuwait—even after

69. *Ibid.*
70. *SCMP*, no. 2288:50 (June 30, 1960).
71. *SCMP*, no. 2292:27 (July 8, 1960).
72. *PR*, no. 44:4 (Oct. 30, 1964).
73. *SCMP*, no. 2292:26, 27 (July 8, 1960).
74. See note 51 above.
75. *WCC 1961*, vol. VIII (1962), p. 202. See also *SCMP*, no. 2531:41 (July 6, 1961).

the Soviet Union had done so on March 11, 1963—arose from its respect for Iraq's claims to the territory now occupied by Kuwait.[76] If this is true, then it was one of the few cases in which the PRC has permitted political considerations to interfere with its recognition practice in the *present* period.

A number of factors appear to underscore Peking's more relaxed practice of recognition in the post-1966 period. Peking apparently suffered from a growing sense of political isolation as a result of the entrenchment of the Sino-Soviet conflict, and the coming into statehood of former (Western) colonies was a welcome sign of the receding influence of colonialism and "imperialism." Recognition of the new states could, therefore, mean a vote in support of the forces of "self-determination." This feeling has already been noted in Chou's message on Southern Yemen's independence in November 1967.

CERTAIN LEGAL ISSUES OF RECOGNITION

Recognition of States and Governments

Recognition of a state and recognition of its government are not the same thing under general international law. It is oftentimes difficult to draw a distinction, however, and, in a majority of cases, recognition of a new state also means recognition of its government. "The state is perpetual and survives the form of its government," as *Lehigh Valley Railroad Co.* v. *the State of Russia* has indicated.[77] The recognition of a state continues beyond changes in its government. No question of recognition arises when a new government comes into being as the heir of a deceased king succeeds to the throne or, in the case of a republic, as a newly elected chief executive constitutionally assumes office. A classical view, which by and large still holds good, is that "the recognition of a new government within a State arises in practice only when a government has been changed or established by revolution or *coup d'état*."[78]

The question of recognition of a new government arises as a practical consequence of the fact that, although rights under international law are attributable to the state rather than to its government, the emer-

76. Refer to Harold Hinton, *Communist China in World Politics* (Boston: Houghton Mifflin, 1966), p. 184.
77. *Lehigh Valley RR* vs. *The State of Russia*, reproduced in Briggs, *The Law of Nations*, p. 194.
78. Stimson, Secretary of State, February 6, 1931, quoted in Briggs, *ibid.*, p. 121.

gence of a new regime by other than peaceful means creates uncertainty as to its effectiveness, stability, and ability as well as its willingness to commit the state to the observance of international obligations. Furthermore, in a world divided by differing social systems and ideologies, the question becomes more complicated as a new government, which came into being either by revolution or by the normal procedures of succession, may adopt a social system or ideological outlook so completely different that the world is in effect confronted with virtually a new entity. The law seems still fluid on this point as it has been ever since the appearance of the Soviet Union in 1917. In doctrine, the PRC does not seem to endorse the view that a drastic change in the domestic social system results in a new state. On occasion it considers itself to have succeeded to the same state of China, but under a new government. At least this cloak of continuity has been used to back its claims to China's membership in the United Nations.[79] Nevertheless, the PRC follows the practice of extending recognition anew to a new government in an already recognized state if that government has drastically changed its organizational and/or ideological complexion. A few cases can be cited.

The PRC recognized the Kingdom of Yemen in August 1956 and maintained diplomatic relations with it at the legation level.[80] Upon the death of the old Imam in 1962, a Republic of Yemen was proclaimed under a new government oriented to Nasser-type nationalism, ushering in a new era for the country. On October 6, 1962, the PRC recognized the new Yemeni government.[81] (Subsequently, from January 1967, the legation in each other's capital was elevated to the status of embassy.[82]) Burma and the PRC exchanged recognition in October 1949. In a coup d'état staged by General Ne Win in March 1962, the neutralist government of Prime Minister U Nu was toppled. Pushing aside representative government, the new army established a Revolutionary Council of seventeen army officers, with Ne Win as the chairman, to function as the

79. See, for example, PRC communications to the United Nations, UN Doc. A/1123 (Nov. 18, 1949), and UN Security Council, *Official Records*, 5th year, 459th meeting (Jan. 10, 1950), no. 1, p. 2; also T'ang Ming-chao, "Oppose United States Schemes to Obstruct China's Rights in the United Nations," *China Reconstructs*, no. 12:7–9 (Dec. 1961); and Hsiung, "Communist China's Conception of World Public Order," pp. 78–83. See also comments by Jerome Alan Cohen, ASIL *Proceedings* (1968), p. 211.

80. *WCC 1956–1957*, vol. IV (1958), p. 101.

81. *WCC 1962*, vol. IX (1964), p. 367.

82. The first Yemeni Ambassador presented his credentials on February 6, 1967. *SCMP*, no. 3879:38 (Feb. 14, 1967).

new government. Quite promptly, on March 6, 1962, Foreign Minister Ch'en Yi notified General Ne Win of Peking's decision to recognize his new regime.[83]

As noted above, the PRC expressly recognized Iraq following Kassem's palace coup in July 1958. Then on February 8, 1963, Kassem's government was violently overthrown by the Ba'athists. Four days later Peking expressly recognized the new Iraqi government.[84] In November 1963 President Aref expelled the Ba'athist elements from his government, but the action did not affect the PRC's recognition, apparently because no serious break of continuity resulted. Peking had exchanged recognition with Syria in July 1956.[85] On September 28, 1961, the Arab Republic of Syria was proclaimed and, in a note sent two days later, it requested Peking's recognition, which was granted on October 11. A new Ba'athist government was formed in Syria on March 8, 1963, and the PRC accorded it recognition one week later.[86] The Republic of Zanzibar was recognized on December 9, 1963. Shortly afterwards a coup placed a leftist government in power. On January 17, 1964, Foreign Minister Ch'en Yi recognized the new regime on behalf of his government.[87]

In these cases, Peking's practice did not depart much from that of most other states. Each time Peking implied in its wording that its recognition was extended to the new government. The question remains, however, whether the recognition could also apply to the state where drastic changes had put its continuity in doubt. Considering Peking's position regarding the perpetuity of the state of China after the Communist government took power by revolution in 1949, one would assume that Peking probably accepted the theory that, while the emergence of a new government marking a clear break from the past gives rise to an occasion for recognition, the state, being perpetual in nature, remains recognized as before.

De Facto and De Jure Recognition

The distinction between de facto and de jure recognition was first drawn in the British practice in the 19th century; it was necessitated by the independence movement in Latin America against the claims

83. *WCC 1962*, vol. IX (1964), p. 309.
84. *Ibid*, p. 158.
85. *WCC 1956–1957*, vol. IV (1958), p. 93.
86. *WCC 1963*, vol. X (1965), p. 183.
87. *SCMP*, no. 3143:51 (Jan. 21, 1964).

of Spain and Portugal. The terms fell into disuse for a time until they were readopted in this century.[88] The very fact that their distinction has even crept into Soviet juristic vocabulary indicates how widely the two concepts have been accepted in international practice.[89] However, the legal consequences of the distinction are far from clear. While it is generally agreed that recognition de jure implies an unconditional acceptance of the stability, effectiveness, and legitimacy of the recognized entity or government, it is also a fact that regimes tottering on the brink of extinction are sometimes accorded recognition de jure for political reasons.

Most scholars agree that it is hard to tell whether an expressly accorded de facto recognition differs much in legal consequences from those of de jure recognition.[90] In *Luther* v. *Sagor* the British Court of Appeals found that Her Majesty's government had explicitly recognized the Soviet government de facto and noted that, although de facto recognition was "for some purposes" distinct from de jure recognition, "for the present purpose . . . no distinction can be drawn."[91] As a result of the thin distinction, the two terms have often been confused or used interchangeably even by distinguished legal authorities.[92] The situation led McNair to suggest that "it is not the recognition which is *de jure* or *de facto,* but the Government or situation. On that understanding, we may use the convenient expression recognition *de jure* and recognition *de facto*."[93] Even then, the confusion does not end, because in cases of conflict between a de jure authority in jeopardy and a newly recognized de facto authority in a given country, foreign courts (especially British) have at times decided in favor of the latter in settling claims. *Arantzazu Mendi* (1939) and *Bank of Ethiopia* v. *National Bank of Egypt and*

88. Lauterpacht, *Recognition,* p. 329.
89. Academy of Sciences of the USSR, *International Law,* p. 118.
90. Lissitzyn, *International Law,* pp. 12–13.
91. Briggs, *The Law of Nations,* p. 161.
92. In 1948, while extending recognition to Israel, the President of the United States stated: "The United States recognizes the provisional government as the *de facto* authority of the new State of Israel." Although recognition of a *de facto* government as such does not necessarily qualify the act of recognition itself, the US delegate in the Security Council, Philip Jessup, said in the Council that "the United States did extend *de facto* recognition to the Provisional Government of Israel." "*De facto* recognition" used here does not, strictly speaking, do justice to what was conveyed in the President's statement above. Denis P. Myers, "Contemporary Practice of the United States Relating to International Law," *AJIL* 55:697 (1961).
93. Sir Arnold D. McNair, *Legal Effects of War* (Cambridge, Eng.: Cambridge University Press, 1948), p. 353.

Liquori (1937) have demonstrated that the rights and status of an authority recognized de jure do not always prevail over those of another recognized de facto.

Precisely because of the confusion, some states—India, for example—avoid expressly granting a recognition de facto.[94] The PRC, to the best of my knowledge, has never expressly recognized any entity de facto. Whether de facto recognition exists in tacit form is hard to tell from available evidence. Given the fact that the PRC, between 1949 and 1955, avoided all mention of recognition, one may question whether its acknowledgment of the express recognition by foreign governments implied a reciprocal recognition de facto.

The question is further complicated by the fact that the PRC maintains rather formal relations, short of express recognition, with many countries. One need not go back to the earlier years; a good recent example can be found in its relations with Ethiopia. The two countries are not known to have expressly recognized each other. (No express mention of recognition was made even in the PRC–Ethiopia announcement of November 24, 1970, that the two countries would henceforth establish diplomatic relations. See postcript below.) Nevertheless, during Chou En-lai's 1964 African trip, he not only visited Addis Ababa as a state guest between January 30 and February 1 but also issued a joint communiqué of serious consequence with Emperor Haile Selassie. Among other things, the Emperor in the communiqué expressed the Ethiopian government's view that the "legitimate rights" of the PRC in the United Nations must be reinstated. Both sides expressed the hope that the discussion held between Premier Chou and Emperor Haile Selassie "would contribute to . . . the future development of friendly relations between the peoples and governments of their two countries." "They further agreed," declared the communiqué, "to make efforts for expanding the economic and cultural exchanges between the two countries."[95] One might infer from this declaration an intention to recognize each other at least de facto as is customary in state practices. But the instance does not alter the fact that the PRC has not yet *expressly* recognized any authority de facto, as, for example, Britain did with regard to the Soviet government in the initial years of its existence.

In extending express recognition to newly independent states, the

94. Misra, *India's Policy of Recognition*, p. 192 and *passim*.

95. PRC-Ethiopia joint communiqué, February 1, 1964, in *PR*, no. 6:31–32 (Feb. 7, 1964).

PRC also shuns the use of the word "de jure." The PRC occasionally refers to the "sole legitimate government" of a country, especially with reference to itself. In January 1964, Peking repeated its claim of being China's "sole legal government" when protesting the temporary continuance of French diplomatic ties with the Nationalist Chinese government after France had switched recognition to the PRC.[96] On another occasion, Peking protested to the Kenyan government over the latter's increasing contacts with the authorities in Taiwan, including a visit there by the Kenyan Minister of State in Charge of Foreign Affairs. In its protest note, Peking recalled that since the establishment of formal diplomatic relations between them in December 1963, the "Kenyan government had repeatedly and solemnly made it known that it recognized only the government of the People's Republic of China as the *sole legitimate government* of China."[97] (Emphasis added.) After the murder of Patrice Lumumba in the Congo (L), Peking, on February 19, 1961, switched recognition from the central government under President Joseph Kasavubu to the short-lived Stanleyville regime of Antoine Gizenga. In an official message, Foreign Minister Ch'en Yi recognized Stanleyville as the "sole legitimate government of the Congo."[98] In each of these instances, Peking was speaking of de jure authority, rather than de jure recognition. Though the two are closely related, they are not the same. In view of Peking's consistent avoidance of the terms "de facto" and "de jure" in its recognition practice, and of its insistence that a government recognizing the PRC must support its claim of being China's "sole legitimate government," one has reason to suspect that perhaps in PRC usage "recognition," at least when expressly accorded, is de jure in nature. An express qualification to the contrary would, of course, vitiate this assumption, but Peking has simply not made its position known.

It can be said with greater certainty, however, that Peking considers that recognition of one regime, where there are two rival regimes in a country, means the automatic withdrawal of recognition from the other if previously recognized. This attitude reflects its intolerance of the "two Chinas" idea, as evidenced in its protests to France and Kenya. In its protest to France, the PRC Foreign Ministry stated: "According to

96. NCNA (Peking) carried a story on January 28, 1964, regarding a PRC Foreign Ministry statement to that effect, in *SCMP*, no. 3151:23 (Jan. 31, 1964).
97. NCNA, Peking, Nov. 23, 1967, in *SCMP*, no. 4067:33 (Nov. 27, 1967).
98. *WCC 1961*, vol. VIII (1962), pp. 141–142.

international practice, recognition of the new government of a country naturally implies *ceasing to recognize the old ruling group overthrown* by the people of that country."[99] (Emphasis added.) When recognizing the Stanleyville regime as the "sole legitimate government of the Congo" in February 1961, the PRC seemed to suggest that the act meant the withdrawal of its previous recognition of the Congolese central government granted on June 26, 1960.[100]

This attitude toward the switching of recognition in a contentious situation accords with the practice of the Soviet Union. When the Soviet government on October 2, 1949, announced its decision to recognize the PRC, formed the previous day, it simultaneously announced that its diplomatic mission accredited to the Nationalist Chinese government was being withdrawn. A Soviet textbook on international law considered that the latter act implied a withdrawal of recognition from a previously recognized regime.[101] As mentioned earlier, Egypt announced its withdrawal of recognition from the Nationalist Chinese authorities when it recognized the Peking regime in May 1956. This example was cited in the same Soviet textbook to show that "the recognition of one government inevitably leads to the withdrawal of recognition from, and the cessation of relations with, the government which previously existed in the given country."[102]

Although the Soviets assert that the "simultaneous de facto or de jure recognition of two governments in one and the same State cannot be considered normal,"[103] their doctrine at least entertains the possibility of such a situation. The PRC doctrine, however, insists that *only* the "sole legitimate government" is to be recognized in a given country. Without doubt, the view reflects a conscious uneasiness over the competition between the "two Chinas." Yet in PRC practice, apart from doctrine, the issue is not so clear-cut. Though it recognizes the East German regime, Peking maintains serious trade ties with West Germany, which is the only major trading partner in Europe that has not exchanged recognition with Peking or at least has not done so expressly. This situation could conceivably be explained away by the fact that Peking openly admits the coexistence of "two Germanys." In showing its support for East Germany's protest against the 1956 treaty between

99. See my note 96.
100. See my note 98. The original wording, I must admit, is by no means clear.
101. Academy of Sciences of the USSR, *International Law*, p. 120.
102. *Ibid.*
103. *Ibid.*

France and the Bonn regime which returned the Saar to (West) Germany, for instance, the official *People's Daily* in an obiter dictum commented that "at the present time, when *two Germanys exist,* the question of the Saar can be reasonably solved only when representatives from the two Germanys participate in the settlement."[104] (Emphasis added.) It is a moot question whether in Peking's view "two Germanys" meant two German "states" or two separate "governments."

TENSION IN THE PRC RECOGNITION PRACTICE

Empirical evidence suggests that tension exists in the PRC's recognition practice between doctrine and practice, between law and policy, and between ideological dictates and foreign policy. The reasons for the phenomenon are not hard to find. As is well known, Communist China is committed to an ideology of revolutionary change in the world. However, in practice its discretion is not unlimited, in view of its modest capabilities, the power configuration in world politics, and the restraining force of existing international law, however tenuous that restraint may be in politically sensitive areas. While the PRC wishes to change the world order in accordance with Marxist ideals, it has to live with the existing deadlocked reality of international life. *Realpolitik* compels Communist China to act with greater prudence than it would if it simply followed its doctrinal impulses.[105]

The phenomenon has resulted in two attitudes in Peking's foreign policy not altogether reconcilable: (a) It shows a minimal acceptance of international law because of the law's functional utility and because of practical considerations given the facts of international life; and (b) it also attempts to exploit "loopholes" in the existing system of world order to further the PRC's own ideological beliefs as well as its national interests. While this conflict between realism and "idealism" is found to haunt all national actors, it is plain that in Peking's case the conflict is more serious.

It is hardly strange that Communist China, with its peculiar blend of Marxist and Chinese perspectives, considers certain norms in the existing framework of international law objectionable, while it accepts

104. *JMJP* (Jan. 2, 1957).

105. Refer to Hsiung, "Communist China's Conception of World Public Order," p. 229 *et seq.;* also Hsiung, "Communist China's Foreign Policy: Ideology, Practical Interests, and Polemics," in *China Today* (Maryknoll, N.Y.: Maryknoll Publications, January 1969).

others for a variety of practical reasons. This selective acceptance of a law that grew largely from the Western background during a time when much of the non-Western world was nonparticipant is by no means a haphazard act. It follows a body of doctrine which reflects not only a commitment to Marxist values but also a reaction (resentment) to China's past and present experience in foreign relations. What is noteworthy here, however, is that the PRC on occasion is found to depart from its own professed doctrine, that is, what it insists ought to be part of a "general" international law binding on all states. Before proceeding further, the PRC doctrine on diplomatic recognition should be examined briefly.

Although Chinese Communist writers seldom discuss in great detail implications of international law—in the way we are accustomed to in the West—a rather systematic treatment of the question of recognition is provided by K'ung Meng. In an article published in the once important *Kuo-chi wen-t'i yen-chiu* (Studies in international problems) in 1960, the author criticized scathingly what he called "the bourgeois doctrine" and presented the PRC's doctrine of recognition. K'ung Meng read an element of "class struggle" into the constitutive theory held by certain "bourgeois" jurists and imputed an intent to submit newly independent states to individual and collective certification by a "bourgeois"-dominated world community. "Conditional recognition" and nonrecognition were, according to the author, vaguely disguised forms of blackmail or, in some cases, even "naked aggression." Although he did not argue specifically for the acceptance of the declaratory view, K'ung Meng laid down four basic principles regarding recognition which, he claimed, constituted "generally accepted norms of international law." These are:

1. Self-determination. Whether a state becomes an international person is determined by the "will of the people" and by the "facts of its actual existence," not by the certification of other nations.

2. Effective control. The independent and effective exercise of authority in a territory is the symbol of existence internationally. Whether a new government comes into existence by constitutional process (in which case, no recognition problem arises) or by coup d'état or revolution (which entails recognition) is not subject to the "review" of any other state, because such review would amount to intervention in internal affairs.

3. Separation of recognition from policy. No state shall either use premature recognition or withhold recognition for the purpose of enforcing "illegitimate interests"—the latter being tantamount to "aggression." Although recognition is a unilateral act by the recognizing state, it is also an institution of international law; therefore, extension of recognition must follow generally accepted norms of that law.

4. Inalienable right to grant recognition. Individual or collective extension of recognition by preexisting states to a new state or government is a right not to be abridged by anyone. Coercion upon other states with the intent to influence or obstruct their recognition of a new state or government ("such as U.S. coercion upon other states to prevent their recognition of [Communist] China") is an act of intervention, a "severe act in violation of [international] law."[106]

The trouble with this recognition doctrine is that it was conceived in what I have called the PRC's "self-oriented" perspective, which sees the question almost exclusively from Peking's concern for other states' recognition of itself. As we shall see, these subjectively conceived tenets cannot always be followed even in Peking's own practice where an outward-directed perspective is called for. For all its relatively consistent recognition practice in the post-1960 period, Peking has professed a nonrecognition policy toward Israel. Its doctrine of effective control notwithstanding, Peking refuses to recognize Nationalist China (although for obvious reasons). In a couple of cases, it appeared even to use premature recognition for political purposes. I have no information as to whether the PRC has ever been engaged in coercing other states into following its own recognition policy; but I assume that it does not yet possess the capability to do so effectively.

Nonrecognition of Israel

Earlier, I noted Israel's recognition of the PRC and Peking's vaguely worded acknowledgment on January 9, 1950. This took place in a period when Peking avoided express mention of "recognition" in its responses to other states' recognition. Throughout its history, Peking has not, with very few exceptions, *explicitly* reciprocated recognition to the recognizing states.[107] Whether Peking considers a recognizing state

106. K'ung Meng, "A Critique of the Bourgeois International Law."
107. In response to Mali's recognition (October 14, 1960), the PRC on October 17, 1960, *expressly* acknowledged Mali's recognition of Peking. In return

to be also recognized by the PRC in return could only be inferred from manifest intention. Yet, it would be hard to judge whether Chou Enlai's acknowledgment of Israel's recognition conveyed an intention to reciprocate in kind.

Peking had never been terribly enthused about Israel because of the latter's close ties with the United States and because of Arab hostility. But the question whether Peking considered Israel to have been recognized did not come up until after the Arab-Israeli "June War" of 1967. In a public denunciation on June 12, 1967, Ch'en Yi condemned Israel as a "lackey" of "U.S. and British imperialism" and called the war an "aggression." He also denounced the Soviet Union for having played "the ignominious role of sham supporter but real betrayer of the Arab people in their resistance" against the "war of aggression."[108]

The word finally came on September 18, 1968. "Israel," stated Ch'en Yi at a Peking reception honoring Saif Ahmad Dhalai, Foreign Minister of South Yemen, "is a tool of U.S. imperialism for aggression, and China will *not* recognize it."[109] It is not clear whether Ch'en's statement represented a revocation of recognition, or a denial of ever having reciprocated Israel's recognition of Peking, or a refusal to recognize the results of the "June War," in which Israel had occupied territories previously under Arab jurisdiction. In any event, the PRC's declared nonrecognition could be based on either an expanded version of the Stimson Doctrine of not recognizing the "fruits of aggression," or a counterpart of the Dulles Doctrine of not recognizing a state or government on moral-ideological grounds, or a combination of the two.

If the PRC rests its policy on the Stimson Doctrine, then its effect should extend only to Israel's newly acquired territories. But the sweeping statement of Ch'en Yi, suggesting a flat nonrecognition of Israel as a state, makes this interpretation quite implausible. If, on the other hand, its nonrecognition is politically motivated, reflecting a disapproval

---

the PRC also *expressly* extended its recognition to the Mali Republic. This is probably the only such instance in which recognition by a foreign government was explicitly acknowledged and responded to in kind by Peking. In all other cases, as already noted, the PRC merely responded by expressing a reciprocal desire for diplomatic or other ties. Besides, the PRC's reciprocal recognition of Mali was phrased in a rather peculiar way: "The Chinese government has decided to *recognize* the Republic of Mali as an *independent, sovereign* state." [Emphasis added.] Text of the PRC note of October 17, 1960, appears in *WCC 1960*, vol. VII (1962), p. 294.

108. NCNA, Peking, June 12, 1967. English text in *SCMP*, no. 3960:28–31 (June 15, 1967).

109. *PR*, no. 39:29 (Sept. 27, 1968).

of the sociopolitical system or of the policies of Israel, then Peking's own doctrine of separating recognition from policy is clearly violated.[110]

"Effective Control" and the Question of Taiwan

The PRC has consistently and vigorously resisted any modus vivendi which might imply recognition of the simultaneous existence of Nationalist China. The PRC apparently prefers remaining outside the United Nations to being seated with the Nationalist delegation under a "two Chinas" solution. Peking has protested to foreign governments that have recognized the PRC when those governments have made contacts with the Nationalist Chinese authorities, even if the contacts were purportedly of a "nonpolitical" character. For example, when a delegation of "Muslim pilgrims" from Taiwan visited Pakistan in 1959, Peking protested to the Pakistani government and accused it of attempting to create "two Chinas."[111] On another occasion, in 1967, Peking disrupted its diplomatic relations with Kenya because, as was noted earlier, a Kenyan minister of state visited Taiwan.

Premature Recognition and Intervention?

PRC doctrine equally condemns premature recognition and withholding of recognition, but its practice is not completely spotless on this score. For example, the PRC in 1958 recognized the Algerian provisional government (GPRA)—a regime in exile—three days after its formation. By "normal" standards, the recognition would be considered both premature and hostile to the French authorities, which the GPRA sought to overthrow by revolutionary means. Traditional international law would permit third states to recognize the Algerian conflict as an insurgency or belligerency, but it would also require them to stay neutral. Neither an insurgent nor a belligerent would be regarded as competent to request military assistance in the name of the state, and the offering of such assistance by an outside state would be regarded as an act of intervention. Not until the insurgent or belligerent group had established general control or an armistice line had been accepted would the occasion arise for recognition by outside states.[112]

110. On the distinction between the Stimson and Dulles Doctrines, see Misra, *India's Policy of Recognition*, p. 9.
111. *WCC 1959*, vol. VI (1961), pp. 79–81.
112. W. E. Hall, *A Treatise on International Law*, 8th ed. (Oxford: Clarendon Press, 1924), Sec. 94.

When it was formed in September 1958, the GPRA had its headquarters in Cairo, far from Algerian territory. Not without reason the French government viewed the GPRA as an "artificial" creation.[113]

Both because of the political complications and the legally shaky grounds of the GPRA's claim to legitimacy, the United States and Britain were among many states (mainly Western) that refrained from recognition. Peking's desire to assist the Algerian revolution and to make it a model for all colonial Africa apparently overrode other considerations. At about the same time that Peking recognized the GPRA, a visiting Algerian delegation headed by Ben Khedda and including Mahmoud Cerif, Minister of Armaments and Supplies, was negotiating in the Chinese capital for arms supplies.[114] Later, as a result of mutual agreement reached in October 1960, the GPRA stationed in Peking a "representative organ,"[115] which was subsequently described as the Algerian "diplomatic delegation."[116] Although Peking's lack of diplomatic relations with France—which continued to recognize the Nationalist Chinese until January 1964—made its support of the GPRA less embarrassing, the fact remains that Peking's recognition was prematurely granted for political reasons.

However, the question was far more complicated than either recognition or intervention as understood in traditional international law. In broad perspective, one finds in the present case, as in many others, a clash between traditional norms given to the preservation of the status quo and the aspiration for self-determination and revolutionary change of peoples having little or no interest in maintaining the status quo. It is worth noting that before it gained independence Algeria was, during the period 1958–1961, recognized by thirty-one states, either de jure or de facto.[117] Contrary to general assumptions, the PRC was *not* the first one to recognize the GPRA. Egypt recognized the provisional Algerian regime on the very day of its formation in Cairo. President Nasser, besides extending recognition, hailed the move as a "glorious historic

113. *The New York Times*, Sept. 20, 1958, p. 1.

114. *SCMP*, no. 1911:41 (Dec. 10, 1958).

115. Joint communiqué issued by Chou En-lai and Abbas Ferhat, October 5, 1960, *SCMP*, no. 2356:28–30 (Oct. 12, 1960).

116. Premier Chou's letter to Premier Ben Hatta of the GPRA, *WCC 1962*, vol. IX (1964), p. 309.

117. According to an official GPRA list, up to December 1961 the GPRA had been recognized de jure by twenty-five states, mostly in the Afro-Asian group but including North Vietnam, North Korea, Yugoslavia, and the PRC. Six other countries, including India, Hungary, Czechoslovakia, Bulgaria, East Germany, and the USSR, were listed as having recognized it de facto. See Misra, *India's Policy of Recognition*, p. 130, n. 54.

moment in the Algerian people's struggle,"[118] as well as offered active support. Prompt recognition was granted also by Morocco, Tunisia, Libya, and Iraq.[119]

Outside the Western bloc, the cause of the Algerian revolution found rather widespread sympathy. Although the Indian government did not overcome its initial hesitancy until November 1961,[120] the delay was due to Nehru's political caution rather than a lack of sympathy. During the prolonged debates in the Indian Parliament, many members offered strong arguments for prompt recognition of the GPRA by India.[121]

With world opinion so divided and many other states also having promptly recognized the GPRA, it would be difficult to sort out Peking alone for condemnation. Whether its premature recognition and material assistance to GPRA amounted to intervention under traditional international law cannot be answered without examining whether all the other recognizing states were also intervening in the Algerian war between 1958 and 1962. Egypt's generosity in permitting GPRA to operate on Egyptian soil would seem, in any event, a more serious challenge to the traditional norms.

The situation was further complicated in another way. Although Peking had recognized the GPRA back in 1958, it explicitly renewed its recognition of the new independent Algerian Republic on July 3, 1962, one day after the French and the Algerians ceased fire in pursuance of the March 18 Evian Agreements.[122] While an Algerian mission had been stationed in Peking at least from October 1960 on, a PRC-Algerian joint communiqué on December 23, 1963, announced an agreement to establish "diplomatic relations."[123] No such renewal of recognition was found in a similar situation in 1960, when Ghana, which Peking had tacitly recognized back in 1958, became a republic from its previous dominion status in the British Commonwealth. The mode of the PRC's response to the independence of Algeria in 1962 raises a few questions: Why was the renewal of recognition necessary? What was the nature of its 1958 recognition of the GPRA? How different was it from the 1962 recognition? What was the difference

118. *The New York Times*, Sept. 20, 1958, p. 18.

119. Michael K. Clark, *Algeria in Turmoil: A History of the Rebellion* (London: Thames, 1960), p. 423.

120. *Hindustan Times* (Nov. 5, 1961), p. 12, quoted in Misra, *India's Policy of Recognition*, p. 129.

121. Misra, *ibid.*, pp. 122–123.

122. *WCC 1962*, vol. IX (1964), p. 342.

123. *WCC 1963*, vol. X (1965), p. 484.

between the new Algerian diplomatic mission subsequent to the agreement of December 23, 1963, and the previous Algerian "diplomatic delegation" in Peking?

As in other cases, the PRC did not provide an explanation for questions of this sort. One can only speculate about some possible answers. Could it be that the 1958 recognition was, so far as Peking was concerned, extended to a belligerent *sui generis*, whereas in 1962 its recognition was addressed to Algeria as an independent state? If so, the Algerian "diplomatic delegation" in Peking prior to Algerian independence would be the representative of a belligerent *sui generis* hard to place under any established categories in international law. Recognition of a belligerent did not, under existing law, permit the recognizing state to give aid to the belligerent or to receive its "diplomatic delegation." An alternative explanation, which appears relatively more plausible, might be that, despite its abstention from the express use of the words, the PRC's 1958 recognition was extended de facto and that of 1962 de jure.

Another example of how Peking made political use of recognition was its recognition of the dissident Stanleyville regime in the Congo (L) in February 1961. On that occasion, Peking appeared to imply that its previous recognition of the Congolese central government headed by President Joseph Kasavubu was withdrawn. Ambassadors were then exchanged with Stanleyville until the latter's collapse in September of that year. The brief and precarious existence of the Gizenga regime only showed that Peking's recognition was premature, being motivated by an intention to intervene in the internal affairs of the Congo. Peking's pretext that its action was "provoked" by Kasavubu's "collusion" with "imperialism" and that its aid to Gizenga was a countermeasure[124] is hardly convincing from the viewpoint of international law.

A number of revolutionary movements in foreign countries are known to have permanent missions in Peking. These missions possibly enjoy a special diplomatic or quasi-diplomatic status. There is a mission of the Palestine Liberation Organization, sent from its headquarters in Cairo. New China News Agency (NCNA) dispatches suggest that the

124. The PRC attitude toward the Leopoldville government of President Kasavubu changed after Patrice Lumumba's murder. See Peking's condemnation of the murder as an "imperialist" plot in *SCMP*, no. 2442:35 (Feb. 23, 1961). For PRC recognition of and establishment of diplomatic relations with the Stanleyville regime, see *WCC 1961*, vol. VIII (1962), pp. 141, 142, 166.

mission's head and deputy head have access to Foreign Minister Ch'en Yi.[125] The Malayan National Liberation League also maintains a mission in Peking.[126] Most spectacular of all is the permanent mission of the South Vietnam National Liberation Front. Its new head, Nguyen Van Quang, was reported by NCNA to have presented his "letter of appointment" to Premier Chou En-lai on December 4, 1967.[127] This appears to be a diluted version of the presentation of credentials by duly accredited diplomatic envoys.

Peking's acceptance of these missions seems to suggest a recognition *sui generis* of the revolutionary movements they represent. Some of these movements are aimed at overthrowing regimes which Peking does not recognize, such as South Vietnam and Israel. It is hard to say whether the PRC is intervening in behalf of these revolutionary movements by receiving their permanent missions in Peking. In other cases, Peking somewhat openly supported native revolutions aimed at governments it had previously recognized, such as in Somalia,[128] Burundi,[129] Indonesia,[130] and so forth.

FURTHER REFLECTIONS AND CONCLUSIONS

We have seen that the PRC's recognition doctrine was founded on its aspiration to be recognized by the world community. In spirit it bore a remote resemblance to the Jeffersonian de factoism, which in its own way reflected the aspirations of the new American nation as well as Thomas Jefferson's empathy for the French Revolution. As Secretary of State, Jefferson on March 12, 1793, made the following statement on whether a government that came to power by revolutionary means should be recognized:

We surely cannot deny to any nation *that right whereon our own Government is founded*—that every one may govern itself according to whatever form it

125. See, for instance, *SCMP*, no. 3660:28 (Mar. 18, 1966); no. 3657:17–19 (Mar. 15, 1966); and no. 3705:31 (May 25, 1966).
126. *SCMP*, no. 3876:32 (Feb. 7, 1967).
127. NCNA, Peking (Dec. 1, 1967) and (Dec. 4, 1967). My attention was called to this by Donald Klein of the East Asian Institute, Columbia University, who offered help freely during the initial stage of my research.
128. I. William Zartman, "Tiger in the Jungle," in Francis Harper, ed., *This Is China* (Hongkong: Dragonfly, 1965), p. 322; also Hinton, *Communist China in World Politics*, pp. 194–195, 196–197.
129. John Cooley, *East Wind in Africa* (New York: Walker, 1965), p. 112.
130. Refer to Justus M. van der Kroef, *The Sino-Indonesia Rupture* (New York: American-Asian Educational Exchange, 1968).

pleases, and change these forms at its own will; and that it may transact its business with foreign nations through whatever organ it thinks proper. . . *The will of the nation* is the *only thing essential* to be regarded.[131] (Emphasis added.)

Jefferson's deference to the "right whereon our own Government is founded" showed a consciousness of America's revolutionary origin not unlike Peking's self-oriented perspective. Again, not unlike Peking's doctrine of self-determination, the Jeffersonian Doctrine with its exclusive concern for the "will of the nation" barred considerations of internal constitutional legitimacy. Following the independence movements in Latin America, however, United States recognition policy gradually shifted away from the Jeffersonian Doctrine, as it became necessary to cope with recurrent coups d'état in the Western Hemisphere. With Woodrow Wilson's insistence on constitutional succession, the issue had run full cycle. In this shift, as in the PRC's subsequent modifications in practice, greater rigidity has replaced the earlier revolutionary idealism of a new nation; the shield has turned into a sword.

In broad historical perspective, the institution of recognition has undergone significant changes with the transformation of international politics. During the period of the "balance of power" system, roughly up until World War I, seldom was recognition withheld on considerations of concern for political advantage to an individual state. As the process of alliance was flexible in that system, rarely did a new state either politically or ideologically represent a definitive threat to one grouping of states and an advantage to another.[132] Although policy considerations then as now always entered into decision-making, recognition once granted served to certify a permanent change in the political status quo. If the matter was simpler than it is today, it was due to the fact that existing international society was geographically and culturally limited to European nations, who had a common base of shared values and sentiments.

The Latin American independence ferment created an unprecedented tension between (past) legitimacy and (present) reality. The emergence and subsequent spread in the practice of states of the distinction

131. A. Moore, *Digest of International Law* (Washington, D.C.: U.S. Government Printing Office, 1906), vol. I, p. 120.

132. Morton Kaplan and Nicholas deB. Katzenbach, *The Political Foundations of International Law* (New York: John Wiley, 1961), p. 125.

between de jure and de facto modes of recognition represented a compromise between the conflicting claims of law and policy.[133]

The bipolar system in the postwar period injected ideological conflicts into the recognition question as in other areas of international politics. Recognition became equated with ideological approval. Besides, there was a practical factor in the equation. The appearance of socialist regimes, because of their belief in the abolition of private capital (both domestic and foreign), severely strained the relative universality of economic principles prevailing in the once predominant capitalist framework. The role of recognition in securing continuity of economic obligations, such as payment of previous debts and protection of foreign investments, ceased to have the significance it once had enjoyed.[134] Ideology thus had as great a bearing on recognition policy as did legal and political considerations. Recognition changed from a "right" to a "political act" to a "privilege." Whereas the criteria for recognition had once been defined as "an established fact of independence" and the "will and capacity to fulfill international obligations," ideological affinity and acceptability became an additional test at least until the early 1960s.[135]

It is a truism, however, that the world since 1960 has been transformed in a number of significant ways: the massive emergence of new nations from former captive status, the expansion of the "nuclear club," and the exacerbation of the Sino-Soviet feud. With the disintegration of the bipolar system recognition is no longer purely calculated on the basis of bloc interests. The three-way tangle between the PRC, the United States, and the Soviet Union, plus the growing importance of the third world, has reintroduced an element of flexibility of alignment, cutting across ideological lines.[136]

133. Refer to Quincy Wright, "Recognition, Intervention, and Ideologies," *Indian Year Book of International Affairs* (New Delhi) *1958*, pp. 89–118, esp. 111.

134. See my note 132. Refer also to Gillian White, *Nationalization of Foreign Property* (London: Stevens; and New York: Praeger, 1961); B. A. Wortley, *Expropriation in Public International Law* (Cambridge, Eng.: Cambridge University Press, 1959); and S. Friedman, *Expropriation in International Law* (London: Stevens, 1953).

135. Percy E. Corbett, *Law in Diplomacy* (Princeton, N.J.: Princeton University Press, 1959; Magnolia, Mass.: Peter Smith, 1967), pp. 68–70.

136. PRC recognition practice after 1960, as noted, stands in contrast to its heightened level of verbal militancy during the same period. The discrepancy might be another reminder that the PRC's redoubled exhortation of armed struggle in the "third world" was an oblique attack on what its leaders believed was a Soviet overemphasis on support to nationalist leaders at the expense of world Communist interests, such as during the Sino-Indian conflict in 1962. In fact, the

The impact of these "systemic" changes upon Peking's recognition practice can be summed up as follows: While its recognition *doctrine* was conceived in the era of bipolar ideological division, its content was by default relatively ideology-free, reflecting an anxiousness to argue that ideological differences should not bar Peking's own recognition by other states. Peking's recognition *practice* toward other new states and governments, on the other hand, was extremely ambivalent, showing a much keener ideological concern than its doctrine said any state should show. Paradoxically, only after the collapse of the bipolar era did it become possible for PRC practice to follow the rather practical dictates that its own recognition doctrine had laid out in self-defense during the previous era.

It is worth reiterating that the ideological factor has not totally vanished in the current period; it has simply ceased to be conceived in terms of bloc interests. It will continue to compete with law and policy considerations in the recognition practices of many states, the PRC included. One might raise a question *de lege ferenda* in this connection. As noted, the existing duality of de jure and de facto recognition has arisen out of the conflicting claims of law and policy. Given the ideological dimension in international conflicts, should there not be a third mode of recognition, *de ideologica*?

In retrospect, recognition *de ideologica* has actually been practiced more widely and longer than we realize. A ready example is the Soviet Union's triangular relations during the 1920s with the warlord government then in Peking (de jure), the Kuomintang opposition in Canton (de facto), and the nascent Communist movement in China (*de ideologica*). The quasi-diplomatic status which the PRC extends to permanent missions from revolutionary movements in foreign countries, especially those whose national governments have been formally recognized by Peking, seems to confer recognition *de ideologica.*

Looking to the future, the PRC's recognition practice, as in the past, is likely to be dominated by the following combination of factors:

Chinese Communists in 1963 openly accused the Soviet leaders of having betrayed "proletarian internationalism" by their support of Nehru during the Sino-Indian boundary dispute. Observer, "The Indian Reactionary in the Anti-Chinese Chorus," *JMJP*, July 16, 1963; also CCP reply on June 14, 1963 to the March 30, 1963 letter from the CPSU ("A Proposal Concerning the General Line of the International Communist Movement"), English translation in *PR*, no. 30:10–26 (July 26, 1963). See also W. W. Kulski, *International Politics in a Revolutionary Age* (New York: Lippincott, 1964), p. 378; and Hsiung, "Communist China's Foreign Policy."

the conflict between the self-oriented and the outward-directed perspectives, the trichotomy of law, policy, and ideology, and the impact of "systemic" changes upon the PRC's international posture.

POSTSCRIPT

Beginning from the latter part of 1970, the PRC entered into diplomatic relations with an increasing number of states, including such important allies of the United States as Canada and Italy. A number of reasons may account for the changing trend. The dust of the Cultural Revolution had finally settled, and China was turning outward again. The US-PRC thaw ever since the Ping Pong Diplomacy offered encouragement for some pro-US countries to move toward the recognition of Peking. Furthermore, a compromise solution to the ticklish Taiwan question was found in the PRC's prolonged negotiations with Canada, serving as a model for others to follow. In an announcement issued on October 13, 1970, Canada "takes note" of the PRC's claim to Taiwan. "The Chinese Government reaffirms that Taiwan is an inalienable part of the territory of the People's Republic of China. The Canadian Government *takes note* of this position of the Chinese Government."[137] (Emphasis added.)

The bilateral accord on "mutual recognition" made it plain that the PRC and Canada *exchanged* recognition, as distinct from unilaterally extending recognition. As such, the act represented a departure from a practice frequently followed by the PRC of not explicitly acknowledging or reciprocating recognition. The Canadian government on its part recognized the PRC as the "sole legal government of China." Both parties agreed to establish diplomatic relations immediately, in accordance with "the principles of mutual respect for sovereignty and territorial integrity, non-interference in each other's internal affairs, and equality and mutual benefit."[138] These recall Mao's 1949 triad for guiding the PRC's foreign relations.[139]

The Canadian formula was promptly followed in a number of other cases. The "take note" form of dispensing with the Taiwan issue, the "sole legal government of China" clause, and the three principles for diplomatic relations were repeated almost in identical language in Peking's agreements with Italy (November 6, 1970) and Chile (Decem-

137. *PR*, no. 42:12 (October 16, 1970). Emphasis added. Material in this section is drawn from the last part of Chapter XI in my book referred to in note 4.
138. *Ibid.*
139. See note 16.

ber 15, 1970).[140] In the Chile case, there was no mention of "mutual recognition"; and the agreement with Italy specified that ambassadors would be exchanged within three months.

The accord reached with Austria on May 26, 1971, took the form of "mutual recognition," and it adopted the triad mentioned above as the principles governing the relations between the two parties. Austria recognized the PRC as the "sole legal government of China," but the Taiwan issue was not mentioned. The PRC, on its part, pledged to respect Austria's neutrality.[141]

Variations were found in recognition accords reached by the PRC with different states, and some of them did not follow the Canadian formula, strictly speaking. The PRC was recognized as the "sole legal government of China" in separate agreements signed with Equatorial Guinea (October 15, 1970), Ethiopia (November 24, 1970), Nigeria (February 10, 1971), San Marino (May 14, 1971), and Sierra Leone (July 29, 1971).[142] In none of these was the Taiwan question raised. But in these as in the four cases above, the word "recognize" was expressly used, with the exception of the PRC-Ethiopian agreement, which used the term "affirm."[143] The accords with Equatorial Guinea, Ethiopia, Nigeria, Cameroon, and Sierra Leone identified the PRC as "representing the entire Chinese people," which appeared to allude to Taiwan as well. In these cases, the "five principles" of peaceful coexistence, in contrast to the triad, were named the guiding principles of diplomatic relations. However, the recognition accords with Kuwait and San Marino made no mention of either set of principles.

It is not clear why the "mutual recognition" form was used in certain cases but not in others; nor why the "five principles" were included in some accords and the triad in some others. The "five principles" are probably reserved for states which show a greater degree of affinity to the PRC, though this explanation may not be valid in all cases. An editorial in the *People's Daily*, commenting on the PRC-Canadian accord, which used the triad, made enthusiastic references to the "five principles of peaceful coexistence."[144] Did the editorial intend to place

140. For PRC-Italian agreement see *PR*, no. 46:6 (Nov. 13, 1970); and for PRC-Chilean agreement, *PR*, no. 2:11 (Jan. 8, 1971).

141. *PR*, no. 23:11 (June 4, 1971).

142. See *PR*, no. 43:10 (Oct. 23. 1970); no. 50:6 (Dec. 11, 1970); no. 8:5 (Feb. 19, 1971); no. 14:16 (Apr. 2, 1971); no. 15:7 (Apr. 9, 1971); no. 20:11 (May 14, 1971); and no. 32:22 (Aug. 6. 1971).

143. *PR*, no. 50:7 (Dec. 11, 1970). See also text at reference for note 95 above.

144. "Welcome the Establishment of Diplomatic Relations between China and Canada," *JMJP*, Oct. 15, 1970; English translation in *PR*, no. 42:13 (Oct. 16,

the two sets of principles on the same footing, or was it expressing an unrealized hope, in that the accord, minus the "take note" clause, would have come close to the spirit of the "five principles"? In other words, do the differences, if any, between the two sets of principles hinge upon the other party's attitude on the Taiwan issue?

Besides the "five principles," Peking's recognition accords with countries such as Equatorial Guinea, Ethiopia, Nigeria, Cameroon, and Sierra Leone also provided a standing Chinese pledge of support for the other party's struggle against "imperialism, colonialism, and neocolonialism." One is tempted to link the "five principles" with the anti-imperialist and anticolonial cause. The link, however, is by no means a firm one, for in the agreement with Kuwait, which mentioned neither the "five principles" nor the triad, the PRC expressed its support for the "Arab struggle against imperialism and Zionism." An editorial in the *People's Daily,* which hailed the PRC-Kuwait accord as paving the way for diplomatic relations "on the basis of the five principles of . . . peaceful coexistence," seems to further complicate the matter.[145]

On balance, the variations in wording among the recognition agreements may suggest a hierarchy of varying types of relations between the PRC and its co-signatories, probably determined by three considerations. In the first place, the "five principles" were cited with relative consistency in those accords reached with states that are ideologically antiimperialist and anticolonial. The triad, on the other hand, was largely reserved for Western countries or their allies. Second, states that had to accept the "take note" formula in regard to Taiwan—Canada, Italy, and Chile—were those which had continued to recognize and maintain diplomatic relations with Nationalist China until the switch of recognition. Last of all, when a state fell under neither of the two groups, as was the case with San Marino and Kuwait, the recognition agreement skipped mention of either set of the principles. In the final analysis, the recognition of the PRC as the "sole legal government of China" is the most crucial test on which all potential recognition agreements with Peking depend.

1970). The "five principles" are mutual respect for sovereignty and territorial integrity, mutual nonaggression, mutual noninterference in internal affairs, equality and mutual benefit, and peaceful coexistence. I have dealt with the changing meanings of the "five principles" in the PRC's usage and application, in Chapter 11 of my book cited in note 4 above.

145. "Greeting the Establishment of Diplomatic Relations between China and Kuwait," *JMJP,* Mar. 31, 1971; English translation in *PR,* no. 14:16 (Apr. 2, 1971).

2 / The Establishment of Diplomatic Relations and the Scope of Diplomatic Immunity: The Dutch Experience with China

Ko Swan Sik

INTRODUCTION

Relations between the People's Republic of China (PRC) and the Netherlands have been limited. An attempt at a critical analysis of such relations is a rather perilous task, made more so since I have had no access to Chinese sources nor to Dutch archives. Notwithstanding these obstacles, however, a factual survey of some events and the posing of a few questions regarding Chinese legal attitudes can offer interesting material and be an inducement to further study, comparison, and thought.

The matter of PRC legal attitudes with regard to specific international relationships may be approached from two different angles. First, one can merely determine whether certain behavior is or is not in accordance with "established" or "generally accepted" rules of international law. The real problem there is to ascertain whether such rules really exist in the field concerned and what they, in fact, decree, bearing in mind the upheaval in which international law has found itself as a result of the changing structure of international society after the Second World War. Second, one could ask whether, in so far as Peking's behavior contradicts such "generally accepted" rules, this constitutes evidence of a Chinese wish to have the specific relationship governed by a rule different from the generally accepted one. Before, however, drawing a conclusion, one should first look at the past practice of the PRC, since one isolated act can hardly be considered sufficient evidence of a legal conviction unless other supporting evidence is available. It is equally important to compare the deviating

NOTE: Basically, the article was finished in the autumn of 1968, and subsequent data have only been summarily added afterwards, mostly in footnotes.

Chinese behavior with the past and present practice of other, "older" subjects of international law with regard to the rule in question: How have similar deviating acts of other subjects of international law been denominated? Such comparison should prevent an isolated contemplation of Chinese practice, which could lead to erroneous conclusions. Finally, in assessing the implications of deviating Chinese behavior, one should take into account the motives underlying that behavior and other determining factors. Knowledge of such motives and determining factors leads to better and more understanding of otherwise less comprehensible behavior. It is submitted that among such determining factors are the following:

1. The widespread feeling of dissatisfaction with traditional rules, often resulting in revolt against the status quo, which exists among many of the so-called "new states." This group of states could, by way of a general denominator, be defined by the following criteria: economically weak, spiritually and often also materially suffering from a recent colonial or semicolonial past, and therefore often fiercely nationalistic. It is suggested that China is one of this group of states.
2. China's heritage of social structures and values and consequently of legal and political values.
3. A collectivist idea of society, prevailing in a Marxist, or Maoist, structure but not necessarily a unique feature of Communist-inspired societies.
4. Pure Marxist-Leninist-Maoist ideas (if any) of international law and relations.

No one of these factors should a priori be seen as the sole factor determining PRC behavior. Although lack of resources and space prevents a thorough investigation herein of each of the factors, only a detailed analysis of China's behavior along the aforementioned lines can warrant conclusions which could fairly be said to be objective.

RECOGNITION AND THE ESTABLISHMENT OF DIPLOMATIC RELATIONS

Relations during the Period between Recognition and the Exchange of Diplomatic Representatives[1]

Dutch recognition of the Central People's Government of the PRC

1. The experiences of the Netherlands described here, it should be borne in mind from the outset, are in no way unique.

as the de jure government of China[2] took place by means of a note of March 28, 1950,[3] presented to the Chinese Ministry of Foreign Affairs by the representative in Peking of the Netherlands embassy, which was at that time still located at Nanking. The Dutch representative also informed the Chinese government orally[4] that diplomatic relations with the Nationalist government had been severed.[5]

In accordance with traditional custom, the Dutch note expressed the wish "to establish normal relations between the Central People's Government of the People's Republic of China and the Government of the Kingdom of the Netherlands, based on principles of equality, mutual benefit and mutual respect of territorial integrity and sovereignty."[6] Apparently the Dutch view was that change of government would in no way affect the level of mutual diplomatic representation. The note contained the following phrase: "I have also been requested to propose to Your Excellency to exchange diplomatic representatives between the Netherlands Government and the Central People's Government. *Pending the appointment of an Ambassador,* it is the intention of the Netherlands Government to nominate Mr. . . . , now at Nanking, as chargé d'affaires *ad interim.*" (Emphasis added.) However, neither the level of diplomatic representation nor the exchange of standing diplomatic representatives itself was considered by the Chinese government self-evident consequences of recognition. This is clearly, though subtly, formulated in the Chinese reply of April 4, 1950:

2. The Netherlands was the twenty-sixth state to grant recognition.

3. Text in *Jaarboek van het Ministerie van Buitenlandse Zaken,* 1949–1950 (Yearbook of the Netherlands Ministry of Foreign Affairs, 1949–1950), p. 298. Hereafter cited as *Jaarboek.*

4. Cited in the reply of the Chinese Ministry of Foreign Affairs of April 4, 1950. Text of unofficial English translation in *Jaarboek,* 1949–1950, p. 299. See also the German translation in *Verträge der Volksrepublik China mit anderen Staaten* (Treaties of the People's Republic of China with other states; Berlin: Metzner Verlag, 1965), vol. III, p. 58. Hereafter, *Verträge.*

5. For the Dutch withdrawal of the *de jure* recognition of the Chinese Nationalist government and the severance of diplomatic relations, see the exchange of notes in *Jaarboek,* 1949–1950, pp. 300–301.

6. Compare the Danish government telegram, January 8, 1950, in *Verträge,* vol. III (1965), p. 11; the telegram of the Norwegian Consul-General in Shanghai, January 7, 1950, *ibid.,* p. 61; the telegram of the Swedish government, January 14, 1950, *ibid.,* p. 73; telegram of the Swiss government, January 17, 1950, *ibid.,* p. 79; telegram of the British government, January 6, 1950, *ibid.,* p. 84; telegram of the Burmese government, December 16, 1949, *ibid.,* I (1962), p. 14; telegram of the Ceylonese government, January 7, 1950, *ibid.,* p. 49; telegram of the Indian government, December 30, 1949, *ibid.,* p. 79; letter of the Cambodian government, July 18, 1958, *ibid.,* p. 172; note of the ambassador of Pakistan in Moscow, January 29, 1950, *ibid.,* p. 228.

I am now instructed to request you to inform the Government of [the] Netherlands that the Central People's Government of the People's Republic of China is willing to establish, with the Government of [the] Netherlands normal diplomatic relations between the People's Republic of China and the Kingdom of [the] Netherlands on the basis [of] equality, mutual benefit and mutual respect for territory and sovereignty, and is willing to accept Mr. . . . , designated as Chargé d'Affaires *ad interim* by the Government of [the] Netherlands, *as the representative of the Government of [the] Netherlands to Peking for negotiations on the question of establishing diplomatic relations* between the Kingdom of the Netherlands and the People's Republic of China.[7] (Emphasis added.)

Thus the Chinese reply, seemingly an affirmative answer, actually turned out to be a rejection of the Dutch proposals. Although willing in principle to establish normal diplomatic relations, this was in fact made an object for negotiations and could be effectuated only if some Chinese conditions would be fulfilled. The man designated by the Dutch note would not be considered the acting head of a permanent diplomatic mission, as intended by the Netherlands, but a special ad hoc representative with a strictly defined task.

Chinese Conditions for the Normal Exchange of Diplomatic Representatives

As Dutch-Chinese negotiations started in Peking,[8] the Chinese, in accord with their usual practice, presented the Netherlands representa-

7. See footnote 4 above. In the Danish telegram, the Chinese government was informed that the plenipotentiary envoy, staying in Shanghai for the time being, was waiting to be received. As in the Dutch case, the Chinese government replied that it was willing to receive him as the representative sent by the Danish government to Peking for negotiations on the question of establishing diplomatic relations. See *Verträge*, vol. III (1965), p. 12. To the Norwegian statement that Norway is prepared to send a chargé d'affaires to Peking as soon as possible, the Chinese replied: "After Your Government has severed relations with the remnants of the Chinese Kuomintang reactionaries, the Central Government of the PRC is prepared . . . to establish diplomatic relations . . . , and requests the sending of a representative to Peking for negotiations on this question." See *ibid.*, p. 62. The same wording was used in the replies to Sweden, *ibid.*, p. 74, and to Switzerland, *ibid.*, p. 81. The case of the United Kingdom was quite similar to the Dutch case, also in its wording, *ibid.*, p. 85. The Chinese reply to Burma said: "On the condition that Your Government severs relations with the Kuomintang remnants, the Central People's Government of the PRC is willing to establish diplomatic relations." *Verträge*, vol. I (1962), p. 14. As Ceylon in its telegram of recognition already mentioned the severance of its relations with the Nationalist government, the Chinese replied: "[The Chinese foreign minister] expects the sending of a representative of the Ceylonese Government to negotiate the matter [of diplomatic relations]," *ibid.*, p. 50. The same or similar wording was used in the replies to India, *ibid.*, p. 80, and to Pakistan, *ibid.*, p. 229.

8. These negotiations were mainly conducted in written form and with long

tive with a questionnaire in which particular stress was laid on the rupture of all relations with the Nationalist regime on Taiwan.[9] This was elucidated in a statement by a spokesman of the Chinese Foreign Ministry pointing out the contradiction inherent in the behavior of those states which, while recognizing the PRC government as the de jure Chinese government, did not act to expel the Kuomintang representatives from the various UN organs.[10] Here, indeed, one finds the reason why the Chinese government considered the Dutch answer on the Chinese questionnaire unsatisfactory, in view of the Dutch attitude in the UN specialized agencies during that period.[11] It is clear that the possibility of establishing normal diplomatic intercourse became even more remote when the Dutch attitude toward admittance of PRC representatives into the UN grew still more unfavorable as a result of the UN resolution branding the PRC an aggressor,[12] and when the Netherlands became a party to the embargo measures.

Neither side, however, wished to break off the negotiations officially,

---

intervals. See the Netherlands Minister of Foreign Affairs in the Second Chamber of Parliament on January 18, 1951, in *Verslag der Handelingen van de Tweede Kamer der Staten-Generaal gedurende het zittingsjaar 1950–1951* (Proceedings of the Second Chamber of the States-General during the parliamentary year 1950–1951), p. 139. Hereafter cited as:

Hand. I (Proceedings First Chamber)
Hand. II (Proceedings Second Chamber)
Bijl. Hand. I (Annex to Proceedings First Chamber)
Bijl. Hand. II (Annex to Proceedings Second Chamber)
Aanh. Hand. I (Addenda to Proceedings First Chamber)
Aanh. Hand. II (Addenda to Proceedings Second Chamber)

9. *Jaarbook*, 1950–1951, p. 130.

10. *Ibid.;* see pp. 65–66 below.

11. While not recognizing the Nationalist government at Taiwan as the *de jure* government of China, the Dutch government held the view that the matter of admitting the PRC (government) into the UN and into its specialized agencies should be decided by the highest UN organs: the Security Council and the General Assembly. Consequently, in the specialized agencies, the Netherlands voted in favor of the rulings of the respective chairmen, who declared "out of order" any proposal aimed at the removal of the Nationalist representative and the admission of a PRC representative. When, in spite of such rulings, the proposals were put to a vote, the Netherlands abstained from voting. In the General Assembly, however, the Netherlands voted to admit the Central People's Government, up to the time (February 1, 1951) when the General Assembly adopted resolution 498 (V) branding the PRC an aggressor. See *Jaarboek*, 1950–1951, pp. 130–131. See also the Minister of Foreign Affairs in the Second Chamber on January 18, 1951, *Hand. II*, 1950–1951, p. 1139; and *Verslag over de vijfde Algemene Vergadering van de Verenigde Naties* (Report on the Fifth General Assembly of the United Nations), Ministry of Foreign Affairs publication no. 25 (The Hague: Government Printing Office), p. 51.

12. Note of Reply of the Dutch Minister of Foreign Affairs to the Second Chamber, December 2, 1952, in *Bijl. Hand. II* 1953–1954, 2800 III, no. 14, p. 17.

although they were in fact suspended until 1954. China continued to pay the rent for the (former Nationalist Chinese) embassy building in The Hague,[13] and the Netherlands even changed its representative in Peking twice during that period.

It was the general détente in China's foreign policy in 1954, or, according to a French professor, the beginning of the third phase of China's foreign policy,[14] which at last created the proper political climate for more normal Chinese-Western relations. On November 19, 1954, the Chinese and the Dutch agreed to exchange permanent diplomatic representatives in spite of the fact that the Netherlands had not given in to the Chinese view of relating diplomatic relations to the question of Chinese representation in the UN.

In accordance with Chinese wishes,[15] the exchange of representatives was to take place at the chargé d'affaires level. Why the Chinese preferred this lowest level of representation is not readily explained, but as late as 1964 the Dutch Minister of Foreign Affairs said that the absence of Dutch support for the PRC claim to exclusive representation of China in the UN might be one of the reasons for Chinese reluctance to exchange diplomatic missions at the ambassadorial level.[16] In this

13. *Jaarboek*, 1950–1951, p. 131.

14. Lazar Focsaneanu, "Les grands traités de la République Populaire de Chine," *Annuaire français de droit international*, 1962 (Paris: Centre National de la Recherche Scientifique), p. 151. Focsaneanu distinguishes six phases: (1) from the founding of the PRC until the conclusion of the Sino-Soviet treaties in February 1950; (2) 1950 to 1954, when China attempted to extend its influence and to establish its domination in Asia through an aggressive expansionist policy; (3) 1954 to 1956, which was the period of the "good neighbor policy," of the five principles of peaceful coexistence, and of the Bandung Conference; (4) 1956 to 1958, which showed the increasing prestige of China within the Communist bloc; (5) 1958 to 1960, showing a stiffening of China's foreign policy; and (6) from 1960, when relations between the PRC and other Communist states continued to deteriorate. It could be fairly suggested that the Cultural Revolution marked a further stiffening of attitude toward the outside world since 1966. (Later developments after 1966 are not included.)

15. Dutch Minister of Foreign Affairs on November 13, 1964, in answer to parliamentary questions in *Aanh. Hand. II*, 1964–1965, no. 62, p. 73.

16. Statement in the Second Chamber of Parliament on December 10, 1964, in *Hand. II*, 1964–1965, p. C 813. Exchanges on the ambassadorial level have taken place with the following Western European states: Denmark, Finland, Norway, Sweden, and France; on the level of legation with Switzerland, and on the chargé d'affaires level with the United Kingdom. Refer to footnote 30 below. As a result of the Dutch stand in the matter of China's representation in the UN in 1971, the two governments agreed to raise the level of their respective diplomatic missions to the ambassadorial level, by joint communiqué of May 16, 1972. Text in *Nederlandse Staatscourant* (State gazette), no. 94 (May 17, 1972). The wording shows a further development compared to the Sino-Canadian example: The Chinese government "reaffirms" that Taiwan is a province of the PRC, which stand is

same discourse, the Minister told Parliament that during a visit to China by a Dutch private economic mission Chou En-lai complained about the Dutch attitude toward Taiwan's position in the UN.[17]

Legal Status and Competence of the Dutch Representative in Peking during the Interim Period

Although the Dutch representative was admitted solely as an ad hoc negotiator, the Chinese government did not adhere too strictly to the consequences of their position. The suspension of the negotiations for three years was no reason for the Chinese to request the mission's recall. Moreover, the Chinese government sometimes tacitly consented to the Dutch representative taking up matters that had no direct connections with the establishment of diplomatic relations as such. The members of the representative's staff, though not officially holding diplomatic status, were permitted to make service-journeys *as if* they held such status.[18]

On the other hand, and apart from the question of whether a state is legally dutybound to do so, the Chinese government never informed the Dutch representative of arrests of Dutch citizens (missionaries and priests) because in the Chinese view the representative had no competence in the field of diplomatic protection.[19] Nor did the Chinese government react in any way when the Dutch representative presented a note on the treatment of arrested Dutch citizens.[20] It is a moot question, however, whether such a note would be answered if the representative were recognized as a permanent diplomatic representative.

"respected" by the Netherlands government. This government further "reaffirms that it recognizes the Government of the PRC as the sole legal Government of China."

17. In March 1971, the Chinese government announced its refusal to receive a similar Dutch private economic mission although an invitation for the visit was extended in 1970. It was assumed in the Netherlands that the cause of the withdrawal of the invitation lay in a government-supported motion of the Second Chamber of Parliament, according to which the Netherlands should support the occupation of China's seat in the UN by the Peking government, without, however, implying the expulsion of the "other" Chinese representation. See the questions from Parliament and the reply of the Minister for Foreign Affairs in *Aanh. Hand. II*, 1970–1971, no. 919, p. 1847. See also *NRC-Handelsblad*, March 6, 1971, p. 7.

18. Note of reply of the Dutch Minister of Foreign Affairs to the Second Chamber, December 2, 1952, in *Bijl. Hand. II*, 1952–1953, 2800 III, no. 14, p. 17.

19. *Ibid.*

20. *Jaarboek*, 1951–1952, p. 134.

The Chinese Legal Attitude Toward and Conditions on the Establishment of Regular Diplomatic Relations

State practice and doctrine show that no unanimity exists on the question of whether a newly recognized government is obliged to consent to the establishment of diplomatic relations with the recognizing state.[21] Neither is this the case with the establishment of permanent diplomatic missions. The freedom which results from this is best formulated in article 2 of the Vienna Convention on Diplomatic Relations (1961): "The establishment of diplomatic relations between States, and of permanent diplomatic missions, takes place by mutual consent." Oppenheim, while agreeing that "obviously a State is not bound to send diplomatic envoys or to receive permanent envoys," maintains that for practical reasons a state cannot refuse to receive ad hoc missions or to make possible the holding of negotiations on various points and the conveyance of messages. This is a consequence of the very existence of a community of states.[22] In its behavior toward the Netherlands, China has done no more than avail itself of the discretion accorded to it by traditional international law.

We have now reached the stage for looking at the conditions posed by China. In making these conditions, the Chinese government neatly carried out article 56 of the "Common Program," adopted by the first plenary session of the Chinese People's Political Consultative Conference, the provisional parliament, in September 1949. This article reads: "The Central People's Government of the People's Republic of China may on the basis of equality, mutual benefit and mutual respect for

21. J. Mervyn Jones rightly distinguishes as follows: "Many of the problems concerning the legal effects of recognition are caused by the confusion between recognition properly so called and the establishment of diplomatic relations. The latter always implies recognition; but recognition is not always accompanied or immediately followed by the establishment of diplomatic relations." See J. Mervyn Jones, "The Retroactive Effect of the Recognition of States and Governments," *British Yearbook of International Law* 16:53 (1935). D. P. O'Connell, *International Law* (Dobbs Ferry, N.Y.: Oceana, 1965), vol. I, p. 349, says that "if there is a right to sever diplomatic relations there must surely be a right to non-reception." See also P. Fauchille, *Traité de droit international public* (Paris: A. Rousseau et Cie, 1926), vol. 1, part 3, p. 32; G. Dahm, *Völkerrecht* (Stuttgart: W. Kohlhammer Verlag, 1958), p. 314; C. Calvo, *Le Droit international théorique et pratique,* 5th ed. (Paris: A. Rousseau et Cie, 1896), vol. III, p. 177; B. Sen, *A Diplomat's Handbook on International Law and Practice* (The Hague: M. Nijhoff, 1965), pp. 8–9; L. Oppenheim, *International Law,* 8th. ed., H. Lauterpacht, ed. (London: Longmans, Green and Co., 1955), vol. I, par. 360; M. Sibert, *Traité de droit international public* (Paris: Dalloz, 1951), vol. II, par. 711, p. 12; Ernest M. Satow, *Guide to Diplomatic Practice,* 4th ed. (London: Longmans, Green and Co., 1958), p. 116.

22. Oppenheim, *International Law,* vol. I, par. 360.

territory and sovereignty, negotiate with foreign governments which have severed relations with the Kuomintang reactionary clique and which adopt a friendly attitude toward the People's Republic of China, and may establish diplomatic relations with them."[23]

Although the full contents of the Chinese questionnaire are not available to the author, it is clear that the main condition made by the Chinese was an unambiguous stand on the issue of Chinese representation. The PRC government has consistently rejected the idea of "two Chinas." All Chinese territory being an integral part of the Chinese state, there could not be more than one government representing it—and that is the Central People's Government at Peking. Recognition of this government as the de jure government of China implied that no other government, even when in factual possession of any part of the territory of the Chinese state, could be considered having legal authority to represent China. Any act to the contrary is thus seen as an unfriendly act, to say the least. Now if "acute disagreement [having] arisen between the two States"[24] is sufficient grounds to break off diplomatic relations, one could hardly contest the right of a government to demand exclusive recognition in all fields as the only legitimate authority of the state concerned, as a prerequisite for the establishment of normal diplomatic relations.[25] This attitude has always been maintained by the PRC in its dealings with other countries and is made explicit when necessary.[26] Besides the wording of the Chinese reply to the announcements of recognition by Norway, Sweden, Switzerland, Great Britain, and Burma,[27] the text of a statement of May 22, 1950, by a spokesman of the Chinese Foreign Ministry on the course of the Anglo-Chinese negotiations is quite illuminating.[28] Again, the Chinese

23. Text in *Documents on International Affairs 1949–1950* (London: Milford, 1953), p. 539. See also H. A. Steiner, "Mainsprings of Chinese Communist Foreign Policy," *AJIL* 44:91–93 (1950).

24. Oppenheim, *International Law*, vol. I, par. 362a, p. 775.

25. For the arguments for and against this viewpoint, see J. Beauté, "La République Populaire de Chine et le droit international," *Revue générale de droit international public* 68:360–362 (1964).

26. See H. A. Steiner, "Communist China in the World Community," *International Conciliation*, no. 533:437–439 (May 1964). In *International Legal Materials* 9:244 (1970), we find that of the 58 states that have recognized the PRC government, eight have not established diplomatic relations, among which two, namely Nigeria and Senegal, recognize "both Chinas." This is fully in accord with the Chinese attitude described in the text. See also my footnote 17.

27. See my footnote 7.

28. The text of the statement was originally published in *WCC 1949–1950*, vol. I (1957), pp. 122–124, and translated into German in *Verträge*, vol. III (1965), pp. 87–89.

stand has been formulated more recently in a statement of January 28, 1964, on the question of diplomatic relations with France.[29, 30]

It may thus be concluded that the only exceptional feature in the Chinese case is that whereas other newly recognized governments are all too eager to enter into diplomatic relations, this is not the case with the PRC. Such an attitude, however, cannot be said to be a violation of the existing legal rules.

As suggested above, the Chinese reply to the Netherlands of April 4, 1950, implied that China was only prepared to receive the Dutch-designated chargé d'affaires ad interim as "representative . . . for negotiations on the question of establishing diplomatic relations," therefore, as a diplomat "with special functions."[31] Since the Netherlands did not react aversely to the Chinese note and did send the designated gentleman to Peking, we may assume that the Netherlands, in fact, accepted the Chinese proposal as to the formal status of the representative, if

29. "It was in the capacity of the sole legal Government representing all the Chinese people that the Government of the People's Republic of China entered into negotiations and reached agreement with the Government of the French Republic on the establishment of diplomatic relations between the two countries. According to international practice, recognition of the new government of a country naturally implies ceasing to recognize the old ruling group overthrown by the people of that country. Consequently, the representatives of the old ruling group can no longer be regarded as representatives of that country to be present side by side with the representative of the new government in one and the same country or international organization. It was with this understanding that the Government of the People's Republic of China reached agreement with the Government of the French Republic on the establishment of diplomatic relations and the exchange of ambassadors between China and France. The Chinese Government deems it necessary to reaffirm that Taiwan is part of Chinese territory and that any attempt to detach Taiwan from China or otherwise to create two Chinas is absolutely unacceptable to the Chinese Government and people." *PR*, no. 5:10 (1964). See also Stephen Erasmus, "General De Gaulle's Recognition of Peking," *China Quarterly*, no. 18:195–197 (Apr.–June 1964).

30. With the Canadian recognition of October 13, 1970, a new development seems to have started. The recognition of the Peking government "as the sole legal government" (in contradistinction to factual?) of China (as such) seems to be no problem anymore. It is even explicitly mentioned in the Sino-Canadian joint communiqué. Instead China stressed their position that Taiwan is an inalienable part of China's territory and insisted on endorsement of this position by the other side. This was refused by the Canadian government who did not consider it appropriate either to endorse or to challenge the Chinese government's position. Finally, both parties agreed that China reaffirms its position while Canada "takes note" of it. Thus was the formulation in the joint communiqué. For the text of the joint communiqué, see *International Legal Materials*, vol. 9 (1970), pp. 1244–1245. One wonders whether the PRC foresaw that after the "two-Chinas" idea failed to materialize, the adversaries of Peking authority over the island of Taiwan would support the "secession" of a separate "Taiwan state."

31. Milan Bartoš, "Report on Special Missions," *Yearbook of the International Law Commission*, 1964, vol. II, p. 83.

only by acquiescence. What are the specific characteristics of the status and competence of such a diplomat in traditional international law, and how far did China conform with or deviate from such norms, if there are any?

Although ad hoc diplomacy preceded the rise of standing missions, it is in the field of the latter that customary rules crystallized in international law. A recent writer complained that, in general, doctrine does not deal with the subject of ad hoc diplomacy, and that one can say, without mistake, that no customary rules exist.[32] In the face of this, we may well avail ourselves of the research done by the International Law Commission.[33] The relevant draft articles in Mr. Bartoš's first report on the subject (later accepted by the Commission) are articles 1, 2, 3, and 11.

Article 1 determines the right to send special missions, the necessary consent thereto of the receiving state, and the possibility of sending such a mission without the existence of regular diplomatic or consular relations.

Of article 2, the first three sections are relevant here. Whereas section 1 states that the assignment of the mission must be *specified by the sending state* and *consented to by the receiving state,* exactly the opposite happened in the Sino-Dutch case. However, since agreement on the scope of the assignment forms the essence of this section, as is amply set forth in the commentary, the Sino-Dutch practice is wholly in accordance with it. Section 2 states that the special mission may carry out on behalf of the sending state only those assignments which are within its competence. Section 3 then follows by saying that the assignment of the mission may be exceeded only by the mutual consent of the states concerned.

As just noted, the Chinese government in some cases agreed—and in other cases refused to agree—to the handling of matters by the Dutch

32. Philippe Cahier, *Le droit diplomatique contemporain,* 2nd ed. (Geneva: Librarie Droz, 1964), pp. 361 and 362: "The term *ad hoc* diplomacy was first used by the International Law Commission and during the discussions of the Sixth Committee of the UN General Assembly. No trace of this term has been found in the past, while doctrine generally does not deal with the subject. . . . It may be stated without error, that in the field of *ad hoc* diplomacy there are no rules of customary law." See also M. Hardy, *Modern Diplomatic Law* (Dobbs Ferry, N.Y.: Oceana, 1968), pp. 89–91.

33. See the report mentioned in my footnote 31. Refer to the Convention on Special Missions, adopted by UN General Assembly Resolution 2530 (XXIV) on December 8, 1969, and opened for signature since December 16, 1969. *International Legal Materials* 9:127 (1970).

representative falling outside the area of his duty as formulated in the Chinese reply. Mention was also made of the fact that, although the mission consisted only of one person, members of the representative's staff, probably employees of the former Netherlands embassy in China, were, at least in some respects, treated de facto as if they held diplomatic status. From these facts we may conclude that whereas the Chinese, in cases convenient to them, rightly held strictly to the limited competence of the special representative, they were quite lenient in other cases. In any case, there is no ground whatsoever to accuse them of any act contrary to the rights of the sending state as formulated in the Bartoš draft.[34]

Article 3 of the draft deals with the appointment of the head of the special mission and its members, for which, the article says, it is normally unnecessary to request *agrément*. The particular genesis of the Dutch special mission was such that the problem of *agrément* did not arise as a separate question. The task and the status of the representative were determined *after* agreement was reached on the person of the representative. The point not covered by the draft articles, but which did play a role in the present case, was the change of the person of the representative. Although it is not clear whether the Netherlands government formally asked for an *agrément* or succeeded in settling the matter informally, the fact is that the Chinese government did give its approval.

The last article of the draft which may be relevant is article 11 under (c), stating that the function of the special mission shall come to an end, inter alia, "upon the interruption or formal suspension of negotiations or deliberations within the competence of the mission."[35] As noted above, however, the Dutch mission did remain in existence despite a three-year suspension of the talks. There is no indication that either party regarded the mission as being terminated and later reinstalled. But even if the facts should be so interpreted, there is no reason to assume that the rule as contained in the draft was in any way meant to be *jus cogens*. Thus none of the facts really contravened the law as interpreted by the Bartoš report.

34. This leniency is also apparent if the Chinese behavior is judged by the standards put forward by Hardy, *Modern Diplomatic Law*, p. 93.

35. The same in the (first) report by Karl Sandström, the International Law Commission's Special Rapporteur at the time, in *Yearbook of the International Law Commission*, 1960, vol. II, p. 113, draft-article 15. See also Satow, *Guide to Diplomatic Practice*, p. 274.

DIPLOMATIC IMMUNITIES AND ACTS OF STATE ON FOREIGN TERRITORY: THE CASE OF THE CHINESE WELDING ENGINEERS

Chronology of Events[36]

In the summer of 1966, the PRC took part in the Nineteenth Conference of the International Welding Institute, which was held in Delft, Holland. The nine members of the Chinese delegation were holders of service-passports[37] and provided with Netherlands visas, valid till July 31, 1966.[38] Through the Chinese diplomatic mission they were lodged in a three-story house in The Hague, which formed part of the mission's official premises.

In the afternoon of Saturday, July 16, one of the delegation members, Mr. Hsu Tsu-ts'ai, was found, lying heavily wounded, on the sidewalk in front of the house. After an ambulance had been summoned by bystanders, Mr. Hsu was transported to the Red Cross hospital in the company of two other Chinese gentlemen at that time present in the house.[39] While Mr. Hsu was being examined and x-rayed, another company of Chinese, among whom was at least one member of the diplomatic staff, arrived at the hospital grounds by a *corps diplomatique* car. The physician in charge thereupon informed the diplomat that Mr. Hsu, suffering from a fracture of the skull and serious damage to the vertebral column, must be kept in the hospital. Meanwhile, however, without the knowledge either of the hospital staff or the police detectives present, Mr. Hsu was carried out of the building by his fellow citizens and transported in the diplomatic car to the main building of the Chinese diplomatic mission.[40]

The "abduction" alarmed the Dutch police who suspected criminal acts to be involved in the event. Since at least one member of the diplomatic staff seemed to have taken part in the incident at the hos-

36. See also *Revue générale de droit international public* 71:180–182 (1967); *The Times,* July 21, 22, 23, 26, and 29, Aug. 1, 2, 3, 4, 5, 6, 22, and 25, Oct. 14, Nov. 18, Dec. 2, 24, 30 and 31, 1966; and *The New York Times,* July 20, 21, 22, 23, and 29, Aug. 2, 3, 4, and 20, Sept. 8, Oct. 22 and 28, Nov. 16, Dec. 2 and 31, 1966.

37. See the survey of the incident, as given by the Dutch Minister of Foreign Affairs on written questions from the Second Chamber, January 16, 1967 (hereafter to be called Survey), in *Aanh. Hand. II,* 1966–1967, no. 189, pp. 381–382.

38. *Algemeen Dagblad,* July 29, 1966.

39. Police information, in *NRC,* July 19, 1966, p. 1.

40. *Ibid.* See also Survey and the press release of the Netherlands Ministry of Foreign Affairs of July 19, 1966.

pital and since the "abduction" was carried out by means of a diplomatic car, the Dutch government held the Chinese chargé d'affaires responsible.[41] That same night he was summoned to the Ministry of Foreign Affairs and was asked for a clarification. The chargé d'affaires apparently refused both to give a satisfactory explanation and to have Mr. Hsu hospitalized, while taking the position that the case was an "internal matter."[42]

Mr. Hsu died in the diplomatic chancellery on Sunday, which fact was reported by the chargé d'affaires in a note to the Dutch Ministry of Foreign Affairs on Monday, July 18. On that occasion the chargé d'affaires was informed that at the request of the district attorney of The Hague, a judicial investigation would be opened to ascertain what really had happened at the hospital grounds and the causes of Mr. Hsu's death. This implied that the eight other members of the welders' delegation, who had at that time all moved from their original housing to the main building of the diplomatic mission, would be summoned as witnesses.[43] The chargé d'affaires, however, refused to cooperate, whereupon the Dutch government declared him persona non grata and requested him to leave the country within twenty-four hours.[44]

The Chinese government reacted immediately by means of a note of July 20,[45] which the Dutch government refused to accept. The note contained the following points:

1. Mr. Hsu was injured as he fell from the window in an attempt to escape the Chinese building. This attempt to desert was the result of incitement by special agents of the US, who acted during the welding conference with the connivance of the Dutch government. These facts were purposely distorted by the Dutch.[46]

2. The Sino-Dutch incident was an extremely serious one, staged by the Dutch government in order to undermine Sino-Dutch relations. All this fitted in with the imperialist anti-Chinese activity of the US.[47]

3. The Dutch demand that the remaining engineers give testimony was illegal, provocative, and an insult to their dignity.[48] All these accusations were categorically denied by the Netherlands.

On July 22, the Chinese government declared the Dutch chargé

41. See Survey.
42. *NRC*, July 19, 1966, p. 2.
43. See Survey.
44. *Ibid.*
45. *Ibid.*
46. *Ibid.*
47. *NRC*, July 20, 1966, p. 1.
48. See Survey.

d'affaires in Peking persona non grata. On that occasion, he was told that for a long time the Netherlands had been closely following American imperialism and had pursued an anti-Chinese policy. Since the attitude of the Netherlands government was most unreasonable, the Chinese government had no choice but to declare him persona non grata. His diplomatic identity card was revoked, but he was not allowed to leave the country until the Chinese welders' delegation received permission to leave the Netherlands.[49]

In the Netherlands, meanwhile, a judicial autopsy was carried out on the body of Hsu Tsu-ts'ai. When interviewed as to the result of his investigation, the pathologist-anatomist declared later that the Chinese engineer was neither poisoned nor maltreated.[50]

As the judicial investigation on the circumstances of the mysterious death started, the judge of instruction summoned the eight remaining delegation members to testify. Since they were staying in the building of the Chinese diplomatic mission, the writ had to be served through the intermediary of the head of the mission.[51] The latter, however, refused to receive the writ, so that it could not be served.[52] The Dutch police then put up a permanent cordon around the premises to prevent the engineers from being smuggled out of the building and eventually out of the country without having fulfilled their legal obligation. Thus began the five-month siege of the Chinese legation, which even became a new attraction for tourists in the otherwise rather staid atmosphere of The Hague.

The development of the case from July to December 1966 centered on three issues: the stay of the eight Chinese engineers in the Netherlands; the criminal investigation and the requirements of the Dutch law of criminal procedure; and the detainment of the Netherlands chargé d'affaires in China.

The first issue became imminent as the July 31 expiration date of the visas neared. However, the visas were extended until August 4. It would be interesting to know whether this was accorded at the request of the Chinese or on the initiative of the Dutch government itself.[53]

49. *NRC*, July 22, 1966, p. 1.
50. *NRC*, Aug. 4, 1966, p. 1.
51. Circular letter of the Netherlands Minister of Justice of Feb. 3, 1922, in *Laws and Regulations regarding Diplomatic and Consular Privileges and Immunities* (U.N., N.Y.: United Nations Publications Office, 1958), p. 200.
52. *Ibid.*
53. See "Ons Commentaar" (editorial comment) in *Eindhovens Dagblad*, Aug. 2, 1966. Here the supposition was made that the extension was given on the initiative of the Dutch government.

In any case, as of August 4, the Chinese engineers were no longer in possession of a valid permit to be in the Netherlands so that their stay from that date on must be considered illegal. The Dutch government did not fail to inform the acting chargé d'affaires that the engineers were to leave the country but that they first had to comply with the requirements prescribed by Dutch law.

With regard to the second issue, one may wonder, first of all, if the public prosecutor acted with the knowledge of the attorney general and the Ministry of Foreign Affairs when he requested the judge of instruction to begin a judicial investigation.[54] However this may be, the judge complied with the request and summoned the engineers to testify. When this failed as a result of the uncooperative attitude of the Chinese chargé d'affaires, the problem shifted to the question of how a compromise could be reached without completely disavowing the formal judicial requirements. Apart from their view that examination of the engineers as witnesses would be "an insult to their dignity," the Chinese denied any breach of Dutch law and refused to cooperate. According to them the incident had a political character and could consequently not be solved juridically.

During the ensuing months negotiations were held many times in attempts to reach a compromise. On August 2, the possibility of an agreement occurred when the Chinese chargé d'affaires ad interim handed to the Netherlands Ministry of Foreign Affairs a written statement from the engineers which referred to the explanation already given in the official Chinese note of July 20. The written statement was not, however, considered by the Dutch authorities sufficient to replace a formal hearing.[55]

In December, almost five months after the Saturday afternoon incident in July, an agreement was finally reached. On December 10, the Netherlands government proposed to examine the engineers within the building of the diplomatic mission. Six days later, the Chinese government agreed to give Dutch officials the opportunity to "ask questions" of the engineers in the diplomatic mansion, which was accepted by the Dutch.[56] The agreement implied that a "conversation"

54. The possibility of a difference of opinion between the Netherlands Ministries of Foreign Affairs and of Justice as to the handling of the case was expressed in the editorial comment cited in my footnote 53. In it the impression was given that Foreign Affairs preferred not to hold too strongly to the legal requirements, whereas Justice insisted on a strictly legal settlement.
55. *NRC*, Aug. 4, 1966, p. 1.
56. See Survey.

would take place between the engineers and the public prosecutor, the latter to be accompanied by the judge of instruction, the head of the cabinet and protocol section of the Ministry of Foreign Affairs, and one more official of the same ministry acting as an interpreter. The "conversation" would not have the character of an "examination," which meant that the engineers would not answer under oath, as prescribed by the law.[57] The meeting took place on December 29, lasting about half an hour,[58] whereupon the public prosecutor and the judge of instruction declared that as far as the investigation was concerned the presence of the engineers was no longer necessary.[58]

At the request of the Minister of Foreign Affairs, the Chinese chargé d'affaires ad interim promised that the engineers would leave the country, which they did that same day. Meanwhile, in China the former Netherlands chargé d'affaires was immediately granted an exit permit, and he left Peking the following day.

CHINA'S LEGAL ATTITUDE: THE ABDUCTION

Three events in the Hsu case attract attention because of their deviation from the normally accepted pattern of behavior in contemporary Western international practice. They are the abduction of the injured engineer; the refusal to give testimony and to cooperate; and the keeping of the Dutch diplomat as a hostage. The relationship between the three facts can be construed as follows: rightly or wrongly the Chinese felt themselves entitled to exercise authority over their injured fellow citizen. That is why, when the Dutch reacted by launching a criminal investigation, the Chinese objected. Since the Dutch persevered and even declared the Chinese chargé d'affaires persona non grata, China retaliated by preventing the Dutch chargé d'affaires from leaving while at the same time also declaring him persona non grata. Thus, the starting point for any further attempts to deduce a legal attitude from the facts is the act of abduction.

Since the events preceding Mr. Hsu's mysterious fall from the window will probably never be wholly disclosed, one may also speculate at will about the real motives behind the Chinese reluctance to have him treated by competent physicians. No consideration of care for his

57. Article 216 of the Dutch Code of Criminal Procedure prescribes that, if in the opinion of the judge of instruction the witness is not likely to appear at the future court session, such witness should testify under oath at the preliminary hearing.

58. *NRC*, Dec. 30, 1966, p. 1.

physical well-being is demonstrable and was never a point in the Chinese arguments. On the other hand, if Mr. Hsu had, as the Chinese stated, sustained his injuries in an attempt to defect, the Chinese must have tried desperately to prevent him from succeeding, thereby consciously disregarding any legal obstacle. If, moreover, members of the Chinese diplomatic mission or of the welders' delegation were involved in the cause of Mr. Hsu's injuries, he would have to be prevented at all cost from giving testimony on such facts to the Dutch authorities. In both cases, prolonged hospital treatment had to be avoided. Other motives are hard to find. But, be that as it may, it is quite improbable that any international legal considerations were at the time present in the minds of the abductors. Nevertheless, the point is whether the facts can be placed in an international legal setting, be it interpreted by the Chinese or by the West.

The crucial question is whether the abduction took place with or without the victim's approval. Any evidence of such approval would, it is suggested, radically alter the whole picture from the legal point of view. It is generally accepted that a state is fully entitled to exercise the *jus avocandi* over its citizens abroad. Factual enforcement of that right, however, would only be permitted when the person in question gives his consent. In the Hsu case, it was striking that the Chinese side did not even make an attempt to prove that such consent was given.[59] Mr. Hsu's physical condition at the critical moment as well as the above speculation about the real motives underlying the abduction lead to the conclusion that some kind of fundamental disagreement must have existed between Mr. Hsu and his fellow citizens, which makes any assumption of consent very improbable indeed.

If then the abduction, carried out by fellow aliens with the connivance or even approval of a diplomatic staff member, occurred without the approval or even against the will of the victim, the question arises whether a state can claim any extraterritorial personal (enforcement) jurisdiction, including police power, over its citizens abroad.

It is generally accepted that the bond of nationality provides a legally sound basis for the personal (legislative) jurisdiction of a state, even when its citizens happen to be outside its territory. Thus, a state is fully entitled to subject its citizens to its legal prescriptions, wher-

59. Compare this with the Soviet allegations in the *Kasenkina* case. See Lawrence Preuss, "Consular Immunities: The Kasenkina Case (US–USSR)," *AJIL* 43:37–39 (1949).

ever they are. It is quite another question, however, whether a state is also entitled to enforce its laws against its citizens on foreign territory. Modern doctrine is fairly unanimous in its opinion that no such right can be recognized in customary international law. Thus Oppenheim says:

> Personal supremacy does not give unlimited liberty of action. . . . Although the citizens of a State remain under its power when abroad, such State is restricted in the exercise of this power with regard to all those matters in which the foreign State on whose territory these citizens reside is competent in consequence of its territorial supremacy. The duty to respect the territorial supremacy of a foreign State must prevent a State from performing acts which, although they are according to its personal supremacy within its competence, would violate the territorial supremacy of this foreign State. A State must not perform acts of sovereignty in the territory of another State. Thus, for instance, a State is prevented from requiring such acts from its citizens abroad as are forbidden to them by the Municipal law of the land in which they reside, and from ordering them not to commit such acts as they are bound to commit according to the Municipal law of the land in which they reside.[60]

Another modern authority, D. P. O'Connell, sums up the contemporary Western position on the subject as follows: "When speaking of jurisdiction, then, one must be careful to distinguish the jurisdiction to enforce from the jurisdiction to prescribe. The former is inherently territorial. . . . The personal jurisdiction, then, is restricted territorially only so far as enforcement is concerned."[61] Finally a "highly qualified publicist"[62] like Clive Parry says: "It is likewise universally agreed that measures of execution in pursuance of personal jurisdiction cannot be taken within the territory of a foreign State."[63]

This priority of territorial jurisdiction over personal jurisdiction, as far as enforcement is concerned, may also be seen in accord with the granting of immunity of (territorial) jurisdiction to foreign diplomats. If there were any general rule whereby foreigners would normally fall under the jurisdiction of their home state, then no useful purpose would be served by introducing a whole set of exceptions to the jurisdic-

60. Oppenheim, *International Law*, vol. I, par. 128, pp. 294–296. See also, for a survey of the concept of jurisdiction in international law, F. A. Mann, "The Doctrine of Jurisdiction in International Law," in *Recueil des Cours de l'Académie de droit international* 111:1–162 (1964–I).

61. O'Connell, *International Law*, vol. II, p. 659.

62. Art. 38, Statute of the I.C.J.

63. "Plural Nationality and Citizenship with Special Reference to the Commonwealth," *British Yearbook of International Law* 30:260 (1953).

tion of the territorial state in favor of diplomats. Such exceptions being recognized for an explicitly limited category of persons, it is irrelevant whether persons not falling in that category are private persons or government officials.

The Oppenheim and O'Connell passages just cited were cautiously referred to as the contemporary Western position on the subject. From a historical point of view, however, practice and opinion have not always and not everywhere been in accordance with those quotations. If only by way of illustration I cite Keeton, who in his chapter on the history of extraterritoriality in general wrote, inter alia: "The conception of sovereignty as absolute over all persons within a defined territory . . . is essentially a modern one. In theory it is scarcely older than the Renaissance, and in practice, even in Europe, it was not general before the French Revolution."[64] In this connection, mention should also be made of the vast complex of "treaty" and "capitulatory" rules governing extraterritorial treatment, often including enforcement power, which existed in vast parts of Asia.

Put against this background of the law of jurisdiction, the essential legal point in all the known cases of kidnapping and abduction on foreign territory is not whether the victim is or is not physically brought across the frontiers of the territorial state. What is relevant is that the person is withdrawn from the jurisdiction of that state.[65]

How then should the Hague abduction be judged? When the event is tested against past behavior of the PRC since its founding in 1949, we find that never before had the PRC claimed enforcement authority over its citizens abroad. But then there probably had never been an occasion necessitating such a claim. It seems, however, that the strong

64. G.W. Keeton, *The Development of Extraterritoriality in China* (London: Longmans, Green, 1928), vol II, p. 155. See also W. L. Tung, *China and Some Phases of International Law* (London: Oxford University Press, 1940), p. 70: "It is the general rule of international law that an alien, after his entrance into a State, is subject to its jurisdiction and responsible to it for all acts he commits on its territory. That is, however, not the case of the nationals of many States which are entitled to the right of extraterritoriality in China." For ancient Chinese practice, see C.H. Alexandrowicz-Alexander, "The Continuity of the Sovereign Status of China in International Law," *Indian Yearbook of International Affairs* 5:84–86 (1956): "Following an ancient Asian tradition China conceded also some measures of extraterritoriality to foreigners and granted concessions to merchants of other nations. These were based on the assumption of equality of nations unlike in the post-1842 treaties which tended to convert them into limitations of sovereignty imposed on the grantor" (p. 85).

65. Compare Elmar F. Bauer, *Die völkerrechtswidrige Entführung in Schriften zum Völkerrecht Band 7* (Berlin: Duncker and Humblot, 1968).

emphasis generally laid by Communist states on the principle of territorial sovereignty and integrity is difficult to reconcile with a claim of personal jurisdiction over citizens on foreign territory to the extent of enforcement authority.

If contemporary Western doctrine refuses enforcement authority on foreign soil, and if PRC practice in general does not give enough reason to think that the PRC maintains a fundamentally different view on the matter, would it be possible to find an answer to our question in the law on diplomatic or consular functions? According to traditional doctrine, consuls often have some competence to act as a public officer of their state, but such competence has always been conditioned on and limited by the consent of the receiving state.[66] In the past, ambassadors and envoys, on the basis of their status as diplomatic representatives of their states (that is, not on the basis of a general extraterritorial regime), were sometimes accorded the right to exercise jurisdiction over their suite, but even then recognition of such competence has always been controversial.[67] However this may be, it should be remembered that in its past behavior the PRC had not shown any indication that it would hold a view contrary to traditional doctrine.

It is peculiar, however, that among the reported cases of abduction similar to the present one, there are two with particular features. In the *Sun Yat-sen* case of 1896,[68] this future founder of the Chinese Republic was kidnapped in London and held a prisoner in the Chinese legation on the charge of having been engaged in a conspiracy against the Manchu dynasty. He was apparently held with the intention of sending him to China. On a strong protest by the British foreign minister, the prisoner was released by the legation. Whereas this case had a "Chinese" element, the so-called *Kasenkina* case of 1948 had a "Communist" one.[69] Here a Soviet teacher in New York, Oksana S. Kasenkina, who had sought refuge with a local White Russian organization to

66. See, for example, Luke T. Lee, *Vienna Convention on Consular Relations* (Leyden: A.W. Sijthoff, 1966), pp. 51–53; and the Vienna Convention 1963, art. 5, particularly under (f) and (m).

67. See the often cited case of the French envoy to London, Sully, in 1605, in Charles de Martens, *Causes célèbres de droit international*, 2nd ed. (Leipzig, 1858), vol. I, pp. 331–333. See also the posthumous notes of B. M. Telders, "Ontwikkeling van het Gezantschapsrecht in de 15e, 16e en 17e eeuw," *Verzamelde Geschriften* (Collected papers; The Hague, Martinus Nijhoff, 1948), vol. II, pp. 159 and 164; and Charles de Martens, *Manuel diplomatique* (Paris, 1822), pp. 55–57.

68. J.B. Moore, *A Digest of International Law* (Washington, D.C.: Government Printing Office, 1906), vol. IV, p. 555.

69. Preuss, "The Kasenkina Case"; see also E. Borchard in *AJIL* 42:858 (1948).

escape repatriation, was abducted by the Soviet consul general and brought into the consulate where she was held a prisoner. After a few days, she tried to escape by jumping out a third-floor window. The event eventually led to the rupture of US-Soviet consular relations.

Although it is tempting to deduce from these two precedents some legal characterization of the Hague abduction, it is submitted that it is impossible to do so. It would be as rash to say that the *Sun Yat-sen* case constituted evidence of Chinese legal thinking as it would be to describe the *Kasenkina* case as evidence of Communist legal views. The most that could be said is that the international and internal political atmosphere may in certain circumstances promote state acts and attitudes that fall outside the pattern of legal behavior normally accepted by the state concerned. Such acts and attitudes can, of course, change from exceptions to established practice. Only when this stage is reached could one say that they represent the state's legal standpoint. The same emergence of a clear general legal stand could occur when the state formally pronounces its legal attitude, as by way of declaration. Meanwhile, however, the sole act of abduction seems not to warrant any definitive conclusion.

If the above proposition is true, we must accept the conclusion that the abduction was, even in the Chinese view, prima facie illegal in international law, being a violation of the territorial sovereignty of the Netherlands. The final question then to be answered is whether, generally speaking or from the Chinese point of view, a defense of justification is possible for the commission of the illegal act. What meaning should be given to the words of the Chinese chargé d'affaires, according to which the case of Mr. Hsu was an "internal matter," and to the first two points of the Chinese note of July 20, in effect accusing the Netherlands, rightly or wrongly, of purposely conducting or at least permitting acts which could be interpreted as undermining the safety of the Chinese state, or, for that matter, subversively hurting China's technical capacity? We here reach a point where analysis of acts becomes hypothetical. On the basis of the Chinese accusations, could the abduction then be considered an emergency action, illegal as such but justified by the circumstances, with the aim of defending some real or imaginary fundamental interests of the state? That such may generally be possible without legalizing the illegality of the act itself is indicated by Oppenheim on the right of self-preservation: "It is a fact that in certain cases violations committed in self-preservation are not prohibited by the Law of Nations. But, nevertheless, they remain violations, may therefore be repelled, and indemnities may be demanded for damages done."[70]

The Refusal to Cooperate in the Hearing of Witnesses

The only official indication of the real motives behind the refusal to cooperate with the Dutch authorities on the judicial investigation is to be found in the Chinese note of July 20, particularly in its third point.[71] The speculations put forward in the foregoing paragraph could also apply here. If the diplomatic staff or other members of the welders' delegation were directly or indirectly involved in Mr. Hsu's injuries and death, everything had to be done to conceal that fact from the outside world. In this connection, the supposition made in a newspaper comment[72] that the Chinese apparently did not realize the difference between being summoned as a witness and as a suspect seems highly improbable. On the contrary, the Chinese must have understood quite well that, as is the case in most, if not all, legal systems, a witness may for a variety of reasons become a suspect in a later stage of the investigation. Here again, however, what interests us in the first place is how the events should be looked at from the legal point of view.

According to Dutch municipal law, the launching of the judicial investigation, apart from its expediency, was legally correct.[73] The Chinese argument that they had not violated the Dutch law does not hold in this respect, because this was exactly the question that the investigation was intended to solve.

In international law the question of whether the demand to hear the engineers as witnesses was permissible must be put to the tests of the international penal jurisdiction of a state and of the principles governing the treatment of aliens. It seems unnecessary to dwell at length on these two tests. The principle of territoriality in penal law, which does not distinguish between nationals and aliens, is so well established, also in Communist states, that any doubt as to Dutch competence in this respect could not be taken seriously. Neither is a precedent to be found to the effect that being an alien, not falling under the category of persons enjoying diplomatic or consular immunity, would in any way

70. *International Law*, vol. I, par. 129, p. 298.
71. See p. 70 above.
72. *NRC*, Dec. 30, 1966, p. 1.
73. See the Netherlands Code of Criminal Procedure, articles 149, 181, 210, 213, and 541, sect. 2; Penal Code, articles 282, 300, 450.

debar the territorial authorities from subjecting a person to investigation with respect to an event occurring within their territory.

Still, the Chinese note characterized the Dutch attitude as "illegal, provocative, and an insult to their [the welders'] dignity." It is difficult to consider the investigation illegal, measured either by municipal or international standards, even from the point of view of general PRC practice. Furthermore, the investigation was not considered an insult to the Chinese state but to the welders' dignity. This would point to a right of aliens as such or to a fundamental human right. Neither of these alternatives, however, leads anywhere, so that the argument must consequently be classified as of nonlegal character.[74] So should, in my opinion, the "provocation" argument.

My conclusion is that the whole Chinese attitude vis-à-vis the Dutch demand to hear the engineers was inspired by nonlegal motives that were considered important enough to risk the blame of illegality. This is also the only possible explanation both for the blunt refusal by the Chinese chargé d'affaires to lend his mediation in the service of the summons and for the use of the diplomatic mission building to prevent the Dutch authorities from enforcing their jurisdiction over the non-diplomatic engineers. It is, furthermore, in accordance with the Chinese characterization of the whole incident as a "political" one. Finally, it is noteworthy that the Chinese did not attempt to construe the hiding of the engineers in the building as a case of diplomatic asylum. Their point of view seems simply to have been that the interests of the state and the individual Chinese were one and indivisible. On the other hand, there is no factual indication whatsoever to justify the presumption that the engineers were held as prisoners against their will.

The Keeping of the Dutch Chargé d'affaires as a Hostage[75]

It is clear that the declaration of persona non grata must be distinguished from the prohibition on leaving the country. In law, a state

74. We are told that a Chinese author on international law "calls the emphasis on human rights in 'capitalist international law' a malicious trick . . . used by the imperialists . . . as a pretext to sabotage other nations' sovereignty internationally." See Shao-chuan Leng, "Chinese Law" in A. Larson *et al.*, *Sovereignty within the Law* (Dobbs Ferry, N.Y.: Oceana, 1965), pp. 260–261, thereby citing Ch'ien Szu, "A criticism of the view of bourgeois international law on the domicile problem" (in Chinese).

75. See also Jurisprude, "The Legal Options," *Far Eastern Economic Review*, no. 1:236–238 (Aug. 1, 1968).

need not even explain the reasons why it considers a head of a mission persona non grata.[76] Practice and the principle of reciprocity have led to the custom that any non grata declaration almost automatically results in a similar act from the other side.[77] The PRC has been shown to adhere faithfully to this custom.

Thus, while the non grata declaration constitutes no legal question for us, it is also generally accepted that, as put by Satow, after the termination of the mission, "the minister remains in possession of the immunities and privileges attached to his public character until he leaves the country to which he has been accredited within such reasonable time as may be necessary to complete and dispose of the affairs of his mission."[78] The inviolability of an envoy has become so self-evident that the *right to leave* after termination of the mission is usually not even mentioned. When article 44 of the Vienna Convention still deems it necessary to point out that the receiving state must grant facilities in order to enable the diplomat concerned to leave at the earliest possible moment, it is suggested that the provision meant to emphasize the granting of *special* facilities.[79] It is against this background that the quote of Satow or article 39 of the Convention should be read: while the right to leave doubtlessly exists, international law on the contrary prescribes that the diplomat must be allowed a sufficient period to prepare for his departure.

Since the Dutch case, accusations about diplomats being held hostage were made during the Sino-Indonesian incident in 1966–1967,[80] while as a result of the Sino-British incident of 1967 British diplomats in Peking were refused exit permits.[81] One might ask whether all these instances really point to a new Chinese view of the law of diplomatic inviola-

76. Vienna Convention on Diplomatic Relations 1961, article 9; see also the commentary on the International Law Commission draft-article 8, in *Yearbook of the International Law Commission,* 1958, vol. II, p. 91. Formerly a different opinion was prevalent. See Satow, *Guide to Diplomatic Practice*, p. 301.

77. For refusal to recall a diplomat, see Satow, *Guide to Diplomatic Practice,* pp. 284–286, 294, 300, 301.

78. *Ibid.*, p. 276; Cahier, *Le droit diplomatique contemporain,* pp. 321–322; see also Vienna Convention, article 39.

79. See Cahier, *ibid.*, p. 322.

80. See J.M. van der Kroef, "The Sino-Indonesian Rupture," *China Quarterly*, no. 33:45 (1968).

81. The requirement of an exit permit, even for diplomats, is regulated in the (Chinese) decree of May 13, 1964, concerning the control regulations on entry, departure and transit, residence, and travel of foreigners. See the German translation in *Die wichtigsten Gesetzgebungsakte in den Ländern Ost-, Südosteuropas und in den ostasiatischen Volksdemokratien* 7:57–59 (1955).

bility. Before drawing a general conclusion, however, I shall first attempt to construe legally the Chinese act in the Dutch case.

The Dutch demand to hear the engineers apparently offended the Chinese government to such an extent that very strong retaliation was considered appropriate, regardless of the legal or illegal character of the retaliatory act itself. If, however, the act is illegal, this is precisely what is understood in international law by an *act of reprisal.*[82] One could raise the objection that reprisals are only admissible as a reaction to an earlier illegal act by the other side. Since the Dutch demand to hear the engineers cannot be considered illegal in international law, so no reprisal against the Netherlands would be legally possible. Without denying the correctness of this reasoning, I propose to find out what the juridical qualification of the Chinese act could be, if the Dutch demand were indeed an internationally illegal act.

While in principle international law does not impose a limitation on the kinds of illegal acts suitable to be met with reprisals, violation of the dignity of a state not only constitutes such a valid reason,[83] but is in practice often used as a pretext for reprisal measures.[84] Anything and everything that belongs to the delinquent state or its citizens may in principle be made the object of reprisals, provided that these measures are proportional to the wrong retaliated against.[85] In this connection

82. Oppenheim, *International Law,* vol. II, par. 33, p. 136: "Reprisals are such injurious and otherwise internationally illegal acts of one State against another as are exceptionally permitted for the purpose of compelling the latter to consent to a satisfactory settlement of a difference created by its own international delinquency." According to Yves de la Brière, "Evolution de la doctrine et de la pratique en matière de représailles," in *Recueil des Cours de l'Académie de droit international* 22:241 (1928): "Reprisals, we might say, are acts of constraint and violence infringing the ordinary rules of the law of nations, and committed with a view to make the adversary repair or, at least, cease forthwith the unjustified acts of violence for which he is responsible." De la Brière then mentions as one of the essential elements of reprisal "voluntary, and intentional, derogation to rules which are recognized as normally and usually obligatory." See also article 1 of the resolution of the Institut de droit international on the regime of reprisals in time of peace: "Reprisals are measures of coercion derogatory to the ordinary rules of the law of nations, taken by a State in consequence of illegal acts committed to its prejudice by another State, and intended to impose on that other State respect of the law, by causing damage [to it]," in *Annuaire* 38:708 (1934). See also C. C. Hyde, *International Law,* 2nd ed. (Boston: Little, Brown, 1945), vol. II, p. 1660; P. Guggenheim, *Traité de droit international public,* II (Geneva: Georg and Cie, 1954), p. 87; and G. Dahm, *Völkerrecht,* vol. II, p. 427.

83. Oppenheim, *International Law,* vol. II, par. 33, pp. 136–137.

84. E. S. Colbert, *Retaliation in International Law* (New York: Columbia University Press, 1948), pp. 68–69.

85. Oppenheim, *International Law,* vol. II, par. 39, p. 141; de la Brière, "Evolution de la doctrine," p. 247. The principle has been clearly formulated by the

Oppenheim says: "The persons of officials . . . of the delinquent State are possible objects of reprisals . . . But it must be emphasized that the only act of reprisal admissible against foreign officials or citizens is arrest; they must be treated, not like criminals, *but like hostages,* and in no circumstances may they be executed or subjected to punishment."[86] (Emphasis added.)

Here the conformity of the Chinese measure with general international law ends. There are exceptions to the rule that the persons of officials of the delinquent state may be made objects of reprisals. One exception is "individuals enjoying the privilege of extraterritoriality while abroad, such as heads of States and diplomatic envoys."[87] This priority of diplomatic immunity over the right of reprisal seems to be generally accepted in traditional doctrine. Apart from the possibility that the PRC in this respect again considered its interests, namely the return of the welding engineers without having been heard by the Dutch authorities, sufficiently threatened so as to require drastic pressure, irrespective of its illegality, what other factors could have played a role in the formation of the Chinese attitude? On this question, one could suggest that the ideology and the collectivist state-structure of the PRC favor the idea of indivisibility between the state and the individual and blurring of the distinction between diplomatic and other state officials.[88] One

---

Mixed Arbitral Commission in the German-Portuguese "Naulilea" case, in *Reports of International Arbitral Awards* (UN, N.Y.: United Nations Publication Office, 1949), vol. II, pp. 1025–1027. See, however, Colbert, *Retaliation in International Law,* p. 76: "This view, although reflecting the opinions of international lawyers, has little to support it in the practice of states."

86. Par. 37, pp. 139–140. See also de la Brière, "Evolution de la doctrine," p. 272. In an interview after his arrival in Hong Kong, the Dutch chargé d'affaires said that after the non grata declaration he refused to leave the legation building and that the Chinese government had not imposed upon him any limitation on his freedom of movement within China. Since he had lost diplomatic status, however, he considered himself in fact a prisoner. See *NRC,* Jan. 2, 1967, p. 1.

87. Oppenheim, *International Law,* par. 37, p. 140; G. Dahm, *Völkerrecht,* vol. II, p. 433; A. Müller, *Wandlungen in Repressalienrecht* (Göttingen, 1933), p. 61. For seventeenth, eighteenth, and nineteenth century instances of diplomats and other state officials kept hostage, see P. Lafargue, *Les représailles en temps de paix* (Paris, 1898), pp. 80–81, and A. Lutteroth, *Der Geisel im Rechtsleben* (Breslau: Marcus, 1922), p. 229. On former Turkish practice, see Charles de Martens, *Manuel diplomatique,* p. 45, note 7.

88. On the other hand, however, the PRC has on several occasions sought agreements with other countries for the granting of diplomatic status to her commercial agents, such as in the Sino-Nepalese and Sino-Soviet commercial treaties of September 20, 1956, and April 2, 1958, respectively, and also in the unofficial Sino-Japanese trade agreement of May 4, 1955. See Shao-chuan Leng, "Chinese Law," p. 263. This is in accord with Soviet practice. See Korovin *et al., International Law* (Moscow: Academy of Sciences of the USSR, 1960), pp. 305–307.

should further bear in mind that the keeping of hostages is in fact related to the idea of collective responsibility, which is again not unfamiliar in collectivist societies. In this connection, it is also interesting to note that during its first year of existence the Soviet Union made use of the same kind of reprisal measure, namely refusing the right of free departure to foreign diplomats.[89]

These considerations, together with the Indonesian and British experiences, while not yet sufficient to warrant a conclusion to the effect that the PRC considers itself legally entitled to sacrifice diplomatic inviolability in case of reprisal, could very well be indicative of constitutive elements for a future Chinese or Communist legal conception.

If, on the other hand, one chooses just to characterize the Chinese behavior as an illegal act, reasonableness demands that we not forget that abuse, and especially abuse of the right of reprisal, by great powers has always been a familiar feature in the history of international relations. Suffice it to refer to the long lists of reprisal cases that more competent writers have drawn up.[90]

CONCLUSION

The case of the welding engineers showed a number of acts on the part of the Chinese which could be characterized as violations of the traditional rules. This in itself, however, is in no way spectacular. When each of the Chinese acts is viewed separately, there are a few precedents to be found both in ancient (not necessarily Chinese) and in Chinese pre-PRC practice, in Western practice in China, and in Communist practice. Technically speaking, some of the acts can to some extent even rely on existing international law precepts. However this may be, it is suggested that the acts have in fact been motivated by nonlegal considerations. These considerations stem from the exigencies of the moment. This too is not a unique feature of PRC behavior. Violation of international law as a result of such considerations is not exceptional in the practice of states.[91] In the Chinese case, it is facilitated

89. See T.A. Taracouzio, *The Soviet Union and International Law* (New York: Macmillan, 1935), p. 187.

90. See A. Haumant, *Les représailles* (Paris: Marcel Giard, 1934), pp. 177–178 for the period 1753–1914; see also de la Brière, "Evolution de la doctrine," p. 273, and Colbert, *Retaliation in International Law*, pp. 76–78.

91. O. Lissitzyn, "International Law in a Divided World," *International Conciliation*, no. 542:24 (March 1963): "Even the most legal-minded Western nations have at times admittedly violated international law."

by social tradition,[92] political experience (former Western practice in China), internal upheavals, and external strains.

The *first crucial* question, however, is whether the welders' case presents evidence that Chinese normative conceptions concerning international intercourse substantially differ from the traditional rules. This, it is submitted, must—as yet—be answered negatively. On the matter of diplomatic inviolability, one could at most speculate as to the eventual emergence of a new legal attitude in case of reprisal. But even if it were clear that the PRC favors different contents for existing rules of international intercourse, the *second crucial* question may be whether law as a motive for behavior takes the same position in China as it is supposed to in Western society.

92. *Fa* (law) was in China traditionally subordinate to *li* (moral codes). If this is so, "even the Peking regime's policy of subordinating the law to politics is, in a curious way, consistent with the classical Chinese practice of elevating the rule of *li* over the rule of law." Another feature of the traditional Chinese view on the law, was, it is said, that "law in traditional China was mainly designed to protect political and social order rather than individual rights." See Shao-chuan Leng, "Chinese Law," pp. 242, 256–257, 243. See also the interesting paraphrase by Luke T. Lee in his "Chinese Communist Law: Its Background and Development," *Michigan Law Review* 60:448 (1961–1962), when he discusses the relation between *fa* and the "Communist *li*": "Where a gap does exist, the Chinese Communists have not hesitated to follow the centuries-old tradition of elevating *li* (the communist *li*, of course) over *fa*."

3 / Chinese Diplomatic Practice during the Cultural Revolution

Philippe Ardant

INTRODUCTION

Between 1949 and 1962, China established diplomatic relations with approximately forty states. Diplomatic missions have been installed in Peking,[1] and Chinese diplomatic agencies have opened their doors in a number of foreign capitals. During this period, with the many changes that have occurred over time, some influenced by sensational international events, China has developed a diplomatic tradition that merits attention. The behavior of Chinese authorities in conducting diplomatic relations is difficult to understand in terms of the norms and customs currently accepted in international society. Indeed, foreign diplomats

NOTE: This essay was previously published in French in the *Revue générale de droit international public*, no. 4 (1968), pp. 991–1042. The English version here contains only minor changes. It was translated by Andrew D. Strupp.

The references to Chinese documents are taken from the official daily Bulletin published in French by the NCNA. Occasionally, a documentary source is taken from the English language edition of the same bulletin, which is generally more complete. Documents after August 1967 are extracts from the London edition of the NCNA Bulletin, published in English.

1. The states which maintain a diplomatic mission in Peking as of September 1967 are: the USSR, Bulgaria, Rumania, Hungary, North Korea, Czechoslovakia, Poland, Mongolia, East Germany, Albania, North Vietnam, India, Indonesia, Sweden, Denmark, Burma, Switzerland, Finland, Pakistan, Norway, Yugoslavia, Afghanistan, Nepal, the United Arab Republic, Syria, Yemen, Ceylon, Cambodia, Iraq, Morocco, Algeria, Sudan, Guinea, Cuba, Mali, Somalia, Laos, Uganda, Kenya, Tunisia, France, the Congo (Brazzaville), Tanzania, Zambia, and Mauritania, as well as Britain and Holland which are represented by chargé d'affaires.

Tunisia, Uganda, Somalia, and Zambia appear on the diplomatic list published in Peking, but without designated personnel. The Sudan has a designated but always absent ambassador, and no embassy. Indonesia and Kenya have withdrawn all of their personnel.

Some countries have recognized China without feeling a need to establish diplomatic relations (e.g., Senegal). China has representatives in some countries which do not maintain an embassy in Peking (Tunisia, until October 1967).

stationed in Peking find themselves in a peculiar and uncomfortable situation. In Peking, they do not receive the treatment to which they are accustomed. Their position ensures them of few special considerations or facilities and is instead a source of frequent unpleasantness. Sometimes, they face annoying or even tragic circumstances without being able to rely on the sympathy or protection of the state to which they are accredited. In the same way, the attitude of Chinese diplomats in the service of their country often appears surprising: Their language contrasts with traditional diplomatic parlance, and some of their actions and initiatives are characterized by a taste for the spectacular, sometimes the provocative, which at times seems like a deliberate breach of the reserve generally characteristic of embassies.

A series of offensive episodes and the permanence of this provocative behavior denote an obvious unwillingness to bend to the rules of diplomatic life that have been refined by international practice. This refusal is not the expression of a pragmatism considered a better guarantee of effective diplomatic action. It is, instead, a strategy based on a coherent, original conception of diplomatic relations. The Chinese believe their attitude is dictated by the actual state of international society and is, therefore, the only proper one. The practices they have chosen must contribute to opening a path to the kind of world they dream of and toward which they labor.

At this point, Chinese diplomacy goes beyond the framework of China's foreign relations; it would appear to be a model intended as a substitute for the diplomatic rules consecrated by the Convention of Vienna of 1961.

In effect, China's policy tends to make the People's Republic the center of world revolution, a title to which the Soviet Union, "corrupted by revisionism," can no longer pretend. While Chinese policymakers may at one time have fancied forming an international organization rivalling the United Nations, they are no longer attached to the concrete realization of this design, and the hopes given birth by the departure of Indonesia from the UN in 1965 have been disappointed. For the moment, they strive to display an active concern toward the malcontents in the present international order. They exploit and seek to amplify all the antagonisms: poor peoples against rich nations, exploited masses against "corrupt governments," colored peoples against white societies, the Afro-Asian countries against Western states, and so forth. They place themselves at the heart of associations which are under their protection and are without ties to the United Nations, such as Afro-

Asian writers and journalists, athletes of the "newly emerging forces," and so forth.

To all those who rise or seek to rise against the current international order, China exemplifies a course of action destined to overthrow this order. At the same time and by another viewpoint, it prefigures relations which conform to Chinese beliefs. Present Chinese diplomatic practice is only one element of this attitude. Chinese diplomacy is thus an instrument in the service of world revolution, and as such, it cannot obey the same rules as Western or Soviet diplomacy.

Therein resides the essential explanation of the conduct of diplomatic relations by the Chinese authorities. If they do not bend to the traditional rules of diplomacy, if they have never displayed an interest in the Convention of Vienna of 1961, the reason is that, from their viewpoint, these customs and this document correspond to the requirements of contemporary international society and are fashioned by "the bourgeoisie and other exploitative classes to ascertain and perpetuate their domination." At their core, the Soviet Union and the people's democracies are progressively more influenced by revisionism. As the fruit of bourgeois ideology, approved by these deviant revisionists, traditional diplomatic practice is challenged by China.

All of this notwithstanding—and a priori this is one of the paradoxes of the Chinese attitude—the Peking government attaches great importance to the adherence by nonrevolutionary states to the traditional rules of diplomacy in their relations with China. The Chinese Ministry of Foreign Affairs thus frequently takes the position of a censor, an intransigent guardian of bourgeois legality; it puts into practice the duality of attitude toward liberty espoused by Louis Veuillot: "I demand liberty from you in the name of your principles, but I refuse it to you in the name of mine." Chinese authorities demand for their diplomats all the facilities and privileges springing from international practice. At the same time, they refuse to place themselves under corresponding obligations or to accord the same facilities and privileges to the members of foreign diplomatic missions in China. One no longer counts the notes in which the Chinese accuse a foreign state of "overt violation of the principles governing diplomatic relations,"[2] of "total contempt for international diplomatic usage,"[3] of "violation of interna-

2. See, for example, declaration to the chargé d'affaires of Indonesia at Peking on April 24, 1967, NCNA, no. 2246 (Apr. 25, 1967).
3. NCNA, no. 2169 (Feb. 7, 1967).

tional diplomatic practice,"[4] and "scorning" or "trampling under foot" the most fundamental principles governing international relations,[5] "to a shocking degree."[6] International society has created a number of rules for itself; there is no reason to ignore them in its relations with China. Is there here perhaps an unconscious suggestion of the adage, *patere legem*?

But, and this complicates the picture one wants to draw, the Chinese have never—to my knowledge—declared openly and officially that they considered the rules of traditional diplomatic practice not binding upon them.[7] Moreover, on occasion they assert that their conduct conforms to the "guiding principles of international relations"[8] or to "international usage."[9] This declaration generally appears in those cases where Chinese diplomats have suffered harassment or persecution by authorities of the state to which they are accredited. In such instances, they protest that nothing in their behavior can be considered so irregular as to justify the treatment they have received. Their submission to traditional practice, then, seems like a convenient argument without general significance.

Moreover, analysis of the behavior of Chinese authorities clearly verifies the impression that China has no intention of submitting to the "norms of international law." It has its own conception of diplomatic relations, which, it is true, is not opposed to a conditional reference to "international usage" when this usage is favorable to Chinese interests and world revolution.

China's attitude, furthermore, cannot be explained solely by its current ideology or by the role it wishes to play in the world; history has a part in all that astonishes a Westener in the scheme we have just drawn.

It should not be forgotten that until recently China had little experience with relations between equal states or political groups.[10] China

4. Protest against the USSR, NCNA, no. 2174 (Feb. 12, 1967).

5. Protest delivered to the ambassador of the Democratic Republic of Germany at Peking, NCNA, no. 2181 (Feb. 19, 1967).

6. Note to the Indonesian government, January 24, 1967.

7. Except on one occasion, with regard to diplomatic privileges and immunities, see below at p. 93–94.

8. Note of the Chinese embassy to the Minister of Foreign Affairs of Ghana, March 19, 1966.

9. Protest of the chargé d'affaires at Moscow, March 18, 1967, NCNA, no. 2213 (Mar. 23, 1967): "All of our activities conform to international usage, to the norms of international law, and are unchallengeable."

10. Refer to C. P. FitzGerald, *The Chinese View of Their Place in the World*

was the center of the world, the Middle Kingdom, and other powers were inferior to it. It was accustomed to relations like those that arise between a suzerain and a vassal, a master and a slave, a combatant and an enemy. China was a nation without a friend, an ally, or a neighbor who was worthy of being treated as an equal. Certainly, during the centuries, the Chinese were dominated and their territory was conquered by invaders. But although it was the Chinese who were reduced to vassalage, they rapidly assimilated their conquerors. Even during the period from the nineteenth century onward when China had to endure an always expanding Western presence in its territory, it habitually affected a condescension approaching contempt toward foreign powers and submitted their representatives to a long series of annoyances and humiliations. Arrogance took the place of power, and Chinese authorities flaunted a superb ignorance about the rest of the world. When the Prussian mission, led by the Count of Eulenburg, came to China in 1861 to establish relations, the Chinese were surprised, for they did not know about Prussia, and they requested information from the French legation whether this was a "great power."[11] This delegation then had to endure a series of rebuffs before the signing of a treaty; the negotiators could not manage to find translators; a Prussian delegate who had been designated envoy to Peking was ordered to return to Tientsin by the Chinese government. The presence of foreigners in Peking was shocking because it was the Emperor's place of residence; the delegates should have waited to be invited to present themselves.[12] The Chinese hoped, furthermore, that the treaty would provide for a delay of ten years before a Prussian representative would reside at Peking. They had to be satisfied with a five-year guarantee, but this question of residence in the imperial city was to raise difficulties in the conclusion of diplomatic treaties with most foreign powers.

Have things changed very much since the end of the nineteenth century? Knowledge of the foreign now comes in a simplistic vision, implanted by daily propaganda, of a world divided between good and evil, where truth is incarnated in the thought of Mao Tse-tung. China

(London: Oxford University Press, 1966). I think this point is partially valid, but Chinese diplomacy was much more flexible *in practice* than is generally supposed. China even assumed an inferior status briefly *vis à vis* various nomad nations.

11. Henri Cordier, *Histoire des relations de la Chine avec les puissances occidentales, 1860–1900,* 3 vols. (Paris, 1901–1902), vol. I, p. 134.

12. *Ibid.* In the same fashion, when the Dutch negotiator, Van de Hoeven, expressed the desire in 1863 to visit Peking after the signing of the Sino-Dutch Treaty, the Chinese set such stringent conditions that he had to withdraw his proposal.

is the leader of world revolution; other peoples must study its example and be inspired by its methods and achievements. Not a day passes without the world being invited to pay attention to the Chinese experience. The old superiority complex of the Middle Kingdom fits this new role well.[13]

At the same time, the China of today is ill at ease in international society. It suffers, more or less consciously, from having been rejected by the UN for twenty-two years and ignored by other international institutions, from being recognized by a minority of states, and from being slandered and vilified by the others. A newcomer in 1949 to an international order which was constructed without it and where its place was contested, China does not always know its rules and does not willingly make an effort to assimilate them. To Chinese diplomats, the fabric of the practices observed by other states seems antiquated and bourgeois; and they seem to be afraid of not knowing how to operate in this traditional diplomatic context. Sometimes China gives the impression of being an unexpected guest at a reception, or of someone entering a club whose customs are unfamiliar. Confronted by this strange environment, certain individuals—often because of personal idiosyncrasies—exaggerate their awkwardness or behave in an insolent or rude manner.

Under these conditions, the personnel representing foreign states in Peking and those who deal with Chinese diplomats are confronted daily by a diplomatic practice that questions the traditional definition of diplomatic status and that challenges the customary notion of embassy functions. The Chinese, in effect, propose an original model of diplomatic relations with respect to both the position of a diplomatic mission and its agents and the delimitation of their activities.[14]

DIPLOMATIC STATUS

Chinese practice recognizes a special status for diplomats as well as for diplomatic missions. During these last few years, a certain number of

13. John K. Fairbank, Statement for the Committee on Foreign Relations, US Senate, March 10, 1966.

14. It is not my purpose here to report all aspects of recent Chinese diplomatic practice so much as to draft a treatise on diplomatic practice. Correspondences with customs of traditional international society will not be mentioned except when they seem helpful in understanding the Chinese conception. With this reservation, I consider only those areas where the practice followed by the Peking government diverges clearly and voluntarily from customary norms.

crises and difficulties make it possible to take the measure of the peculiar situation defined by the Chinese.

Diplomats

The status of diplomats is a projection of the Chinese authorities' conception of the diplomat's mission. This is profoundly original since the Chinese consider the diplomat a "fighter."

The Chinese press has frequently characterized China's diplomats as "red fighters on the diplomatic front" or "red diplomatic fighters." These phrases may be found in particular in an editorial in the *People's Daily*[15] —a newspaper thought to reveal official opinions—of June 28, 1967, and entitled "Salute the Red Fighters for Chairman Mao's Revolutionary Diplomatic Line."[16] A passage from this article conveys particularly well the Chinese conception of diplomacy, the state of mind they inculcate into their representatives abroad, and the climate in which these questions are envisaged in Peking:

> The diplomatic personnel of great socialist China are proletarian diplomatic fighters. At any time and in any place, they conscientiously study Mao Tse-tung's thought, resolutely put it into practice, earnestly propagate it and valiantly defend it. With Mao Tse-tung's thought, that matchless weapon, in their hands they show a dauntless revolutionary spirit, a firm and correct political orientation, an unconquerable fighting will. They are capable of accomplishing all the missions of proletarian revolutionary diplomacy however complicated or perilous the situation.[17]

Hence, diplomacy is but one element in the vast struggle undertaken by the Chinese authorities to achieve the triumph of world revolution, inspired by the Thought of Mao Tse-tung. As a result, the behavior of Chinese diplomats reflects the position taken toward this revolution by the country in which they are stationed. The rest of the editorial states unequivocally:

> The proletarian fighters on the diplomatic front . . . can distinguish friends from enemies. They are most modest in their attitude toward revolutionary

15. See also *People's Daily*, Nov. 4, 1967 and NCNA, no. 3571 (Nov. 5, 1967), in regard to Indonesia; NCNA, no. 3534 (Sept. 29, 1967) in regard to Tunisia; and NCNA, July 2, 1967, regarding India.

16. Concerning the return to Peking of some Chinese diplomats who had been mauled and injured by demonstrators in New Delhi.

17. See NCNA, no. 2310 (June 28, 1967); *SCMP*, no. 3971:32–33 (June 30, 1967).

people and countries; they respect them; they resolutely support their revolutionary struggles, displaying the proletarian internationalist spirit. They repudiate all manifestations of great-power chauvinism. They wage a firm, blow-for-blow struggle against the imperialists, modern revisionists and all reactionaries, and relentlessly rebuff their provocations.

In the exercise of their functions, then, Chinese diplomats need not content themselves with maintaining reserve, with observing, and with informing. They must participate in revolutionary struggles in a friendly country that receives them, spread the Thought of Mao Tse-tung, and put it into practice. In a hostile society, their task of spreading revolutionary ideas remains, but they must be wary of the "sugar-coated bullets of the bourgeoisie," not plunge themselves "into acclamation and blandishments," and their loyalty to revolutionary principles may lead them into violent confrontations in which they need not necessarily remain on the defensive. "The style of revolutionary diplomacy" thus defined by the *People's Daily* differs profoundly from that of traditional diplomacy. The attitude of the Chinese authorities with regard to the privileges and immunities of diplomats flows naturally from this conception.

Although in all circumstances China demands that foreign governments respect the rules which those governments recognize in these matters and which they impose upon other accredited diplomats in their territory,[18] China does not consider itself bound by international principles in matters of diplomatic privileges and immunity. China's conception of reciprocity does not lead it to concede to a foreign country's diplomats stationed in Peking a status identical with that granted Peking's diplomats stationed in that foreign country. For the Chinese, the principle of reciprocity is geographic and not bilateral: Chinese diplomatic agents in a foreign state must have the same privileges and immunities as are to be granted the diplomats of other foreign missions, just as all diplomats stationed in Peking supposedly receive the same treatment from Chinese authorities.

But this absence of discrimination to which the Chinese proclaim themselves so firmly attached is merely theoretical.[19] Moreover, the

18. See, for example, notes of the Chinese Minister of Foreign Affairs to the Indonesian embassy, February 27, 1966, March 10, 1966, and January 24, 1967; note of the Chinese embassy at Djakarta to the Indonesian Minister of Foreign Affairs, February 15, 1966.

19. It was affirmed in particular when Chinese authorities, having closed the universities in the summer of 1966, sent home foreign students who were originally admitted under cultural accords. See the note of June 10, 1967, from the Chinese

notion of "privileges and immunities" is contested by China. Thus, during an audience at the Ministry of Foreign Affairs in February 1967, the Mongolian ambassador in Peking heard it declared that diplomatic immunities were of bourgeois origin and that they had no place in a socialist society.[20] In practice, the status of foreign diplomats provides more or less protection to their person and property in proportion to the warmth of the relations between China and their national state. Thus, the degree of protection granted their person and property fluctuates accordingly.

Indeed, is this relatively not in keeping with the conception of diplomacy which has been described here? Since Chinese diplomats are "fighters," does not China's analysis of the role of foreign diplomats ineluctably lead the Chinese to consider all diplomats to be engaged in a battle, either on China's side, or, conversely, against the Revolution? The treatment they receive is dependent upon their qualifications as allies in combat, as doubters whom one hopes to convince, or as enemies. Enemies, at most, are entitled only to the residual humanitarian status that the modern law of war recognizes in individuals under the domination of the adversary.

Inasmuch as this is the point of view of Chinese authorities—and the practice followed by China in recent years, the *People's Daily* editorial just cited and other declarations do, in fact, verify the assumption[21]—the status of the foreign diplomat in China offers few guaranties of his well-being. From day to day, he is subject to distrust depending on the evolution of relations between China and the state he represents. In this sense, the most important diplomatic immunities do not exist in China since they disappear in time of crisis, that is, precisely at the time when they should demonstrate their utility.

Minister of Foreign Affairs to the Bulgarian embassy, NCNA, no. 2294 (June 12, 1967). See also the note from the Chinese government to the Soviet government on October 22, 1966. It was publicly known in Peking, however, that the students of certain foreign nations continued to pursue their studies at the Institute of Languages in Peking.

20. This point of view was never formulated officially in writing, and the Chinese press, to my knowledge, never echoed it. Mr. Tsevegnid, meanwhile, is explicit concerning the tenor of the resolutions divulged to him which, furthermore, are in line with the Chinese conception of international law.

21. In this connection China affirmed its recognition of the diplomatic privileges of Ghanaian representatives during a period of tension in a note from the Chinese embassy at Accra to the Ghanaian government, March 19, 1966. Likewise, in their dealings with "revisionists," Chinese authorities often announce their regret that they cannot recognize privileged status. See, for example, *People's Daily,* Feb. 6, 1967, and NCNA, no. 2169 (Feb. 8, 1967).

The status of the foreign diplomat in China must be considered a relative matter. An analysis of diplomatic practice in the most important areas—facilities for coming and going, inviolability, and immunity from jurisdiction—demonstrates how, in those cases one can characterize as pathological, the traditional rights of the diplomat are ignored and his status diminished.

LIMITATIONS ON THE FACILITIES FOR TRAVELING WITHIN THE COUNTRY

Classic doctrine, confirmed on this point by the Vienna Convention, grants the members of diplomatic missions freedom of movement and circulation in the territory of the state to which they are accredited, subject to the imperatives of national security.[22] The appearance of the socialist states created a gap in this principle, a breach rendered more significant by measures of reciprocity. China, for its part, has reverted to, and sometimes aggravated, the practice of other socialist states.[23] At present, nearly all of China's territory is normally and permanently closed to foreign diplomats; sometimes diplomats are subjected to travel regulations that are even stricter than the existing rules.

It is paradoxical, first of all, that foreign diplomats are governed by travel restrictions much more severe than those applied to tourists, businessmen, technicians, or experts invited by China. The system is based on the existence of a certain number of "open towns."[24] Forty-eight hours prior to entering any of these towns, entrance authorization must be applied for. Theoretically, it is granted automatically. Aside from these "open towns," it is also possible, though exceptional, to obtain the right to travel in other regions. Exceptional authorizations are liberally granted for some towns and regions, but there are entire provinces—Sinkiang, Tibet, and Inner Mongolia—which foreign diplomats may not visit, and this has been the case for several years. Since the closing of the Soviet consulates in Urumchi and Kuldja in Sinkiang

22. See the Convention of Vienna, article 26, in Philippe Cahier, *Le Droit diplomatique contemporain* (2nd. ed., Paris, 1964).

23. It is fair to note that the Chinese have not necessarily initiated this limitation. Since 1951, for example, Indonesian authorities have sought to restrict the travel of Chinese diplomats. See Lea E. Williams, "Sino-Indonesian Diplomacy: A Study of Revolutionary International Politics," *China Quarterly*, no. 11:185 (1962).

24. Peking, Tientsin, Shanghai, Nanking, Wuhan, Canton, Hangchow, and Soochow.

in 1962, probably no foreigner has entered these provinces.[25] Chinese territory, then, is divided into three zones: those which one may visit normally, those which a diplomat may visit occasionally with special permission, and those which are totally closed to foreigners.

Authorizations are granted for a fixed period; however, it is sometimes possible to obtain an extension on the spot after local authorities most probably have consulted Peking security officials. The journey must be made by train or airplane, sometimes by bus, and must conform to the mode of transportation specified in the request for travel. The only route that may be traveled in a private automobile is the road between Peking and Tientsin. Control posts, located in railroad stations, air terminals, or at the exits of towns, watch over the arrival and departure of foreigners and stamp their travel authorization papers.

Chinese authorities do not willingly invoke reasons of internal security to justify these restrictions imposed upon the travel of foreign diplomats. They prefer to mention the difficulties of transportation, reception, and lodging. According to them, travel restrictions are maintained in the interest of the traveler.

To compensate for the evident frustration and sense of claustrophobia among foreign diplomats, the Chinese organize train tours for them which permit a visit to one or more provinces and provide an occasion for propagandizing. In principle, each year two trips are proposed to the chiefs of missions and their wives, another to military attachés, and, in 1965, one for counselors and cultural attachés. However, these trips are designed just for a few high-ranking diplomats. If embassies with a limited staff profit extensively from this kind of travel, the solution hardly appears democratic to embassies with a larger staff since their subordinate agents never benefit from it.

The travel situation that has just been described exists during normal periods. In the period of crisis that China has gone through since the beginning of the Cultural Revolution, even more severe limitations have appeared.

In the first place, the authorization to visit "open towns" has been suspended at certain times. A formal demand for travel authorization is not generally rejected—since this runs counter to a well-established tradition of avoiding, as often as possible, formal official refusals—but is left unanswered until the projected time of the journey, which pro-

25. See "Chronique des faits internationaux," *Revue générale de droit international public* 67:144 (1963).

vides an excuse for not answering. Or else the Ministry of Foreign Affairs shifts the burden to the official travel agency, China Travel Service (Luxingshe), the necessary intermediary for all travel in China, which then indicates that there are neither train nor airplane accommodations available for the departure dates requested. Certain towns, then, have been only intermittently open, while at the same time authorization to visit unusual places has been almost systematically withheld.

On the other hand, discrimination has appeared in the treatment reserved for different embassies. English diplomats, particularly after the Hong Kong incidents in the spring of 1967, received practically no authorizations to travel in the provinces. The British chargé d'affaires, Donald Hopson, was excluded from the June 1967 trip reserved for chiefs of missions. When a mob invaded the British mission in Shanghai and the apartment of the British representative was sacked, the English had great difficulty in sending an agent from Peking to Shanghai. They received a travel authorization for only a very short period since the agent was regarded by the Chinese as a courier.

Restrictions imposed upon diplomats not only concern travel across China but also affect travel in Peking and environs. Theoretically, foreign diplomatic personnel may circulate freely within the capital and in a peripheral zone with a radius of fifteen or twenty-five kilometers. They may without authorization make excursions outside this perimeter to the Great Wall and to the valley of the Ming tombs. Signboards,[26] control posts, and the vigilance of the population ensure that they do not stray beyond these open areas. Within these limits, there are military zones that the foreigner may not enter. The fact that they generally are not marked exposes the automobile driver to the risk of involuntary incursions, followed by a delay of several hours for identity checks and an admonition—most often courteous. These limitations are found in all towns open to foreign diplomats.

This regime is tightened considerably for the representatives of a state in crisis with China. Their freedom of movement is restrained and sometimes entirely suppressed. Accordingly, when difficulties arose between China and Holland in 1966,[27] the Dutch chargé d'affaires,

26. The signboards say in various languages: "Out of bounds for foreigners without special permits."

27. See below. See also "Chronique des faits internationaux," *Revue générale de droit international public* 71:180–182 (1967).

Mr. Jongejans, found his diplomatic card, that is, his identity card as a diplomat, withdrawn. He had to confine himself to his residence for several months because each time he would have left it he would have been subject to questioning.[28] He was not expressly forbidden to travel, but the Chinese deprived him of the document that gave him permission to reside in China; he was thus in an irregular situation in Chinese territory.[29] After the anti-British demonstrations in August 1967, the movement of British diplomats was restricted to trips between the office of the chargé d'affaires and their residences. An authorization had to be solicited to leave the diplomatic quarters in the Foreign Diplomats Building where the English families had been installed. This permission, which was not automatically granted, specified the hours during which the diplomat could leave his residence and where he was allowed to go. In another case,[30] no travel prohibition was explicitly issued, but the Chinese authorities demanded that the chief of the Indian mission resettle the diplomats and their families at the embassy. This was done under the pretext that their security could no longer be assured. Thus, during June 1967 about sixty people spent several days enclosed in the Indian embassy.

Abridgement of freedom of movement, then, is particularly harsh, and, in certain cases, can lead to a complete restriction to residence. Nevertheless, Chinese authorities appear to be very attached to this freedom for their own diplomats in foreign posts and do not miss an opportunity to protest that their movements are being restricted. For example, the Tunisian government found itself the recipient of a protest note when in September 1967 it decided to make the issuance of an authorization a condition for allowing Chinese diplomats to travel in the country.[31]

28. A police car was stationed in front of his door for the duration of his confinement in order apparently to intervene should he make an unexpected exit.

29. The freedom of the other members of the Dutch embassy to travel in Peking was also restricted.

30. See the note of the Chinese government to the Indian government, June 17, 1967, in NCNA, June 18, 1967.

31. Note of September 14, 1967, in NCNA, no. 3522 (Sept. 16, 1967); *SCMP*, no. 4025:31 (Sept. 21, 1967). See also an oral protest issued June 15, 1967, to the Indian chargé d'affaires regarding "unreasonable restrictions" on the freedom of movement of members of the Chinese embassy and their families in New Delhi, NCNA, June 16, 1967; *SCMP*, no. 3963:32 (June 20, 1967). This protest stresses the discriminatory character of this measure.

THE ATTACKS ON DIPLOMATIC IMMUNITY FROM JURISDICTION

In principle, diplomats cannot be tried by the courts of the state to which they are accredited. It is a question of guaranteeing their independence to exercise their mission.

The Chinese do not readily recognize such an immunity for foreign diplomats. Whether it is a question of private acts or official ones, they frequently subject them to a judicial proceeding. The results of automobile accidents in which diplomats are implicated are adjudicated, indeed, according to a complex process the judicial character of which appears nonetheless established. In principle, if the dossier is compiled by the police authorities who also direct the investigation,[32] a decision is reached after an adversary proceeding which assesses damages between the diplomat who caused the accident and the victim. This decision is final and cannot be contested through litigation. The diplomat has no choice but to accept the share of responsibility thus distributed.[33]

It is true that the Chinese authorities make an effort to present the proceeding as a transaction carried out under the arbitration of the police. But the authoritarian character of the decision, its obligatory force, and its semiclandestine procedure[34] negate much of the force of this argument. Moreover, it should be added that frequently the decision is not restricted to sentencing the diplomat to pay damages; his driver's license may also be revoked. This measure, it seems, reinforces the idea of the judicial character of the decision.

Foreign diplomats, in effect, must surrender their national driver's license to the Chinese authorities if they desire to drive a car while in

32. To our knowledge, the locally competent police authority investigates the matter initially, but the different stages of the investigation unfold under the supervision of representatives of the Office of Security for Foreigners. This office orally notifies the diplomat of the conditions of settlement. The two parties to the proceedings never confront each other. The foreign diplomat may present an explanation when he meets with the Office of Security, but this appears to be futile because after he has presented his explanation, a decision is read to him, which was prepared in advance. He may not contest either the facts as presented in the decision or its conclusions.

33. The text of the decision is read aloud. While during this dictation it is possible to make notes of the terms of the decision, a copy of the decision cannot be obtained. This attitude of the Chinese poses serious problems to foreigners who seek to receive reimbursement from their insurance company for damages required to be paid.

34. It is impossible to review one's dossier.

China. They go through a medical examination and are granted an authorization to drive which is valid for one year. In the case of an accident, this document is confiscated by the police, who can return it almost immediately—if the consequences are not serious—or who can hold it until the final decree. In the latter situation, the final decree will decide the fate of the driver's license; a suspension of several months may be ordered. However, and this is a point which deserves emphasis, the Chinese authorities keep the national driver's license of the convicted diplomat for the duration of his sentence. If he leaves China to go on vacation, he will not be able to recover it. In this way, the conviction tends to reach beyond the limits of Chinese territory.

Similarly, retention of the national driver's license seems to be a lever intended to force the diplomat to pay the damages imposed on him. The license is returned to a diplomat who is leaving China permanently only if he shows a receipt for having complied with the decision.[35]

This procedure, no matter how unusual or disagreeable, is only one small part of China's normal treatment of diplomats. The principle of jurisdictional immunity was manhandled much more severely during the events of June 1967, when the official activity of a diplomat actually led to his trial before a Chinese court.

The Raghunath Affair

On June 12, 1967, the Indian embassy at Peking was informed by the Ministry of Foreign Affairs that the Chinese government would henceforth no longer recognize the diplomatic status of M.K. Raghunath, second secretary of the embassy, and that he could not leave Chinese territory until Chinese judicial authorities had punished him according to law for the "crimes" with which he had been charged.

M.K. Raghunath was accused of espionage. He had been "collecting everywhere" political and military intelligence about China "in brazen violation of Chinese laws and decrees." In particular, it was said, a few days earlier he had been surprised while in the act of taking photos in a military zone; the films which were confiscated proved

35. It should also be mentioned that the Chinese authorization to drive may at any time be withdrawn as a political sanction. British diplomats suffered this experience in August 1967.

beyond doubt his espionage activity.[36] The same evening, Mr. Raghunath was told to appear the next afternoon before a tribunal called the "Peking Municipal Higher People's Court." This tribunal, which may have been created for the occasion, was presented as an extension of the normal jurisdiction of Chinese courts.

The hearing took place in the covered Workers' Stadium in Peking in front of 15,000 representatives of the "revolutionary masses"; the accused was absent.[37] During this "meeting," the masses "condemned with indignation" the grave crimes of Raghunath and demanded that the court mete out a severe penalty to him. The preliminary examination having "demonstrated [that] under the cover of diplomatic status . . . the accused . . . for a long time . . . had deliberately engaged in espionage activities," the court condemned him to expulsion. Mr. Raghunath was to be conducted to the frontier under the escort of public security personnel and the Red Guards.[38]

It is certain that this affair carries the mark of the events of this period; some of its aspects, like the meeting for people's judgment and the intervention of the Red Guards, must be placed in the perspective of the Cultural Revolution during the month of June 1967. Very likely, by these actions the Chinese wanted to deliver a blow to curb the curiosity of diplomats who, for Chinese tastes, were too closely interested in the development of China's internal politics. Nevertheless, the significance of the case derives from the fact that the Chinese did not hesitate to impeach diplomats, even for diplomatic acts, when the authorities felt that these acts were illegal and amounted to the crime of espionage. Moreover, these cases were handled by a judicial process under particularly unpleasant conditions and without any guarantee of impartiality. And the authorities did not hesitate to

36. The Chinese press published a series of photos seized from Raghunath and presented them as incontrovertible documents. The only one which was reproduced in its entirety showed the Indian diplomat standing under a sign that indicated the limits beyond which foreigners could not pass without authorization. Most of the foreign diplomats in Peking have such a souvenir photo.

37. The Indian chargé d'affaires forbade him to attend. NCNA reported: "Fearing punishment, the accused, K. Raghunath dared not appear at the tribunal," *SCMP*, no. 3961:31 (June 16, 1967).

38. Raghunath was put in the custody of his Chinese escort at the Peking airport and taken to the Hong Kong border after having suffered all sorts of brutalities and humiliations. He was subsequently made responsible for Chinese affairs at the Indian Ministry of Foreign Affairs; the Indians have a sense of humor. For details of this affair, see "Chronique des faits internationaux," *Revue générale de droit international public* 72:173–175 (1968).

pronounce a decision of expulsion, which was executed *manu militari* and without delay.

The same result could have been achieved by declaring Raghunath persona non grata and setting a date by which he had to leave Chinese territory.[39] In this way, the principles of jurisdictional immunity and immunity from punishment could have been safeguarded. China's actions manifested an apparent desire to break away from one of the essential rules for the protection of diplomats.

This proposition, however, has delicate nuances. Paradoxically, Chinese authorities, to the degree possible, gave the appearance of legality to the handling of this affair. The accused was summoned to appear, guarantees of personal security were given to him,[40] and the tribunal charged with his case was linked to the regular jurisdictional order. And, above all, should it not be considered homage to the traditional rules that Mr. Raghunath was deprived of his "quality as a diplomat" before being deferred to the tribunal? Did not the Chinese wish to indicate by this that they were not judging a diplomat but simply a private individual accused of espionage? Legalism and respect for form are features of the Chinese Communist mentality today; this interpretation, then, is not unreasonable, and we can deduce from it that the Chinese intend to respect the principle of jurisdictional immunity.

Nevertheless, this point of view seems specious. Jurisdictional immunity, above all, is emptied of all significance if the accrediting state can turn at its pleasure and deprive the accused of his diplomatic status in order to try him before a court. But even supposing that a state can remove diplomatic status in this manner, is not the essential point that the person in question possessed this diplomatic status at the moment he performed the acts for which he is being reproached? This second view of jurisdictional immunity is acknowledged in doctrine and consecrated by the Vienna Convention.[41] The subtleties of the Chinese authorities cannot hide the fact that in the Raghunath affair they violated the principle of jurisdictional immunity.

39. It is noteworthy that the same day the Ministry of Foreign Affairs declared another agent of the Indian embassy persona non grata for "collusion" with Raghunath.

40. It is true that their value should be eyed with caution. The same guarantees were given for Raghunath's departure, and they did not protect him from the excesses he suffered.

41. See Cahier, *Le Droit diplomatique contemporain*, p. 252.

Prohibition Against Leaving Chinese Territory: The Jongejans Affair

Chinese authorities maintain a strict control over the coming and going of diplomats. For each voyage, the diplomat stationed in Peking must solicit an exit visa from China, which is valid only for a limited period and only at the border station or airport mentioned in the document. He must also obtain a return visa, under the same conditions, in order to resume his Peking post. This administrative formality, contrary to traditional practice, allows the Chinese government to prohibit the departure of that state's diplomats from Chinese territory if a crisis occurs between China and an accredited state.

In July 1966, a Chinese engineer who was attending the International Welding Congress in Holland died under suspicious circumstances in the villa of the Chinese chargé d'affaires at The Hague. He had arrived there after having been forcibly removed from a hospital to which he had been taken after having been found unconscious on a public road. As a result, the Chinese chargé d'affaires was declared persona non grata and left Dutch territory on July 18.

In response, the Chinese government on July 20 declared Mr. Gerrit Jongejans, the Dutch chargé d'affaires, persona non grata. But the Chinese note further specified that the Dutch diplomat was not authorized to leave China inasmuch as the members of the Chinese delegation visiting Holland had not been guaranteed a safe return to China.[42] In effect, they remained secluded in their legation building at The Hague, refusing to answer the summons of the examining judge charged with obtaining their testimony about the affair. The Chinese government considered that the Dutch "without valid reason" were preventing the Chinese technicians from leaving Holland and that they had "issued an order for a court appearance to [the technicians] with the intention of making them stand trial illegally." This action of the Dutch government, it was said, "grossly violated the elementary principles governing international relations." After long negotiations, the Chinese technicians agreed to interrogation by the judge, and Mr. Jongejans obtained an authorization to leave China at the end of December 1966, after more than five months of confinement.

Chinese authorities always emphasized the element of reprisal in the measures taken against Mr. Jongejans. The Chinese technicians in

42. As we have seen above, they also withdrew Mr. Jongejans' diplomatic identity card.

Holland held service passports, which seemed sufficient to the Chinese to justify an act of retortion against an agent holding diplomatic status.

The reasoning of the Chinese is difficult to support. A service passport gives no particular privileges to its holder and does not confer diplomatic status on him. Furthermore, the Chinese chargé d'affaires had been able to leave Holland without undergoing harassment after being declared persona non grata; if a parallel could be established, it should have been between his situation and that of Mr. Jongejans.

Certainly the action taken against the Dutch chargé d'affaires is among the most serious that can be ordered by a government; it imperils the liberty of all diplomats stationed in Peking and manifestly violates the rules of international society. Yet, this conduct was not to remain an isolated case; rather, it has become established practice for the Chinese authorities systematically to refuse to grant exit visas to diplomats whose governments are in conflict with China.

At the time of the Jongejans affair, the wives and children of other Dutch diplomats had already been forced to wait several weeks for their exit visas.[43] Shortly thereafter, following the sacking of the British embassy in August 1967, authorization to leave Chinese territory was refused British diplomats and their families. Only pregnant women and children who had come to China to spend their vacation with their parents were permitted to leave.[44]

Moreover, Chinese authorities do not need to play on the necessity of an exit visa in order effectively to impede the departure of any foreign diplomat from Chinese territory. They can see to it that the competent organizations, particularly the China Travel Service, do not deliver travel tickets to persons who request them. This subterfuge was employed in the month of July 1967 with regard to Anthony Grey, the Reuters correspondent, who did not enjoy diplomatic status[45]; but

43. The same delay was imposed on Ghanaian diplomats at the end of the summer of 1966. The June 29, 1967, declaration of the government of the People's Republic of China expressly mentioned the prohibition against the return of the Burmese ambassador in Peking to his own country. See NCNA, June 30, 1967.

44. As of late summer 1968, this prohibition against leaving still existed. Thirteen members of the British mission, notably women and children, were still awaiting their visas, according to a statement of the British chargé d'affaires, Sir Donald Hopson, on his arrival in Hong Kong, August 14, 1968. All were subsequently granted visas.

45. Mr. Grey was put under house arrest in reprisal for the arrest of Chinese journalists in Hong Kong and was cut off from all outside contact. He was finally released in October 1969.

the procedure could be used equally well with a diplomat. If a diplomat wishes to take a vacation outside of China, the Chinese can simply inform him that there are no available places on the trains and planes leaving Peking for foreign destinations.

Within the diplomat's general situation outlined above, no matter what its severity, there is room for a multitude of variations in pestering, harassment, punishment, humiliation, and revenge. In a society where the strike theoretically does not exist, it makes an appearance when the employer is a foreign diplomat—the domestic personnel use it to protest the conduct of their employer's government. After having resumed work, the same personnel will eventually refuse, at some time, to serve their employer's guests. Stores will receive an order to refuse to sell to foreigners of a certain nationality; taxis will refuse to service the residence. If the foreign diplomat is transferred to another country, the official services will refuse to help him move his furniture, and he will have to leave his effects in China.

But even more serious is the fact that in certain circumstances Chinese authorities do not guarantee the security of foreign diplomats. During mass demonstrations, the police, though present, do not intervene to protect diplomats trapped by the mob; when the police intercede, it is only after a long delay. The British experienced this in the burning of their legation in Peking in August 1967. They were beaten, injured, thrown to the ground, trampled, and undressed under the impassive eyes of the public security forces. No penalty was imposed on any of the demonstrators who injured the diplomats and destroyed the property of the diplomatic mission. The absence of control and the guarantee of impunity it carries with it can only encourage excesses; it is also a striking indication of the complicity of the authorities.[46]

The departure of diplomats required by the deterioration of relations between their countries and China also give rise to distressing scenes; nothing occurs in China without the consent or even the initiative of the public authorities. The departures of Mr. Raghunath and of the wives and children of the Soviet diplomats in March 1967 remain serious incidents because of the dishonorable conditions, in the memory of all those who were involved, under which they occurred.

46. This impunity contrasts markedly with the unreasonable demands for sanctions made by the Chinese each time one of their embassies is attacked by a mob. For the incidents of August 22 and 29, see the "Chronique des faits internationaux," *Revue générale de droit international public* 72:409–414 (1968).

The trip to Canton in the spring of 1967 of the Indonesian chargé d'affaires and his wife, who had been declared personae non gratae and who were returning to Djakarta, took place under equally infamous conditions.

The repetition of events of this kind has considerably aggravated the distrust of many governments with regard to China. The concept of reciprocity is reinforced by the idea of simultaneity: out of prudence, a country could not allow a Chinese diplomat whom it declared to be persona non grata to leave its territory unless it knew the fate reserved by Chinese authorities for his counterpart in Peking. In the case of reprisals, the two diplomats would leave the same day at the same hour. It takes on the appearance of exchange of prisoners or hostages at a border.[47]

Foreign diplomats are somewhat like vouchers for the good conduct of their government. But it must be recognized that at times China has had good reason to subject diplomats to strict control, a control justified, until now, by the necessity of protecting their lives. The situation of Chinese diplomats in Indonesia, Burma, and India during 1967 was even less enviable than the position of their foreign colleagues in Peking.[48] The governments of these countries allowed dramatic events to develop in which the Chinese embassy was the principal target; these events overwhelmed diplomatic status and put into question the status of diplomatic buildings.

The Diplomatic Mission

The diplomatic mission seems like a foreign implantation on Chinese territory. This is true, at least, in a country that still suffers retrospectively from the memory of the conditions imposed on China by Westerners in the nineteenth century. China does not want foreigners to become involved in its internal problems nor to mingle with its population, and the authorities try to limit as much as possible the presence of foreigners in the country.

The socialization of land brought about the eviction of former property holders, and foreign states did not escape this. They no

47. See, for example, the declaration of the spokesman of the Indian government, June 21, 1967, Agence France Press and NCNA, June 24, 1967.

48. The treatment imposed on Chinese diplomats in Moscow and Ulan Bator under some circumstances during 1967 did not always conform to international usage. But can it be said that their attitude was free of provocation?

longer own the land on which their embassies and the housing of their agents are constructed. Chinese authorities took advantage of this situation to regroup the foreign embassies in two new districts away from the center of Peking.[49] Countries with embassies in the former legation quarter gradually had to abandon them. The Chinese state, through a long term lease, put a piece of land at their disposal on which the new embassy was to be built at the cost of the tenant.[50] It is also possible—and many states which do not want to incur the construction costs use this formula—to rent a building specially built to house an embassy.

The diplomats had to follow the embassies in this migration to the periphery. Those who lived in Chinese houses situated in the old areas of Peking were compelled to leave or, more simply, could not renew their leases.[51] Four "diplomatic buildings" intended for the housing of diplomats[52] were built near the new embassies; the Chinese authorities certainly intended to confine in two "diplomatic districts" all the activities of foreign officials in Peking.

Geographically, then, the diplomatic missions are already situated apart. This should make it easier to grant them a special status, and, in particular, should favor the protection of diplomatic buildings. What happens in practice?

The Embassy Building

We know that the principle of inviolability dominates the status of the embassy building. The authorities must guarantee to respect and

49. Only the Soviet Union, during the time of Sino-Soviet amity, was allowed to construct an immense embassy, housing both services and personnel, outside of the quarters assigned to the other embassies.

50. The eviction of the foreign state from its previous quarters is recompensed with an indemnity. The same principle applies to the purchase of any buildings that these foreign states owned in China before 1949. With rare exceptions, diplomatic missions and consulates no longer exist outside of Peking; the fate of the buildings formerly belonging to the consulates gives rise to delicate negotiations with Chinese authorities. Some shipping companies and airlines may maintain offices outside of the capital.

51. Leases were actually concluded with the Service Bureau by the foreign state and not by the diplomats who occupied the premises in behalf of that state. The unstable condition of the buildings and their state of decay are invoked by Chinese authorities to justify the change of location.

52. The rents are relatively high and the construction, though remarkable for China, is mediocre by Western standards. Post office, hairdresser, tailor, and grocery stores are available in the buildings where the diplomats live, and the general effect is that of a ghetto.

protect it; they take it upon themselves not to enter the embassy, and they guard to see that individuals do not enter contrary to the wish of the chief of the mission.

The Chinese government seemingly adheres to this rule of the inviolability of embassy grounds when violations of this principle occur in other countries. During 1967, Chinese authorities had several occasions to reaffirm their point of view. Successively, their embassies in Moscow, New Delhi, Rangoon, and Djakarta were attacked by mobs, with no attempt by the local police to stop the demonstrators from invading the diplomatic quarters.[53] These events gave rise to some dramatic scenes: a Chinese expert was killed in Rangoon, a diplomat injured in New Delhi, and several diplomatic agents were seriously beaten in Djakarta.

In each of these cases, the Chinese government vigorously protested, basing its charges on the rules of international law. Thus, on June 19, 1967, the Ministry of Foreign Affairs addressed a note to the Indian embassy in Peking regarding the invasion of the Chinese embassy in New Delhi and charged that the incident was "one more striking example of the [Indian government's] flagrant transgression of international law and violation of the principles guiding international relations."[54] The official New China News Agency specified in its June 21 comments that the entrance of the demonstrators into the embassy violated the norms of international relations which prohibit entry into a foreign embassy.[55]

Even when demonstrations do not involve incidents of this magnitude, Chinese authorities remind foreign governments of their duty to protect the embassy and its property.[56] They were indignant that snowballs, eggs, and apples were thrown during a demonstration,[57]

53. The Chinese maintain that the police were in league with the demonstrators and that they even directed the operations. See the Chinese note to the Indian embassy in Peking dated June 19, 1967. For these various incidents, see "Chronique des faits internationaux," *Revue générale de droit international public* 71:751–752 and 1066–1067 (1967) and 72:160–161, 174–176, and 419 (1968).

54. NCNA, June 19, 1967; *SCMP*, no. 3965:18 (June 22, 1967).

55. NCNA, June 22, 1967.

56. See note from the Chinese embassy at Djakarta to the Indonesian government, June 13, 1967, NCNA, June 16, 1967; note of the Chinese Ministry of Foreign Affairs to the Burmese embassy at Peking, June 28, 1967, NCNA, June 29, 1967.

57. Protest against the Soviet Union on February 9, 1967, NCNA, no. 2174 (Feb. 12, 1967). These acts were characterized as violations of "international diplomatic practice." Note of the Chinese embassy in Indonesia to the Indonesian government on June 29, 1966, NCNA, July 3, 1966 regarding stones thrown into the embassy garden.

and that "reactionary signs" were stuck to the doors of the embassy.[58]

The Chinese, then, feel that host governments are obligated to protect the Chinese embassies established on their territory, and they base these obligations on international law and practice. Their attitude toward diplomatic missions established in Peking, however, barely takes these rules into consideration.[59]

Foreign embassies in Peking, in effect, are the top places for the Chinese "masses," invited by the authorities, to shout their indignation or affirm their solidarity. The embassy building has a symbolic value as a monument erected by a foreign nation; the people can desecrate it or cover it with flowers. Thousands, even millions, of people will file past the building in an orderly way for days or weeks at a time. During the night preceding the beginning of the demonstration, the immediate area is fitted out with first aid stations, water, and toilets. The demonstrators will shout slogans, brandish small paper posters on which expressions of hate, contempt, or sympathy are printed, wave pennants, and exhibit caricatures. Their attitude will be adjusted in proportion to the degree of the offense. The masses' total lack of spontaneity and the efficiency of the whole operation reflect absolute control over the unfolding of the demonstration. In a sense, demonstrations can be divided into several classes. In the mildest case, the mob contents itself with marching in front of the embassy, pasting up signs of protest, and trying to deliver petitions to the foreign diplomats.[60] As one gradually advances up the hierarchy of offenses that must be avenged, the acts necessary to expiate the sin become correspondingly more extreme. The chief of state and other high-level foreign personalities will be hung in effigy at the front gate, and the dummies which represent them will be burned;[61] the windows will be broken by stones; the face of the building will be defiled with ink and

58. Note from the Chinese embassy at Djakarta to the Indonesian government, June 29, 1966, NCNA, no. 1950 (July 3, 1966).

59. It is interesting to note the following passage in the aforementioned note to the Indonesian Minister for Foreign Affairs on June 13, 1967: "The whole world knows that it is not in China . . . that guarantee[s] to the security of foreign representative organs and the life and property of their members [have] completely disappeared. Incidents of foreign representative organs being attacked, sabotaged and searched by the armed forces of the country where they are stationed do not occur in China. . . ."

60. About ten embassies were targets of such demonstrations in 1967: France, the Soviet Union (6 million demonstrators,), Yugoslavia, Mongolia, Bulgaria, Indonesia, India, Burma (5 million demonstratoars), Great Britain (several million demonstrators), Kenya.

61. Soviet Union, January 1967; Great Britain, June 1967; Burma, July 1967.

rotten fruit;[62] a group of demonstrators will invade the diplomatic settlements and then withdraw quickly after having broken everything in their path;[63] and finally, the embassy will be sacked,[64] the archives scatter , the diplomats manhandled, beaten, and humiliated, and the building burned.[65]

Nothing about these demonstrations is unforeseeable or spontaneous; they are organized by the public authorities. Police forces, sometimes numerous, are stationed in front of the embassy to channel the mob and to see that the demonstration remains within the previously determined limits. In no case do they interfere if the demonstrators follow the pre-established scenario.

The Chinese authorities, then, have a peculiar conception of their duty to protect diplomatic missions. Protests drawn up by the chiefs of missions involved are always abruptly dismissed. The Ministry of Foreign Affairs invariably responds, in effect, that "the action of the revolutionary masses is entirely justified,"[66] or that "one can do nothing against the legitimate anger of the masses."[67]

The material consequences of these demonstrations remain. Chinese authorities have no intention of assuming any responsibility for the events that have occurred, and they do not contemplate repairing the damage caused.[68] The repair of these premises usually has a dual aspect: First, the Chinese government must consent to the repairs, and then the foreign state must bear the costs. The largest and most important repairs can only be undertaken with the consent of the Chinese authorities. In a socialist society, it is impossible to deal directly with a contractor; consequently, the foreign mission must request that the Ministry of Foreign Affairs send it some workers. The Ministry, which never takes the initiative in repair operations, may then allow the work to be assigned to qualified professionals. Its intervention is usually characterized as a favor, because it must "appease the anger of the

62. India, June 1967; Burma, July 1967. In February 1967, a window of the French embassy was broken by demonstrators.

63. Great Britain, June 7, 1967; on June 9, an English diplomat was wounded.

64. British consulate, Shanghai, May 1967; local Soviet consulates in Peking, August 17, 1967.

65. Great Britain, August 23, 1967.

66. Response to the protest note from the British chargé d'affaires, June 8, 1967.

67. Response given at the time of the sacking of the British consulate in Shanghai in May 1967.

68. But they do not hesitate to demand reparations for damages suffered by their embassies. See, for example, the declaration of the government of the People's Republic of China, February 5, 1967, NCNA, no. 2168 (Feb. 6, 1967).

masses." But, in all cases, Chinese authorities carefully specify that the work is to be undertaken at the expense of the foreign state and that, in their opinion, this financing corresponds to an avowal of responsibility on the part of the foreign embassy.[69]

Also, well after the demonstrations have ended, ink still stains the face of the building, and the walls of the embassy remain covered with slogans and signs that proclaim the indignation of the people and their rulers. The rules of diplomatic practice concerning the respect due an embassy building have little value for Chinese authorities; the situation concerning other attributes of a diplomatic mission is scarcely more favorable.

The Annexes and Various Attributes of a Diplomatic Mission

Duality also characterizes the attitude of the Chinese government regarding the annexes and attributes of the diplomatic mission. The Chinese protest when the offices of their commercial services, or of their military attaches, their consulates, or the installations of the New China News Agency[70]—which does not enjoy diplomatic status—are besieged or attacked. The annexes of the Chinese diplomatic mission, then, in the opinion of the Chinese, are entitled to the same protection as the main embassy building. But it must be pointed out that they did nothing in May 1967 to protect the British mission in Shanghai from invasion by a mob. During that incident, the home of the British representative, Mr. Hewitt, was completely sacked by the demonstrators, and his wife and children were terrorized without any intervention by the Chinese police. The same lack of responsibility was observed during the sacking and burning of the residence of the British chargé d' affaires in August 1967. On the other hand, the Chinese government demands no less than that the residences of its agents abroad receive the same protection as the embassy. For example, the Chinese characterized the occupation of eight diplomatic buildings in Djakarta

69. Under the contractual plan, in light of their obligation to provide the tenant with premises suitable as a diplomatic building, it is arguable that, because the Chinese authorities are the owners of the building, they thereby accept the responsibility of repairing the walls. A demand based on this concept, however, has been rejected.

70. Declaration of the government of the PRC, June 29, 1967, NCNA, June 30, 1967, regarding Burma.

as a "violent fascist act which tramples underfoot the principles which govern international relations and international law."[71]

The Chinese also demand a special status for the attributes of their diplomatic missions abroad. They react violently to any offense committed against the Chinese flag—which happened in June 1967 in both New Delhi[72] and Rangoon[73]—referring to "universally recognized principles regulating international relations," and invoking "standards governing international relations" to affirm their right to raise their national colors over their consulate buildings.[74] At the same time, Chinese authorities have allowed demonstrators to seize and publicly burn the British flag.[75]

All attempts to control automotive vehicles belonging to the Chinese embassy are also denounced in the name of international law,[76] and constant quarrels concerning window displays of photographs or documents on embassy walls pit the Chinese embassy against local authorities. Use of window displays for propaganda seems to have great importance for the Chinese in spite of the small number of people affected. In certain countries where the dissemination of ideas, theories, and information from China is restricted by the public authorities, this is the only public way to achieve at least a minimum of propaganda, and Chinese diplomats are very attached to it. But these display cases are also the first targets on which the anger of demonstrators is vented, and local police do not always protect them with great conviction.[77] The Chinese government will then redouble its protests

71. Protest of the Chinese embassy at Djakarta addressed to the Indonesian government, July 3, 1966. In the same vein, another note to the Indonesian government, January 27, 1967, NCNA, no. 2163 (Feb. 1, 1967), characterized the occupation by the Indonesian Army of a dormitory belonging to the Chinese embassy as an "impudent infringement on the rights of diplomatic institutions" and as an "illegal occupation."

72. Note of the Ministry of Foreign Affairs to the Indian embassy at Peking, June 19, 1967, NCNA, June 20, 1967.

73. Refer to note of the Ministry of Foreign Affairs to the Burmese embassy at Peking, June 28, 1967, NCNA, June 29, 1967.

74. NCNA, no. 2261 (May 10, 1967). At the consulate at Medan in Indonesia, the Chinese presented in their showcases a photographic report of police repression.

75. Peking, June 1967.

76. Note of the Chinese Ministry of Foreign Affairs to the Indian embassy in Peking on June 17, 1967. The Indian police had wanted to search the car of the Chinese chargé d'affaires *ad interim* in New Delhi. This desire was characterized as "illegal" in the Chinese note and as a "violation of diplomatic immunity." NCNA, June 18, 1967.

77. Sometimes the Chinese embassy uses them to attack the authorities of the host state. This was the case when Chinese students were manhandled in Red Square in Moscow in January 1967.

because it believes that it has a right to install and safeguard these display cases; besides, it allows these displays on the walls of foreign embassies in Peking.[78]

DIPLOMATIC ACTIVITY

The conception of the normal activity of an embassy is evidently not the same in the socialist sphere as in the Western world. In the Marxist democracies, the freedom of action of each diplomatic mission is limited by the necessity of defending the socialist society from ill-intentioned curiosity and subversive foreign enterprises. At a time when the theory that there are a variety of paths to communism is no longer considered heresy and nationalism influences the people's democracies, the "fraternal countries" themselves are suffering a reduction in their embassies' freedom of action, and their status is approaching that of Western diplomatic missions.

With respect to diplomatic activities, China displays a defensive attitude at home, placing restrictions and prohibitions on diplomatic missions located on its territory. At the same time, it uses its embassies abroad in an "evangelical" manner.

The ancient Chinese tradition of secrecy reinforces the suspicion of Chinese authorities toward representatives of reactionary or revisionist ideologies; a "cordon sanitaire" is established around those embassies and diplomats. Any attempt to break loose from it is mistrusted and nourishes the climate of "espionage" which the regime carefully maintains. Similarly, the usages of diplomatic courtesy are ignored; Chinese authorities deliberately assume an air of superiority toward foreign missions which hardly conforms to the attitude that should govern relations between equal sovereign states. But here again China's recent past, as well as her earlier history, may explain the difference.

The Chinese, in practice, have a very restricted conception of the activity of embassies established on their territory. They hope to

78. Note of the Ministry of Foreign Affairs to the Kenyan government, July 1, 1967, NCNA, July 2, 1967; NCNA, Feb. 2, 1967; NCNA, no. 2166 (Feb. 4, 1967). The breaking of the windows was pictured as a "violation of the sovereignty of the People's Republic of China." Protest to the East German government, February 18, 1967, NCNA, no. 2181 (Feb. 19, 1967) that the destruction resulted in "contempt for the most elementary principles governing international relations." Declaration of the government of the PRC, February 5, 1967, NCNA, no. 2168 (Feb. 6, 1967): "The diplomatic privileges which the Chinese embassy enjoys in the Soviet Union are sacred and inviolable." Note to the Yugoslav government, January 30, 1967. Note of protest to the Indian government, June 15, 1967, NCNA, June 16, 1967.

confine them to a decorative role which does not go much beyond formal diplomatic protocol. Chinese authorities would like the embassies to do no more than organize receptions for national holidays, or serve as witnesses, preferably dazzled, of the government's displays and achievements.

The establishment of Chinese diplomatic missions abroad has an entirely different purpose. Though they certainly act as sources of information for the Chinese government, they respond above all to a desire to make known to the outside world China's brand of Marxism-Leninism, the Thought of Mao Tse-tung, and the transformation taking place in Chinese society. It is a question, as we have seen, of a fighter-diplomat; Chinese diplomats are propagandists of the good word, and they assert their freedom of action in order to disseminate it. Their initiatives frequently displease foreign governments. As a result, these governments often attempt to fetter them, each time provoking a note of protest that firmly claims "guarantees to function normally" for the Chinese embassy.[79]

But this normality is not the same in China's closed society as it is in the open societies of the West; in China, the Chinese impose their point of view on others, while at the same time they challenge foreigners to respect the rules they have set for themselves in their own countries. Thus, most of the traditional rules arising from international practice have become points of contention in Peking.

Relations with the Authorities

In their relations with Chinese authorities, foreign states have a natural tendency to adopt a mode of behavior familiar and normal to them in international relations. They consider their partner an equal, avoid involvement in his internal affairs, minimize the difficulties that can arise with him, and employ understatement, euphemism, or allusive forms in order not to shock the other party. Certainly, this ideal is frequently ignored, but it remains true, at least, that the majority of states consider it to be the correct attitude in matters of diplomatic relations.

China ignores these niceties and, moreover, tends to consider them hypocrisies. The Chinese infuse their foreign relations with a particular

79. Refer particularly to the notes to the Burmese embassy in Peking, July 4 and 5, 1967, NCNA, July 5 and 6, 1967.

style, perhaps one of the most remarkable features of which is its aspects of inequality.

The Chinese authorities are still profoundly affected by memories of the semicolonial period which preceded the advent of communism. The contempt endured and humiliations suffered weigh heavily today on relations with foreign countries. An analysis of Chinese diplomatic notes thus reveals certain profound currents in the psychology of the Chinese leaders. Familiarity with the diplomatic notes prepared by Western embassies and knowledge of the attention, the meticulousness and prudence with which they are drafted make one feel a great sense of estrangement upon reading Chinese documents, for they reveal the width of the chasm that separates two kinds of diplomacy.

The mentality of the Chinese rulers approaches the attitude of decolonized peoples and is shown in the violent, polemical tone of their protest notes. Things are said clearly, crudely, and without compromise in terminology. At each opportunity, they affirm that "the Chinese people will not permit themselves to be humiliated or mistreated,"[80] and that "the Chinese people will never allow the dignity of their great homeland to be offended."[81] This essential principle is reaffirmed like a challenge. China never "requests"; instead, it "demands" or announces that it cannot "tolerate" disrespect. These notes are followed by a series of threats leading to the Chinese criticism that the accused state "will assume total responsibility for all consequences"[82] or the familiar statement of Chairman Mao Tse-tung on the "imbeciles who lift a rock in order to drop it on their feet."[83]

The concept of "offended dignity" justifies the insistence with which Chinese notes clamour for the satisfactions of amour-propre. Foreign authorities are summoned, in effect, to "recognize their responsibility" and to present "public apologies." It is not sufficient in the end for China to win on the merits of the case material damages or a guarantee of safety for its agents. Rather, the propriety of its behavior must be proclaimed, China must gain face, and its adversary must be humiliated. This is more important for China, perhaps, than a material settlement.

80. See, for example, the note to the Indian embassy, June 17, 1967, NCNA, June 18, 1967.

81. See, for example, the note from the Chinese embassy to the Indonesian Minister of Foreign Affairs, June 13, 1967, NCNA, no. 2298 (June 16, 1967).

82. For example, see the end of the declaration of the government of the PRC, June 29, 1967, NCNA, June 30, 1967.

83. Note of June 9, 1967 to the Indonesian Minister of Foreign Affairs, NCNA, June 16, 1967.

Also, the possibility of compromise is miniscule in discussions with Chinese authorities.

The terminology of the Chinese notes is itself confusing. It makes for an interesting and tasteful comparison, for example, to examine the manner in which the Chinese describe a demonstration directed against a Chinese embassy abroad and, in contrast, the Chinese description of an attack against a foreign embassy in China. In the one case, "delegations" demonstrate in a "just and natural" fashion and come to deliver "resolutions" or "letters of protest" to the chief of the foreign mission. But, in the case of a demonstration against a Chinese embassy, there are "riff-raff," "hooligans," or "ruffians" whose "frenzy" is "engineered" by foreign authorities; the crowd "shouts savagely" and "hurls provocations" while the police accord it "their protection and encouragement."

All told, this is very human and somewhat amusing; however, the expressions used in some notes are so grave that they constitute an insult to foreign authorities, which in turn often reject them because of their unacceptable terminology.[84] For example, a spokesman of the Chinese Foreign Ministry referred to Soviet Defense Minister Malinowski as a "liar" during a declaration on May 3, 1966. On another occasion, the Mongolian Minister of Foreign Affairs was called a "Mongol Fox,"[85] and in a note to the Burmese government on July 5, 1967, the Chinese characterized the foreign spokesman as a "clown"[86] after having called him an "assassin" two days earlier.[87]

The audiences during which these verbal notes are delivered to the interested parties give rise to official reports in which the attitude of the foreign diplomat or functionary is described in a humiliating fashion. Sometimes "he did not have the courage to accept the note"; more often, "he did not know what to say," "he had no response," "he remained quiet," "he did not dare raise his head," or "he had the guilty conscience of a thief"; if absolutely necessary, he found "pitiful excuses" or replied "absurdly."

A similar attitude may be found in all the activities of the Chinese

84. See, for example, the note of the Chinese Minister of Foreign Affairs to the Indonesian embassy in Peking, September 19, 1966, NCNA, no. 2029 (Sept. 19, 1966).

85. See NCNA, May 24, 1967, English edition.

86. NCNA, July 6, 1967. "Clown" was also used in reference to the Bulgarian government in a note on June 10, 1967, NCNA, no. 2294 (June 12, 1967); *SCMP*, no. 3959:39 (June 14, 1967).

87. Note of July 3, 1967, NCNA, July 5, 1967.

diplomatic service. Their hypersensitivity, always intense, leads Chinese diplomats to recall at each available opportunity that "the China of today is not the China of yesterday, exploited and dominated by colonialism and imperialism," and that the "China of today intends to be respected."

Chinese agents abroad do not maintain a discreet reserve toward the authorities of the country that has welcomed them. They do not hesitate to write a letter to the press actively attacking a minister.[88] At times, they have announced that a chief of state is a slanderer,[89] and they have refused to shake his hand during an official ceremony.[90] This attitude seems perfectly legitimate and normal to Chinese authorities. In their eyes, they are challenging the customs which form part of a bourgeois code of politeness and decency. They will not shrink from proclaiming what appears to them to be the truth, and they act without regard for conventions. The Chinese also do not consider themselves any longer bound by a notion of domestic affairs that might preclude them from criticizing what takes place in the host country.

Nevertheless, they themselves are extremely touchy about any meddling in their own affairs. For example, the Chinese addressed a note to the Tunisian government on February 16, 1967, characterizing the "two China" policy practiced by the Tunisian authorities as a "flagrant interference in Chinese internal affairs and a scandalous provocation of the Chinese people." The note continued: "In active connivance with imperialists, revisionists, and reactionaries against China, it is evident that you act against the interests of the Tunisian people and this will end badly."[91]

Chinese diplomats sometimes embarrass the authorities of the state to which they are accredited by criticizing the authorities or politics of a third state. In the month of February 1967, for example, the diplomatic missions in Ceylon received an open letter from the Chinese chargé d'affaires to the Soviet ambassador insulting the "pigs called Brezhnev and Kosygin." Similarly, a Chinese diplomat in Pakistan publicly insulted his French and Soviet colleagues during a reception

88. Letter of the Chinese embassy at Nairobi criticizing a discussion of the Kenyan Minister of Planning, NCNA, no. 2315 (July 3, 1967).
89. Note of the Chinese embassy in Tunis, September 14, 1967, NCNA, no. 3422 (Sept. 17, 1967).
90. See *L'Analyste*, March 1967, p. 21.
91. *Ibid.* See also note of November 22, 1967, to the Indonesian government, NCNA, no. 3590 (Nov. 24, 1967).

held February 7, 1967, at the Rawalpindi airport, for the King of Afghanistan.[92]

These activities frequently result in difficulties for Chinese diplomats who find themselves declared personae non gratae. The surprise and indignation of Chinese authorities are indicated by notes of protest; they are manifest particularly when the expelled diplomat leaves the foreign country and when he arrives back in China. When a member of a Chinese embassy is requested to leave a country, the embassy personnel accompany him to the station or airport and organize a demonstration of sympathy and solidarity for the traveler. The discretion which usually governs departures is transformed here into a propaganda operation.[93] At his arrival in Peking, the diplomat is welcomed by important personalities and representatives of the masses; he is treated as a hero, covered—literally—with flowers, and he pronounces violent declarations against the government of the country from which he has come.[94] Sometimes the demonstrations are held in front of the embassy of the former host country, and the press, for a certain time, retraces the heroic exploits of this "red fighter on the diplomatic front."[95]

Besides this style and these unusual acts, the state of mind of the Chinese leaders is also shown by the inequality of the relationship which they seek to establish with the foreign embassies in China.[96]

92. *Ibid.* See also *Revue générale de droit international public* 71:743 (1967).

93. Chinese press reports of the departure are always constructed according to the same scheme: (1) restatement of the facts and a protest against the ruling; (2) the arrival of the Chinese at the airport and a reading in unison from the Thought of Mao Tse-tung; a part of the crowd obviously sympathetic; (3) a statement of the incorrect or brutal attitude of the foreign authorities; (4) at the time of departure, no matter what the reaction of the crowd, an old woman, a young man, or a worker is called forward to disapprove of the departure and the circumstances leading to it and to announce his solidarity with China and Chairman Mao. This is very characteristic of Chinese politics, which tend to contrast the attitude of the government with the sentiment of the people.

94. These ceremonies were frequent in the spring and early summer of 1967, a period during which Chinese diplomats were scandalously mistreated in certain countries. The staging of the welcome was remarkable. Many of the diplomats, having been wounded, returned on stretchers and were covered with bandages. The airplane had hardly landed when doctors and nurses—sometimes about thirty—rushed into the plane. The diplomats then emerged, each waving the "little red book" and chanting slogans. They then lined up, passed in review, and were covered with flowers while the crowd shouted patriotic slogans and chanted the Thoughts of Mao Tse-tung. Despite the condition of some of the returning diplomats, the ceremony lasted a long time before anyone thought of taking them to a hospital. Also, some of the passengers who accompanied the diplomats suddenly felt inclined to lie down on stretchers—although they had made the trip seated.

95. See, for example, NCNA, July 7, 1967.

96. It is interesting to recall that the Preamble of the Constitution of 1954 provided for the Chinese state "to establish and develop diplomatic relations with all

During the contacts in Peking between the embassies and the Chinese authorities, the Chinese consciously adopt an attitude of superiority toward the foreign diplomats, not so much in the tone of their human relations as in the procedure which governs the encounters and interviews. One must realize, first of all, that it is at times extremely difficult to arrange a meeting even at a very modest level. Sometimes it requires many telephone calls and weeks or even months before a date is set. In all cases, it is necessary to specify the purpose of the meeting. Occasionally, in spite of the insistence of the applicant, the department in question does not respond.[97] Conversely, however, when a Chinese functionary desires a meeting with a foreign diplomat, he arranges a rendezvous by telephone for the next day, the same day, or sometimes immediately without considering the hours or the vacation periods of the embassy, and it is usually impossible to know the subject of the interview in advance.[98] The Chinese are the sole judges of the urgency of an appeal whether it is made by them or by a foreign diplomat. They will easily revert to threats[99] if the spokesman explains that he is not available.[100] Finally, the meeting is always held at the office of the Chinese department; this conforms to traditional practice.

The same difficulties of receiving permission for an appointment and of setting a date arise when the question of a conversation with a high-ranking official is involved. The Chinese have reinvented the rule of leisure: the Chinese personality takes his time in responding, and if he does not wish to receive the foreign diplomat, he prolongs his silence so long that the meaning is clear. If he decides to respond to the request for an interview, the Chinese official often does not state the time of the meeting precisely but simply the half-day during which it will be held; the foreign ambassador must then await the disposi-

---

countries . . . on the principles of equality, reciprocal benefit, and mutual respect for national sovereignty and national integrity." See *Constitution of the People's Republic of China* (Peking: Foreign Languages Press, 1961), p. 85.

97. Apparently, the Chinese rules of conduct oppose the expression of a formal refusal. Rather than give a negative response, the Chinese authority does not respond.

98. When the same treatment is given them abroad, the Chinese protest vigorously. See the protest of the chargé d'affaires *ad interim* in Moscow, March 18, 1967, NCNA, no. 2213 (Mar. 23, 1967): "The time of the meeting must be determined by both parties."

99. The formula used is sometimes as follows: "If you do not arrive immediately, you and your embassy must bear the consequences."

100. Once a meeting is arranged, it generally takes place in a courteous way: One talks about the weather and about the comfort of the family, sugarless green tea and cigarettes are offered, and so forth, and a secretary always takes verbatim notes of the meeting.

tion of the Chinese leader until a last-minute phone call informs him and his aides of the exact time of the meeting. In other cases, the Chinese personality lets the ambassador know that he will visit him, that he will dine with him, or that he will receive him on a certain day. The chief of the foreign mission will have to stop all work and make himself available.[101]

The receptions that traditionally mark national holidays also give rise to demonstrations of the inequality which Chinese authorities apparently want to impose on their relations with the embassies. The chiefs of foreign missions organize a reception at the embassy or in the salon of a Peking hotel to celebrate their country's national holiday. Invitations are addressed to high-ranking Chinese personalities and to the functionaries with whom the embassy deals. The Chinese never respond to these invitations; until the last minute the ambassador will not know the rank and the number of his guests. The protocol functionaries, who always arrive first, do not reveal the name of the luminary whom the Chinese government has delegated to represent it; the chief of the foreign mission will not know who it is until the notable has arrived.[102]

In the case of many embassies, the reception involves mutual speeches. The Chinese have set a rule that the foreign ambassador must communicate the text of his speech to the Foreign Ministry several days in advance of the event, but there is no reciprocity. The response of the person representing the Chinese government will become known only at the moment it is pronounced.

This inequality would be merely discourteous if the Chinese representative would content himself with making small talk fit for the occasion, or if he would confine his talk to friendly comments or to stereotyped or neutral conversation. But Chinese authorities do not stick to the usual amenities. Rather, they use this occasion, with its assembled diplomatic corps and attending reporters, as a pretext to

101. On occasion, Chinese authorities, wishing to hold a traditional farewell reception for an ambassador, have requested his schedule and then have set the reception for one of the two days on which the ambassador declared he would not be free.

102. The rank of this personality fluctuates according to the state of relations between China and the country under consideration. In general, Ch'en Yi, Minister of Foreign Affairs, will represent China; but, if the Chinese wish to honor a friendly country, Chou En-lai, the Prime Minister, replaces him. If relations with the host country are in doubt, China will be represented by a lesser functionary such as the director of European affairs of the Foreign Ministry, rather than a political personality.

touch on political problems which lie outside the bilateral relations between China and the host state. And they do it with no regard for the sensibilities of the state receiving them and with no concern for the guests of the chief of the foreign mission. Sometimes the Chinese will direct violent remarks against countries whose representatives are present or who are allies of the celebrating state.[103] The host ambassador whose guests have been offended must look on without reacting either to these comments[104] or to the icy departure of his offended colleagues. Westerners consider this behavior a sign of poor education and a violation of the laws of hospitality. The Chinese must have some other conception of politeness. They seem to enjoy provoking these small scandals and eagerly seize this rostrum offered them openly to speak their piece to representatives of foreign states.[105]

Relations with the Citizenry

While maintaining relations with the citizens of the accrediting state is not part of the official function of embassies, this activity is nevertheless a normal, current, and obligatory aspect of their work. The

103. For example, during the French national holiday celebration in 1966, Ch'en Yi vigorously attacked American imperialism.

104. At the beginning of the speech, the translation of the Chinese statement is distributed to the assistants of the foreign ambassadors by the protocol department. Each diplomat, beginning with the host ambassador, hurriedly reads the translation so that he can compose his face, prepare his departure, or restrain his relief. It all looks very much like a group of students at the distribution of prizes, but at least it injects some animation into these ceremonies, which, after all, are so stiff and formal that there is little semblance of the festive air of a national holiday. At the end of the speech, the Chinese representative proposes a toast to the audience. Generally, he drinks the toast only with the ambassadors while lower-ranking personnel are ignored.

105. The number of times foreign diplomats have had to leave receptions because of the speech of a Chinese representative is countless. The representatives of states that have had difficulties with China these last few years at one time or another have all had to depart in this fashion. In 1967, those most frequently taken to task were the "revisionists" and the British. For a time, the condemnation of "revisionism" did not insult the diplomats of the Eastern states, who thought they were not concerned. The Chinese spokesman had to specify the "Soviet" revisionists before the Russian and other diplomats of the people's democracies, except Rumania, would leave the room. The English very politely stopped to say good-by to the host ambassador while two steps away the Chinese representative, unintimidated, continued his speech. The increasing number of such incidents has caused the embassies to reduce speeches to a bare minimum. Since 1967, particularly in the Western embassies, the speakers limit themselves to an exchange of toasts. These toasts, however, also pose a delicate problem of protocol. In principle, they should mention President of the Republic Liu Shao-ch'i, even though Liu has been violently attacked by the other Chinese leaders and by the Chinese press.

diplomatic mission is thrust into the foreign society and necessarily makes contact with the people. Questions of everyday life or those arising out of the embassy's work (for example, issues of public information) can bring about this contact. Here also a great many restrictions are placed on diplomats, and it is up to them to control themselves because the accrediting state can always remind them of this rule. The accrediting state normally restricts but does not entirely prevent contact with its citizens.

Chinese authorities have no confidence in the self-regulation of diplomats. Instead they place a screen around them in an effort to reduce their contacts with the Chinese people to a strict minimum.

Naturally, the diplomatic missions and their agents may recruit Chinese personnel: interpreters, chauffeurs, and servants. But the selection of these people is made by a subsection of the Ministry of Foreign Affairs, the Service Bureau. A request must be submitted to this organization, which, after a delay of varying length, will provide the desired person.[106]

Personnel thus recruited sign a contract with their employer that is a conventional form identical for all embassies.[107] The Chinese labor law[108] applies to the interpretation and the writing up of this contract. But, at the same time, the employee remains under the authority of the Service Bureau[109] which, as a result, can terminate his services at any time. A further point deserves emphasis: while in all circumstances the employer must respect the conventional arrangements and regulations concerning his employees, the Service Bureau can break away from them in a discretionary fashion by simply invoking a "particular case" of which it is the sole judge and which it does not even try to justify to the embassy or to the foreign diplomat.[110] This is another example of the unequal attitude of the Chinese authorities.

106. In practice, a single candidate is presented and it is best to accept him if one wants to avoid a wait of several months for another applicant. On the other hand, it is nearly impossible to obtain the services of a Chinese employee whose competence is known and who is available.

107. The salaries, however, vary from one embassy to another. An employee of the French embassy, for example, earns much more than one who works for the Vietnamese embassy. It is unlikely though that he is allowed to keep all of his earnings.

108. It is impossible to obtain copies of the law governing these matters.

109. In all likelihood, he transmits information about the life of the embassy and the diplomat.

110. The service bureau, then, can terminate the work of a Chinese employee within an hour while the employer must give one month's notice. This permits the Chinese to occasionally sanction an employee who does not render to the Chinese authorities the services they expect.

Furthermore, the Chinese do their best to make difficult the creation of ties, other than professional ones, and the development of friendships between the Chinese employees and their foreign employer. In this connection, in case of difficulties between China and the government of the employer, the Chinese employees are induced to be in the vanguard of the demonstrators who pass in front of the embassy, to deliver letters of protest to the chief of mission, and to declare a strike.[111] When the period of crisis is over, the employees resume their work as though nothing had happened, but the climate of their relations with the foreign diplomats is permanently affected. In a totalitarian society, can the employees remain outside of these demonstrations without compromising their position? The essential point here, however, is that their behavior coincides with the wish of the Chinese authorities to dehumanize relations between the Chinese people and foreigners.

This desire also explains the barriers set between the diplomats and the Chinese people in general. Police control is maintained over all Chinese who enter an embassy or the home of a foreigner. A permanent police check point is installed at the entrances of all these buildings to monitor all Chinese visitors. Chinese employees in the service of the embassies arrange for an identification card; apparently, those without this document are turned back.[112] The reason given by Chinese officials for this police measure is the protection of the security of the embassies and of their personnel. This concern is paradoxical when one considers that this security is scarcely enforced when the embassy is made the target of a demonstration by the "masses" and that the police do not attempt to prevent violent raids against diplomatic places by demonstrators. To admit that it is permissible for some elements of the population, and not for others, to violate the security of diplomatic missions is to concede that this control tends essentially to hinder Chinese citizens from calling on the embassies.

In effect, all Chinese who enter into contact with a foreigner are suspect. A Chinese citizen whose profession does not bring him into contact with the embassies can have no legitimate reason to meet foreign diplomats.

The obsession with espionage is always present, reinforced by the extensive conception which the Chinese authorities have of it. There are several incidents which help to show how the Chinese define the

111. In principle, the right to strike is not recognized by Chinese law, but in practice it is currently employed by the Chinese personnel of embassies.

112. The Chinese who arrive in the company of a foreigner are not checked, however.

notions of information and espionage. In the Raghunath affair, for example, the Indian diplomat was reproached for having sought to collect not only military information, but also "political information."[113] Following this, in a verbal protest of July 3, 1967, made to the Soviet chargé d'affaires Razhudov, two agents of the Soviet embassy were accused of having "read and copied surreptitiously" posters and of having collected "openly or secretly" printed materials and information about "the Great Proletarian Cultural Revolution." The Chinese authorities declared them guilty of "stealing information." Ancient China's taste for mystery is tied effortlessly to the rule of silence of Marxist powers. Information for internal consumption is controlled and sparse; it is not always best to speak the truth; foreign diplomats, like all others who live in China, should obtain their information solely from the official Chinese press.

Diplomats may subscribe to only three daily newspapers—two in Peking, one in Shanghai—whose sale is authorized to foreigners. They are not allowed to procure copies of the provincial press[114] nor the countless "Red Guard papers" which flourished during the Cultural Revolution. The prohibition against selling newspapers to foreigners was not always strictly enforced, but at the end of 1966 the Service Bureau ordered the Chinese translators who had been assigned to the embassies to refuse to translate any newspaper other than the three authorized ones. Evidently, this decision was never relayed to the chiefs of mission, but it became known when the Chinese translators in each embassy simultaneously declared themselves incapable of reading or understanding the texts submitted to them.

Peking's peculiar conception of the embassy's activity consists in making these diplomatic missions agents whose only job is to transmit official Chinese ideas and viewpoints. It is not only discourteous but also forbidden to be dissatisfied with the officially labeled "truth" and to seek verification of information disseminated by the government. By definition everything the public powers say is correct; anything they do not say is a state secret. To venture beyond the official facade is to adopt the attitude of a spy.

As a result of all this, a void envelops the diplomats. It is out of the question for them to maintain friendly relations with the Chinese

113. See note, already cited, of June 12, 1967.

114. The Soviets still benefit from the previous situation and receive a certain number of provincial journals.

officials they encounter professionally, and they do not have many opportunities for chance encounters with Chinese citizens. Fear, mutual surveillance, and social pressure stifle all desire that would normally arise for a dialogue. Moreover, for the Chinese citizen, the act of "maintaining relations with foreign diplomats" may be an actual misdemeanor. Fragmentary evidence indicates that a real legal barrier is placed between Chinese citizens and foreigners.[115]

An extension of this attitude is found in the regulations concerning photography, which are applicable to all foreigners, diplomats or not. Although many things may not be photographed at all (airports, bridges, aerial views, military material, etc.),[116] others are restricted only under certain circumstances. For example, when the Soviet families departed in February 1967, the foreign diplomats who accompanied them were given information notices announcing in three languages that they could not take pictures.[117] Similarly, during the turbulent days of the Cultural Revolution, photographs could not be taken of the large wall posters or of the processions of demonstrators leading persons under criticism who were wearing dunces' caps. These restrictions, enforced by the authorities, are based on the fear of foreigners gathering information relating to China's internal politics and on the fear that these photographs will be used against China abroad.

If foreign nationals are mixed with the Chinese people, all sorts of obstacles are created to cut them off from relations with their embassy. With few exceptions, the Chinese no longer accept the principle of stationing consular representatives on Chinese territory. Rather, the embassies themselves normally exercise consular jurisdiction. The last Soviet consulates, located in Sinkiang, were abolished in 1963. In May 1967, Chinese authorities unilaterally and forcibly closed the British office in Shanghai, which, although technically not a consulate, nevertheless fulfilled consular functions.[118] Under these conditions, it is

115. Such a rule would not be exceptional if one can believe Mr. Cahier (*Le Droit diplomatique contemporain*, p. 149, n. 11) who refers to a *Le Monde* article regarding East Germany.

116. A military truck or a soldier's water flask may not be photographed.

117. It is interesting to recall that in a protest note of February 1967 addressed to the Soviet Ministry of Foreign Affairs from the Chinese embassy in Moscow, an affirmation is found that "the ruling Soviet clique . . . was mortally frightened by several photographs showing the true nature of the bloody incident which took place in Red Square. This is because they are afraid of the truth and of the people, that they are frightened of the Soviet people knowing the truth."

118. The Chinese employed a "Jesuit-like" procedure to give an aura of legitimacy to their decision. They declared that no Sino-British agreement existed and

very difficult effectively to protect foreigners who are in trouble with Chinese authorities, especially since these officials can always refuse a travel authorization to an embassy representative who wants to visit the scene of the incident. This occurred, for example, when two British sailors were arrested at the port of Dairen in May 1967 and charged with "political provocation."[119]

When the occasion arises, however, the Chinese demand the "inalienable and universally recognized right of each sovereign state to protect its nationals."[120] The existence of an important Chinese minority in Indonesia frequently obligates the Chinese government to intervene on behalf of its own nationals in order to protect them against bullying and violence, which are gradually turning into persecution by the Indonesian authorities. The Chinese send frequent notes pointing out their right to protect their nationals, and they strongly resist the Indonesian government each time it seeks to obstruct relations between the embassy and the Chinese in Indonesia. One privilege is particularly close to their hearts; this is the right to send, when they wish, a consular agency to the scene.[121] In the same connection, the Chinese embassy in Burma is always presented as a natural defender of the Chinese in that country.[122]

Apparently, the duality in the attitude of the Chinese authorities in this area is caused less by a desire to hinder foreign embassies in China from protecting their nationals, who are not very numerous anyway, than by the fear that the protecting mission will double as an information gatherer. For all purposes, China is still a closed country. The restriction on movement of diplomats is a demonstration of this.

---

that the Chinese government merely "acknowledged" a British demand to open an office in Shanghai. On May 22, 1967, the Director of the European Section of the Ministry of Foreign Affairs, Lo Kuei-po, upon receiving the British chargé d'affaires, Mr. Hopson, told him: "As a consequence of the hostile attitude adopted by the British government toward the Chinese people [the bloody events of May 1967 in Hong Kong] . . . the arrangements made in 1954 by the Chinese government, acknowledging a demand of the British government for the presence of personnel in Shanghai sent by the office of the British chargé d'affaires in China and responsible for all affairs coming under British jurisdiction in this city, have lost all value. Consequently, the Chinese government has decided to annul these arrangements and to order Mr. Hewitt to leave Shanghai within 48 hours." NCNA, no. 2274 (May 23,1967).

119. See NCNA, no. 2274 (May 23, 1967).

120. Note of the Chinese embassy at Djakarta, August 31, 1966, NCNA, no. 2014 (Sept. 5, 1966).

121. See in particular note of the Ministry of Foreign Affairs, September 12, 1966, NCNA, no. 2022 (Sept. 13, 1966).

122. Particularly during the crisis in the summer of 1967.

The Chinese authorities do not want the embassies to employ their nationals as information gatherers or to establish consulates elsewhere in China to act as observation posts. Also, they do not want the travel of consular agents to bring them into contact with the real China. Their attitude then is perfectly coherent, but they do not contest the principle of the right to protect nationals, and they intend to apply it outside China.

CONCLUSION

Many of the aspects of Chinese diplomatic practice which have just been traced, including those which are most shocking to a Western jurist, must be viewed from the perspective of the most tempestuous vicissitudes of the Cultural Revolution, of the crisis of authority that accompanied it, and of the battle over basic principles on which it was based.

But these excesses have resulted only in a particularly vigorous formulation of a new conception of diplomatic relations arising from the perspective of world revolution. The Chinese leaders adjust their conduct according to the interests of this revolution in the contemporary world. The foreign states and their representatives in Chinese territory must not expect to be esteemed and humored simply because they are foreigners; rather, they will be treated according to their objective attitude toward the revolution. And this revolution is taking place every day; the Chinese live it. While the battle is in progress, diplomacy can only be a diplomacy of combat which makes "good manners" of value only to the embassies of the bourgeois states.

Furthermore, the Chinese leaders cannot forget that they are Chinese. They are animated by the feeling that they are the spokesmen for a Great Power, and they have a wrong to avenge. They want to lower the heads of powers that were respected yesterday, to submit them to humiliating treatment, and to challenge the rules of their societies. All this confirms them in their power, and they can show condescension and paternalism toward the representatives of the Third World.

Foreign states do not have the same reasons as China to rally around this revolutionary conception of diplomatic practice, and one would think that violent reactions and protests of all sorts would appear each time the Chinese breached the customary rules.

Unhappily, the behavior of foreign states is hardly such as to brake the Chinese authorities in their actions. A tacit consensus as to the treatment China will receive characterizes the attitude of most of the embassies. During these last few years, no collective steps have been taken by the diplomatic corps or by its doyen toward the Chinese government even after the most marked attacks on customary diplomatic practice. All the initiatives that were drafted ran afoul of the passivity or uncooperativeness of the majority of the chiefs of missions.

The representatives of the states of the Third World, who make up a majority of the diplomatic corps, do not want to assume any responsibility in this area. It is not even certain that they recommend to their governments what attitude to take. They do not realize that, in the short or long run, they compromise their own situation, they acquiesce in advance to difficulties which they some day will have to face, and finally they hinder international law from taking root in China, especially those aspects of it which are least debatable. The representatives of Europe and the Soviet Union see the problem with more realism and courage. But even in the best of cases, their governments show their disapproval essentially with well-chosen adjectives that decorate their protest notes. Affronts are avenged by verbalism.

One thus gets the curious impression that foreign states do not want to run afoul of the Chinese, that they humor them, and that they accept from them what they never would suffer in their relations with one another. Perhaps they are afraid. More simply, perhaps they believe that China is going through a crisis of adolescence experienced by all nations, and that they must guard against the future. The debate is open. But what here and now can be seen as a positive aspect of this behavior is the attenuation of the notion of *casus belli*. Many of the incidents which have unfolded in Peking in recent years would formerly have met their answer through gunboat diplomacy, led to an ultimatum, and given the signal for hostilities. In our time, most states feel such actions are not even a reason for cutting off diplomatic relations. We can only congratulate ourselves to see these inclinations lessening, to see sovereignty becoming less supercilious, and to see wisdom rising above the spirit of vengeance. In a sense, this is a sign of the maturity of international society. But we cannot be certain whether this is a day when the great powers practice as much moderation in their relations with the small states and the new states as they show among themselves or whether this conduct is simply due to the mounting shadow of China's power.

4 / Nonrecognition and Trade: A Case Study of the Fourth Sino-Japanese Trade Agreement*

Gene T. Hsiao

Sino-Japanese trade has now entered its twentieth year since the conclusion of the first agreement between trading groups of the two countries in 1952. Economically, Japan has become China's leading trade partner. The annual volume of two-way transactions increased from US $15 million in 1952 to nearly US $900 million in 1971.[1] Politically, however, relations between the two countries have deteriorated steadily since the breakdown of the fourth Sino-Japanese trade agreement of March 5, 1958, and the resultant interruption of trade in the succeeding four years.

When the two countries resumed large-scale trade under the Liao-Takasaki Memorandum of November 9, 1962, Peking laid down a set of political conditions to govern its trade relations with Japan. These include the principle of "nonseparation of politics from economics" as well as propositions requiring the Japanese government not to adopt any hostile attitude toward the Peking government, not to follow the United States in the "two Chinas" plot, and not to obstruct the development of Sino-Japanese relations in the direction of normalization.[2] Since

NOTE: This is a product of my project on "Legal Aspects of China's Foreign Trade." I wish to thank the Joint Committee on Contemporary China of the Social Science Research Council and the American Council of Learned Societies for its support of my undertaking.

1. Released by the Japanese Ministry of Finance on January 22, 1972, the figures for 1969 and 1970 were U.S. $625 million and U.S. $824 million respectively. For reference to the trade figures prior to 1969, see Robert F. Dernberger, "Prospects for Trade Between China and the United States," in Alexander Eckstein, ed., *China Trade Prospects and U.S. Policy* (New York: Praeger, 1971).

2. These principles were enunciated by Peking soon after the breakdown of the fourth trade agreement in May 1958. Subsequently, they were formulated into the Peking government's policy toward Japan. See "Premier Chou En-lai on the

the expiration of the Memorandum in 1967, Peking has persistently demanded that the Japanese negotiators of the annual trade agreements not only accept the above principles but also denounce their own government in most humiliating terms.[3]

More recently, after concluding the trade agreements for 1970, Premier Chou En-lai presented the visiting Japanese delegation with four additional conditions of trade with Japan: China would not trade with (1) those firms that help Taiwan to invade the mainland and South Korea to invade North Korea, (2) those that have large investments in Taiwan and South Korea, (3) those that supply arms and munitions to United States "imperialism" to wage aggression against Vietnam, Laos and Cambodia, and (4) the joint American-Japanese enterprises and American subsidiaries in Japan.[4]

In line with this general policy, a trade official of the Peking government specified that China would henceforth examine all transactions with Japan according to the four new conditions; would refuse to enter into any trade contract with Japan inconsistent with any one of these conditions; and would even cancel already concluded contracts if they failed to conform to these conditions. To demonstrate Peking's determination to enforce this policy, he identified four Japanese manufacturers, including a subsidiary of the Dow Chemical Company, as disqualified to trade with China.[5] Furthermore, Peking demanded that the so-called "dummy firms" set up by the four biggest Japanese trading

---

Three Principles of Sino-Japanese Trade, September 10, 1960," in *Jih-pen wen-t'i wen-chien chi* (Collection of documents on the question of Japan; Peking: Shih-chieh chih-shih ch'u-pan-she, 1961), vol. III (1961), pp. 135–137; "Premier Chou En-lai's Restatement on the Principles of Sino-Japanese Relations, September 19, 1962," in *ibid.*, vol. IV (1963), pp. 17–19. Hereafter cited as *Jih-pen wen-t'i.*

3. "Chinese and Japanese Trade Organizations Sign Minutes of Talks in Peking," in *PR*, no. 13:9 (Mar. 29, 1968); "Communiqué on Talks between Chinese and Japanese Representatives of Memorandum Trade Offices, April 4, 1969," in *PR*, no. 15:38 (Apr. 11, 1969); "Joint Statement of China Council for Promotion of International Trade and Six Other Japanese Organizations for Friendly Trade, April 14, 1970," in *PR*, no. 17:29 (Apr. 24, 1970); "Communiqué on Talks between Representatives of China-Japan Memorandum Trade Office and Japan-China Memorandum Office, April 19, 1970," in *PR*, no. 17:31 (Apr. 24, 1970).

4. Chou's statement was first reported by a Kyodo correspondent in "Chou Attacks Japan for Militarism," *Japan Times*, Apr. 21, 1970, pp. 1, 5. The Japanese report, however, was slightly different from the Chinese version released by the Peking-controlled *Ta-kung pao*, Hong Kong, May 3, 1970, p. 2. The above translation is based on the Chinese report.

5. *Ta-kung pao*, Hong Kong, May 3, 1970, p. 2; "Four Japanese Firms Barred from Red China Trade," *Japan Times*, May 3, 1970, p. 13. The four manufacturers are Sumitomo Chemical Co., Mitsubishi Heavy Industries, Teijin Ltd., and Asahi-Dow Co.

companies to deal with China sever business ties with their parent companies, which had interests in Taiwan.[6] Many leading Japanese industrial firms and trading companies have yielded to Peking's demand.[7] Others that have rejected it have lost their contracts.[8]

For two decades, Japan and the NATO powers, except Iceland, have embargoed trade in strategic goods with all socialist countries except Yugoslavia.[9] Trade discrimination on political grounds is thus by no means Peking's invention. The significance of Premier Chou's policy is that this is the first time Peking has openly barred Japanese firms from trading with it on the conditions mentioned above. There are, of course, many reasons for this policy. In broad terms, its immediate cause is Japan's new economic and political role in Asia, as outlined in the Nixon-Sato communiqué of November 21, 1969.[10] Specifically, the key issue remains Japan's nonrecognition of the Peking government despite an ever-growing trade relationship with it.

Interstate trade demands orderly arrangements for transactions, and mutual concessions in matters relating to national sovereignty—such as the freedom of entry, travel, and residence, and other pertinent rights of individual traders in the receiving state. Under normal circumstances, these concessions can be made only on the basis of intergovernmental agreements through mutual recognition of the international personalities of the parties involved. Law, as a rule of conduct, plays a positive role in making these arrangements.

Nonrecognition, on the other hand, denies the existence of the other party as an international person. Consequently, it also denies to two mutually unrecognized states the possibility of making legal transactions and thereby deprives the traders of both states of the usual legal

6. "Fertilizer Firms OK Peking's Principles," *Japan Times*, May 12, 1970, pp. 1, 5; "Far East: So Long at the Fair," *Newsweek*, June 8, 1970, p. 82. These companies are Mitsubishi Shoji Kaisha, Ltd., Mitsui and Co., Marubeni-Iida Co., and C. Itoh and Co.

7. E.g., "Firms Cut Ties Due to Peking Pressure," *Japan Times*, May 8, 1970, p. 12; "Sumitomo Metal Gives Red China Assurances," *Japan Times*, May 10, 1970, p. 13; "Two Firms Here Clarify Stand on Chou Rules," *Japan Times*, May 13, 1970, pp. 1, 5; "Nippon Steel Adopts Peking 'Principles'," *Japan Times*, May 15, 1970, p. 12; "Peking Ban Dropped on Sumitomo Chemical," *Japan Times*, June 5, 1970, p. 11. As of December 1970, nearly 700 Japanese companies had accepted Chou's conditions. See L. B. Weed, "Japan Looks to China for Trade," *St. Louis Post Dispatch*, Dec. 17, 1970, p. 13A.

8. See "Uemura Spurns Chou Principles," *Japan Times*, May 16, 1970, p. 10.

9. See Gunnar Adler-Karlsson, *Western Economic Warfare, 1947–1967* (Stockholm: Almqvist & Wiksell, 1968).

10. In *The New York Times*, Nov. 22, 1969, p. 14.

protections. In short, although nonrecognition and trade are not entirely incompatible, there is an obvious conflict involved. This conflict, in turn, is not devoid of legal consequences.

While it is too early to evaluate the implications of Chou's new policy for the legal aspects of Sino-Japanese trade relations, it is possible to study the significance that nonrecognition has had for those relations in the past. The case of the fourth Sino-Japanese trade agreement, concluded in 1958, offers a classic example of the legal problems which can arise when trade takes place in a context of mutual nonrecognition. The following, then, is a discussion of three important aspects of this case: the negotiation of the agreement, its form and content, and its nullification.[11]

NEGOTIATIONS

Negotiations for the fourth agreement started with the unsolved issues of the third agreement. A brief review of this earlier document is therefore necessary in order to understand the present case.

The third agreement was signed in Tokyo on May 4, 1955, after month-long negotiations between the two parties. Representing the Chinese side was a thirty-eight-member delegation headed by Vice-Minister of Foreign Trade Lei Jen-min and Minister of Light Industry Li Chu-ch'en.[12] Their Japanese counterparts were Shozo Murata, president of the Japan Association for the Promotion of International Trade (JAPIT), and Masanosuke Ikeda, a senior member of the House of Representatives, who also served as Vice-Secretary General of the ruling Democratic Party and director of the Japanese Dietmen's League for the Promotion of Japan-China Trade. The Japanese government itself did not take direct part in the negotiations and the signing of the document. However, it entrusted three cabinet ministers in charge of foreign affairs, finance, and international trade and industry to assist Murata and Ikeda "behind the scenes."[13]

11. For a discussion of the political aspects of the case, see Gene T. Hsiao, "The Role of Trade in China's Diplomacy with Japan," in Jerome A. Cohen, ed., *The Dynamics of China's Foreign Relations* (Cambridge, Mass.: East Asian Research Center, Harvard University, 1970), pp. 41–56.

12. This was the first Chinese trade delegation to visit Japan since the founding of the People's Republic. They arrived in Tokyo on March 29, 1955, upon an invitation from their Japanese sponsors. "Chinese Trade Mission to Japan," *People's China*, no. 8:39 (Apr. 16, 1955).

13. The names of these ministers were Manuro Shigenitsu, Hisato Ichimada and Tanzan Ishibashi respectively. See *Nippon Times*, Tokyo, Apr. 27, 1955, p. 1.

The principal issues were expressed in the Chinese demand for the conclusion of a government trade agreement, the signing of a payments agreement between the two state banks, the exchange of permanent trade missions vested with diplomatic immunity, and the abolition of Japan's embargo against China.[14] The Japanese, however, were unable to accept these demands due to the absence of diplomatic relations between the two countries and the Japanese government's commitment to the embargo policy. A compromise clause was finally introduced into the agreement, stating that both parties would "urge their own governments to conduct intergovernmental negotiations as early as possible" for the conclusion of official agreements.[15] At the same time, in compliance with a Chinese request, the Japanese signatories formally pledged in a letter that the agreement had Premier Ichiro Hatoyama's "support."[16]

The Chinese accepted the letter as government recognition of the agreement. However, only a few hours after the conclusion of the agreement, Chief Secretary of the Hatoyama cabinet, Ryutaro Nemoto, denied that the letter had his government's prior approval.[17] At this point, the Japanese Premier was "vacationing" in Kamakura and the Chinese delegation was about to leave after the Japanese Ministry of Foreign Affairs had refused to extend their visiting visa.[18] The matter was thus put off for further discussion.

When the third agreement was due to expire on May 4, 1956, the Japanese asked for an extension of one year. The Chinese complied and urged the Japanese to solve the pending issues within the extended period.[19] The Japanese failed to do that. Moreover, the requirement

14. These terms were later disclosed by the Chinese chief negotiator and signatory Lei Jen-min, "The Key to the Development of Sino-Japanese Trade (September 3, 1955)," in *Jih-pen wen-t'i*, vol. II (1958), pp. 171, 174.

15. See China-Japan Trade Agreement, arts. 5, 10, 11, May 4, 1955, in *TYC 1955*, vol. IV (1960), pp. 258–260.

16. See Correspondence between China and Japan Concerning the Japanese Government's Support and Assistance to the China-Japan Trade Agreement, May 4, 1955, in *TYC*, vol. IV, pp. 262–263. Also see "Red China Trade Points Conceded by Hatoyama," *Nippon Times*, Apr. 28, 1955, p. 6.

17. *Nippon Times*, May 5, 1955, p. 1.

18. "Red Traders Draw A 'No' on Extension," *Nippon Times*, Apr. 27, 1955, p. 1. The Chinese delegation left Japan on May 6, a day after the signing of the agreement. See *Nippon Times*, May 7, 1955, p. 9.

19. See the letter of Murata and Ikeda to Nan Han-ch'en, April 24, 1956, in *Jih-pen wen-t'i*, vol. II (1958), p. 175; Reply of Lei Jen-min to Murata and Ikeda, May 18, 1956, in *ibid.*, p. 176; Joint Statement of the China Council for the Promotion of International Trade with the JAPIT and the Dietmen's League for the Promotion of China-Japan Trade, October 15, 1956, in *ibid.*, pp. 179–

of the Japanese government that Chinese traders visiting Japan for a period of over two months be fingerprinted provoked a new issue.

The Chinese traders, of course, were state officials. Accordingly, the Peking government rejected the Japanese demand, contending that such a requirement was an "insult" to the Chinese state and an obstacle to the development of Sino-Japanese trade, since the law had its origin in preventing opium and other smugglers from entering Japan after World War II.[20] This controversy caused the delay of negotiations for a fourth agreement in the fall of 1956 as well as the postponement of the exchange of trade missions and of two Chinese fairs scheduled to be held in Nagoya and Fukuoka a year later.

Then, in July 1957, the Japanese government succeeded in removing 272 strategic items from its embargo list. With Premier Nobusuke Kishi's approval, a twenty-four-member Japanese delegation representing the Dietmen's League, the JAPIT, and the Japan Association for Japan-China Exports and Imports (JAJCEI) finally arrived in Peking on September 17, 1957, to reopen the negotiations for a fourth agreement. The Chinese described the mission as "official" (*Jih-pen fang-Hua t'ung-shang shih-chieh t'uan*),[21] and the Japanese accepted the description without comment. Moving up from the status as an assistant in the negotiations for the third agreement, Dietman Ikeda now acted as top negotiator with Vice-Minister of Foreign Trade Lei Jen-min as his counterpart.

In view of their experience with the third agreement and its still pending issues, prior to Ikeda's departure for Peking, leaders of the Japanese government and the ruling Liberal-Democratic Party had made a four-point decision regarding any new agreement. Two of these points were important. First, the number of Peking trade mission officials who would be allowed entry without going through the process of fingerprinting would be limited to five. Second, no formal diplomatic privileges would be granted to the trade mission members, but "every convenience" would be accorded to them, such as diplomatic treatment in regard to customs, the use of ciphers, and exemption from business and income taxes.[22]

180; "Welcome the Opening of the Japanese Commodities Fair in Peking," *JMJP* editorial, Oct. 16, 1956, reproduced in *ibid.*, pp. 177–179.

20. Commentator, "Trade and Fingerprinting," *JMJP*, Aug. 7, 1957, reproduced in *Jih-pen wen-t'i*, vol. II (1958), pp. 182–184.

21. See *Ta-kung pao*, Peking, Sept. 18, 1957, p. 4.

22. The other two points were establishment of the trade mission in the form

On the basis of this decision, Ikeda proceeded to negotiate with the Chinese. Three committees were established to discuss the pending issues. The first was in charge of "institutional arrangements," namely commodity inspection, arbitration, and the exchange of trade fairs and trade missions; the second, commodity classification; and the third, payments settlement.[23]

As soon as the committees met, however, differences arose over the number and status of Chinese trade representatives in Tokyo. The Japanese, as already indicated, limited the number who would have the privilege of enjoying some "convenience" to five. The Chinese, on the other hand, insisted on giving official status to thirty.[24] A deadlock developed, which resulted in a one week's adjournment of the committee meeting on institutional arrangements.

Resumption of the meeting on October 17 did not solve the issue. By October 25, the Ikeda delegation had decided to return home in time to attend an extraordinary session of the Diet and to discuss the trade mission problem.[25] Two days before their scheduled departure on November 1, however, the Chinese offered unexpected concessions to the Japanese in other aspects of the negotiations. First, the Chinese fixed the yearly trade volume at thirty-five million pounds sterling each way. This was five million pounds more than the Japanese had expected. Second, the Chinese consented to settle payments through correspondence contracts with private exchange banks before the conclusion of a payments agreement between the two state banks of China and Japan.[26] Thus, according to the Chinese chief negotiator Lei Jen-min, the remaining differences boiled down to the number of mission members to be exchanged, the fingerprinting of Chinese mission members, the guaranteeing of their physical safety, and the provision of work facilities for their activities.[27]

Negotiations over these terms were tedious, often lasting until

---

of a "trade office" and the increase of trade volumes. Officials who participated in making this decision included Secretary General of the ruling Liberal-Democratic Party Shojiro Kawashima, chief policy-maker Takeo Miki, Foreign Minister Aiichiro Fujiyama, Minister of International Trade and Industry Shigesaburo Maeo, and Dietman Ikeda. Later, Secretary General of the Japanese Socialist Party, Inejiro Asanuma, was also informed of the decision and reportedly endorsed it. See "Policy Fixed for Peiping Trade Talks," *Japan Times*, Sept. 14, 1957, p. 6.

23. *Ta-kung pao*, Peking, Oct. 18, 1957, p. 4.
24. *Japan Times*, Nov. 1, 1957, p. 6.
25. *Ibid.*, Oct. 27, 1957, p. 6.
26. *Ibid.*, Oct. 31, 1957, p. 6.
27. *Ibid.*

dawn. Finally, after a plenary session attended by eight Chinese and eleven Japanese representatives,[28] on November 1 a joint statement was issued, announcing that (1) both parties had discussed the draft of the fourth agreement proposed by the Chinese side and reached an agreement on that document; (2) both parties had agreed to a memorandum concerning the establishment of trade missions at the "people's" level; and (3) the Chinese side had consented to the Japanese proposal for adjournment of the meeting so that the Japanese could return home for consultation.[29]

The Japanese left Peking on schedule. The Chinese, while hoping for a final agreement on the pending issues, pointed out that they could not make an exception for Japan insofar as the trade mission issue was concerned. They also regretted that while a total of 584 Japanese had been allowed to visit China during the previous year, no Chinese trader had been permitted to enter Japan in the corresponding period. This, in Peking's view, was clearly a failure of the Japanese to reciprocate and consequently a violation of the principle of mutuality in international trade.[30]

After a nearly four-month consultation in Tokyo, Ikeda returned to Peking on February 25, 1958, with a twelve-member delegation. He was under orders not to compromise the Japanese government's nonrecognition policy toward mainland China and to assert that the proposed Peking trade mission in Tokyo would not be turned into a base for political activities. In addition, he received a new four-point instruction from his party as the basis of negotiations for the Peking-drafted memorandum attached to the draft agreement. These points were: criminal jurisdiction over the proposed trade mission and its members should rest with the receiving state; the clause permitting the mission to raise its national flag should be deleted; the number of mission members should be limited to the minimum necessary for the performance of duties; and Japanese governmental approval would be necessary for enforcing the trade agreement.[31]

When the Ikeda delegation arrived in Peking the Chinese suddenly announced the successful conclusion of a five-year barter agreement

28. *Ta-kung pao*, Peking, Nov. 2, 1957, p. 4.

29. See Joint Statement of the China Council for the Promotion of International Trade and the Visiting Japanese Official Trade Delegation, November 1, 1957, in *Jih-pen wen-t'i*, vol. II (1958), p. 184.

30. *Japan Times*, November 3, 1957, p. 6.

31. *Ibid.*, Feb. 23, 1958, p. 1.

with the Japanese steel industry in the total amount of 200 million pounds sterling both ways.[32] So smooth and swift were the negotiations for the agreement that it took the visiting Japanese steel delegation less than twelve days to conclude the deal. And so reasonable were the terms of the agreement that both the Japanese government and the steel industry expressed great satisfaction.[33] No political strings were attached to the agreement.[34] On the contrary, Premier Chou En-lai declared to the Japanese steel delegation that since his country was annually importing at least one million tons of steel products, he would be willing to consider extension of the barter agreement from the agreed five years to ten years at some future time without any specific conditions.[35]

Overwhelmed by Peking's combination of pressure and temptation on the one hand, and restricted by Tokyo's four-point instruction on the other, members of the Ikeda delegation were unable to meet their Chinese counterparts in a full session for nearly a week after their arrival. In several individual sessions with Lei Jen-min, Ikeda tried to amend the clause of the draft memorandum that stipulated that the trade mission would have the "right" to fly its national flag. In his opinion, since the negotiations were held on a "private" basis, it was not proper to use the word "right." This proposal drew an immediate rebuttal from Lei, who declared that he could not accept it because he had previously reached an agreement with Premier Chou En-lai on this matter.[36]

In order to break the impasse, Socialist Katsumata, who served as Ikeda's chief advisor, offered a compromise.[37] This, too, was rejected by Lei Jen-min as being a plan to hamstring the proposed trade agreement and memorandum.[38]

32. *JMJP*, Feb. 27, 1958, p. 4.
33. *Japan Times*, Feb. 27, 1958, p. 1.
34. See the text of the Barter Agreement of the China National Minerals Corporation and the China National Metals Import Corporation with the Japanese Steel Delegation, February 26, 1958, in *JMJP*, Feb. 27, 1958, p. 4.
35. *Japan Times*, Feb. 27, 1958, p. 1.
36. According to the Japanese, this was the first time that the Chinese negotiators quoted Premier Chou in their trade talks. *Japan Times*, Mar. 2, 1958, p. 6.
37. The salient points of this compromise were limits on the changes of wording to those required for a correct translation, to have frank exchange of views, to make arrangements on concrete matters concerning the enforcement of the agreement and the memorandum, and to explain to the Chinese the doubtful points of the memorandum, including Tokyo's four-point instruction. See *Japan Times*, Mar. 3, 1958, p. 6.
38. *Japan Times*, Mar. 4, 1958, p. 6.

Finally, on March 3, Lei held a press conference with Chinese and foreign correspondents in Peking and declared that, as evidenced by the joint statement of November 1, 1957,[39] the Japanese had already accepted the draft fourth agreement, including the memorandum attached to it, before their return to Tokyo for consultation the previous autumn. The present delay in the signing of the document, Lei pointed out, was due to the Japanese attempt to eliminate the clause concerning the right of the Chinese trade mission to fly its national flag, to evade the issue of guaranteeing the enforcement of the agreement by the Japanese government, and to limit the number of Chinese trade mission members. He warned that the whole matter was now "a test of the good faith of the official Japanese trade delegation."[40] This statement was clearly a total rejection of Tokyo's four-point plan and an ultimatum to the Japanese delegation.

Unable to resist the mounting Chinese pressure, and without prior consultation with Tokyo, Ikeda met with members of his delegation on the following day and decided to give in.[41]

FORM AND CONTENT

The final form of the document was written in two equally authentic versions. The Chinese version bore the designation "*Chung-Jih mao-i hsieh-ting*" or "China-Japan Trade Agreement"; the Japanese version "*Nichu boeki kyotei*" or "Japan-China Trade Agreement."[42] The entire document consisted of three parts: the text of the agreement, which comprised a preamble and fifteen articles; one export schedule of classified commodities for each party; and a memorandum which constituted an inseparable part of the agreement.[43]

The preamble and a statement of Foreign Minister Ch'en Yi to the Japanese delegation characterized the agreement as an instrument to promote trade and friendship.[44] Subsequently, the Chinese Ministry of Foreign Affairs even included the document in its official treaty series

39. See note 29 above.
40. *JMJP,* Mar. 4, 1958, p. 4.
41. *Japan Times,* Mar. 5, 1958, p. 1.
42. For the Chinese text, see *TYC 1958,* vol. VII (1959), p. 197; for the Japanese text, the Dietmen's League for the Promotion of Japan-China Trade, *Nichu kankei shiryo shu* (Collection of materials on Japan-China relations; Tokyo, The Dietmen's League for the Promotion of Japan-China Trade, 1967), p. 173.
43. The text of the memorandum, dated March 5, 1958, in *TYC 1958,* vol. VII (1959), p. 201; the export schedules in *Jih-pen wen-t'i,* vol. II (1958), p. 190.
44. Ch'en's statement was later disclosed in *JMJP,* Apr. 2, 1958, p. 1.

as an "appendix," thus endowing it with a treaty character. In reality, however, both parties signed the agreement in their capacities as representatives of their respective associations, not as government agents. On the Chinese side, the chief signatory was Nan Han-ch'en, who identified himself as chairman of the China Council for the Promotion of International Trade (CCPIT).[45] He was seconded by three vice-chairmen of the CCPIT and five negotiating representatives.[46] The Japanese chief signatory was Masanosuke Ikeda who, with five other members of the Diet, signed as representatives of the Dietmen's League. These were followed by the signatures of four representatives of the two other Japanese organizations.[47]

Despite the active participation of high state officials in the negotiations, the agreement was nongovernmental in form: Neither side had to concern itself with the procedures prescribed by the domestic law of each country for the approval of governmental commitments, such as treaties or other agreements. Chinese law requires that a treaty with a foreign state be ratified by the standing committee of the National People's Congress and chairman of the People's Republic.[48] An agreement, which does not require ratification, must be approved by the State Council.[49] Similarly, under Japanese law, a treaty requires ratification by the Diet, but executive agreements may be concluded independently by the Cabinet under its general power to administer foreign relations.[50]

The content of the agreement dealt with three major subjects: trade, payments, and institutional arrangements. On the first question, the volume was set at thirty-five million pounds sterling each way for

45. Among other affiliations, Nan was also a member of the Chinese Communist Party and the Standing Committee of the National People's Congress. See Union Research Institute, *Who's Who in China* (Hong Kong: Union Research Institute, 1966), p. 459.

46. The three vice-chairmen were Vice-Minister of Foreign Trade Lei Jen-min, Minister of Light Industry Li Chu-ch'en, and Deputy Director-General of the Bank of China Chi Ch'ao-ting.

47. Kumaichi Yamamoto and Den Kawakatsu for the JAPIT and Saburo Nango and Hiroshi Nita for the JAJCEI.

48. See *Constitution of the People's Republic of China*, art. 31, par. 12, and art. 41 (1954).

49. See Standing Committee of the National People's Congress Decision on the Procedures of Ratification of Treaties with Foreign States, October 16, 1954, in *Chung-hua jen-min kung-ho-kuo fa-kuei hui-pien 1954–1955* (Compilation of laws and regulations of the People's Republic of China; Peking), vol. I (1956), p. 207.

50. *Constitution of Japan*, art. 73, pars. 3 and 4 (1947). Also see Harold S. Quigley and John E. Turner, *The New Japan* (Minneapolis, Minn.: University of Minnesota Press, 1956), pp. 206–207.

one year (articles 1 and 14), as had already been disclosed during the negotiations. Commodities were classified into two categories for each export schedule. Category A, comprising mainly minerals on the Chinese side and steel products on the Japanese side, accounted for 40 percent of the total volume. Category B, consisting of miscellaneous items, accounted for 60 percent (article 2). Prices for individual items listed in the export schedules were not mentioned, but the parties concurred that prices should be calculated in pounds sterling or in other mutually acceptable third nation currencies (article 4). Transportation and delivery were to be arranged later when the transactions were actually concluded (article 6).

The civil law textbook that was published in Peking in 1958 outlined the principal terms of a sales contract as "object, amount, price, and time."[51] In the absence of any of these terms, a sales contract would be incomplete. The fourth China-Japan trade agreement dealt with these terms only in generalities. It was not specific enough to be enforceable.[52] Thus, although the parties to the agreement were all legal persons capable of making contracts, the agreement was nothing more than a precontract arrangement.[53] Its realization would depend upon "the conclusion of concrete trade contracts between China's state foreign trade corporations, state-private joint foreign trade corporations, and private foreign trade corporations on the one hand, and Japanese manufacturers and business firms on the other" (article 3).

On the questions relating to payment and clearing, article 5 of the agreement called for the conclusion of a payments agreement and the establishment of clearing accounts between the Chinese People's Bank and the Bank of Japan; however, before the conclusion of such an agreement, it provided that matters should be handled by the two official foreign exchange banks (the Bank of China and the Bank of Tokyo) through the establishment of direct business relations; transactions were all to be paid in hard currencies. This was an improvement

51. Central Political-Legal Cadres' School, *Chung-hua jen-min kung-ho-kuo min-fa chi-pen wen-t'i* (Basic problems in the civil law of the People's Republic of China; Peking: Fa-lü ch'u-pan-she, 1958), p. 206.

52. For reference to a sample of sales contracts between the Chinese and Japanese, see Gene T. Hsiao, "Communist China's Foreign Trade Contracts and Means of Settling Disputes," *Vanderbilt Law Review* 22.3:503,521 (1969).

53. For a discussion of the legal personality of the CCPIT, see "China's Foreign Trade Organizations," *PR*, no. 28:13 (Nov. 9, 1958). On the Japanese side, the sources were based on my interview with the Japanese in February 1967. It should be noted that the actual capacity of both the Chinese and Japanese associations to assume liability was not known.

for both parties, as compared with practice under the third agreement according to which the settlement of payments had to be made through London banks.[54]

Finally, in treating the question of so-called "institutional arrangements," the agreement touched on three topics: commodity inspection, arbitration, and the exchange of trade fairs and trade missions. Article 7 provided that the commodity inspection agency of the seller's country was to issue certificates of quality and weight as the basis of payment; the buyer had the right to have his own country's agency reinspect the commodities at his own cost and to make claims if the quality or weight was inconsistent with the contract.

When compared with the pertinent provision of the third agreement, this was a concession to the Japanese, as the Chinese chief negotiator Lei Jen-min claimed. Under that provision, the Chinese state commodity inspection agency had been exclusively qualified to inspect Chinese exports and to reinspect Japanese imports if necessary, whereas the qualifications of a Japanese agency to inspect Japanese exports and to reinspect Chinese imports were subject to the agreement of the actual trading parties.[55]

In regard to the issue of arbitration, prior to the third agreement China was designated the sole location for the conduct of hearings, irrespective of which party was the defendant, although the arbitration tribunal was to be jointly organized by both parties.[56] This meant that, whenever an arbitration proceeding became necessary, it would be an obligation of the Peking government to allow the Japanese party to enter its country and to provide him with all necessary facilities. More important from the Japanese perspective, the Japanese party would

54. Under the third agreement, art. 5, both parties expressed the desire to conclude a payments agreement between the two state banks. This desire, however, was never realized because of the lack of diplomatic relations between the two countries. Moreover, as the Japanese chief negotiator Shozo Murata (for the third agreement) pointed out, all major Japanese bankers were "dead set against dealing with" the Chinese because they were aware of United States regulations about Japanese firms doing business with the mainland. See *Nippon Times,* Apr. 26, 1955, p. 2.

55. See China-Japan Trade Agreement, art. 7, May 4, 1955, in *TYC 1955,* vol. IV (1960), pp. 258, 259. It should be noted that the commodity inspection clause of the second China-Japan Trade Agreement, October 29, 1953, was substantially the same as that of the fourth agreement. In *TYC 1952–1953,* vol. II (1957), pp. 369, 370. Thus, the Chinese concession was in essence a reinstatement of the Japanese position in 1953.

56. China-Japan Trade Agreement, art. 6, June 1, 1952, and art. 7, Oct. 29, 1953, in *TYC 1952–1953,* vol. II (1957), pp. 367, 368 and pp. 369, 370 respectively.

always have the disadvantage of being heard in a possibly hostile atmosphere.[57]

Presumably for the latter reason, in the third agreement the two parties modified the arbitration clause by designating the country of domicile of the defendant as the location of hearing. They also agreed upon another provision that appears to have been designed to enhance the impartiality of the arbitration tribunal—that it be composed of an equal number of arbitrators of Chinese and Japanese nationality appointed by the disputing parties, plus a third person (presumably to serve as umpire) agreed upon by the arbitrators chosen by the parties.[58]

Article 8 of the fourth agreement substantially modified the arbitration clause by permitting the national foreign trade arbitration association (as distinguished from a joint tribunal) of the defendant's country to conduct the hearing according to its own procedures and rules. However, there was a major difference in the composition of tribunals. In the case of a Chinese tribunal, the arbitrators were to be all Chinese. In the case of a Japanese tribunal, the arbitrators were not to be limited to those listed by the Japan Association for International Commercial Arbitration, but were to be limited to persons of Chinese and Japanese nationality as well as persons of a third nationality agreed upon by the disputing parties.

The relative advantages and disadvantages to the Chinese and Japanese in this arbitration clause, however, should be evaluated in terms of its enforceability. As indicated earlier, when the first official Chinese trade delegation led by Vice-Minister of Foreign Trade Lei Jen-min visited Japan in the spring of 1955, the Japanese Ministry of Foreign Affairs refused to extend the visas of its members. They were able to stay a few days more than the permitted period mainly due to Premier Hatoyama's "unofficial understanding."[59] In view of this fact, whether or not the Japanese government was prepared to allow the entry of a Chinese plaintiff, his counsel, and witnesses under the fourth agreement remained a question.

Furthermore, although arbitration is a private proceeding, there is always the possibility that the Nationalist Chinese embassy in Tokyo may interfere with the proceeding when it involves Peking as a plaintiff.

57. For a discussion of this matter, see Gene T. Hsiao, "Communist China's Foreign Trade Contracts," pp. 503, 511.

58. See China-Japan Trade Agreement, art. 8, May 4, 1955, in *TYC 1955*, vol. IV (1960), pp. 258, 260.

59. See "Peiping Hits Trade Delay," *Nippon Times*, Apr. 30, 1955, p. 9.

In February 1967, when I questioned some responsible officials of the Japanese Ministry of International Trade and Industry about the feasibility of holding such a proceeding in Japan, the reply was that "we have not thought about that problem."

If the holding of an arbitral proceeding in Tokyo was difficult because of the Japanese government's political policy toward Peking, the problems involved in the exchange of trade fairs and missions were even more formidable. The Chinese had in 1957 postponed two fairs because of the fingerprinting requirement of the Japanese government. Now the signatories of the fourth agreement again agreed to hold two Chinese fairs in Nagoya and Fukuoka in exchange for two Japanese fairs in Wuhan and Canton before the end of 1958 (article 12). In addition, they further agreed to establish trade missions at the "people's" level in Peking and Tokyo (article 11). The functions of these missions were described as follows: handling matters arising from the execution of the agreement, reporting the market conditions of each country, investigating and gathering information concerning the trade and market of the receiving state, assisting manufacturers and business firms of each country in the conduct of transactions, promoting the technological intercourse of both states, and handling other commercial matters assigned to the trade missions by their appointing agencies.

In order to implement these functions, the memorandum of March 5, 1958—a part of the fourth agreement—provided each trade mission and its members with the following treatment: protection of the physical safety of the trade mission and its members, choice of methods for settling legal disputes after agreement between the two parties, facilitation of the procedures for the entry and exit of trade mission members, favorable treatment of mission members by customs authorities, freedom of travel for the purpose of carrying out trade activities, use of ciphers for the conduct of business, the right of the trade mission to fly its national flag on its buildings, and exemption from fingerprinting of trade mission members and their dependents. The number of mission members was left to each party to decide on the basis of its own needs.[60]

Most of these provisions are so-called "establishment provisions" that appear in a modern commercial treaty.[61] They are essential to the

60. In *TYC 1958*, vol. VII (1959), pp. 201–203.

61. See Herman Walker, Jr., "Modern Treaties of Friendship, Commerce and Navigation," in *Minnesota Law Review* 42.5:805 (1958).

successful conduct of international trade. However, enforcement of these provisions involves consideration of diplomatic relations and national sovereignty. Without governmental approval and support, execution of the agreement would be impossible. For this reason, the agreement made it an obligation of each party to obtain the consent of its own government to enforce all the provisions stated above. On the Chinese side, foreign trade is a sovereign function of the state, and the CCPIT a front organization of the government.[62] There was no doubt that Peking was prepared to honor the agreement. The Japanese, on the other hand, had to have formal approval from their government. This difference in the actual capacity of the parties to make promises and discharge obligations was to be the primary source of controversy in the execution of the agreement.

NULLIFICATION

The proposal for the exchange of trade missions came originally from Koichi Uda, a Japanese negotiator of the second (1953) agreement.[63] This coincidentally suited the needs of the socialist system of foreign trade.[64] In principle, therefore, both sides were receptive to the idea. The exchange stipulated in the third agreement was postponed because of the Japanese government's fingerprinting requirement. For the fourth agreement, as has been indicated earlier in the discussion of Tokyo's four-point decision of September 1957 and its second four-point instruction of February 1958 to the Ikeda delegation, the Kishi cabinet was prepared to grant the trade mission of Peking almost all privileges provided in the memorandum of March 5, 1958, except for the right of the trade mission to fly its national flag in Japan. This, then, was the key issue in question.

Premier Kishi's position on this issue was not entirely invulnerable. First, when the first Chinese trade fair was held in Tokyo in 1955, the Japanese government permitted the flying of Peking's national flag. Rejection of the present clause would undoubtedly contradict that precedent and provide Peking with a legitimate reason to question Tokyo's sincerity in improving mutual trade relations. Second, in 1956,

62. See Gene T. Hsiao, "Communist China's Foreign Trade Organization," in *Vanderbilt Law Review* 20.2:303 (1967).

63. Observer, "Who Is After All Destroying Sino-Japanese Trade," *JMJP*, Apr. 25, 1958, p. 5.

64. See Gene T. Hsiao, "Communist China's Trade Treaties and Agreements (1949–1964)," in *Vanderbilt Law Review* 21.5:623, 637 (1968).

as a member of the Diet, Kishi sponsored two resolutions jointly with the Socialist leader Inejiro Asanuma and others for the expansion of trade with mainland China.[65] It was also under the Kishi administration that the Japanese government successfully concluded a formal treaty of commerce with the Soviet Union on December 6, 1957, with an annex defining the juridical status of Soviet trade representation in Japan.[66] Third, the Japanese Socialist Party then held one third of the seats in each house of the Diet, and a general election was already set for May 1958.[67] Since trade expansion was a popular desire of the Japanese, failure to reach an accord with Peking on the terms of the fourth agreement could possibly jeopardize Premier Kishi's re-election.

Finally, and perhaps most important, the reality of Japan's foreign trade was such that for more than ten years in succession, it had suffered heavy deficits.[68] For 1957 alone, Japan's total trade amounted to about US $7 billion, with an unfavorable balance of nearly US $1.5 billion. Trade with Peking accounted for US $140 million, with a deficit of US $20 million; and trade with the United States, US $2.2 billion, with a deficit of over US $1 billion. In that same year, Japan also suffered a depression in its domestic steel market.[69] Consequently, the fourth agreement totalling 70 million pounds sterling and the five-year steel deal in the total amount of 200 million pounds sterling became very important sources of trade for the Japanese.

Thus, despite the fact that the agreement had been concluded without his prior approval, Premier Kishi subsequently supported the position of the Ikeda delegation.[70] But in reply to Taipei's diplomatic protests and economic sanctions against Japan for its trade agreement with Peking, Premier Kishi did state that the flying of a Peking flag in Japan would not be recognized by the Japanese government as a "right";[71] consequently, he would not protect the Peking flag according to the Penal Code, article 92, which provides that

65. These resolutions were dated March 30 and December 12, 1956, respectively. In *Nichu kankei shryo shu*, pp. 23–24.
66. In *Japanese Annual of International Law* (Tokyo, 1958), II, 173.
67. "An Important Contribution to Sino-Japanese Relations," *People's China*, no. 10:39 (May 16, 1957).
68. See Warren S. Hunsberger, *Japan and the United States in World Trade* (New York: Harper & Row, 1964), p. 106.
69. *Japan Times*, Feb. 27, 1958, p. 1.
70. Premier Kishi's initial reaction to the conclusion of the fourth agreement was that it would be "difficult" for the Japanese government to approve it if the flag clause was not deleted. See *Japan Times*, Mar. 6, 1958, p. 1.
71. *Japan Times*, Mar. 30, 1958, p. 1.

> A person who, for the purpose of insulting a foreign state, damages, destroys, removes or defiles the national flag or other national emblem of that state shall be punished with imprisonment of forced labor for not more than two years or a fine of not more than 200 yen, but the crime shall be dealt with only on the request of the government of such state.[72]

At the same time, however, Premier Kishi pointed out that Japan did not have a law forbidding the hoisting of foreign flags.[73]

In response to American pressure against Japan's dealing with Peking,[74] Foreign Minister Fujiyama regretted "recent movements" in the United States to restrict Japanese imports. He declared that "I do not need to point out that Japan's trade with the United States is a matter of life and death to the Japanese people." However, he noted that there was a need for Japan "to lessen the gap now existing in the two–one ratio in favor of the United States" in the two countries' trade.[75]

When Kishi's position on the flag issue failed to satisfy Taipei, whose relations with Tokyo had already neared a breaking point, and the pressure from the United States became even more intense,[76] Premier Kishi finally on April 9 issued a three-point statement in reply to a request of the three Japanese organizations (the Dietmen's League, JAPIT, and JAJCEI) for approval of the trade agreement. He denied the proposed trade mission of Peking the *right* to fly its national flag and to enjoy any privileges and official status. While reassuring Peking that the Japanese government would support the agreement within the limits of Japan's domestic law, Premier Kishi also reminded Peking of the fact of nonrecognition and Japan's consideration for existing international relations.[77] In a separate statement of the same day, Premier Kishi reiterated that in case of damage to the Peking flag, the Japanese government would not invoke article 92 of the Penal Code to protect it; rather, he would consider such an act destruction of private property and

72. In Supreme Court of Japan, *The Constitution of Japan and Criminal Statutes* (Tokyo, 1958), p. 73.

73. In *Chung-yang jih-pao* (Central daily), Taipei, Mar. 31, 1958, p. 1.

74. For a discussion of this and Taipei's protests, see Gene T. Hsiao, "The Role of Trade in China's Diplomacy," pp. 43–47.

75. *Japan Times*, Apr. 8, 1958, p. 1.

76. This culminated in the publication of a full-page public notice in *Japan Times*, Apr. 9, 1958, by the Committee of One Million, calling Japan's trade with Peking "an act of insanity and potential national and international suicide."

77. *Japan Times*, Apr. 10, 1958, p. 1. Premier Kishi personally delivered the reply to Dietman Ikeda. The version of his statement forwarded to Peking by the three Japanese organizations, however, was in the name of Chief Cabinet Secretary Kiichi Aichi. See *Jih-pen wen-t'i*, vol. II (1958), p. 209.

handle the case accordingly. Foreign Minister Fujiyama supplemented Kishi's statement by saying that "in the event any troubles should arise over the flying of the [Peking] flag, I think they should be settled between the parties concerned, because the trade agreement after all is a private one."[78]

Taipei promptly accepted Premier Kishi's statement and resumed normal relations with Tokyo.[79] Mainland China, however, would not yield to Japan's settlement with the Nationalists. For nearly one month after the conclusion of the trade agreement, Peking had waited for Premier Kishi's decision without making any official comment on his quarrel with Taipei and Washington. In fact, the value of Peking's monthly trade contracts with Japan in March had increased to an unprecedented level—over six million pounds sterling in basic commodities and nearly 800,000 pounds sterling in ordinary goods.[80] Furthermore, by the end of that month, a trade delegation from Peking had arrived in Tokyo to negotiate with the Japanese steel industry for individual contracts on the basis of the five-year barter agreement.[81] Both sides had expressed confidence that the negotiations would be concluded in about one week, and all indications pointed to the fact that Peking meant to do business with the Japanese.

At this juncture, however, the Japanese government's attitude toward the question of protecting the Peking flag under the provisions of the Japanese Penal Code had already become public knowledge. In Peking's view, this attitude not only denied the 1955 precedent, where a trade fair of Peking in Tokyo was permitted to fly its national flag, but also violated international practice according to which alien citizens are normally permitted to fly their own national flag. Moreover, in Peking's opinion, Premier Kishi's refusal to protect its national flag according to article 92 of the Japanese Penal Code was testimony of his intention to condone destructive acts against the flag and, consequently, to insult the People's Republic.[82] As a warning, four days before Premier Kishi's statement of April 9, Vice-Minister of Foreign Trade Lei Jen-min announced the postponement of two trade fairs scheduled to be held in

78. *Japan Times*, Apr. 10, 1958, p. 1.
79. "Communiqué of the Ministry of Foreign Affairs, April 9, 1958," in *Chung-yang jih-pao*, Apr. 10, 1958, p. 1.
80. *Japan Times*, Apr. 6. 1958, p. 7.
81. *Ibid.*, Mar. 29, 1958, p. 6.
82. Editorial, "[We] Cannot Allow the Kishi Government to Destroy the Sino-Japanese Trade Agreement," *JMJP*, Apr. 3, 1958, p. 1.

Nagoya and Fukuoka, pending clarification of Tokyo's attitude toward the fourth agreement.[83]

When the three Japanese organizations that signed the agreement finally forwarded Kishi's decision of April 9 to Peking, the Chinese chief signatory, Nan Han-ch'en, refused to accept it on the ground that the Japanese government had failed to provide any assurance for the enforcement of the agreement. Legally, Nan contended that Premier Kishi's statement regarding the national flag of the People's Republic as private property not entitled to the protection of article 92 of the Japanese Penal Code was a discrimination in the application of Japan's domestic law. Nan's argument apparently ignored the fact that application of that article was contingent upon the existence of diplomatic relations between Japan and the insulted foreign state. Nevertheless, it was on this basis that he raised the further question as to whether or not the Japanese government really intended to protect other rights and privileges of the proposed trade mission of Peking, such as exemption from fingerprinting requirements and protection of the mission members' physical safety.[84]

On the question of recognition, Nan declared that the basic spirit of the agreement was "friendship," but that the Japanese government's nonrecognition policy and pro-Nationalist attitude had destroyed that spirit. He attacked Premier Kishi's policy of "separating trade from politics" as being hypocritical since the Japanese government had always linked the problem of trade with Peking to the question of nonrecognition. Moreover, he pointed out that by unilaterally denying the Chinese trade mission the rights and privileges stipulated in the agreement, the Japanese government had in fact violated the principles of equality, mutual benefit, and mutual respect, since the Japanese trade delegation holding fairs in Wuhan and Canton was enjoying such rights and privileges, including the right to fly the Japanese national flag.

Finally, with respect to Japan's consideration for existing international relations, Nan reminded Tokyo that the trade agreement was concluded with Peking, not with Taipei or Washington. Consequently, he contended that Japan should first of all consider its relations with the People's Republic and the enforcement of the agreement, so as to pave

83. See Lei's press conference with Chinese and Japanese correspondents in Wuhan, April 4, 1958, in *JMJP*, Apr. 6, 1958, pp. 1–2.

84. See Nan Han-ch'en's Telegram to the Three Japanese Organizations, April 13, 1958, in *Jih-pen wen-t'i*, vol. II (1958), pp. 204–208.

the way for the restoration of diplomatic relations between the two countries. He noted that China would not trade with Japan under any humiliating and unequal terms and that until all barriers created by the Japanese government were removed, the Chinese side would not enforce the agreement.[85]

The execution of the fourth agreement was thus indefinitely delayed. However, negotiations for individual contracts to carry out the 200 million pound steel deal continued in Tokyo. There were some indications that Peking wanted to save both the agreement and the steel deal without losing too much face.[86] But, as all parties concerned had anticipated, an incident involving the destruction of a Peking flag soon occurred in Nagasaki.

The incident took place on May 2 in the Hamaya Department Store at a mainland Chinese postage-stamp and paper-cut exhibition sponsored by the Nagasaki chapter of the Japan-China Friendship Association. Two young Japanese, To Seki and Kiyoshi Ishibashi, walked into the store and ripped down one of the Peking flags on display. The sponsor of the exhibition filed a charge against Seki for destruction of property. After questioning him on motives, the local police released Seki, pending consultation with the Nagasaki district prosecutors' office.[87]

Earlier, the Nationalist embassy in Tokyo and its consulate in Nagasaki had protested against the display of the Peking flag at the Hamaya store. But the Japanese government could not find legal grounds to compel the store to remove the flag.[88] After the incident, the Japanese Ministry of Foreign Affairs reiterated its previous position that article 92 of the penal code would not apply to the Seki case.[89]

At this time, the second plenum of the Eighth Central Committee of the Chinese Communist Party was being held in Peking. Presumably the Nagasaki incident received careful consideration by the top party leadership, for the official reaction of the Peking government did not come until May 7. On that day, the Peking government simultaneously took three actions. First, it linked the flag incident to the Nationalist protests, thus implying the existence of collusion between the National-

85. *Ibid.* For Peking's further argument along these lines, see Observer's comment, "Who Is After All Destroying the Sino-Japanese Trade Agreement," *JMJP*, Apr. 25, 1958, p. 5.

86. For example, an editorial of *JMJP*, Apr. 25, 1958, still maintained an optimistic view of the future of Sino-Japanese trade.

87. *Japan Times*, May 4, 1958, p. 3.

88. *Ibid.*, May 2, 1958, p. 2, and May 3, 1958, p. 1.

89. *Chung-yang jih-pao*, May 4, 1958, p. 1.

ists and the Japanese government.[90] Second, it seized fourteen Japanese fishing boats about 100 miles north of Taiwan.[91] Third, it suspended all import and export licenses for Japan, discontinued all commercial negotiations with the Japanese at the trade fair in Canton, and recalled the Chinese trade delegation that had been negotiating the steel deal in Tokyo.[92]

Following these actions, the Chinese chief signatory Nan Han-ch'en sent a telegram to his Japanese counterparts, holding the Kishi government responsible for the incident and "all the consequences arising therefrom"—the breakdown of Sino-Japanese trade, including trade under the fourth agreement and the steel barter deal.[93] At the same time, Foreign Minister Ch'en Yi issued a similar statement repeating the charges made by Nan Han-ch'en. In addition, he pointed out that Premier Kishi's refusal to recognize the People's Republic as an independent state and his interpretation that its flag was private property was "extremely ridiculous."[94]

Japanese businessmen quickly apologized for the "unfortunate" incident at Nagasaki.[95] The Japanese government, however, refused to change its policy on the flag issue. Instead, it expressed the view that since Peking "badly" needed iron and steel for its Second Five-Year Plan (1958–1962), its decision to suspend trade with Japan would not last very long. Moreover, Premier Kishi believed that Peking's trade ban was basically intended to hamper his re-election and to aid the Japanese Socialists. Thus, in reply to Ch'en Yi's accusations, the Japanese government issued an "unofficial" statement saying:

> 1. The Japanese government adheres to the basic policy of not recognizing Communist China; however, it has taken steps to conduct trade and cultural exchange. Communist China's repeated attacks against the Japanese government, starting with the flag issue, indicate that China does not fully understand Japan's policy or it is deliberately misinterpreting Japan's stand for political reasons.
>
> 2. Ch'en's accusation that Japan is unfriendly to China is not true. The Kishi cabinet has authorized the establishment of a Communist Chinese trade mission in Japan for implementing the fourth private trade agreement and

90. *JMJP*, May 7, 1958, p. 5.
91. *Japan Times*, May 8, 1958, p. 1.
92. *JMJP*, May 11, 1958, p. 1; *Japan Times*, May 9, 1958, p. 1.
93. See the CCPIT's Telegram to the Three Japanese Organizations, May 9, 1958, in *Jih-pen wen-t'i*, vol. II (1958), pp. 214–215.
94. Foreign Minister Ch'en Yi's Interview with Hsinhua Correspondents, May 9, 1958, in *ibid.*, pp. 87–89.
95. *Japan Times*, May 9, 1958, p. 1.

waived fingerprinting requirements for the mission members—a controversial issue pending since the Hatoyama cabinet.

3. Communist China insists there can be no trade until it is allowed to fly its flag over the Red Chinese trade mission building in Tokyo. It is deliberately bringing up an issue that has no direct relations with trade.

4. Communist China is trying to make a big political issue out of the flag ripping incident in Nagasaki. While the incident is a regrettable one, it is to be deplored that Communist China should for political purposes exploit an act by an individual.[96]

In addition, Premier Kishi contended that it was against the principles of international law to treat the flag of a nation with which Japan had no diplomatic ties in a similar manner to that of a nation with which his country had formal relations.[97] Specifically, on the Nagasaki flag incident, Chief Cabinet Secretary Kiichi Aichi explained that he was doubtful "whether the man responsible could be punished under provisions of the penal code, even if diplomatic relations existed between the two countries."[98] He pointed out that the national flag of any country would not be treated as such if it was not flown by an official organization of that country. Referring to a similar incident on May 11 in which an array of flags of various nations, including Nationalist China's, were insulted by pro- and anti-Communist elements in Yokohama, Aichi said that the Japanese government received a protest from the Nationalist government but did not refer the case to prosecutors, because the Japanese Ministry of Justice reasoned that the flags involved in that incident were not of such a nature as to officially demonstrate the dignity of the nations involved.[99]

Peking interpreted the situation in a different way. It maintained that the fourth trade agreement was actually "destroyed" by Premier Kishi's statement of April 9, which denied the three Japanese organizations' request for approval of the entire agreement, including the flag clause. By this very act, Peking contended, the Japanese government showed bad faith in its avowed support for the improvement of Sino-Japanese trade relations and practically made the agreement unenforceable. Con-

96. *Ibid.*, May 11, 1958, p. 1.

97. *Ibid.*

98. *Japan Times*, May 14, 1958, p. 1. It should be noted that under Peking's pressure, To Seki, the man responsible for the Nagasaki incident, paid a 500-yen fine many months later. This, however, was too late to satisfy the Chinese who contended that the fine was nothing more than "lip service." See Observer's comment, "Kishi's Posture Cannot Deceive Any One," *JMJP*, Feb. 16, 1959, reproduced in *Jih-pen wen-t'i*, vol. III (1961), pp. 42–45.

99. *Japan Times*, May 13, 1958, p. 1; *ibid.*, May 14, 1958, p. 1.

sequently, the party at fault was not the Japanese signatories but the Kishi administration. Indeed, throughout the debate Peking never charged the three Japanese organizations with the failure to obtain the consent of the Japanese government in order to discharge their obligations.[100]

As to the Nagasaki flag incident, Peking believed it was the result of a Tokyo-Taipei plot. As such, it provided further evidence of the Japanese government's hostility toward the People's Republic. In the absence of a friendly relationship between the two countries and some assurance from the Japanese government for the fulfillment of the agreement, Peking had no choice but to suspend trade relations with Japan in order to "maintain the dignity of an independent sovereign state and to protect its rights."[101]

CONCLUSION

As the foregoing analysis demonstrates, the question of recognition was the central problem of both the negotiations and the implementation of the fourth China-Japan trade agreement. In reaching and administering the agreement, China sought to maximize its potential for implicit diplomatic recognition, and Japan sought to minimize that potential. The agreement itself represented an unstable compromise that elicited an ambivalent response from the Japanese government and that broke down as Tokyo became increasingly sensitive to its implications.

Some degree of recognition may be thought to have been implied by Premier Kishi's initial approval of all the terms of the Peking-drafted agreement except for the flag clause. Kishi was even inclined to approve this last point, since Japanese law did not forbid the flying of the national flag of a foreign state with which Japan had no formal diplomatic relations. Yet, in his final decision of April 9, 1958, he denied Peking's proposed trade mission any form of official status, including the right to fly its national flag. This reversal of his position should not be seen as a decision made solely by the Japanese government, for third-state pressure from Taipei and Washington also played an important role. The fact that Tokyo succumbed to such "interference" explains some of the political wrath that Peking displayed against the Japanese government in succeeding years.

100. Commentator, "Why Was Sino-Japanese Trade Interrupted?" *JMJP*, May 20, 1958, reproduced in *Jih-pen wen-t'i*, vol. II (1958), pp. 216–220.
101. *Ibid.*

As to the Nagasaki flag incident, Premier Kishi's earlier statements, which indicated his anticipation of trouble, demonstrated political and diplomatic insensitivity. Legally, however, Peking's charge that the Japanese government condoned the incident in order to insult the People's Republic appears groundless. Dignity cannot be accorded to a state symbol if there is no recognition of that state's international personality. Since Premier Kishi ultimately refused to grant the Peking government any form of recognition, his decision not to protect the Peking flag according to article 92 of the Japanese Penal Code was consistent with the accepted norms of international law.[102]

102. See L. Oppenheim, *International Law,* ed. H. Lauterpacht (New York: David McKay, 1967), vol. I, p. 282.

5 / Negotiating with China: A Minor Episode

Gilbert P. Verbit

Disconcerting as it may be for the reader, it is necessary to begin this short paper with a disclaimer. I claim no expertise in international law or Sinology. The sole reason for my presence among the distinguished group of scholars whose contributions make up the body of this volume is the fact that from September 1962 until June 1964, I served as legal adviser to the Ministry of External Affairs of the Republic of Tanzania.[1] During that period I was called upon from time to time to participate in the negotiation of various international agreements. This memorandum records the experience of one such negotiation—an Agreement on Cultural Co-operation between the Government of the Republic of Tanzania and the Government of the People's Republic of China, done at Dar es Salaam, December 13, 1962.

Those who expect from this paper a detailed analysis of protracted negotiations á la Kenneth Young or Arthur Lall will be disappointed. The negotiations in which the writer participated were both brief and noncontentious. Moreover, the resulting agreement is much like others to which the People's Republic of China is a party so that the text of the agreement is of no more than passing interest. The significance of the negotiations, if any, therefore depends on factors extraneous to the actual negotiations. The writer would identify two such factors: first, the negotiations were conducted and the agreement signed during the time that the border dispute between China and India was in a state

1. From Independence on December 9, 1961 until December 9, 1962, the name of the country was Tanganyika. On December 9, 1962, it became the Republic of Tanganyika. Following the union with Zanzibar on April 24, 1964, the proper name was first the Union Republic of Tanganyika and Zanzibar, shortened in October 1964, to the Republic of Tanzania.

of open conflict, and second, the position of the People's Republic of China in the array of states with which Tanzania enjoyed diplomatic relations. For unlike the unique position China enjoys, or more correctly, holds in the eyes of most Americans, both private and official, the Tanzania government viewed China as one of the group of major powers with which it dealt on various matters—no better and no worse. Why it is that Tanzania deals with China as just another great power—an attitude which has earned for the Tanzanians the label "pro-Chinese"—is too long a story to relate here. The little episode which follows, however, is a part of that story.

Prior to the attainment of independence on December 9, 1961, the experience of the Tanzanians with the Chinese was rather scant. There was, for some years, in the capital, Dar es Salaam, a restaurant operated by a man named Harry Lin. As well as providing some variety from the otherwise drab British-style cuisine available at the local restaurants and hotels, Harry Lin provided the only real contact that Tanzanians had with anything Chinese. Harry Lin's restaurant and attached grocery shop, located on the fringes of the African section of the city, were places where one could see rotogravure pictures of China and buy Chinese bowls and chopsticks. In short, if one wanted to learn about China, one could drop by at Harry Lin's for a "look-see." At times the lonely figures of Harry Lin and his family were supplemented by sailors, usually from British-flag ships with Hong Kong–recruited crews, who found a little piece of home at the bar of Harry's restaurant. In addition to Harry Lin, the Dar population included a legendary figure known as "the Chinese carpenter." The Chinese carpenter, also a long-time resident, lived in the midst of an African village in the suburbs of Dar, where he plied his trade of carpentry in general, and in particular prepared the wooden crates so necessary to transport the personal effects of colonial civil servants on their way to and from their periodic long leaves. These two figures represented, to my knowledge, the extent of the Chinese presence in Dar es Salaam prior to independence.

There was, however, an image of China prevalent in the government. This was the image created by the British civil servants who, until independence and for some time thereafter, staffed the key ministries of the Tanzanian government. The image was, to say the least, most unsophisticated. It might be summarized by noting that the British conveyed to their African compatriots the view that the Chinese represented a "yellow peril" that would seek, in East Africa, a place to settle their surplus population. Despite the fact that the British maintained relations with China, the prevailing view among the colonial servants seemed to be that Communists were bad in general, and Chinese Communists were worst of all. This attitude was, of course, directly related to the social groups who staffed the colonial service. It manifested itself in policies designed to "protect" the Tanzanians from the Chinese, both by restricting travel to China and Chinese contacts in Dar, and in efforts to persuade the Africans to treat the Chinese with great circumspection.

At the time of independence, the situation changed, for the Tanzanian government decided to recognize the People's Republic of China as the representative of the Chinese people and gave permission for the Chinese to establish an embassy in Dar es Salaam.[2] At the same time, however, the Tanzanian government announced that its policy with regard to foreign missions was that those missions would be limited to ten accredited personnel. The announced reason for this limitation was that the Tanzanian Foreign Ministry was so new and so small that it could not cope with too large a number of diplomats in the city.[3] The limitation, while not directed against China, placed a special burden on that country, since China has long followed a policy of employing no local staff in its missions.[4] While the opening of the mission thus increased the Chinese population of Dar es Salaam by 500 percent, in actual numbers the total was insignificant. This was particularly true when compared with the great numbers of British civil servants still in the government, and the rapidly increasing population of American technical advisers, Peace Corps volunteers, teachers in East Africa, and so forth.

The opening of the embassy did little to enhance the image of the Chinese. Both the embassy and the residences were surrounded by walls, in one case topped with wire. These rather forbidding structures were in sharp contrast with the missions of other countries which were much more accessible and inviting. Moreover, just as was the case in

2. The government of Tanzania did not establish a mission in China until some years later due to a shortage of financial and human resources.

3. The limitation did not apply to Commonwealth countries.

4. See Arthur Lall, *How Communist China Negotiates* (New York: Columbia University Press, 1968), p. 193. The limitation may have penalized the Chinese in another way. Lall suggests that the present Chinese leadership takes great pride in the population of China (p. 2) and that large Chinese delegations to international meetings and large overseas missions represent an effort to impress on others China's great population (p. 7).

other countries, Chinese embassy personnel were never observed alone. Wives and dependents of diplomatic personnel, as well as the diplomats themselves, always traveled in groups on those occasions when they went shopping or when they went swimming in the ocean.[5] In addition, the image of the People's Republic certainly was not enhanced by the ambassador's car. There were, at the time of independence, two black Lincoln Continentals in Dar es Salaam. One was the car of the American ambassador; the other, the car of the ambassador of the People's Republic of China. While everyone expected that the ambassador of the world's leading capitalist country would travel in great luxury, this was not the case with regard to the shining light of the socialist world. And it was a favorite joke among government officials in Dar es Salaam that the Chinese ambassador should favor an American luxury car.

So it was that at the time the negotiations for the first formal international agreement between the People's Republic of China and Tanzania were about to take place, the image of People's China was not a particularly good one among the ranks of the Tanzanian government officials. If it could be characterized briefly, the attitude of the Tanzanians was one of suspicion, tempered by curiosity. And this suspicion *should have been* reinforced by the events occupying the newspapers at the time that the Chinese cultural delegation arrived, for the delegation—led by Chu Kuang, then Vice-Chairman of the Chinese Commission for Cultural Relations with Foreign Countries—arrived in Tanzania in December of 1962. The reader may recall that on October 20 of that year Chinese forces moved against India on the common border between the two countries. That the Tanzanian government was well aware of what was happening on the China-India border is evident from the attempt of the Tanzanian government to bring peace to the area on the basis of a five-point plan announced on November 8.[6] Despite Tanzania's best efforts, however, the *East African Standard* of November 17 announced "Battle Raging on Frontier." On December 6, Mrs. L. N. Menon of the Indian Ministry of External Affairs arrived in East Africa to proclaim, "China could threaten the world." Shortly after Mrs. Menon arrived in Nairobi, then under British rule, the cultural delegation of the People's Republic of China began negotiations with representatives of the Tanzanian government.

In such circumstances, one might have expected that the negotiations

5. See Lall, p. 5: "Always they operate in groups."
6. Reported in the *Tanganyika Standard*, Nov. 8, 1962.

would have been postponed, if only to protect the sensibilities of the large population (over 100,000) of Indian origin in Tanzania. But the fact that the Indians had a constituency in Tanzania, whereas the Chinese did not, did not lead to a postponement of the negotiations. This may be surprising to those unfamiliar with the position of the Indian community in Tanzania and East Africa generally. The Indians had been brought to East Africa to help in the construction of the railways and to staff the lower echelons of the civil service during the early days of British administration. They had stayed to become the prosperous middle class controlling virtually all wholesale and retail trade and such manufacturing as existed in Tanzania. They occupied positions in the civil service between the Africans who were at the lowest rungs of the ladder—mainly messengers and janitors—and the British expatriates who occupied the senior positions. The British permitted the Indians to maintain separate schools and generally encouraged them to maintain a way of life separate from the Africans. The result is that most Africans intensely dislike—to put it mildly—the Indians. Since independence, this attitude has manifested itself in many ways, not the least of which was the long exclusion of Tanzanians of Indian descent from the government ruling party, TANU, and the government efforts to "Africanize" the civil service and the economy. One may surmise that this dislike of the Indians in East Africa is carried to the point that India, being the homeland of this group, is similarly not viewed with great affection.[7]

Lest the case be overstated, however, it is safe to assume that, in fact, the government of Tanzania leaned toward neither side in the border dispute and wished only that it would be settled as quickly as possible. To have turned away the Chinese delegation might have been interpreted in some quarters as taking sides. In such circumstances, the best course would seem to have been to ignore the border dispute and to allow events to proceed as scheduled.

As scheduled, therefore, the Chinese delegation arrived at the Ministry of Education (Tanzania not then having a Ministry of Culture) to negotiate a cultural cooperation agreement. The Chinese delegation consisted of about seven men, mainly senior civil servants from ministries concerned with the subjects to be covered in the agreement. There was thus no attempt to impress Tanzania with China's power by sending a massive delegation, a technique apparently reserved for more

7. This attitude is reinforced by the unhappy experiences of many Africans who received their advanced education in India. On the position of the Indian community in East Africa see Dharam Ghai, *Portrait of a Minority* (London: Oxford University Press, 1965).

contentious negotiations.[8] On the Tanzanian side, the delegation consisted of civil servants, the chairman being a senior civil servant in the Ministry of Education. Although other members of the Tanzanian delegation were expatriates of either British or, in my own case, American nationality, it was apparent to all that the chairman, who was African, was in firm control of the negotiations on the Tanzanian side. Thus, however disconcerting it may have been for the Chinese to come to Tanzania and face British and American civil servants across the negotiating table, it was immediately apparent once the negotiations commenced that Chinese-Tanzanian relations were not in any way to be prejudiced by these expatriates.

The negotiations were themselves a rather simple affair. Both sides began with a common desire to strengthen their existing relationships. As indicated in the press release, the purpose was to "establish the framework within which future exchanges of cultural materials and outstanding personalities would take place . . . in the hope that the agreement would lead to a greater mutual understanding and enrichment of their respective cultures." Moreover, there were no surprises on either side. The negotiations proceeded from a draft which had been submitted in advance by the Chinese as the initiating party. Although this was the first cultural exchange agreement that Tanzania was to enter into, and was, in fact, one of its first bilateral agreements since the attainment of independence, the Tanzanian delegation had access to various treaty collections, including the *United Nations Treaty Series,* which reprinted cultural exchange agreements. The draft fitted into the general form of such agreements.

The smooth course of these negotiations—final agreement was arrived at in the course of a few days' negotiation—is in sharp contrast to observations of Chinese negotiating techniques in more contentious situations. Kenneth Young has noted, for example, that "[as] Chinese and Maoists, they negotiate with a very different conception of time, showing endless patience and imperturbability."[9] In the Tanzanian-Chinese negotiations, it was the Tanzanian side which enjoyed the luxury of time, while the Chinese delegation was probably interested in consummating an agreement as quickly as possible. Young also notes with regard to the Panmunjom negotiations, "[no] one ever left the table."[10]

8. See my note 4.

9. Kenneth Young, *Negotiating with the Chinese Communists* (New York: McGraw-Hill, 1968), p. 21.

10. *Ibid.,* p. 26.

Again the Tanzanian–Chinese negotiations proceeded in a more normal way, with tea breaks during which members of the two delegations mixed freely and engaged in light conversation characteristic of such interludes. What seems obvious is that the behavior I observed and that observed by Ambassador Young were conditioned by the context of the particular negotiation.

In my experience, it appears dangerous to attempt to generalize on the negotiating characteristics of the Chinese or any other nation. During my two years in Tanzania, I had the good fortune to participate in a number of negotiations with governments of countries of varying ideologies. Every negotiation was difficult or easy, lengthy or short, successful or not, depending on the substance of what was being negotiated. Every characteristic of so-called Chinese negotiating behavior and techniques could have been applied, in my own experience, to every party with whom Tanzania negotiated. In some negotiations, ambassadors had wide discretion to reach agreement. In others, ambassadors were restricted by Foreign Ministry directives. States that were belligerent in some negotiations were pacific in others. There was neither a "typical" negotiating technique nor a "typical" negotiation. So it was that the Tanzanian–Chinese Agreement on Cultural Co-operation was negotiated in as relaxed and friendly a manner as either side could have wished. The agreement that was the product of these negotiations is as follows:

AGREEMENT ON CULTURAL CO-OPERATION
BETWEEN
THE GOVERNMENT OF THE PEOPLE'S REPUBLIC OF CHINA
AND
THE GOVERNMENT OF THE REPUBLIC OF TANGANYIKA

The Government of the People's Republic of China and the Government of the Republic of Tanganyika, with a view to promoting mutual understanding and friendly relations between the peoples of the two countries, and being desirous to develop cultural exchange and co-operation between the two countries, have decided, in the spirit of respect for each other's national culture, to conclude the present Agreement, the articles of which are as follows:

ARTICLE I

The two Contracting Parties shall consult together concerning the exchange of visits by delegations or personalities of their educational, scientific, literary, medical, public health and religious circles.

ARTICLE II

The two Contracting Parties shall consult together concerning the exchange of visits and performances by their art ensembles and artistes.

ARTICLE III

The two Contracting Parties shall consult together concerning the exchange of visits and holding of friendly matches between their sportsmen and sport teams.

ARTICLE IV

The two Contracting Parties shall consult together concerning the technical problems involved in the dissemination of news, broadcasting and film production, and encourage the exchange of visits by delegations or personalities working in these fields.

ARTICLE V

The two Contracting Parties shall consult together with a view to preparing an acceptable programme for the exchange of students.

ARTICLE VI

The two Contracting Parties shall consult together concerning the exchange of cultural, art and other publications, works of art, lantern slides, phonographic records and tape recordings; the exchange of pictorial, cultural and art exhibitions and film shows; and the recommendation of outstanding works of literature and art of each country for translation and publication in the other.

ARTICLE VII

For the implementation of this Agreement, each Contracting Party may, at the end of the year from the date of entry into force of this Agreement, submit its suggestions as to the operational plan for the next year, which shall be discussed and decided upon through diplomatic channels.

ARTICLE VIII

The present Agreement shall be ratified by the Governments of the two Contracting Parties and shall enter into force on the date of the exchange of instruments of ratification, which shall take place as soon as possible in Dar es Salaam.

The present Agreement shall remain in force for three (3) years from the date of the exchange of instruments of ratification and shall continue in force thereafter, provided that it shall be terminated on the date of expiry of the above-mentioned three (3) years' period or thereafter, if the Government of either Contracting Party has previously given to the other at least six months' written notice of its intention to terminate the present Agreement.

The present Agreement may be amended by common consent of the two Contracting Parties.

Done in duplicate in Dar es Salaam on the Thirteenth day of December in the year One Thousand Nine Hundred and Sixty Two in the Chinese and English languages, both texts being equally authentic.

(Signed) HO YING Plenipotentiary of the Government of the People's Republic of China	(Signed) L. NANG'WANDA SIJAONA Plenipotentiary of the Government of the Republic of Tanganyika

It is important to note three features of this agreement. First, it is not typically Chinese. By that I mean there is nothing about the agreement which would distinguish a cultural exchange agreement to which the People's Republic of China is a party from any other cultural exchange agreement. If one looks at the subjects covered in it, one finds that they are usually present in cultural exchange agreements. A sample of such agreements concluded between 1959 and 1962 to which Brazil, Cambodia, Czechoslovakia, the Republic of China, India, Israel, Norway, El Salvador, and the USSR are parties, shows provisions dealing with the general exchange of "delegations or personalities,"[11] "artistes,"[12] "sportsmen and sport teams,"[13] "news, broadcasting and film production,"[14] "students,"[15] and "works of art, etc."[16] Nor is the idea of an annual "operational plan" at all unusual.[17] Finally, the implementation

11. See Agreement on Cultural Co-operation between the Czechoslovak Socialist Republic and the Kingdom of Cambodia, done at Prague, November 27, 1960, article 2, *UNTS* 410:263, 276 (1961); Cultural Agreement Between the State of Israel and the United States of Brazil, done at Rio de Janeiro, June 24, 1959, article 2, *UNTS* 515:151, 162 (1964); Agreement on Cultural Co-operation Between the Government of the Republic of Cuba and the Government of the Democratic People's Republic of Korea, done at Havana, August 29, 1960, article 1, *UNTS* 473:117 (1963); Cultural Agreement Between Norway and India, done at Oslo, April 19, 1961, Article la, *UNTS* 404:307, 308 (1961).

12. See Israel–Brazil Agreement, article 3, p. 162; Cuba–Korea Agreement, article 3, p. 124; Norway–India Agreement, article 1e, p. 308; Cultural Convention Between the Republic of China and the Republic of El Salvador, done in San Salvador, November 27, 1961, article 4 (1), *UNTS* 437:161, 168 (1962); Agreement Concerning Cultural Co-operation Between the Union of Soviet Socialist Republics and the Syrian Arab Republic, done at Damascus, August 19, 1962, article 8b, *UNTS* 457:285, 294 (1963).

13. See, for example, Israel–Brazil Agreement, articles 1, 2, p. 162; Cuba–Korea Agreement, article 4, p. 126; China (ROC)–El Salvador Agreement, article 4 (5), p. 170; USSR–Syria Agreement, article 10, p. 296.

14. See, for example, Agreement Concerning Cultural Co-operation Between the Government of the Polish People's Republic and the Revolutionary Government of the Republic of Cuba, done at Havana, March 6, 1961, article 5, *UNTS* 484:123, 132 (1963–1964); Cuba–Korea Agreement, article 5, p. 126; Norway–India Agreement, article 1e, p. 308; Agreement of Cultural Co-operation Between the Rumanian People's Republic and the Republic of Ghana, done at Bucharest, September 30, 1961, article 5, *UNTS* 457:3, 6 (1963).

15. Poland–Cuba Agreement, article 4, p. 132; Israel–Brazil Agreement, article 4, p. 163; Norway–India Agreement, article 1b, p. 308; Cultural Agreement Between the State of Israel and the Federal Republic of Cameroon, done at Jerusalem, October 24, 1962, article 1, *UNTS* 449:15, 19 (1962); Rumania–Ghana Agreement, article 1, p. 4.

16. See, for example, Israel–Brazil Agreement, article 5, p. 163; Cuba–Korea Agreement, article 4, p. 126; India–Norway Agreement, article 1d, p. 308; Israel–Cameroon Agreement, article 2, p. 19; China (ROC)–El Salvador Agreement, article 4 (1, 6), p. 170.

17. See, for example, Czechoslovakia–Cambodian Agreement, article 8 (1), p. 277; Poland–Cuban Agreement, article 7, p. 132; Cuba–Korea Agreement, article 9, p. 126.

of the agreement through meetings of diplomatic representatives is typical of this species of agreement.[18]

The second point of interest, at least from the viewpoint of an American lawyer, is that the final agreement is somewhat vague. There are no specifics on numbers of persons who are to be exchanged, how such exchanges are to be administered, and, most important for a poor country such as Tanzania, how costs are to be allocated. The agreement is, however, again typical of its genre. The established pattern for cultural agreements seems to be a series of articles expressing the interest of both parties in exchanges of scholars, publications, etc. The 1962 Cultural Exchange Agreement between the USSR and Syria provides, in article 2, that the "Contracting Parties shall *bring about* an interchange of experience in achievements in the fields of literature, science, art, education and public health, arranging the dispatch of groups and individuals . . ."[19] Other cultural agreements state that the parties "will facilitate the co-operation between,"[20] "shall endeavor to promote . . . ,"[21] "shall endeavor, according to their needs and potentialities, to develop the interchange of . . . ,"[22] or "shall consider the possibility of."[23]

The very generality of these agreements suggests that their value to at least one if not both of the parties may be somewhat different than appears from a reading of the agreement. Because they involve no significant commitment by either party, cultural exchange agreements are easy to negotiate. The expeditious and friendly manner in which the negotiations proceed serves to create an image in each other's eyes of reasonable, well-meaning people with whom one can do business. In the early stages of relations between two states the establishment of such an image may be far more important than the subject of the agreement itself. In the present case, as has been indicated, the agreement may have conferred an additional benefit to the Chinese party. At a time when China was being widely condemned as an aggressor on the India-China border, the Chinese were able to enter into an agreement with another state as if the Chinese-Indian dispute did not exist. If China was considered an outlaw in the international community at that time,

18. See, for example, Czechoslovakia–Cambodia Agreement, article 8 (2), p. 277; Norway–India Agreement, article 6, p. 310.
19. USSR–Syria Agreement, p. 292 (emphasis added).
20. Rumania–Ghana Agreement, article 1, p. 4.
21. China (ROC)–El Salvador Agreement, article 1, p. 168.
22. Czechoslovakia–Cambodia Agreement, article 2, p. 276.
23. Israel–Brazil Agreement, article 4, p. 163.

at least one state indicated by signing an agreement that it did not hold this view.

The third interesting aspect of this agreement is the omission of reference to the Five Principles, since one of the features characteristic of China's international agreements during the period in which these negotiations took place was the incorporation, in the preamble, of the Five Principles of Peaceful Co-existence. The principles were first set out in an agreement between India and China done in 1954.[24] The strong irony of what was happening between those parties may well have created an atmosphere in which their inclusion in the Chinese-Tanzanian agreement was considered unwise. Alternatively, the Five Principles may have been considered uniquely Asian, both in origin and meaning,[25] and therefore out of place in an agreement between an Asian and African state.[26] Whatever the reason, the Five Principles do not appear in the preamble to the Tanzanian-Chinese cultural agreement. Instead the preamble contains the kind of friendly generalities one associates with agreements of this type.[27]

The final texts of the agreements were prepared, in English and Chinese, by the respective parties and were signed on December 13, 1962, by L. N. Sijaona and Ho Ying.[28] The agreement did not, however, enter into force that day. Tanzania had earlier adopted the policy of requiring ratification of international agreements by the cabinet. This policy was adopted for the usual reason that any commitment which was to bind the country ought to be carefully considered by the government as a whole. The ratification procedure presented Tanzania with an added benefit in the present case.

As noted above, the final texts were in English and Chinese, both

24. Lall, *How Communist China Negotiates*, p. 195.

25. *Ibid.*, pp. 31, 195.

26. That the Chinese may consider the Five Principles applicable to their relations with non-Asian states, however, is indicated by their draft of a proposed joint announcement to be made by China and the United States concerning the exchange of newsmen, September 6, 1960. That draft incorporated the Five Principles in its preamble. See Young, *Negotiating with the Chinese Communists*, p. 232.

27. Just as the Five Principles are characteristic of the agreements of the People's Republic of China, the agreements of the Republic of China are unusual in that their preambles typically contain a reference to the United Nations Charter. See, for example, the China (ROC)–El Salvador Agreement, and the Cultural Agreement Between the Republic of China and the Republic of Nicaragua, done at Taipei, April 25, 1961, *UNTS* 423:139, 146 (1962).

28. On that day, the *East African Standard* carried a front page story with the headline "India Lists Border Losses."

being equally authentic. While no state can legitimately quarrel with a text in the other's official language being equally authentic, for Tanzania, as I suspect, for many other developing countries, the Chinese text presented a practical problem. The government of Tanzania had no one in its civil service who possessed a knowledge of the Chinese language. Nor was it possible to locate an independent outside agent who could make a definitive translation. Being aware that the Chinese and English languages may not have exact equivalents in all cases,[29] good practice required that Tanzania obtain an independent translation of the Chinese text. The Chinese text was forwarded to the Permanent Mission of Tanzania to the United Nations, which in turn obtained such a translation. Following receipt of the translation, and following Cabinet approval, instruments of ratification were duly exchanged and the agreement entered into force.

Both parties have benefited substantially from the agreement. The people of Tanzania have had the pleasure of a visit from a renowned Chinese acrobatic troupe. The Tanzanian National Museum, whose central attraction is an exhibit on the origin of *homo sapiens,* has had its collection greatly enhanced by the gift of an ancient skull excavated by Chinese archaeologists. Perhaps of even more importance, the negotiations and subsequent implementation of the agreement have enabled both sides to test each other's bona fides. Like many other states that have entered into agreements with China, Tanzania has found that China scrupulously abides by its international commitments.[30] This initial experience undoubtedly paved the way for such future agreements as the agreement to establish a joint shipping line, and the Chinese financing of the rail line between Tanzania and Zambia.

Tanzania's experience under its Cultural Exchange Agreement with China should serve to qualify sweeping statements about China's attitude toward international law, such as, "International law does not even receive its lip-service."[31] It is particularly appropriate that, in this pub-

29. See Young, *Negotiating with the Chinese Communists,* p. 390.

30. Luke T. Lee, "Treaty Relations of the People's Republic of China: A Study of Compliance," *University of Pennsylvania Law Review* 116:244, 293 (1967) (Finland); Lall, *How Communist China Negotiates,* p. 187 (Burma), p. 200 (Nepal); Douglas M. Johnston, "Treaty Analysis and Communist China: Preliminary Observations," ASIL *Proceedings* (1967), pp. 126, 132.

31. E. L. Katzenbach, Jr., and G. Z. Hanrahan, "The Revolutionary Strategy of Mao Tse-tung," *Political Science Quarterly* 70 (Sept. 1955), quoted in Young, *Negotiating with the Chinese Communists,* p. 376.

lication, sponsored by the American Society of International Law, an effort has begun to look at China as others see her—not the maverick of the international community but a state which abides by its international agreements.

6 / The Genesis of the Territorial Issue in the Sino-Soviet Dialogue: Substantive Dispute or Ideological Pas de Deux?

George Ginsburgs and Carl Pinkele

Perhaps the most intriguing aspect of the current political quarrel between Moscow and Peking is the territorial one. Since the rest of the Sino-Soviet verbal exchange is usually couched in esoteric terms while disagreements over frontiers tend, by their very complexion, to be concrete and juridically assessable, we felt that focusing on this facet of the problem could produce a valid legal analysis of the parties' respective claims while shedding added light on the nature or at least the mechanics of the more general controversy. Thus, the purpose of this paper is threefold: (1) to trace the early course of the two countries' recent debate over border questions; (2) to examine the component elements of each regime's case at the germinating stage, from the standpoint both of matter and form; and (3) to evaluate, if possible, the significance of the territorial rights then asserted by the opponents as an independent source of contention and as an index to the quality of the broader clash of views and interests which has led to their present confrontation.

BACKGROUND

As we now know, the topic of frontier "adjustments" is not an entirely new item on the record of the Soviet and Chinese Communist governments' diplomatic business with one another.

NOTE: This is a revised and updated version of a paper originally prepared for the panel on "China and International Order" of the American Society of International Law and discussed at its meeting of December 7, 1968. The authors gratefully acknowledge their indebtedness to the participants for the many constructive remarks and suggestions concerning the essay's substance and organization. These have been incorporated into the present article to the extent that the space and format limitations have permitted.

In principle, the advent of the Chinese Communist Party to power on the mainland should not have caused any undue difficulties along the Sino-Soviet border. True, article 55 of the Common Program of the Chinese People's Political Consultative Conference of September 29, 1949,[1] declaring that the "Central People's Government of the People's Republic of China shall study the treaties and agreements concluded between the Kuomintang and foreign governments, and shall recognize, abrogate, revise, or renegotiate them according to their respective contents," presumably applied to all the states concerned, not exempting the Soviet Union, and to all manner of agreements, frontier pacts included. Yet, the precise effect of that clause on the position of the USSR's existing borders with China remains unclear.

This key formula expressly encompassed only "the treaties and agreements concluded between the Kuomintang and foreign governments." The Soviet Union's operative boundary line with China does not owe its origins to any accords entered into with the Kuomintang administration (the Mongolian question will be dealt with below). Indeed, even in their Agreement on General Principles for the Settlement of Problems of May 31, 1924[2] (which, though signed with a predecessor of the Kuomintang [KMT] regime, nevertheless continued to regulate relations between the USSR and China following the KMT's accession to power), the contracting states merely confirmed that they would "redemarcate their national boundaries" at a conference to be held within one month from that day to "conclude and carry out the detailed arrangements." These arrangements, in turn, would be completed as soon as possible and, in any case, not later than six months from the date of the opening of the parley. "Pending such redemarcation," the parties agreed "to maintain the present boundaries." However, the conference, which should have met almost at once, was only staged in 1925 and, it is now

1. Text in *The Important Documents of the First Plenary Session of the Chinese PPCC* (Peking: Foreign Languages Press, 1949), and A. P. Blaustein, ed., *Fundamental Legal Documents of Communist China* (South Hackensack, N.J.: Rothman, 1962), pp. 34–53; text in Russian in E. F. Kovalev, ed., *Zakonodatelnye akty Kitaiskoi Narodnoi Respubliki* (Legislative acts of the Chinese People's Republic; Moscow: Inlitizdat, 1952), pp. 50–65, and *Obrazovanie Kitaiskoi Narodnoi Respubliki, dokumenty i materialy* (Creation of the Chinese People's Republic, documents and materials; Moscow: Gospolitizdat, 1950), pp. 30–49.

2. *Sbornik deistvuyushchikh dogovorov, soglashenii i konventsii, zaklyuchennykh SSSR s inostrannymi gosudarstvami* (Collection of treaties, agreements, and conventions concluded by the USSR with foreign states and in force; Moscow: Gospolitizdat, 1925), vol. II, pp. 16–23 (hereafter, *SDD*); *League of Nations Treaty Series* 37:175–191; L. Shapiro, ed., *Soviet Treaty Series* (Washington, D.C.: Georgetown University Press, 1950), vol. I, pp. 242–243.

recalled "owing to the historical conditions at the time, no agreement was reached by the two sides on the boundary question, no redemarcation of the boundary between the two countries was made and no new equal treaty was concluded by the two countries."[3]

Thus, while the 1924 agreement spoke elsewhere of the decision of the parties to annul at the proposed session "all conventions, treaties, agreements, protocols, contracts, etc., concluded between the Government of China and the Tsarist Government and to replace them with new treaties, agreements, etc., on the basis of equality, reciprocity and justice, as well as the spirit of the Declarations of the Soviet Government of the years 1919 and 1920," nothing came of these grandiose plans and the old location of the frontier stayed unchanged. Manchukuo rose and fell, pitched battles were fought between Soviet and Japanese forces over where the boundary should run in certain sections, but to no avail: the territorial *status quo* was not seriously disturbed throughout.

The Mongolian affair constitutes an exception. By agreeing in the August 14, 1945, exchange of notes[4] with the USSR to recognize the independence of Outer Mongolia "in her existing boundaries," if a plebiscite conducted after the defeat of Japan showed it to be the wish of the local population, and by honoring its promise when that condition was subsequently fulfilled, the Kuomintang regime, in concert with the Soviet authorities, sanctioned the removal of the issue of defining the

3. "Statement of the Government of the People's Republic of China, May 24, 1969," *China Reconstructs*, no. 7, Suppl.:4 (1969); *PR*, no. 22:6 (1969).

According to M. S. Kapitsa, *Sovetsko-Kitaiskie otnosheniya* (Soviet-Chinese relations; Moscow: Gospolitizdat, 1958), pp. 154–155, citing Soviet archives, the conference opened in August 1925. The subcommissions which it created sat more or less regularly until April 1926. The text of a consular convention was drafted. The only item left unresolved was the Soviet proposal that the consuls have the right concurrently to function as personnel of the People's Commissariat for Foreign Trade, the right to include in the staff of the consulate the necessary number of employees, and the right to dispatch diplomatic couriers. A Chinese draft of a trade treaty was discussed, but since it did not take into account the USSR's monopoly of foreign trade it proved unacceptable to the Russians, whereas the Soviet draft submitted at the end of 1925 was rejected by the Chinese. Beginning in March 1926, the subcommissions dealing with the trade treaty and the consular convention no longer met due to the illness of the Chinese representative. The juridical subcommission drafted a convention on the extradition of criminals and a treaty on legal assistance in civil matters. A convention on inheritance also raised no difficulties. The subcommission on the demarcation of the frontier only held three meetings. The subcommission on claims was presented a Chinese claim in the amount of forty million gold rubles, primarily in compensation for material losses suffered by Chinese traders in connection with the revolution in Russia and the devaluation of the ruble.

4. *Pravda*, Aug. 27, 1945, and *Izvestiya*, Aug. 28, 1945; *Vedomosti Verkhovnogo Soveta SSSR*, no. 59 (1945); *UNTS* 10:322–323, 314–315, 342–344 (1947).

central portion of the erstwhile Sino-Soviet frontier from their common agenda. Henceforth, the Soviet Union and the People's Republic of Mongolia (PRM) would be responsible for determining the configuration of the PRM's northern contour, and China and Mongolia would fix the limits of the latter's southern confines.

This 1945 transaction clearly lay within the scope of article 55 and, in fact, the USSR and the People's Republic of China (PRC), in an exchange of notes on February 14, 1950,[5] thought it advisable tacitly to reconfirm the arrangement. This was done by arriving at a fresh understanding in which both countries formally acknowledged that "the independent status of the People's Republic of Mongolia is fully guaranteed as a result of the referendum held in Outer Mongolia in 1945, which attested to its desire for independence and as a result of the People's Republic of China's establishment of diplomatic relations with it." In roundabout fashion, the Soviets thus got the Communist Chinese to sanction, if not the letter, at least the juridical consequences of the 1945 correspondence pertaining to Mongolia. While the Treaty of Friendship and Alliance and the Agreement on the Chinese Eastern Railroad, Dairen and Port Arthur of August 14, 1945, and all the documents appended thereto, were now explicitly cancelled, the companion communications concerning Mongolia were never mentioned and, instead, Peking's constructive acquiescence in the outcome of the 1945 plebiscite amounted practically to acceptance on its part "to inherit" the underlying agreement. That may explain the otherwise anomalous passage encountered in Vice-Premier Ch'en Yi's remarks at a press conference summoned on September 29, 1965, and attended by Chinese and foreign newsmen. Recalling that "in 1945 Chiang Kai-shek's government concluded a treaty with the Government of the Soviet Union recognizing the Mongolian People's Republic," he observed that "after its founding, New China *succeeded to the commitment* and recognized Mongolia as a socialist country."[6] (Emphasis added.) Significantly, the latest messages did not repeat the earlier reference to (and ensuing endorsement of) Mongolia's "existing borders." The core problem of Mongolia's right to its own legal personality, though, seemed finally to have been put to rest.

5. *Vedomosti Verkhovnogo Soveta SSSR*, no. 36 (1950); *SDD* (Moscow: Gospolitizdat, 1957), vol. XIV, pp. 17–19; *UNTS* 226:10–11, 16–19 (1956).

6. *Vice-Premier Chen Yi Answers Questions Put by Correspondents* (Peking: Foreign Languages Press, 1966), p. 21.

The language of article 55 is permissive, not mandatory. The successor regime thereby simply served notice on all states which had in the past signed treaties and agreements with the Kuomintang administration that it now considered itself free to scrutinize the substance of these instruments and to reach appropriate conclusions whether to keep them in force, amend them, or supplant them with a different text. No a priori or automatic negation of the international obligations incurred by the preceding sovereign was presently envisaged, but rather an *ad hoc* process of critical review of the pertinent materials would objectively disclose which of these agreements could be retained by the PRC, which had to undergo minor surgery to fit its revolutionary philosophy, and which were beyond salvation. Since no time limit was set for accomplishing the "sorting out" procedure, the fate of these treaties from the KMT era meanwhile remained in doubt.

Still, the impression one gathers is that, technically, all such agreements remained valid until properly denounced or suitably modified by the PRC leadership. This observation holds doubly true for the category of border pacts. Indeed, no less a figure than Chou En-lai reportedly indicated as much in a 1957 statement in which he said that "it was the opinion of our government that, on the question of boundary lines, demands made on the basis of formal treaties [concluded by former Chinese governments] should be respected according to general international practice."[7] This did not mean that the old boundary treaties would necessarily be permitted to function forever. On the contrary, the real expectation was that, at a propitious moment, China and each of its neighbors would work out a mutually more satisfactory and precise graph of their joint periphery, as evidenced by the premier's accompanying comment that the admitted willingness of the Peking authorities to countenance the current situation on the PRC's frontiers "by no means excluded the seeking by two friendly countries of a settlement fair and reasonable for both sides through peaceful negotiations between their governments."[8] In short, the new regime was prepared in principle to tolerate China's factual frontiers, but also anticipated their proximate segmentary resurvey at the diplomatic table.[9]

7. Quoted by Hungdah Chiu, "Certain Legal Aspects of Communist China's Treaty Practice," ASIL *Proceedings* (1967), p. 124.

8. *Ibid.*

9. Refer to Neville Maxwell, "Simmering Dispute along the Sino-Soviet Border," *The Times*, Sept. 30, 1968, p. 9: "That is the approach China has taken to the question of boundary settlement with all her neighbors. She has insisted in every

On neither count, then, did the Russians appear to have grounds for worry about the essential soundness of their operative frontier with China.[10] To be sure, this does not imply that the Soviet title to the lands acquired from the Chinese empire over the centuries was unassailable. For that matter, if need be, the charge of "unequal treaties" could always be leveled to impugn the legitimacy of Russian possession of these territories. Again, though, the Chinese Communist government displayed no inclination to resort to that nihilistic weapon indiscriminately, so here, too, the Russians saw no immediate cause for anxiety.

Nevertheless, even before the political frictions between Moscow and Peking degenerated into today's open split, the Chinese, on three separate occasions, managed to bring up the potentially explosive item of boundary "corrections." Not too surprisingly, the subject of Mongolia was the earliest to crop up: It was an issue in private Sino-Soviet discussions in Peking in 1954. The published accounts of what transpired differ, since the parties now recall the event in order to accuse each other of bad faith or worse. To hear Peking tell the story, "according to the Yalta agreement, the Soviet Union, under the pretext of guaranteeing the independence of Mongolia, has actually placed that country under its domination . . . In 1954, when Khrushchev and Bulganin came to China, we raised this question, but they refused to talk with us."[11] In rebuttal, the Soviets contend that

---

case that the boundaries should be negotiated anew. But while refusing to accept the legality of boundaries imposed by the imperialists, she has in every case shown herself willing to accept the general alignments drawn by those imperialists. Such was the case in China's boundary settlements with Burma, Pakistan and Afghanistan; and in her settlements with Mongolia and Nepal, China agreed to the boundaries that those smaller neighbours claimed. All these governments found that her interest was not in regaining territory but in removing what the Chinese saw as the stains of history. They found China tough but reasonable at the negotiating table and they emerged with their boundaries confirmed on the alignments they claimed, with minor variations upon which they had agreed with the Chinese in a pragmatic process of give and take."

10. Except, of course, that a proximate physical demarcation of the boundary line between the two countries was urgently needed since only short sections of it were ever surveyed and properly defined and riverine boundaries, especially on major navigational waterways and in fluvial basins which provide much of the livelihood for a relatively dense population on both banks of the stream, are notoriously productive of disputes and require complex, up-to-date treaties to sanction them. As a matter of practical importance, then, an on-the-spot delimitation of their joint frontier was long overdue.

11. *Sekai shūhō,* Tokyo, Aug. 11, 1964; *Pravda,* Sept. 2, 1964; *Current Digest of the Soviet Press,* no. 34:6–7 (1964). The July 11, 1964, issue of the *People's Daily* merely reported that on the previous day (July 10) Chairman Mao received thirty Japanese friends and had a "personal and friendly talk with them." No mention was made of the contents of the conversation, however.

> They [the Chinese leaders] would like to deprive the M.P.R. of independence and make it a Chinese province. It was precisely on this that the C.P.R. leaders proposed the "reaching of agreement" to N.S. Khrushchev and other Soviet comrades during their visit to Peking in 1954. N.S. Khrushchev naturally refused to discuss this question and told the Chinese leaders that the destiny of the Mongolian people was determined not in Peking and not in Moscow but in Ulan-Bator, that the question of Mongolia's statehood could be settled only by the country's working people themselves and by nobody else.[12]

The timing of the encounter is suggestive, for it coincides with the end of Soviet influence in Sinkiang. Once again involved in various vital sectors of the region's economy long monopolized by the Russians, the Chinese Communists in four brief years engineered their reversion to Peking's sole control. Khrushchev's trip to the PRC in 1954 to all intents and purposes marked the close of an epoch as, with his acquiescence in the dissolution of the Sino-Soviet joint-stock corporations, the curtain rang down on the last reminders of the once preponderant Soviet "presence" in this corner of Inner Asia. With that as an example, one can easily imagine the Chinese next pressing the Soviets to relax their grip on Mongolia and arrive at a modus vivendi that would give the Chinese an equal voice in Mongolian affairs, in the hope that ultimately Mongolia, just as Sinkiang previously, would slip out of the Soviet orbit and gravitate toward China. There is little doubt that Chinese aspirations ran in the direction of the imminent "voluntary return" of Mongolia to its traditional association with the Chinese nation. After all, as everyone is fond of pointing out, back in 1936, Mao, not noted for a short memory, had explained to Edgar Snow that "when the people's revolution has been victorious in China, the Outer Mongolian republic will automatically become a part of the Chinese federation, at their own will."[13]

12. *Pravda*, Sept. 2, 1964; *In Connection with Mao Tse-tung's Talk with a Group of Japanese Socialists* (Moscow: Novosti, 1964), pp. 11–12; *International Affairs*, no. 10:83; *Current Digest of the Soviet Press*, no. 34:5 (1964).

13. Edgar Snow, *Red Star Over China* (rev. ed., New York: Random House, 1938), pp. 88–89, note 1. More recently, the exchange of letters between the PRC and the USSR of February 14, 1950, which confirmed Mongolia's right to self-rule used, interestingly enough, the expression "independent status" (*tu-li ti-wei* in the Chinese original; *nezavisimoe polozhenie* in the Russian text) in describing Mongolia's current position, not plain "independence." This may be a normal circumlocution in the Chinese language, but sounds strange in both Russian and English: "independent status" and "nezavisimoe polozhenie" intimate a temporal quality, a de facto phenomenon, with distinct undertones of impermanence. "Independence" conveys the flavor of something fixed, crystallized; "status" evolves, changes, emerges, grows, declines, and vanishes—in sum, fluctuates. An-

Thus, what the Chinese probably wanted was a fair share in the management of Mongolia and a chance to convert the Mongols to the idea of a "free reunion" of their country with the Chinese Motherland. The Soviets, at a guess, wished to preserve Mongolia's strong ties with Moscow and blocked the Chinese bid for a deal by appealing to Mongolia's sovereignty, which on balance spelled the maintenance of the system now in existence, together with its pro-Russian orientation. Doubtless, neither side was in this instance guilty of the horrible designs the other was later to impute to it: The Russians did not "occupy" Mongolia and insist on perpetuating their hegemony over the area; conversely, the Chinese did not try to persuade the Soviets to consent to a unilateral incorporation of Mongolia into the Chinese domain. More subtle tactics were employed by both to promote their local ambitions, nicely cloaked behind technical talk of border rectifications.

Of the second occasion on which the Chinese brought up the question of boundary corrections, there is only the Chinese version, and this account, too, is retrospective. "At the interview with Premier Khrushchev in January 1957," Chou En-lai is quoted as saying, "I requested that the U.S.S.R. make proper arrangements for the territorial issues covering Japan, China, the Middle East, and the Eastern European countries including Finland. I could not get a satisfactory answer from him then, but the announcement of the issue was kept secret because the Sino-Soviet dispute was not public at the time."[14] Not much can be gleaned from this alone, but the highly unusual circumstances in which the statement was made furnish plenty of food for thought. In effect, Chou En-lai's visit to Moscow followed upon his tour of Eastern Europe ostensibly launched in an attempt to heal the widening rift between the Soviet Union and the neighboring Communist regimes in

---

other possible—and more innocuous—explanation for the choice of words might lie in the wish to avoid any suggestion that "independence" was now being granted by the PRC to Mongolia and, instead, to stress the point that the present correspondence merely aimed at confirming the *existing* "independent status" of Outer Mongolia stemming from the 1945 referendum and ratified by the establishment in the meantime of diplomatic relations between the two countries.

To compound the uncertainty, this particular diplomatic exchange (which the Chinese Communists formally designate as a joint "public statement") is not published in the PRC's official treaty series, although it does appear in the compilation *WCC 1949–1950*, vol. I (1957), pp. 74–75.

The authors are grateful to Gene T. Hsiao, Professor, Southern Illinois University, for the above information and help with the Chinese sources.

14. *Asahi shimbun*, Tokyo, Aug. 1, 1964; Dennis J. Doolin, *Territorial Claims in the Sino-Soviet Conflict* (Stanford, Calif.: Hoover Institution Studies No. 7, 1965), pp. 45–46.

the wake of the Polish and Hungarian events. Outwardly playing the part of neutral moderator and urging both sides to tone down their demands and settle their quarrels amicably, he meanwhile assiduously cultivated in his audiences the image of China as an impartial arbiter on the correct terms of association between "proletarian nations" and an authority on the etiquette of state conduct within the self-styled "socialist Commonwealth," with judicious praise and criticism for everybody involved.

The East Europeans were wisely counseled not to indulge in Russian-baiting and not to push the Kremlin to where it might lose patience and turn violent, applauded for their awareness of the "activities and danger of reactionary elements" in their midst, and pressed to eradicate these "enemies" ruthlessly. And, in the next breath, the Soviet leaders were chided, by inference, for neglecting "the principle of equality among nations in their mutual relations," warned that "such a mistake, by nature, is the error of bourgeois chauvinism," that, particularly when committed by a big country, it "inevitably results in serious damage to the solidarity and common cause of the socialist countries," and, by example, exhorted to eternal vigilance "to prevent the error of big nation chauvinism in relations with socialist countries and others."[15]

In short, with the Soviets in disarray, the Chinese seized the opportunity to pose simultaneously as champions of the "just aspirations" of the smaller Communist states vis-à-vis the Soviet colossus and staunch defenders of the "integral unity of the socialist camp." Presumably, for these sterling services, Moscow would be heavily indebted to Peking for helping restore order and discipline in Russia's front-yard, the East European states would feel grateful to it for espousing their cause against unreasonable Soviet pretensions, and, as a consequence, Chinese influence in the region would be immeasurably enhanced. Whether or not the Chinese really fancied themselves in the role of official partner of the Russians in setting the general policy in Communist East Europe is hard to tell. Such calculations do not lie beyond the realm of credibility. At any rate, whatever their ulterior objectives, the Chinese at this point did not hesitate to lecture their "Western allies" on the accepted norms of international "socialist" behavior or recommend to them specific solutions for their present difficulties.

15. Statement by the Government of the People's Republic of China on the Declaration of the Soviet Government on Relations among Socialist States, November 1, 1956, in P. E. Zinner, ed., *National Communism and Popular Revolt in Eastern Europe* (New York: Columbia University Press, 1956), pp. 492–495.

No conflicting territorial claims were publicly aired at this stage. The atmosphere was sufficiently heated up without looking for extra aggravations, but the Russians themselves had, all too unwittingly, introduced the subject, at least in a manner of speaking, when they issued the famous "Declaration on the Foundations of Development and Further Consolidation of Friendship and Cooperation between the Soviet Union and Other Socialist States" of October 30, 1956.[16] Therein Moscow took the unprecedented step of openly endorsing the proposition that "the countries of the great commonwealth of socialist nations can build their relations only on the principle of full equality, respect for territorial integrity, state independence and sovereignty, and non-interference in one another's domestic affairs." The Chinese were quick to pick up the item and the PRC government's Statement of November 1, 1956, in response to the Soviet pronouncement, put stronger emphasis on that theme than had the Russians. For Peking, "mutual relations between socialist countries all the more so should be established on the basis of these five principles," since "only in this way are the socialist countries able to achieve genuine fraternal friendship and solidarity. . . ."[17]

The explicit mention of "respect for territorial integrity" in the Kremlin's manifesto, prominently echoed in the Chinese document, may very well have inspired the Chinese delegation to broach here the question of possible frontier "adjustments" by the USSR in favor of several of the surrounding states. One can readily imagine Chou En-lai suggesting to Khrushchev that, if the modus vivendi between the USSR and its confederates were now to be thoroughly overhauled, a few territorial concessions to members of the inner family, China included, might be a tangible method of demonstrating the new approach and the most effective means of cementing the unity of the "socialist" world. Furthermore, as long as the current Soviet leadership had recognized the value of the "neutralist" countries and was seeking appropriate ways of expressing its support for them and of convincing other peoples to embrace that attitude, suitable border compromises for the benefit of Finland, Japan, and various lands in the Middle East could offer the best answer.

16. *Pravda,* Oct. 31, 1956; *Pod znamenem proletarskogo internatsionalizma, sbornik materialov* (Under the banner of proletarian internationalism, collection of materials; Moscow: Gospolitizdat, 1957), pp. 15–18; *East Europe,* no. 3:51–52 (1957).

17. See note 15.

It is most unlikely that Chou En-lai ever nurtured hopes of detaching large chunks of peripheral Soviet territory and parceling them out among the interested contiguous states or would even have approved then of any scheme of the sort. What he probably did contemplate was a process whereby the Soviet Union would negotiate afresh with its neighbors on where their respective boundary line ought to run, show a spirit of conciliation and subscribe to technical changes in the corresponding section of the border to accommodate the legitimate grievances of the other side. True, the Soviet Union would stand to lose a bit of acreage as a result; in return, though, it would gain frontiers guaranteed by iron-clad treaties concluded between equals and would be trading some space for goodwill, a patch of ground for political advantages accruing from increased confidence, esteem, and loyalty on the part of those handled with such sympathy and understanding.

Not surprisingly, the Russians betrayed little appreciation for their chief ally's undisguised inclination to sound generous with Soviet soil. In fact, this lack of enthusiasm may help explain why the unfortunate reference to relations between "fraternal peoples" resting on the so-called "Five Principles," while it still appears in the joint Soviet-Chinese declaration issued to commemorate Chou En-lai's stay in the Soviet Union,[18] thereafter suddenly dropped out of the official Soviet lexicon. Thenceforth, to capture the essence of the intramural activities of the "socialist" community, "proletarian internationalism" is again deemed to be a more fitting term of art than "peaceful co-existence."

The third probe about border corrections dates back to 1960, when Chou En-lai "at a press conference in Katmandu in Nepal on April 28 . . . was asked whether there were any 'unestablished sections on the Soviet-Chinese frontiers' and he replied: 'There are insignificant discrepancies in the maps, easy to solve peacefully'."[19] Apparently, the incident had a private sequel: On "August 22 and September 21, 1960, the Chinese Government took the initiative in proposing to the Soviet Government that negotiations be held" on the topic of a comprehensive

18. *Izvestiya,* Jan. 19, 1957; *Deklaratsii, zayavleniya i kommyunike Sovetskogo pravitelstva s pravitelstvami inostrannykh gosudarstv 1954–1957gg.* (Declarations, statements, and communiqués of the Soviet government with the governments of foreign states, 1954–1957; Moscow: Gospolitizdat, 1957), pp. 189–197.

19. Statement of the Government of the People's Republic of China, May 24, 1969, *China Reconstructs,* no. 7, Suppl.:6, and *PR,* no. 22:8 (1969); Declaration of the Government of the U.S.S.R. of March 29, 1969, *Pravda,* Mar. 30, 1969, p. 1; *Izvestiya,* Mar. 30, 1969, pp. 1–2; *Soviet News,* no. 5483:3–4, 14 (1969).

boundary settlement.[20] As far as is known, nothing came of thes overtures either.

The above three episodes represent the sum total of hard data on concrete Sino-Soviet discussions that developed during this phase on the status of Russia's boundaries. The available information is meager; yet, the record of these early years already contains the germs of the present situation. First, in all cases the initiative for bringing up the subject of frontier revisions has rested with the Chinese; they are the ones who seem to have shown real interest in talking about the issue, whereas the Soviets consistently have shied away. Second, although Peking's spokesmen have attempted to engage the Russians in serious conversation on the USSR boundary line in certain areas, their efforts have not been made public. Although reportedly the request to keep the conversations quiet emanated from the Kremlin, the Chinese have given their consent with no sign of hesitation and have faithfully abided by the compact. The "indiscretion" at Katmandu is an exception to the rule, but one has reason to believe that what happened on this occasion was not part of the original script, for Chinese sources now describe the episode as having been triggered by "the provocative question of an American correspondent."[21] Still, for a statement voiced in a relatively open forum, it went virtually unheeded. More important, Chou's answer was couched in such deprecatory terms as to make the issue sound almost trivial. Both previous bids to explore the matter further with the Russians were pursued in strict confidence and only leaked out nine years later. Third, while the Chinese evidently felt quite free to raise the border question at opportune moments, they never formulated fixed demands or advanced specific claims in that connection, but dealt only in generalities.

A distinctive pattern thus emerges. The Chinese tender clear notice to their Soviet associates that they view the frontier problem as a live issue. However, they also think of it as a private affair, best left unadvertised, and throughout treat it as a piece of business which, albeit deserving of attention, conveys no sense of imminent crisis. Moreover, Peking consistently advocates a negotiated settlement, without prejudging either the character or the extent of the territorial concessions which the Russians might eventually decide to grant as a

20. Statement of the PRC Government, May 24, 1969, *China Reconstructs*, p. 5; *PR*, no. 22:7 (1969).
21. *China Reconstructs*, no. 7, Suppl.:6 (1969); *PR*, no. 22:8 (1969).

result of such diplomatic pourparlers, so that, by the looks of it, the actual procedure perhaps counts more than the substantive terms of any particular bargain struck by the parties. By contrast, the Soviets simply refuse to debate the topic.

The incidental details likewise fit neatly into the assembled mosaic. For instance, much has recently been made of the fact that the Chinese Communists have on various occasions published maps in which vast tracts of land around China's rim, including portions of Russia, were designated as "lost territories." The most famous episode entails a map featured in a history text printed in Peking in 1954[22] purporting to identify all the nearby areas that once "belonged" to China and of which it was despoiled in the last century by the "imperialist powers," Russia among them. The technique is not new—maps have often served in the past as a convenient method of airing border claims and "scientifically proving" the validity of the rights being asserted. The trouble in this case is that there is no evidence that the Chinese Communist regime ever attempted to use the material in this manner.

First, an obscure volume issued in the Chinese language is hardly a suitable vehicle for such purposes, for if the intention was to let the adversary know how Peking felt about the profile of their common border, the chances of that aim being duly accomplished through this medium are poor. Next, the available data tend to indicate that while the Chinese authorities did not prevent foreigners living in China from picking up copies of the book in question, they made no positive efforts to disseminate it abroad. Indeed, to believe a latter-day Soviet account frankly hostile to the Chinese and calculated to put Chinese conduct in the worst possible light, allegedly "the Chinese leaders . . . for a time kept such books and maps secret from foreigners." True or not, ten years elapsed before Moscow suddenly woke up to the "vital importance" of the message it now discovered in the map. Similarly, the Nepalese government only learned of the chart and its reference to Nepal during a visit of the Nepalese Prime Minister to the PRC, where Nepalese students in Peking brought it to his attention.

Hence, either the PRC officialdom really did restrict the volume's circulation or the map's existence was no mystery to the outside world and nobody then paid much attention to it. Again, none of this

22. Liu Pei-hua, ed., *Chung-kuo chin-tai chien-shih* (Peking: I-ch'ang shu-chü, 1954), following p. 253. Reproduced in Doolin, *Territorial Claims*, p. 16, and *The New York Times*, Sept. 6, 1964, part 4, p. 3.

substantiates the charge that Peking thus counted on laying the groundwork for challenging the legal title of certain adjacent states to a number of regions contiguous to Chinese soil. If that is what the Chinese leadership had in mind, it certainly plumped for a self-defeating procedure to attain this objective. To be sure, plain ineptitude is not ruled out but even in that respect the caliber of Peking's performance would strain credibility. A more intelligent conclusion would be to accept the experience at face value—as a relatively innocuous exercise in patriotic bombast. Otherwise, why in 1963 would the Chinese, when pressed on that score, simply repudiate the map, as though dismissing some insignificant minutia?

Admittedly, a year later at the 1964 trade fair in Mexico City, the Communist Chinese are said to have distributed a booklet containing a map that pictured the USSR's Maritime Provinces as part of China.[23] The circumstances of the occurrence would seem not to deny what we have said, but to support our thesis. Both the place and the modus operandi were utterly inappropriate for framing a legal argument for China's pretensions to territory currently owned by the Russians. Rather, the physical setting hints at a very different explanation. Moscow and Peking were then openly vying for the favor of the Latin Americans, and in that context spreading a diagram of that sort makes excellent sense: At a single stroke, the Russians are portrayed as usurpers of foreign soil, the Latin Americans recall how they themselves suffered from the depredations of US imperialism, and, in their eyes, the Soviets and the Americans are lumped together under the label of arrogant great powers preying on their weaker neighbors. The Chinese, in turn, are perceived as fellow victims of that greed. In sum, it all amounts to a skillful political maneuver, but comes nowhere near constituting any kind of a legal case. In fact, even on a strictly political plane, the move ranks as a minor gambit without serious overtones—a flanking thrust, a probing raid into the opponent's camp, and no more.

This still leaves the problem of whether the Chinese regime was not deliberately trying to manufacture a "revisionist mood" at home by sanctioning the insertion of an "inflammatory" item in a modern history textbook. The suggestion here is that the chart was not earmarked primarily for foreign consumption nor printed as a sign of an impending Chinese drive to "recover territories amputated from the mother

23. "Quarterly Chronicle and Documentation," *China Quarterly*, no. 18:241 (1964).

country," but injected into the mass educational system in order to create a propitious climate of opinion preparatory to launching a diplomatic offensive to wrest drastic territorial concessions from adjoining nations. The tactic is an old one and has much to recommend it, but its effectiveness largely hinges on the leadership's ability and willingness to mount a vocal popular campaign to dramatize and magnify the issue and soften up the intended target. That cardinal element was precisely what was lacking from the mainland scene. On the contrary, from the impression gathered by most outside observers, the experiment was apparently motivated by the same sober wish to cultivate in the younger generation pride in their land's glorious heritage which is often encountered elsewhere and which, in virtually identical guise, was standard fare in the school curricula under the previous Chinese administrations.[24] Use of the theme of a nation's heroic past to stimulate "love of country" is quite a different matter from consciously exploiting it to promote "revanchist" schemes. Since one sometimes degenerates into the other, the problem must be tackled with due caution. However, as yet there are no clues of a shift on this front from an attitude of perhaps prickly, albeit essentially still defensive, nationalism to a policy of militant irredentism.

Actually, the best evidence in support of this proposition may be found in the documented record of the public treatment accorded in Communist China in those days to the early history of Russo-Chinese competition over border districts. Thus, a thorough survey of pre-1962 Communist Chinese literature aimed at establishing the accepted instructional approach to the sensitive topic of the methods by which Russia managed to acquire the Maritime Provinces reports that "the concise histories of China which have been published on the mainland since the beginning of the Communist regime seldom specifically mention Russian expansion into the Maritime territory. Even when such reference is included, efforts are made to avoid elaboration of the Russian episode. Consequently, especially in the books intended for mass consumption, such important events as the conclusion of the Chinese-Russian Treaties of Aigun, Tientsin and Peking have simply been omitted."[25] "Advanced academic treatises," judging by this study, have been less reticent in painting an accurate picture of Russian

24. Li Tsung-jen and Chang Hsin-hai, Letter to the Editors, *The New York Times*, Sept. 18, 1963, p. 38.

25. Peter S.H. Tang, *Russian Expansion into the Maritime Province: The Contemporary Soviet and Chinese Communist Views* (Washington, D.C., 1962), p. 47.

ambitions in this sector and the stratagems used to realize Moscow's goals. On balance, though, the most striking thing here is the obvious

> disparity of presentation of Russian activities in the Maritime territory between the Chinese Communist accounts intended for mass consumption and those of a more scholarly nature. In the former case, the general policy would seem to be one of avoiding mention of the episodes of Russian expansion on the grounds that this is remote in terms of time, having occurred a century ago, and also in terms of space. Russian activities in the Maritime territory were far removed from the center of activities in China and consequently of little concern to the masses in their daily life. The Chinese Communist historians can gloss over these incidents on the safe grounds that this is the proper historical perspective and position for the events. At the same time, they can be sure of avoiding any unnecessary irritation to their present-day Soviet ally. This is entirely in keeping with the great emphasis placed on proletarian internationalism. It is also a means to eliminate any possible grounds for sentiments of great nation chauvinism or small-nation narrow nationalism in Sino-Soviet relations.[26]

A second experience indicates the same desire for discreet mutual accommodation. In this instance, a newspaper story concerning certain cartographic discrepancies between Soviet and Chinese versions of the exact location of the PRC boundary line with the USSR, Mongolia, and Afghanistan dwelled on the likely diplomatic implications of these developments in the context of the widening ideological rift but conceded that

> as Western mapmakers and political experts puzzle over these map differences, there is no indication that either the Soviet Union or Communist China is concerned about the matter. Except for the cartographic evidence, neither side appears to discuss the matter in its official publications.[27]

Finally, the various policy declarations issued in that period dealing with the status of the PRC's frontiers also followed this set pattern. Typical, for instance, were Chou En-lai's remarks at the Bandung Conference to the effect that

> With some of these countries [possessing common borders with the PRC] we have not yet finally fixed our border-line and we are ready to do so with our neighboring countries. But before doing so, we are willing to maintain the present situation by acknowledging that those parts of our border are parts which are undetermined. We are ready to restrain our Government and people from crossing even one step across our border. If such things

26. *Ibid.*
27. *The New York Times*, Feb. 26, 1961, p. 20.

should happen, we would like to admit our mistake. As to the determination of common borders which we are going to undertake with our neighboring countries, we shall use only peaceful means and we shall not permit any other kinds of method. In no case shall we change this.[28]

Then, on October 1, 1959, Chou, in talking about the number of frontiers with other nations that had not been demarcated, reportedly reiterated that China had claims on all of them and that the countries involved comprised the USSR, Mongolia, Pakistan, North Korea, North Vietnam, Burma, and Nepal, but again did not embroider on his statement. More to the point, during the Hundred Flowers interlude in 1957, several prominent Chinese asserted that they saw little to choose between Tsarist and Soviet imperialism, and the Party quickly moved to suppress these heretical views.[29]

In summary, prior to 1963, the Communist Chinese hierarchy lost no opportunity to remind the states abutting on the PRC that frontier questions still remained open. In the process it took good care not to sound either belligerent or menacing as it firmly insisted that each portion of its boundary line must be renegotiated and in some spots drawn anew. While recognizing that until this was accomplished the problem could not be satisfactorily resolved, the Chinese also let it be known that they were nonetheless prepared to live with the existing regime on their borders for the moment and to bide their time. Its claim properly staked out now, Peking could sit back and wait for the other party to tire of the game and head for the bargaining table or, if worst came to worst, put a modicum of pressure in the right place to hasten the conference or, *in extremis,* heat up the local temperature somewhat to convince the opposite camp of the wisdom of attempting to settle the affair in friendly fashion without further delay. None of this impresses the objective onlooker as intrinsically unreasonable, nor will the recorded practice sustain any of the gory tales since circulated which strain to discredit the leaders of the PRC by trying to cast them in the role of megalomaniacs bent on conquering half the world in pursuit of a dream to restore the Middle Kingdom as it stood when at the pinnacle of its power and splendor.

No doubt the outburst of violence on the Sino-Indian border for a

28. Quoted by F. Watson, *The Frontiers of China* (New York: Praeger, 1966), pp. 87–88.
29. See, for example, "Huang Chi-hsiang Unmasked as a Two-faced, Anti-Communist, and Anti-Socialist Monster," NCNA, Peking, July 29, 1957.

while succeeded in injecting a jarring note into this tableau of serenity and self-restraint; it did not, however, seriously discredit the regional image Peking was striving to project, since in the surrounding countries—and, indeed, elsewhere as well—the uneasy feeling often prevailed that the Indians through their own stubbornness had contributed mightily to sparking the explosion and that the Chinese had demonstrated superior tactical skill by winning on the battlefield and then unilaterally withdrawing from the areas they had overrun. Having thus vindicated the status quo by force of arms, they left the other side with no option but to maintain the old de facto boundary line or assume the responsibility for trying to alter it by military means, thereby placing India in a very awkward position in the eyes of the international community.

KHRUSHCHEV'S GAMBIT

The opening salvo in the recent war of words (before they turned into bullets on a few occasions during 1969) was fired by the Russians. Stung to the quick by Peking's accusations of "adventurism" in introducing missiles into Cuba and "capitulationism" in removing them under US pressure, Khrushchev, in his speech before the Supreme Soviet on December 12, 1962, launched a broad counterattack against his Chinese critics. Quoting the relevant passage in his address in full will serve to pinpoint the proper sequence of these events and permit a more precise analysis of the complexion of the ensuing altercation. Said Khrushchev to the detractors of his role during the Caribbean crisis:

> One must be very cautious and not rush in with irresponsible charges, such as that some carry out an orthodox policy while others pursue a mistaken policy, some are attacking imperialism and do not tolerate it, while others allegedly display liberalism. These questions can be rightly understood, and different actions can be correctly assessed, only if one takes into account the time, place and circumstances in which one has to operate.
>
> India, for instance, achieved the liberation of Goa, Diu and Daman. Those were vestiges of colonialism on Indian soil. Even when the British colonialists had been expelled from India, Portugal retained her colonies there, colonies which disseminated the foul stench of colonialism. India, and her government, showed patience and tolerated this for several years, but then threw out the colonialists. Did they act rightly? Of course, they did! Incidentally, when this question was discussed in the Security Council, the United States and Great Britain tried, in point of actual fact, to have India proclaimed an

aggressor. They tried to set the public opinion of the world against India. It was only the veto of the Soviet Union that prevented them from achieving this.

One more example. When Indonesia gained her freedom, the Dutch colonialists tried to retain West Irian. The Indonesian people and their government, however, compelled the colonialists to withdraw from West Irian.

We did what we could to help Indonesia in her struggle, and we welcome the liberation of West Irian, and her reunification with free Indonesia.

Macao is situated at the mouth of the Chuchiang River, on the coast of China. It is a small territory and not easily to be spotted on the map. It was leased by the Portuguese way back in the middle of the sixteenth century and in 1887 they wrested it completely from China and made it their colony. The British colony of Hong Kong is there also—it lies in the Delta of the Hsichiang River, literally below the heart of such an important town as Kwangchow (Canton). The odour coming from these places is by no means sweeter than that which was released by colonialism in Goa.

But no one will denounce the People's Republic of China for leaving these fragments of colonialism intact.

It would be wrong to prod China into actions of some kind which she considers untimely. If the government of the People's Republic of China tolerates Macao and Hong Kong it clearly has good reasons for doing so. It would, therefore, be ridiculous to levy against it the accusation that these are concessions to the British and Portuguese colonialists, that this is appeasement.

But perhaps that is a retreat from Marxism-Leninism? Nothing of the kind! It means that the government of the People's Republic of China is taking into account reality, the actual possibilities.

And this is by no means because the Chinese are less sensitive to colonialism than the Indians, that they are more tolerant towards Salazar than India is. No, our Chinese friends hate colonialism just as every revolutionary does. But they are clearly basing themselves on their conditions, they are acting in accordance with their own views and are showing patience.

But does this mean that we must condemn them for this, that we must claim that they have retreated from Marxism-Leninism? No, it doesn't. That would be ridiculous.

As a result of a variety of conditions, one sometimes has to live not among fragrant roses but amidst thorns and sometimes even in close proximity to the colonialists' outhouses.

But the hour will come when our Chinese friends will find this position intolerable and will tell the colonialists in a loud voice "Get out!" And we shall welcome that step. But it is for our Chinese friends themselves to decide when this is to be done.

We are not hurrying them. On the contrary, we say: "Decide this matter in the way that your country's interests, and the interests of the whole socialist camp, demand.[30]

30. *Zasedaniya Verkhovnogo Soveta SSSR shestogo sozyva, vtoraya sessiya (10–13 dekabrya 1962g.), stenograficheskii otchet* (Sessions of the Supreme Soviet of the USSR, sixth convocation, second session, December 10–13, 1962, stenographic report; Moscow: Izd. Verkhsoveta SSSR, 1963), pp. 492–493; *The Present*

The thrust of the Russian leader's argument thus lay in a plea for a pragmatic approach to vital questions of foreign affairs, eschewing dogmatic judgments and rigid doctrinal slogans in favor of effective tactics and practical considerations. He did more, though, than simply call for a halt to ideological recriminations between China and the USSR and went beyond the mere passive defense of the merits of his administration's past performance in the field of international politics. Indeed, he proceeded to find fault with various aspects of the Communist Chinese diplomatic record. The important dimension here is the stylistic element which offers the best clue to Khrushchev's motivations in now choosing to answer his opponents and his probable intentions in broaching this particular line of inquiry.

A direct confrontation on the main issues was studiously avoided. To be sure, the juxtaposition of Peking's seeming indifference to the persistence of residues of colonialism on Chinese territory and India's and Indonesia's evident determination to wipe out all traces of imperial rule from their soil was hardly flattering to the Chinese ego, especially at a time when relations between the PRC and India were thoroughly spoiled. The invidious comparison was meant to embarrass the Chinese advocates of "revolutionary purism"—and the gambit obviously succeeded. At the same time, Khrushchev was very careful to protect his own flanks. While lauding the Indians and Indonesians, the Soviet chief insisted that he was not lecturing his Chinese allies on how to manage their private business. Nevertheless, the implication was clear—the non-Communist Indians and Indonesians had so far proved more hostile to surviving manifestations of colonialism in their backyard than had the Chinese comrades despite their oft-avowed hatred for all things imperialist.

True, the Soviet Premier professed mild surprise at how accommodating the Chinese government's attitude toward its sworn enemies looked to him, but again hastened to emphasize that he had no desire to advise the PRC leadership on the manner of dealing with the existing anomalous situation and no wish to egg it on into initiating rash measures to eject the British and Portuguese from their footholds in Hong Kong and Macao. Indeed, the closing reference to "the interests

International Situation and the Foreign Policy of the Soviet Union, Report presented by N. S. Khrushchev, First Secretary of the Communist Party of the Soviet Union and Chairman of the USSR Council of Ministers, to the Supreme Soviet, in a joint session of the Soviet of the Union and the Soviet of Nationalities, in the Great Palace of the Kremlin, on December 12th, 1962 (Soviet Booklet No. 104; London, December 1962), pp. 19–20.

of the whole socialist camp" tempered somewhat the previous impression the Soviet head of state had created, inadvertently perhaps, that he was giving his Chinese associates completely free rein in disposing of this problem.

Weighed in substantive terms, Khrushchev's message sounded quite innocuous. What he said was not new; what was significant was how he said it. Reiterating the USSR's unqualified endorsement of the "struggle by the emergent nations to eliminate all local vestiges of the colonial heritage" could not per se be expected to upset the Chinese, although singling out India and Indonesia for elaborate praise in this context was certain to irk the PRC hierarchy because of its running feud with these countries. Expressing the hope that Communist Chna too would some day soon expel the colonialists from Hong Kong and Macao was not, on the face of it, an offensive comment either, even if the accompanying allusion to China's marked slowness in tackling the job was bound to grate on Peking's nerves. Plainly, Khrushchev was throwing a few digs at his Chinese "friends." Yet, the needling was sufficiently subtle that the victim was denied a solid excuse to take umbrage; the wording was unobjectionable, the tone and accent had a cutting edge to them, hence, in the final analysis, it all boiled down to personal interpretation, leaving the responsibility for the next move up to those at whom the remarks were aimed and, in fact, inviting the latter to show their hand by bidding or dropping out of the game, while also deftly shifting onto their shoulders the onus for any ensuing "escalation" of the polemic. Meantime, Khrushchev could easily plead innocence should the Chinese claim they felt affronted by his language; and should they lash back at him he could just as readily protest that his statement had been misunderstood or deliberately distorted by the leaders of the PRC bent on picking a quarrel.

In a technical sense, one further item bears noting, since it reflected an effort by Khrushchev to establish a definite limit to the discussion he was prepared to engage in: He drew a firm distinction between the kinds of territorial problems he had in mind when urging the systematic expulsion of colonial powers from their sundry overseas possessions. He left no doubt that he was now talking about conflicts pitting imperial states endeavoring to keep their dominions and nations from whose land these had originally been carved out. Frontier disputes between two recognized and independent countries fell into an altogether separate category.

Thus, commenting on the recent large-scale fighting between China and India, he unequivocally deplored such use of force and the attendant heavy casualties each belligerent suffered. "This has grieved us deeply," he said. On the question of border disputes, "we maintain Leninist views," he claimed and proceeded to explain that "the forty-five-year experience of the Soviet Union suggests that there are no border disputes which, provided there is a mutual desire to do so, cannot be settled without resort to arms. It is from these positions that Soviet people approach the developments on the Chinese-Indian border."[31] All subsequent Soviet pronouncements on the subject have echoed these parallel themes that no boundary disagreement warrants use of force to impose a solution and that, given a modicum of good will, an acceptable answer can always be worked out through diplomatic media.

Both sides were accordingly blamed in this instance for allowing the argument to degenerate into violence and exhorted to compose their differences amicably, with greater accent, however, on Peking's role in first starting the brawl and later unilaterally suspending hostilities by pulling its troops back to the line they manned before their incursion into India's northern regions. Even so, the Chinese were simultaneously faulted for permitting the situation to get out of hand and praised for demonstrating restraint, "reasonableness," and "wisdom" in promptly terminating the unfortunate affair.

In sum, for the Russians the entire incident was cause for deep regret, and they offered their Chinese allies no material or spiritual aid or comfort in the military confrontation with India. Liquidating colonial regimes was apparently one thing, and to be warmly greeted; handling a border dispute between "friendly states" through recourse to armed might was taboo. Moscow hoped to be able to convince Peking not to confuse the two.

With all due respect for Khrushchev's skill in framing these issues in a manner best calculated to avoid a direct clash with his Communist Chinese confederates—counting on ambiguous formulas and casuistic qualifications to slant the dialogue in his favor or, alternatively, to furnish him with a convenient escape route—one nonetheless wonders at what could have motivated him to inject so dangerous a topic as the territorial issue into the ongoing debate with the Chinese critics of his administration's foreign and domestic policy. Notwithstanding

31. *Zasedaniya Verkhovnogo Soveta SSSR*, p. 504; *The Present International Situation and the Foreign Policy of the Soviet Union*, p. 29.

the multiple semantic precautions he took, springing the territorial question itself in the light of the documented record of past Russo-Chinese history seems a rather foolhardy gesture by most standards. A couple of hypotheses may account for the choice of tactics.

To begin with, the leaders of the PRC had previously made several determined attempts to involve their Soviet counterparts in a substantive discussion of the existing frontiers of the USSR. Soviet officials must have found these recurrent surreptitious efforts to extract what to them looked like consequential territorial concessions from the Soviet Union extremely irritating and possibly Khrushchev finally decided that, under the circumstances, he had nothing to lose and even stood to gain a bit by trying to smoke the Chinese out into the open on this particular item. Since the PRC spokesmen persisted in wanting to deal with this matter in private conversations, perhaps Khrushchev thought he would test their true intentions and give them a chance to air their views properly or stop striving to corral the Russians into debating the proposition. In either case, he ran little risk and, indeed, was sure of posting a propaganda victory over his opponents: if the Chinese rose to the bait, they could then be widely exposed as "territorial revisionists," a potentially serious charge in the overheated atmosphere of third world politics; if they declined, the Soviet head of state would have the satisfaction of having administered a stinging public rebuff to Mao and his associates and forced them to beat a retreat on an important point.

The second theory hinges on a certain amount of available evidence to the effect that at this juncture Khrushchev was under considerable pressure at home from the Stalinist or Maoist wing of the Party and that the "territorial gambit" may have been conceived as a deliberate ploy to outmaneuver his internal enemies: If he could unmask the Chinese hierarchy by showing that it coveted Russian soil, the pro-Peking faction in the Kremlin would *pro tanto* be put on the defensive by virtue of being labeled as ideologically aligned with a regime purportedly bent on tearing vast stretches of land away from Mother Russia. Even if the Chinese refused to take the bait, Khrushchev could still come out ahead: A major setback to the Chinese "leftists" was bound to affect negatively the position of their local adherents. Assuming the above interpretation to be correct, Khrushchev may here have turned one of the neatest tricks of his tortuous career, since he obviously managed to weather the storm and survive a while longer.

Actually, it is hard to tell which of these results the Russian leader hoped for—a concrete Chinese reflex or a success by default. With his temperament and from the perspective of the conditions in which he had to operate, the prospect of pinning his Chinese adversaries down probably attracted him more.

The crucial element in the foregoing picture is its proof of the wholly artificial nature of the controversy's origins. There was no compelling reason for Khrushchev to introduce the territorial issue when he did. That step was dictated by ulterior motives of a purely political order in no guise related to the drift of the earlier comments by the Chinese authorities which presumably triggered the response. Nothing in the episode's genesis conveys the sense of urgency or drama that usually surrounds the outbreak of an earnest territorial dispute, and in assessing the meaning of these events that symptom must certainly be included in the end equation.

On January 9, 1963, the American Communist Party issued its own statement on "The Cuban Crisis and the Struggle for World Peace"[32] in which it repeated Khrushchev's references to Taiwan, Hong Kong, and Macao and lamented China's embroilment in a military conflict with India "at the very moment when imperialism threatened the peace of the entire world." After a protracted silence, the Chinese finally accepted the challenge and an editorial in *People's Daily* of March 8, 1963, took up the cudgels on Peking's behalf.[33] Noting that "some persons have mentioned Taiwan, Hong Kong and Macao," the authors of the piece judged that "we are obliged to discuss a little of the history of imperialist aggression against China," which they did in the following terms:

> In the hundred years or so prior to the victory of the Chinese revolution, the imperialist and colonial powers—the United States, Britain, France, Tsarist Russia, Germany, Japan, Italy, Austria, Belgium, the Netherlands, Spain and Portugal—carried out unbridled aggression against China. They compelled the governments of old China to sign a large number of unequal treaties—the Treaty of Nanking of 1842, the Treaty of Aigun of 1858, the Treaty of Tientsin of 1858, the Treaty of Peking of 1860, the Treaty of Ili of

32. *The Worker*, New York, Jan. 13, 1963; *Political Affairs*, no. 2:1–6 (1963); excerpted in Doolin, *Territorial Claims*, pp. 28–29.

33. English translation in *PR*, nos. 10–11:58–62 (1963); *A Comment on the Statement of the Communist Party of the U.S.A.* (Peking: Foreign Languages Press, 1963); excerpts in A. Dallin, ed., *Diversity in International Communism, A Documentary Record, 1961–1963* (New York: Columbia University Press, 1963) pp. 809–813.

1881, the Protocol of Lisbon of 1887, the Treaty of Shimonoseki of 1895, the Convention for the Extension of Hongkong of 1898, the International Protocol of 1901, etc. By virtue of these unequal treaties, they annexed Chinese territory in the north, south, east and west and held leased territories on the seaboard and in the hinterland of China. Some seized Taiwan and the Penghu Islands, some occupied Hongkong and forcibly leased Kowloon, some put Macao under perpetual occupation, etc., etc.

At the time the People's Republic of China was inaugurated, our government declared that it would examine the treaties concluded by previous Chinese governments with foreign governments, treaties that had been left by history, and would recognize, abrogate, revise or renegotiate them according to their respective contents. In this respect, our policy towards the socialist countries is fundamentally different from our policy towards the imperialist countries. When we deal with various imperialist countries, we take differing circumstances into consideration and make distinctions in our policy. As a matter of fact, many of these treaties concluded in the past either have lost their validity, or have been abrogated or have been replaced by new ones. With regard to the outstanding issues, which are a legacy from the past, we have always held that, when conditions are ripe, they should be settled peacefully through negotiations and that, pending a settlement, the *status quo* should be maintained. Within this category are the questions of Hongkong, Kowloon and Macao and the questions of all those boundaries which have not been formally delimited by the parties concerned in each case. As for Taiwan and the Penghu Islands, they were restored to China in 1945, and the question now is the U.S. imperialist invasion and occupation of them and U.S. imperialist interference in China's internal affairs. We Chinese people are determined to liberate our own territory of Taiwan; at the same time, through the ambassadorial talks between China and the United States in Warsaw we are striving to solve the question of effecting the withdrawal of U.S. armed forces from Taiwan and the Taiwan Straits. Our position as described above accords not only with the interests of the Chinese people but also with the interests of the people of the socialist camp and the people of the world.

You are not unaware that such questions as those of Hongkong and Macao relate to the category of unequal treaties left over by history, treaties which the imperialists imposed on China. It may be asked: In raising questions of this kind, do you intend to raise all the questions of unequal treaties and have a general settlement? Has it ever entered your heads what the consequences would be? Can you seriously believe that this will do you any good?[34]

In short, if the Soviets were eager to talk about territorial problems, the Chinese were ready to accommodate them, but only on their own grounds, which happened not to coincide with those of the Russians. Plainly, the tenor of the Chinese retort constitutes in this respect a net aggravation of the quarrel between the two capitals.

For the first time, the validity of the mode of Russia's acquisition of certain areas once allegedly belonging to China was publicly contested

34. *A Comment on the Statement of the Communist Party of the U.S.A.*, pp. 12–14.

by the PRC official spokesmen. Branding, inter alia, the conventions of Aigun, Tientsin, Peking and Ili—all of which consummated the transfer of chunks of Chinese soil to Russia—unequal treaties, the Chinese leaders let it clearly be known that these agreements as well as the cessions they ratified were in principle *eo ipso* illegal. Then, by quietly altering the wording of article 55 of the Common Programme and insinuating that by dint of this clause the new sovereign had expressly retained the right "to study treaties concluded by *previous Chinese governments* with foreign governments" (emphasis added), instead of, as in the authentic text, just those concluded by the Kuomintang, Peking effectively set the stage for the eventual recognition, abrogation, revision, or renegotiation of any of these pacts that such an examination might entail.

This is not to say, as has often been done, that the Communist Chinese were advancing claims for the immediate reversion to their jurisdiction of large tracts of land incorporated into the USSR's Siberian provinces. To begin with, in adumbrating the subject of "unequal treaties," the writers of the essay were careful to couch their statements in highly tentative tones. Though the treaties in question were duly designated as unequal, Peking's advocates refrained from taking the next normal step of classifying them as automatically null and void. Rather, having made that crucial point, the Chinese now switched around and rhetorically asked their allies whether they really wanted to pursue the topic further, in which case, presumably, the PRC authorities would be prepared to push the argument to its logical extreme. Otherwise, so runs the inference, they were quite disposed to drop the matter on that note.

Why bother to invoke the controversial concept of "unequal treaties" at all, if it was not going to be used to its full extent? In part, one supposes, the act was intended to sound a serious warning for the future, should the Russians persist in their present course: Fresh carping by the Kremlin on the Maoist failure to vindicate the integrity of China's home territory could impel the PRC government to press forthwith for the return of all ancestral lands, including those lost to Russia in the last century, with dire political consequences for the individuals rash enough to incur Peking's wrath. But, the leadership of the PRC may also have had an extra card hidden up its collective sleeve: If sufficiently rattled, perhaps the Russians would blunder into rushing to the defence of the agreements the legitimacy of which was being impugned, thus enabling Peking to score a neat psychological coup by baring to the eyes of the world the Khrushchev "clique's" true face as a self-confessed champion of international documents sanctioning the product of brutal colonial depredations. The risk of earning in the process the sobriquet of "territorial revisionist" would be more than balanced by the advantages accruing from publicly sticking Moscow with the tag of "territorial imperialist."

The scheme was surely worth testing. Either the Soviets would henceforward desist from trying to portray the Chinese as delinquent in protecting the country's physical heritage or their borders with China would become a live issue, forcing them somehow to prove bona fide title to much of their Far Eastern possessions, doctrinally not an easy project in view of the manner in which most of this property was originally obtained, or to fall back on quoting the provisions of the Tsarist conventions, ideologically an altogether thankless task.

Meanwhile, the central thrust of Peking's message lay elsewhere. In practical terms, what the Chinese were telling the Soviets was that the frontier extant between the two states was in no sense final but awaited the same kind of exercise in joint redemarcation for which, according to Peking's version, the other sectors of China's boundaries with neighboring nations had been slated from the very start. The facile illusion, hitherto widely shared, that the operative border-trace separating Soviet from Chinese territory was exempt from fresh scrutiny was now rudely dispelled. The Russians were by no means placed in an inferior position compared with the rest of the states that rubbed shoulders with the PRC. On the contrary, the Chinese took special pains to stress that, "in this respect, our policy towards the socialist countries is fundamentally different from our policy towards the imperialist countries," which at least implied that the path to diplomatic agreement would in this instance be smoother.

Still, the Chinese proposal manifestly envisaged business-like bargaining sessions, a compromise settlement which would carry the signatures of the top leaders of the USSR and the PRC in lieu of the names of representatives of the old order—in short, an official testimonial to the freely granted acquiescence of the PRC authorities in the contours of the ensuing Sino-Soviet frontier line rather than the previous odd situation where everyone simply assumed that the PRC's hands were tied by dusty relics of a distant past. As on earlier occasions, Peking accompanied its bid with standard assurances to the effect that it was in no hurry to tackle the job, that it wished for a peaceful answer to these problems and that, until one could be found, the territorial *status quo* on China's borders would be duly observed. Yet, neither Peking's avowed willingness to tolerate existing conditions nor its pledge not to use coercion to accomplish its goal meant, where it was concerned, that the frontiers with which modern history had saddled it were fixed and immutable. The Russians too were thereby served notice that they would be well advised to mend their fences fast and not lull themselves into falsely believing that the recent shape of the southern perimeter of their Asian flank bore Peking's full endorsement.[35]

That left the next move up to Moscow. Thus far, the Russians had gotten the Chinese to admit that they wanted to redraw the map of China's international boundaries. However, Peking's reply also raised the question for the USSR of what to do with the Chinese offer to sit down at the conference table.

Basically, the Kremlin could proceed in either of two directions. As a first alternative, it could move to counter the Chinese thesis on its merits, even if such an approach did meet with several difficulties of a doctrinal nature. For one, in the literature of the early Soviet phase, the Sino-Russian agreements now attacked in Chinese quarters as "unequal treaties" likewise were frankly so denominated, and no Soviet commentator in those days tried to pretend that the terms of these were won by the Tsarist diplomatic circles through honorable means.[36] Next, certain official Soviet pronouncements of that period had adopted a similar tone and, in fact, erased any doubt that, in the opinion of their authors, the conventions falling into the present category were, for that very reason, voidable at the discretion of the signatories. The Declaration of the Council of People's Commissars of the RSFSR to

35. N. Maxwell, "The basic Chinese position was that the boundaries must be renegotiated. The old, unequal treaties, reminders of China's generations of humiliation, must be replaced by new boundary agreements negotiated between equals. Until that was done, China would regard the Sino-Russian boundaries as not formally delimited. But in the meantime she would respect the status quo—and Peking made it clear that an insistence on renegotiating the boundaries was not at all the same thing as an insistence on changing them. Bitterly as the old injustice of the unequal treaties was resented by the Chinese, they were prepared to accept the boundaries thus established as a fact of life. The lost territories were gone for good. As Mr. Chou En-lai told the late Mr. Nehru in the same context: 'China has [still] a vast expanse of territory, more than half of which is sparsely populated,' and therefore had no interest in an irredentist quest for living space."

36. See, for example, V. Andersen, "Neravnopravnye dogovora Tsarskoi Rossii s Kitaem v XIX veke" (Unequal treaties of tsarist Russia with China in the 19th century), in *Borba klassov* (Struggle of classes), no. 9:102–112 (1936).

the Chinese Nation and the Governments of Southern and Northern China of July 25, 1919,[37] thus already proclaimed that "the Soviet government has renounced all the conquests made by the tsarist government in depriving China of Manchuria and other areas. Let the peoples themselves decide within the frontiers of which state they want to be and what form of government they wish to establish at home."

A little more than a year later, the Note from the People's Commissariat of Foreign Affairs of the RSFSR to the Ministry of Foreign Affairs of China, dated September 27, 1920 (commonly known as the Karakhan Manifesto), again offered the Peking authorities a set of principles on which the Soviet regime was prepared to institute negotiations at once toward normalizing contacts between their countries.[38] The second message contained, inter alia, a draft paragraph to the effect that "the government of the Russian Socialist Federated Soviet Republics declares as without force all treaties concluded by the former government of Russia with China, renounces all seizures of Chinese territory, all Russian concessions in China, and returns to China without compensation and forever all that was rapaciously seized from her by the tsarist government and the Russian bourgeoisie." Finally, it will be remembered, the Sino-Soviet accord of May 31, 1924, confirmed afresh, *expressis verbis*, Moscow's apparent consent to review jointly with the Chinese "all conventions, treaties, agreements, protocols, contracts, etc., concluded between the Government of China and the Tsarist Government and to replace them with new treaties, agreements, etc., on the basis of equality, reciprocity and justice, as well as the spirit of the Declarations of the Soviet Government of 1919 and 1920."

Technical explanations could, of course, minimize the substantive significance of these assorted public commitments, but their derivative importance as a clear statement of official intent was unassailable. While the precise juridical weight of a unilateral policy announcement emanating from a competent agency or of an unfulfilled treaty clause continues to be a hotly debated issue, most international law experts now concede that both possess a modicum of evidentiary value in determining the objectives sought by the party or parties concerned and

37. *Izvestiya*, Aug. 26, 1919; *Dokumenty vneshnei politiki SSSR* (Documents of the foreign policy of the USSR; Moscow: Gospolitizdat, 1958), vol. II, pp. 221–223.

38. *Dokumenty vneshnei politiki SSSR* (Moscow: Gospolitizdat, 1959), vol. III, pp. 213–216; *Sovetsko-kitaiskie otnosheniya, 1917–1957, sbornik dokumentov* (Soviet-Chinese relations, 1917–1957, collection of documents; Moscow: Izd. Vostochnoi Literatury, 1959), pp. 51–53.

the subjacent conception of the rights and duties involved. Still, with proper diligence, a respectable case could be assembled in rebuttal of these various points.

Moscow's twin communications could be discounted, in the way just mentioned, as mere positional papers, thereby raising a serious question as to their ultimate juridical stature. In addition, while the 1919 appeal specified elsewhere that the Soviet regime had from the start called on the Chinese side to hold conversations on the annulment of the treaty of 1896, the Peking protocol of 1901, and all the agreements with Japan from 1907 to 1916, none of which dealt with the territorial problem, on the latter score it remained singularly reticent. The RSFSR's repudiation of the Tsarist conquests in Manchuria was made explicit, but, for the rest, the text spoke only of "other areas" without designating what further regions might fit the bill. Even then the Soviets managed to append an extra qualification by gearing the whole matter to a prospective exercise in self-rule by the local population, a formula that in principle could work out to their advantage as much as to the benefit of the Chinese, save that in the meantime the situation was left up in the air. In the long run this was bound to favor the cause of the power that retained physical mastery of the field, to wit, Russia. The 1920 version quite obviously represented no more than a preliminary invitation to conduct discussions in the near future on a lengthy list of subjects of mutual interest, the frontier issue among them, and the featured reference to that item was equally indefinite with respect to its projected range and focus. In neither instance, it must be emphasized, were those particular pacts which had contributed to drawing the modern outline of the Sino-Soviet border identified by name as scheduled for a thorough overhaul. Moreover, the latest Soviet bid again produced no tangible results.

The relevant provision of the treaty of May 31, 1924, which climaxed these exploratory efforts, brought no change in the existing pattern: While endorsing the familiar proposition that past agreements between the two nations were slated for proximate reassessment, its language carefully eschewed any indication of which of the conventions prescribing the geographic location of their functioning state boundary the signatories here had in mind; in any event, the actual business of sifting through the accumulation of old documents, figuring out what to do with them, which to keep, which to discard, which to amend, and which to replace entirely, was postponed until afterwards, when a special conference would address itself to that enormous task; the talks, when at last they materialized, left the job undone and the status quo lingered on undisturbed.

To complete the picture, the Soviet attitude subsequently shifted. The revolutionary theories expounded at a young age gradually lost ground. A more conservative viewpoint emerged to which jurisprudential doctrine gave tongue by espousing the position that "the external frontiers of the territory inherited by the Soviet state through the process of historical and juridical succession to the former Russian empire were fixed by the frontier treaties of that empire in force on August 1, 1914,"[39] and, since "the treaties . . . with Mongolia on November 5, 1921, and China of May 31, 1924, said nothing of alterations in the former . . . Chinese frontiers, . . . the previous acts in force in 1914 still governed for the purposes of definition or redemarcation (in the event of damage) of the frontiers with . . . China and the Mongolian and Tannu-Tuvian people's republics established astride a portion of the Chinese frontier."[40] Or, in a slightly different version, "one of the species of treaties relating to territory concluded by tsarist Russia was treaties regulating boundary lines with neighboring states. Naturally, the new subject of international law—the Soviet state—could not but take into account the frontiers created by these treaties. In this instance, we speak less of recognition of the treaty itself than of the treaty frontiers."[41]

Or, to quote the most fully developed exposition of these concepts to date,

> The external frontiers of the territory inherited by the Union of Soviet Socialist Republics through the process of historical and juridical succession to the former Russian empire were not infrequently drawn by Russia's treaties concluded in the 17th, 18th and 19th centuries. Among them, one can name the treaty of Nerchinsk of 1689, the treaties of Burin and Kiakhta of 1727, the treaties of Aigun and Tientsin of 1858, the treaty of Peking of 1860 and others in respect to the Far Eastern territories, . . . the conclusion of which had nothing to do with national self-determination in its contemporary sense. However, it would be practically impossible and politically incorrect and in no way justified to deny all significance to these acts of the past.

39. V. N. Durdenevskii, "Sovetskaya territoriya v aktakh mezhdunarodnogo prava za 30 let, 1917–1947gg." (Soviet territory in acts of international law during 30 years, 1917–1947), *Sovetskoe gosudarstvo i pravo* (Soviet state and law), no. 12:58 (1947).

40. *Ibid.*, p. 62.

41. M. M. Avakov, *Pravopreemstvo Sovetskogo gosudarstva* (Succession by the Soviet state; Moscow: Gosyurizdat, 1961), p. 88.

Analysis of international practice demonstrates that some acts of the past are repudiated by the peoples, others retain their significance, in some cases the territorial status quo is reviewed, in others it is preserved.

Inasmuch as today obsolete norms of law cannot serve as a basis for the solution of territorial questions, one must renounce those treaties and the legal foundations of the past stemming therefrom which run counter to the right of nations to self-determination.

Of the former international treaties, those acts keep their significance as legal bases for territorial delimitation which objectively correspond to the principle of national self-determination and, consequently, do not infringe upon the sovereign rights of the interested nations. All depends on the content with which history fills this or that legal form. That is why the old frontiers of the Russian empire with . . . China have remained unchanged. On the other side of the Chinese frontier Mongolian and Tuvinian people's republics came into existence and within the confines of the territory of the former Russian empire along the frontiers referred to arose on the basis of national self-determination the Central Asian national republics which became part of the USSR. The old territorial delimitation won the recognition of the interested peoples and remained unchanged, with the exception of the Tuvinian sector, amended in connection with the voluntary merger in 1943 of the Tuvinian people's republic with the Soviet Union. The juridical title of the Soviet state to the territories located within the state frontiers of the USSR rests on the voluntary and inviolable alliance of the free people of these territories based on the right of all nations to free self-determination guaranteed by the Constitution of the Soviet Union.[42]

What had started out as a purely de facto phenomenon—a genetic outgrowth of historical experience, a legally neutral theme—thus ended up invested with a positive image and a distinct legal rationale. By most odds, a policy pursued with rather impressive consistency over a span of forty-five years and cloaked in an aura of doctrinal legitimacy offers a solid pedestal on which to erect a legal-like argument on one's behalf.

In sum, had the Russians wanted to engage in legal polemics at this juncture, enough ammunition lay at hand to ensure a creditable performance on their part. Yet, as the subsequent record reveals, they held back. This unaccustomed "show of restraint" in turn bears looking into.

An excellent reason for not getting entangled in a legal debate was, of course, the bare fact that, from a jural standpoint, the substantive elements of Tsarist Russia's territorial treaties with China still constituted the strongest single link in the Soviet case. However, no member of the Soviet hierarchy could contemplate with relish the thought of rallying to the defense of these agreements in a public forum, a

42. Yu. G. Barsegov, *Territoriya v mezhdunarodnom prave* (Territory in international law; Moscow: Gosyurizdat, 1958), pp. 118–120.

thoroughly distasteful prospect for an acknowledged Communist in light of Marxist dogma. That in itself would inhibit any tendency to rely on the instrumentalities of the law in handling the affair. For that matter, neither did the Chinese want to get entangled in a legal debate and probably out of calculations not much different from those entertained by their opposites in the Kremlin. The impulse behind the expansion of the Middle Kingdom had, at its peak, been as imperialistic in inspiration as the impetus behind Russia's latter-day drive to the shores of the Pacific ocean. To attempt to prove that China had good title to the remote border regions meant subscribing to the annexationist policies of the dynastic court vis-à-vis the alien peoples surrounding the Han nucleus of the empire, an approach no better suited to the ideological complexion of the new order than the notion of championing the Tsarist regime's land acquisitions at the expense of Russia's weaker neighbors fitted the plans of its revolutionary successors.

More generally, though, the observable behavior of both parties seems to indicate a deliberate effort on their part to keep the dispute from becoming "juridified," from hardening into an object of "legal contention." Consider these items. Khrushchev first raises the territorial question in a speech before his own Parliament; true, his remarks are picked up at once by the mass media and widely disseminated, but they are not directly addressed to the Chinese "comrades" and do not amount to an official communication between the two governments. The Chinese riposte follows an even more roundabout path, taking the shape of an editorial in the Peking press replying to a statement released by the Communist Party of the United States, which had echoed Khrushchev's worst taunts. A face-to-face meeting is thus avoided; the Soviet and Chinese leaderships do not zero in on each other. Rather, they air their views in front of a home audience or criticize a third party, letting the message reach its real destination by an intendedly circuitous route.

Nor is Peking's choice of Party channels to deliver its answer at all accidental. Khrushchev was discussing sundry aspects of the USSR's foreign relations, including the Cuban crisis, and his comments on the PRC also dwelled on Communist China's dealings with various imperialist powers and India, i.e., on select examples of state-to-state diplomacy. The question of the Sino-Soviet frontier, it will be recalled, did not enter into this picture, and the current conflict between Moscow and Peking was portrayed by the speaker essentially as a clash of opinions over doctrinal orthodoxy in matters of global strategy. Under these circumstances, there was nothing wrong with using a state occasion to analyze the situation and spell out the Soviet position on these topics. As against this, the Chinese response focuses squarely on the problem of their shared boundary, but then seeks to soften the blow by putting the whole affair in a Party context, with the dual aim apparently of emphasizing that, within the "socialist brotherhood," an item of this sort was not state business and maintaining a proper degree of balance in the intensity of the verbal counter-thrust—escalation in one sector being compensated for by commensurate relaxation elsewhere. The Chinese Communists were careful and able to keep the exchange of volleys from ballooning forthwith into an interstate confrontation.

The substantive contents of this strange "correspondence" re-enforce the pattern. The concepts of "unequal treaties" and "national self-determination" both sprawl on the outskirts of the legal realm, straddling the thin line between law and politics. Conscious resort to such pseudo-legal devices when superior legal tools were available again suggests a common concern with preventing the dialogue from slipping into the rigid format and the technical patois of a "litigational contest." It also indicates each party's preoccupation with enhancing its own ideological stature by invoking a principle supplied with a certified "socialist" genealogy. In sum, if style accurately reflects the underlying purpose and if a subject's frame of mind can be ascertained from his chosen modus operandi, neither the Soviet nor the Chinese Communist regime played out the opening scene as though its vital interests were endangered. Nobody ran scared or even sounded worried enough to recite his legal rights, which generally happens when events take a serious turn.

This leaves us with the second alternative response to China's March 1963 message—negotiations—and the perplexing question of what considerations held the Russians back from exploring the promise inherent in the Chinese bid that all such issues be settled "peacefully" at the conference table "when conditions are ripe." Personal factors doubtless influenced Soviet official conduct on that score. Having cleverly conjured up the specter of Han imperial ambitions, Khrushchev must have been loath to exorcise that hardy ghost so soon. However, other, more routine impulses probably also had a role. After all, on several previous occasions, similar expressions in diplomatic overtures emanating from Peking had led in short order to fruitful results. Boundary pacts had already been concluded with Burma and Nepal. On December 26, 1962, in the wake of the Sino-Indian hostilities and when the Sino-Soviet border dispute was a-brewing, in a step that can only be described as a grand demonstrative gesture, a frontier treaty was signed with Mongolia, and Chinese commentators were quick to point out the universal lesson to be learned from this experience. The main message was beamed at the Indians, with assurances that

> China's stand on the Sino-Indian boundary question is consistent with her stand on all other boundary questions: she has always striven for a settlement through peaceful negotiations. At the present time, the Chinese frontier guards, having been compelled to strike back in self-defence, have on their own initiative ceased fire along the entire border and are withdrawing. This fact provides still more incontrovertible evidence of China's sincere desire and unshakable stand for a peaceful settlement of the Sino-Indian boundary question.[43]

But the moral of the story applied equally to the Russians and the move was obviously aimed as much at Moscow as at New Delhi, for elsewhere the Chinese waxed no less lyrical about how

> this swift settlement of the Sino-Mongolian boundary question and the successful signing of a boundary treaty provides a fine example of the way socialist countries handle their mutual relations. It shows how fraternal socialist countries find the correct way to solve questions existing between them on the basis of Marxism-Leninism and proletarian internationalism and in accordance with the principles governing mutual relations between fraternal countries as laid down in the Moscow Declaration of 1957 and the Moscow Statement of 1960. It shows how a reasonable solution can be secured for outstanding questions through comradely, friendly consultations. In solving their boundary question, the Chinese and Mongolian Governments are acting not only in the interests of the unity and solidarity of the Chinese and Mongolian peoples, but also in the interests of the unity and solidarity of the peoples of all socialist countries.[44]

Finally, just before the *People's Daily* unleashed its broadside against the Communist Party of the United States for repeating Khrushchev's anti-Chinese remarks, the PRC and Pakistan likewise reached a border accord; and the year had not yet expired when Afghanistan, too, joined the list.

In each instance, of course, the outcome owed a great deal to purely political motives. Chinese interest in putting an early and painless end to the border problem with Burma and Nepal was closely linked with

44. *Ibid.*
43. "The Sino-Mongolian Boundary Treaty: Its Significance," *PR*, no. 52:5 (1962).

the difficulties encountered in resolving the smoldering controversy over the correct shape of the Sino-Indian frontier. Productive talks with these two countries would serve to isolate India, throw into sharp relief China's ability to work out a reciprocally satisfactory arrangement with a pair of smaller neighbors as compared to India's apparent intransigence, and exert pressure on the Indian government also to come to terms. Again, the impact of the timely signature of border agreements with Mongolia and Pakistan transcended the narrow confines of the immediate agenda. The success of the enterprise, in addition to being expected to pry Mongolia from its pro-Moscow orientation and Pakistan from its allegiance to SEATO, was plainly calculated to convince both India and the USSR of the wisdom of following suit and composing their border differences with the PRC without further delay. Furthermore, these samples of constructive international behavior would help offset the poor impression created in the eyes of world public opinion by the perpetual dissension over the matter of the precise silhouette of China's perimeter with the Soviet Union and India.

More à propos, however, is the fact that in the process the Chinese Communist hierarchy managed to evolve a standard diplomatic formula to which the opposite side was in every case so far quite willing to subscribe. Thus, the whole length of the joint frontier was retraced in minute detail. Although the contracting powers invariably professed to be guided in their labors by a wish to preserve the "traditional customary boundary line," their findings coincided in most particulars with the old version of their combined border, except for a few minor adjustments in some spots. In redefining the site of the frontier, no attention was paid to the provisos of past border agreements. Indeed, the very existence of these tainted witnesses to a bygone age was systematically ignored and the lone citation of a treaty harking back to the "colonial epoch" merely fulfilled a reference function. With the entry into force of the latest accords, all previous conventions regulating the location of the corresponding sector of the border lapsed and thereafter any question arising in connection with the format of the frontier would be governed by the appropriate document bearing the names of the PRC representatives.

The official refrain is that the course of the negotiations leading up to the conclusion of each frontier pact was marked by the spirit of mutual understanding and mutual accommodation, cordial consultations, fairness, and reasonableness—expressions that convey the flavor of ad hoc compromise, practical expediency, pragmatic outlook, flexible posture, and opportune improvisation, in short, of proceedings unhampered by punctilio and trivial technicalities. Legal rights were never mentioned. Chinese sources noted with hearty approval, for example, how "the Chinese and Nepalese Governments had agreed that, prior to the overall settlement of the boundary question, they would maintain the status quo of the boundary and not make any territorial claims on each other as pre-conditions for negotiation."[45] The rigid ritual of the law, then, did not set the tone here; instead, we are told, the ancient art of friendly political bargaining dominated the scene and, in an animus of quid pro quo, accomplished the objective in record time.

The end picture sounds almost idyllic. The resulting agreements netly favored the PRC's co-signatories: Their state frontiers with China remained virtually intact and, as an extra bonus, received a formal endorsement from the current mainland regime. Peking, in turn, wound up with a series of agreements which, in a very real sense, erased whole slices of the historical past, together with its many unpleasant memories, and redated China's border relations with the countries involved to start with a new era.

What prevented India and the Soviet Union from at least testing the possibilities of handling their business with Communist China in the same neat fashion? For one, the situation had since deteriorated so much that they probably felt that any such venture entailed an unwarranted amount of risk. To put the fate of their entire frontier with the PRC at stake in the hope that the Communist Chinese authorities would act as they had on earlier occasions and again accept a modus vivendi essentially sanctioning the hitherto operative boundary line called for willingness to take a gamble that the Soviet and Indian governments both apparently thought was excessive. Readiness to engage in unconditional discussions on the status of their respective frontiers with the PRC could be interpreted as an admission of doubt on the part of either as to the intrinsic validity of the effective border, a factor which, if the negotiations failed, might *in fine* gravely prejudice the Soviet Union's or India's title to the disputed areas. So, the Indians, rather unwisely, brought up their biggest legal guns and insisted on making a juridical case of the affair, unheeding of the endless complications, profound bitterness, and inevitable recriminations that a litiga-

45. Mao Sun, "Final Settlement of Sino-Nepalese Boundary Question, Dr. Giri in Peking," *PR*, no. 4:10 (1963).

tional approach tends to engender, and thus only succeeded in blocking every avenue to a compromise arrangement that easily could have met nearly all their demands. The Russians, equally lacking in perspicacity, sought refuge behind a heavy ideological barrage, and by coupling the issue with the ongoing doctrinal controversy just as badly reduced their chances for a quick settlement.

Second, the key to the solution of the border problem between the PRC and Burma, Nepal, Pakistan, Mongolia, and Afghanistan lay in Peking's consent to waive China's traditional claims to peripheral territories once incorporated into the Chinese empire or under its suzerainty. These nations did not object to being cast in the role of beneficiaries of Chinese bounty, judging that the material gains they derived from the deal were fully worth the psychological price they were required to pay and the cost, by any count, was not exorbitant. The Soviet Union and India, however, concerned with their image and prestige as great powers, seemingly concluded that they could not afford to "demean" their rank by allowing themselves to be publicly identified as recipients of Chinese liberality, especially on an item the importance of which was obvious to everybody. Saving "face" can be an expensive proposition; in this instance it probably was.

Communist China was, of course, playing a similar game vis-à-vis its smaller neighbors, and its tactics on that score toward India and the USSR were influenced by comparable considerations. During their protracted debate with the Russians on the subject of their common frontier, for example, at no point until March 1969 did the Chinese invoke the Soviet Declaration of 1919 or the 1920 Karakhan Manifesto, although the tenor of both documents would strengthen their argument, presumably because the latter represented a unilateral gesture of generosity by the Kremlin to which they did not want to be indebted in any way. Peking preferred, without regard to profit, to defend its interests by relying on its own resources rather than using evidence borrowed from Soviet diplomatic archives to dramatize the constancy of China's title to the territory in question and its utter independence of any momentary aberration in the spectrum of Soviet foreign policy. And, even when the mainland regime finally did refer to these texts,[46] it was not for the purpose of adducing some positive right accruing

46. Information Department of the Chinese Foreign Ministry, "Chenpao Island Has Always Been Chinese Territory," *PR*, no. 11:14–15 (1969); *The New York Times*, Mar. 12, 1969, p. 16; Statement of the PRC Government, May 24, 1969, *China Reconstructs*, p. 4.

from their contents but merely to illustrate the inconsistency of Soviet behavior and to spotlight the extent to which the attitude of the current Soviet leadership was at variance with the spirit of Lenin's "great testament."

STALEMATE

A pause followed the first flurry of verbal exchanges. Both capitals used the lull to advantage to launch confidential probes reportedly inspired by a concern to bring the polemics to an early and peaceful close. Thus, many years later, Russian sources revealed how "during that period the Soviet Government took quite a number of constructive steps to avert the sharpening of border friction, to lessen tension. With these aims, the Soviet Government on May 17, 1963, proposed to the PRC Government that bilateral consultations be held between our states."[47] Chinese spokesmen countered with their own version, according to which "on August 23, 1963, the Chinese Government put forward to the Soviet Government a six-point proposal for maintaining the status quo of the boundary and averting conflicts."[48] Interestingly enough, both sides now implied that their particular initiative deserved the credit for paving the way for the convening of the 1964 border talks, although at the time neither betrayed a desire to advertise its efforts, nor does the known record indicate that the overtures met with any measure of success at that juncture.

Regardless of what went on behind the scenes, in the public forum the brief silence was rudely shattered on September 6, 1963, with the publication of a "Comment on the Open Letter [of July 14, 1963] of the Central Committee of the CPSU" by the Editorial Departments of *People's Daily* and *Red Flag*.[49] Analyzing the recent background of the Moscow-Peking conflict, the authors at one point censured the Soviet side for the first time for having "provoked troubles on the Sino-Soviet border"[50] and, elsewhere, took the "leaders of the CPSU" to task for having

47. *Pravda*, Mar. 30, 1969, p. 1; *Izvestiya*, Mar. 30, 1969, pp. 1–2; *USSR Government Statement of March 29, 1969* (Moscow: Novosti, 1969), p. 12.

48. Statement of the Government of the People's Republic of China, May 24, 1969, *China Reconstructs*, no. 7, Suppl.:6 (1969).

49. *The Origin and Development of the Differences between the Leadership of the CPSU and Ourselves* (Peking: Foreign Languages Press, 1963); *PR*, no. 37:6–23 (1963). The July 14 Open Letter from the CPSU did not refer to the frontier controversy.

50. *The Origin and Development*, p. 32.

in April and May 1962 . . . used their organs and personnel in Sinkiang, China, to carry out large-scale subversive activities in the Ili region and enticed and coerced several tens of thousands of Chinese citizens into going to the Soviet Union. The Chinese Government lodged repeated protests and made repeated representations, but the Soviet Government refused to repatriate these Chinese citizens on the pretext of "the sense of Soviet legality" and "humanitarianism." To this day this incident remains unsettled. This is indeed an astounding event, unheard of in the relations between socialist countries.[51]

Mention of "troubles on the Sino-Soviet border" was new. Unfortunately, the Chinese source gave no details on the extent and location of the alleged "troubles" that would permit an assessment of the gravity of the situation. "Troubles" could cover anything from an isolated border crossing to a local armed clash; in concrete terms, the two types of occurrence lie very far apart.

The imputation that the Soviets had a finger or even a few fingers in the Sinkiang pie is probably justified. While not immediately connected with rival territorial claims,[52] the episode at least identified one major arena of political competition and strongly implied that some, perhaps most, of the PRC–USSR frontier problems originated right here. In any case, the Russians stood formally charged by their allies with flagrantly violating Chinese sovereignty in Sinkiang. On the other hand, it should also be remembered that Peking's policies in that remote province had met with the spontaneous resistance of the native population more than once before and that the Chinese, casting around for a convenient scapegoat, were not at all averse to blaming the Russians for their current embarrassment.

51. *Ibid.*, p. 47. In the western press, the Chinese remarks about "Soviet large-scale subversive activities in the Ili region" were in some instances pictured as a charge that the Russians "had attempted to overthrow the Chinese local government at Ili." See *Asian Recorder* (1963), p. 5459. In the absence of other information, the correctness of this interpretation is open to doubt. That the Soviets fomented trouble in the Ili area may be taken for granted; that they went so far as to plot the overthrow of the local government is not clear even from the data furnished by Chinese sources.

More credible are the reports concerning the flow of refugees from Sinkiang to nearby Soviet territory. About 50,000 souls are said to have fled across the border into Soviet Central Asia since the fall of 1962 (estimated as of October 1963). The same number is quoted in *Facts on File,* Sept. 12–18, 1963, p. 324, which attributed the exodus to "hunger and religious persecution."

52. No specific allegations concerning differences of opinion over the profile of the USSR-PRC frontier in the Sinkiang region were aired at this time. The Russians were accused of political meddling in Sinkiang's internal affairs. This interference and the turmoil in the area did, however, occasion collisions on the frontier stemming apparently from Chinese attempts to interdict the flight of refugees into the USSR and Soviet countermeasures against Chinese pursuit of the refugees into Soviet territory.

The Peking regime, however, was still careful to treat the matter as an interparty affair. Hence, the next Soviet move—in the guise of a "government statement" released on September 21, 1963—marks a significant departure in this respect.[53] The ostensible reason for the switch in polemical media was that, upon acquainting itself with the contents of the "statement by a spokesman of the Chinese government" against the treaty banning nuclear weapon tests in the atmosphere, in outer space and under water, circulated in Peking on September 1, 1963—to which the September 21 communication was a response—Moscow now discovered that

> on this occasion, too, a government statement is being used mainly in order to slander the Communist Party of the Soviet Union (C.P.S.U.) and the other Communist Parties in connection with a wide range of questions on which the leadership of the Communist Party of China (C.P.C.) has differences with the international communist movement.[54]

On most of the subjects touched upon in the Soviet policy paper, recourse to official channels was appropriate enough, since they involved diverse aspects of international diplomacy. This applies to the topic of the Sino-Indian border hostilities as well, an item on which the Soviets firmly clung to the old line that "we consider that in frontier disputes, especially in a dispute of the type of the Chinese-Indian clash, one should adhere to the Leninist views according to which it is possible to settle any frontier problems without resorting to armed force, granted that both sides desire to do so."[55] It is where the Kremlin then embarks on a discussion of the growing friction along the Sino-Soviet boundary in the same conceptual frame of reference that the element of novelty emerges. For, with this step, the Soviets virtually raised the issue to a state level, except that they endeavored to make it look as though their Chinese colleagues were liable for this adverse turn of events because they had purportedly instituted the offensive practice of expounding on ideological themes in government documents and left the Russians no choice save to retaliate in kind.

Moscow's assertion is unfounded, needless to say, since that is pre-

53. *Pravda*, Sept. 21–22, 1963; *Vneshnyaya politika Sovetskogo Soyuza i mezhdunarodnye otnosheniya, sbornik dokumentov, 1963 god* (Foreign policy of the Soviet Union and international relations, collection of documents 1963; Moscow: Mezhdunarodnye Otnosheniya, 1964), pp. 236–287; *A Reply to Peking* (Soviet Booklet No. 122, London, 1963); *Soviet News*, no. 4896:159–164 (1963) and no. 4897:167–174 (1963); *Moscow News*, special issue, Sept. 24, 1963.
54. *A Reply to Peking*, p. 3.
55. *Ibid.*, p. 23. Also, *New Times*, no. 39:44 (1963).

cisely the sort of error top PRC circles seemed determined not to commit and to date they had managed to avoid the trap. Yet, none of this prevented the Soviets from premeditatedly trying to saddle the Chinese with full responsibility for stirring up a crisis on the PRC-USSR boundary, which helps explain the strident tones of the accusations hurled by the Kremlin to the effect that

> in recent years, on her borders with neighboring states, the Chinese side has been stooping to acts of a nature which gives us reason to think that the government of the People's Republic of China is departing, on this question, more and more from Leninist positions. The leaders of the People's Republic of China are deliberately concentrating the people's attention on frontier problems, artificially fanning nationalist passions and dislike for other peoples.[56]

To Peking's version of the causes of the border strife, Moscow opposed its own interpretation, noting that

> since 1960, Chinese servicemen and civilians have been systematically violating the Soviet frontier. In the one year of 1962, more than 5,000 violations of the Soviet frontier from the Chinese side have been recorded. Attempts are also being made to "develop" some parts of Soviet territory without permission.
>
> One Chinese citizen who crossed the border had written instructions from the People's Committee of the Heilun Ch'iang province, which said:
>
> "When fish are being caught on the disputed islands of the Amur and the Ussuri, the Soviet border guards often demand that our fishermen leave these islands. We propose that the catching of fish on the disputed islands be continued and that the Soviet border guards be told that these islands belong to China, and that the border is being violated by them, not by us."
>
> And further:
>
> ". . . our fishermen are not to be removed from these islands in any circumstances. We imagine that, in view of the friendly relations between our states, the Soviet side will not resort to force to remove our fishermen from the islands."[57]

The Chinese had condemned the Russians for the deteriorating situation on their common perimeter and the Russians returned the compliment, adding a few extra flourishes, such as that the infractions of the Soviet frontier with China had assumed a "systematic" character and that the estimated number of these incidents already exceeded five thousand. Again, no specific data were furnished so that one has no way

56. *A Reply to Peking*, p. 24. To the same effect, see the front page editorial in *Pravda*, Sept. 23, 1963.
57. *Ibid.*

of knowing when and where the events alluded to took place and what exactly they entailed. Unluckily for the Soviet case, the sole example cited to illustrate Chinese wrongdoing on this score completely misses the target, for genuine disagreement concerning the ownership of these particular islands has evidently persisted for quite a while. Thus, before the territorial issue had even surfaced, a press story dealing with various divergences observed in contemporary Chinese and Soviet charts of their shared boundary featured the following account:

> Less spectacular is a difference in mapping an area on the border between China and the Soviet Union [as compared with the magnitude of the discrepancies pictured on the Sino-Mongolian arc]. In this instance a series of low-lying swampy islands about twenty miles long are claimed by both sides at the confluence of the Amur River and the Ussuri River.
>
> Although the islands adjoin the Siberian metropolitan center of Khabarovsk, they appear to be uninhabited. That is probably why the territorial dispute, if one exists in fact, has not gone beyond the mapping stage.[58]

In light of the above, to describe Chinese efforts to establish a physical presence on the contested islands as an infringement of the Soviet frontier, as though the latter's status here was definitively fixed and put the USSR in absolute possession of the islands, smacks of sheer effrontery.

More pertinent was Moscow's companion disclosure that "the Soviet government has already proposed many times to the government of the People's Republic of China that consultations be held on the question of the demarcation of specific sections of the frontier line, so as to exclude any possibility of misunderstanding," but that, reportedly, "the Chinese side evades such consultations, while at the same time continuing to violate the border." Commented the Russian note: "This cannot but make us wary, especially in view of the fact that Chinese propaganda is giving clear hints alleging that there has been unjust demarcation of some sections of the Soviet-Chinese border in the past."[59]

58. *The New York Times*, Feb. 26, 1961, p. 20. The news item adds that: "Not even scholarly Soviet studies refer to the Amur island discrepancy. For example, a historical review of the formation of the Soviet-Chinese Amur River frontier, reviewed in the July, 1960, issue of *Voprosy istorii*, Soviet historical journal, discussed the history of the frontier in considerable detail but ignored the map differences." The review in question by G.P. Basharin, published in *Voprosy istorii* (Questions of history), no. 7:160–162 (1960), is of the book by P.I. Kabanov, *Amurskii vopros* (The Amur question; Blagoveshchensk: Amurskoe knizhnoe izd., 1959), 254 pp.

59. *A Reply to Peking*, p. 24; *Soviet News*, no. 4987:170 (1963).

In a sense, it is strange that the Russians had waited so long to play this card. Elementary logic dictated the move. In his initial sally, Khrushchev had singled out negotiations as the proper means for settling the Sino-Indian border conflict. The latest manifesto again emphasized that "communists consistently work for the solution of frontier problems through negotiation" and trumpeted the message that "the socialist countries, guided in their relations by the principle of proletarian internationalism, should show other peoples an example in the friendly solution of territorial problems." At some juncture, these brave-sounding words had to be converted into suitable deeds in order to forestall loss of credibility. By advertising that the Soviet chiefs had urged their Chinese counterparts to sit down with them and talk these matters over, in vain we are told, Moscow presently sought to persuade its global audience that it lived by the rules it preached and, by the same token, to cast Peking in the role of the official villain. Furthermore, the very slogan of "peaceful methods of resolving international differences" was altogether too valuable a sales pitch to let the Chinese preempt it without a challenge.

Also quite true to Khrushchev's "style" in the current debate was the careful omission of any hint of a basic divergence between the Soviet and Chinese conceptions of the agenda for such a conference. Peking had indicated from the outset its desire to see the entire extent of the boundary retraced; Moscow mentioned only the "demarcation of specific sections of the frontier-line," totally ignoring known Chinese wishes on that count and then feigning surprise that the leaders of the PRC did not respond with enthusiasm to the "reasonable" Soviet offer. Reasonable it might have been, but it did not fit Peking's plans. And, on the diplomatic scene, advocating a formula that intentionally disregards the other party's point of view is seldom conducive to positive results, unless, of course, the whole purpose of the exercise is to post a propaganda victory and not to strive for a real consensus.

Until now the Soviets had kept busy heaping abuse on their Chinese comrades. They still had not said anything constructive in defense of the existing Sino-Soviet frontier to parry Peking's suggestion that, since that boundary rested on a series of treaties the validity of which, due to their "unequal" nature, was highly dubious, the boundary's own legitimacy was equally impaired. Some kind of a rebuttal was needed, and the Kremlin's communiqué next tackled this difficult job with the plea that

The artificial creation, in our times, of any territorial problems—especially between socialist countries—would amount to entering on a very dangerous path. If, today, countries begin making territorial claims on one another, using as arguments certain ancient data and the graves of their forefathers, if they start fighting to revise the historically developed frontiers, this will lead to no good, but will merely create feuds among all peoples, to the joy of the enemies of peace.

It should not be forgotten that questions of territorial disputes and claims have often in the past been the source of acute friction and conflict between states, a source inflaming nationalist passions. It is common knowledge that territorial disputes and frontier conflicts have been used as pretexts for wars of conquest. . . .

The Soviet Union has no frontier conflict with any of her neighboring states. And we are proud of this, because this situation is in line not only with the interests of the Soviet Union, but also with the interests of all the socialist countries and the interests of world peace.[60]

The brief was a curious one, both for what it contained and what it left out. First, no attempt was made to summon the authority of international law, although its precepts were certainly relevant to the occasion. The Russians might have been willing to reproach the Chinese for turning the "ideological dispute" into a state issue, but they were not about to expose themselves to a similar charge and steered clear of "juridifying" the tenor of the dialogue. So, if the Chinese Communists had banked on maneuvering their Russian allies into flying to the support of the Tsarist agreements, they must have been sorely disappointed. Second, the authors of the Soviet document relied on the shopworn contention of every champion of the status quo—in this instance donning the mask of "historically developed frontiers"—against the protagonists of change, to wit, that any such undertaking owes promise of destroying the civilized world. Third, Moscow's spokesmen, quite advisedly, forebore decrying the dangers of "territorial revisionism" within the narrow frame alone of the Sino-Soviet polemics, since a parochial focus was bound to reduce the force of their argument, but, instead, chose to lecture on general experience and thus, presumably, hoped to universalize the appeal of the Kremlin's case.

We end up with the picture of a Khrushchev administration intent on injecting the "territorial" theme into the mainstream of the mounting

60. *A Reply to Peking*, pp. 24–25. Refer to the statement which appeared in the editorial entitled "Dangerous Seat of Tension in Asia," *Pravda*, Sept. 19, 1963, reprinted in *Soviet News*, no. 4895:157–158 (1963) and no. 4896:165 (1963): "As to the Soviet Union, it treats with respect the countries bordering on it. It understands that good neighborliness is possible only if the frontiers existing between states are respected."

Sino-Soviet doctrinal controversy and of exploiting to the full the advantages perceived in publicizing the "cardinal sin" attributed to the PRC leadership of pursuing a policy of "geographical expansionism." For, one must remember, it was Moscow that was pushing the article. Up to this point, the Chinese had contributed little on the subject, and most of it was couched in the tone of a warning and a query—more or less alerting the Russians to the risk they ran if they insisted on trifling with matches and asking them if they actually wanted to start a fire. Peking moved to block the opening blow and stopped; Moscow carried the fight a step further.

The previous pattern of rhetoric continued to hold. Inasmuch as the Kremlin was waging a propaganda battle, legal devices did not recommend themselves to it. Conversely, an emotional attack on those who succumbed to the evils of militant nationalism, exhibited war-like tendencies, and manufactured frontier incidents offered a double attraction. In the name of "proletarian internationalism," by whose code both capitals professed to regulate their behavior, the Chinese Communist hierarchy could be pilloried for the crime of "nationalist particularism" and its prestige within the so-called "socialist Commonwealth" and the international Communist system effectively undermined as a consequence. In "bourgeois" circles and among nonaligned governments, Peking's influence would also suffer a serious decline if the idea that the PRC regime harbored grandiose plans of conquest and aggression ever took root. That is why the Soviets kept harping on the Sino-Indian border *contretemps:* to cater to the impression that they were more disturbed by Chinese transgressions in this quarter than any possible peril to themselves.[61] Khrushchev's bid for popular sympathy at home and abroad in his anti-Mao campaign was rather obvious. And the parting shot about the USSR not having any other frontier problems both drew an invidious comparison, for foreign consumption, between its record in this domain and that of the PRC and subtly informed anybody else who aspired to "revise" the topography ot the Soviet boundary that the subject was strictly forbidden.

Distortion, willful exaggeration, plain fabrication, assigning to the Chinese leaders sinister designs of territorial aggrandizement without a shred of proof to sustain the accusation—all this, then, was pressed into

61. A vivid illustration of this technique is the long essay cited in the previous footnote devoted entirely to the "disastrous consequences of the Chinese-Indian border conflict for the cause of peace." See *Soviet News*, no. 4895:157 (1963).

service in order to score in a shrewd game of political one-upmanship contrived to strengthen Moscow's hand within the ranks of the Communist club and enhance its stature on the outer stage, a contest in which the business of the frontiers furnished a welcome means toward extraneous ends and swung little weight on its own. In sum, with the Sino-Soviet doctrinal dispute currently rising to a new crescendo, either Khrushchev felt that the territorial issue was too potent a diplomatic weapon not to wield it against his Chinese opponents, or, having once gone to the trouble of digging up a suitable hobby-horse, he was prepared to ride it for all it was worth.

That the drift of the Soviet communication here amounted to a deliberate exacerbation of the tenor of the Moscow-Peking controversy is undeniable. Yet, the "escalation" was a finely calibrated one and retained a due sense of proportion. In particular, although the Soviets were quick to denounce the Chinese comrades for diverting an ideological discussion into governmental channels and used this as a pretext to turn to the same media, they still stopped short of officially "legalizing" the debate. Besides the many factors already mentioned which conspired against such a move, the Kremlin's decision to emphasize the tenets of "proletarian internationalism" and Peking's alleged violation thereof compounded the difficulties of openly resorting to the language of the law: To make a good legal case for the USSR, a "national" approach was a sine qua non—promoting Russia's rights versus China's rights, Russia's claims versus China's claims, Russia's title versus China's title, and so forth, none of which squared with the "internationalist" thesis that Moscow now propounded. Hence, the law was left untouched, and less confining methods were relied upon in prosecuting the waxing war of words.

A few months later, Khrushchev tried a different tack with the dispatch, on December 31, 1963, of a letter to the governments of all countries that called for the conclusion of a convention renouncing the use of force in the settlement of territorial and frontier disputes.[62] In substantive terms, the circular contained no surprises. The old dichotomy between situations in which, for various reasons, recourse to coercion was licensed as an instrumentality for effecting a change in the operative boundary line and those contingencies where such a solution was

62. *Pravda*, Jan. 4, 1964; *Vneshnyaya politika Sovetskogo Soyuza*, pp. 343–357; *A Call for a Treaty Renouncing the Use of Force in the Settlement of Territorial and Frontier Disputes* (Soviet Booklet, Vol. 2, no. 2; London, 1964); *Soviet News*, no. 4938:5–8 (1964).

a priori barred was spelled out once more, in richer detail this time. Thus, territorial claims "associated with the completion of the liberation of this or that people from colonial oppression or foreign occupation," be it the recovery of a portion of the ancestral soil still under imperialist rule or a struggle of an entire nation for independence, fell into the former category. While, according to the Russian head of state, the population of the colonies strove to achieve their goal of political emancipation "by peaceful means," these means often proved inadequate because of the resistance of those determined to preserve their ill-gotten gains—by violence, if necessary—and so "the oppressed peoples have no choice but to take up arms themselves." Indeed, he declared, "this is their sacred right."[63]

Military bases abroad were likewise not immune from the application of duress to secure their liquidation: Though ostensibly sanctioned by treaty clauses, the legality of such installations was nevertheless challenged on grounds that the constitutive pacts were bare *diktats* that allowed stronger powers to trample on the sovereignty and physical integrity of the weaker host countries. Therefore, whenever the latter insisted that "the treaties on military bases be dissolved, that those territories be restored to them, and that the bases be dismantled and the foreign troops withdrawn," then, in the words of the text, "these just demands should be satisfied."[64] If not, compulsion was presumably in order to attain this objective.

Not subject to the above dispensation were the issues stemming from the partition of several countries in the wake of World War II and since. The matter of reunification of these divided lands was also identified "to a certain extent with the territorial question." The Kremlin urged that the desire of the local inhabitants to form a single state be "treated . . . with understanding and respect" provided the problem was "settled by the peoples of these countries and their governments themselves, without any interference or pressure from the outside and, of course, without foreign military intervention. . . ." But, the message cautioned, "no force should be used in settling this question and the peoples of these countries should be given the opportunity to solve the problems of unification by peaceful means," adding that "all other states should contribute to this."[65]

63. *A Call for a Treaty*, pp. 6–8.
64. *Ibid.*, p. 8.
65. *Ibid.*

By Khrushchev's own admission, however, his proposal was primarily focused on another matter, namely, on "how to deal with territorial disputes and claims which arise over the actually existing and well-established frontiers of states." The Soviet note first pinpointed a "special class among such claims" consisting, in its phraseology, of the "demands of the revenge-seeking circles of certain states which were the aggressors in the Second World War." The note further states that these circles "are harboring plans for a revision of the just postwar territorial settlement . . . [and] want to get hold of those territories which went to other states by way of eliminating the consequences of aggression and providing guarantees of security for the future." These "claims," the Kremlin maintained, "must be absolutely rejected, as being incompatible with the interests of peace, because nothing but a new world war can grow out of those claims." As for the rest, which, it conceded, perhaps numbered a majority of the current conflicts generated by rival efforts to assert title to the same piece of territory, plainly enough these "had nothing to do with postwar settlements," and here the parties "put forward arguments and considerations relating to history, ethnography, blood affinity, religion and so on."[66]

In its Statement of September 21, 1963, the Soviet government had already expressed doubts concerning the wisdom of nations seeking to rely on "ancient data and the graves of their forefathers" in pressing for the revision of "historically developed frontiers"; such an attitude merely created deadly feuds between members of the global community. Now, Moscow again queried the validity of that procedure, except that on this occasion its criticism of the practice was formulated in much more elaborate, comprehensive, and sophisticated fashion. To wit:

> It often happens that one state justifies its territorial claim on another state by such arguments, and the second state in its turn finds other arguments from the same sphere, but of an absolutely opposite nature, and itself puts forward a territorial counter-claim. The result is the fomenting of passions and the deepening of mutual strife.
>
> How can one tell which side is right, whose position is just and whose unjust? In some cases this is very difficult, because the existing frontiers came into being as a result of the influence of many factors.
>
> In many cases, references to history are of no assistance. Who can affirm, say, that a reference to the 17th century which one state puts forward in substantiation of its territorial claim, is more valid than, for instance, a reference to the 18th or 19th century by which the other state tries to bolster its own counter-claim?

66. *Ibid.*, p. 9.

> And if one were to take as the basis for the solution of a frontier dispute the whole of history spread over several millennia, all would agree, one would think, that in many cases no real solution could be found. Nor can we forget the fact that not infrequently references to history are made in order to provide a cover for open aggression, as was the case, for instance, with Mussolini's references to the frontiers of the Roman Empire in order to substantiate his seizures of territory in the Mediterranean, which the Italian fascists even christened "*mare nostrum*," i.e., "our sea," in an effort to present themselves as the heirs of the ancient Romans.
>
> Sometimes it is difficult to get one's bearings among the numerous "arguments" based on national or ethnographic grounds, or grounds of blood affinity. The development of mankind has been such that some peoples are now living on the territories of a number of states. On the other hand, there exist states of a multi-national type, sometimes inhabited by dozens of peoples, even belonging to different races.
>
> Unfortunately, disputes about frontiers take place not only between historians and ethnographers, but also between states, each of which possesses armed forces, and sometimes quite large ones. Life itself shows that the majority of territorial disputes are fraught with the danger of relations between the parties becoming complicated, with the possibility of a serious armed conflict, and consequently constitute a potential threat to universal peace. This means that due understanding of frontiers, as they have been formed in the course of history, has to be displayed.[67]

In short, for Khrushchev, the weakness of a tradition-oriented approach to territorial rights was that the data culled from antiquated records could easily be cited both pro and con by either side in a squabble over ownership of some slice of terrain, that the facts so adduced failed to demonstrate the superiority of one advocate's contentions over his competitor's, that the norm itself was largely obsolete and ran counter to modern social conditions which had transcended the constricting limits of a purely ethnic concept of human organization, and that recourse to evidence of this genre only sowed the seeds of international discord. All this counselled reserve in invoking the testimony of the past as a rationale for altering the realities of the present, but the Soviet document was also very careful not to convey the impression of a total repudiation by the USSR of the value of "historical rights" per se: The annals of Soviet diplomacy are replete with examples of resort to historical arguments to vindicate Moscow's actions, and the prospective usefulness of history as an alibi under similar circumstances loomed far too great to discard so handy a tool just yet.

To the Russians, the worst danger from military outbreaks over frontier issues centered on Europe. Elsewhere as well, though, the price of

67. *Ibid.*, pp. 9–10.

wars to decide possession of a contested area was now deemed to be prohibitive and not to warrant these extreme measures. Not unexpectedly, then, the letter concluded that

> There are not, nor can there be, territorial disputes in our times between states already formed, or unresolved frontier questions, of such a kind that it is permissible to use armed force in order to settle them. No, this cannot be allowed to happen, and we must do everything possible to rule out the possibility of events developing in such a way.[68]

The note did acknowledge the occurrence of genuine frontier problems that required concerted attention. Without purporting to ignore these, it simply registered anew its opposition to any "military methods of settling territorial disputes," appealed for a thorough exploration of all peaceful avenues apt to produce a consensus and assured its mass audience, rather truistically, that "life itself shows that whenever states firmly abide by the principles of peaceful coexistence and display good will, restraint and due regard for each other's interests, they are quite capable of extricating themselves from the maze of historical, national, geographic and other factors and finding a satisfactory solution."[69] Mentioned as effective devices in that connection were direct negotiations between the states involved, the use of good offices, requests for assistance from international organizations, the machinery of the United Nations, etc.

Accordingly, the Soviet government called for the signature of a universal convention that would "include the following principal proposition":

1. A solemn undertaking by the states, parties to the agreement, not to resort to force to alter the existing state frontiers;

2. Recognition that the territory of states should not, even temporarily, be the object of any invasion, attack, military occupation or any other forcible measures directly or indirectly undertaken by other states for whatsoever political, economic, strategic, frontier, or any other considerations;

3. A firm declaration that neither differences in social or political systems, nor denial of recognition or the absence of diplomatic relations, nor any other pretexts can serve as justification for the violation by one state of the territorial integrity of another;

68. *Ibid.*, pp. 13–14.
69. *Ibid.*, p. 14.

4. An undertaking to settle all territorial disputes exclusively by peaceful means, such as negotiations, mediation, conciliatory procedure, and also other peaceful means at the choice of the parties concerned in conformity with the United Nations Charter.

A postscript read: "Needless to say, such an international agreement should cover all territorial disputes concerning the existing frontiers between states."[70]

It is not our purpose here to analyze in depth the jural caliber of Khrushchev's message. The exercise would accomplish little in any case, for the chief criticism that can be levelled at its contents was the bland, unimaginative, and stock quality of its prescriptions.[71] Moreover, an elaborate assessment of the legal merits of the project would in this instance be quite irrelevant since this study focuses on the dynamics of the Sino-Soviet controversy and, as will be shown, the Chinese did not bother to comment *ad rem* on the various elements of the plan advanced by Khrushchev and brushed the idea aside after a minimal attempt to deal with just one dimension of the blueprint in semisubstantive fashion. The sole purpose of summing up the highlights of Khrushchev's message, then, was that a survey might indicate what it was that the document featured or omitted that precipitated or colored Peking's brusque refusal to endorse its dicta.

Indeed, the sole official explanation volunteered by the Chinese regime for its negative response to the Russian bid, articulated in Chou En-lai's report on the results of his visit to 14 lands,[72] was that

> This proposal deliberately confused imperialist aggression and occupation of other countries' territories with territorial disputes and boundary questions between nations left over by history. Of course, boundary questions between Asian and African countries should and could find a fair and reasonable solution through peaceful consultations. This was also the case with boundary questions between socialist countries. But imperialist aggression and occupa-

70. *Ibid.*, p. 16. The formalities were left to be worked out later and Khrushchev sounded as though this aspect of the problem would prove relatively simple: "As for the forms of a future international agreement on the renunciation by states of the use of force for settling territorial disputes, and also the procedure for conducting talks on the conclusion of this agreement, it seems to me that it would not be very difficult to reach agreement on this, if, of course, the sides concerned show an interest in it. The Soviet government, for its part, is ready to do everything possible to facilitate the solution of these questions." *Ibid.*, p. 18.

71. *Cf.* F. Monconduit, "La Note Khrouchtchev du 31 décembre 1963 relative au réglement pacifique des litiges territoriaux," *Annuaire francais de droit international, 1964* (Paris: Centre national de la recherche scientifique, 1964), pp. 62–63.

72. *PR*, no. 18:6–12 (1964).

tion of other countries' territories was a matter of a completely different nature. As to countries whose territories had been invaded and occupied by imperialism, they naturally had every right to recover their lost territories by any means. To ask those countries which were subjected to aggression to renounce the use of force in any circumstances was in fact to ask the people of all countries to renounce their struggle against the imperialist policies of aggression and war, placing themselves at the mercy of imperialism and submitting to imperialist enslavement.[73]

From the above passage, the Chinese seemed to take exception to two particular aspects of Moscow's draft formula. First, by inference, they appeared to want to exclude the frontiers between non-Asian, non-African, and non-socialist countries from the workings of the veto against the employment of coercion to amend their present configuration. Second, they argued in favor of a further differentiation between interstate boundary lines born of true historical accident and presumably neutral in a political sense and those tainted with an imperialist association. Khrushchev had drawn a distinction only between the unfinished business of emancipation from colonial rule, in which recourse to compulsion to achieve a final solution was acceptable, and disagreements over the placement of current boundaries in the affairs of recognized, equally sovereign states, where such conduct was barred.

By contrast, the Chinese Communists implied that in the latter category too, the functioning frontiers were not prima facie immune from violent change if imperialism had played a role in determining their complexion and if imperialistic motives still operated to prevent the consummation of an appropriate readjustment in the territorial status quo by pacific means. To illustrate the discrepancy in concreate terms: Under the Soviet concept, the Sino-Indian frontier quarrel automatically fitted the bill of a "dispute opposing established states" in which due attention would have to be paid to today's "historically defined boundaries"; in the Chinese version, if these boundaries were the product of imperialist expansionism and imperialistic appetites stood behind the efforts to maintain them intact, they were not, on those grounds alone, exempt from suitable revision by dint of exertion of physical pressure, if need be. Much the same can be said, of course, of the origins of the Sino-Russian border, save that the principle of proletarian internationalism theoretically supervened to preclude use of force between "fraternal nations"—pursuant to the Chinese thesis, an eventual

73. *Ibid.*, p. 12.

accommodation was imperative here as well, but meantime duress ought not to be applied to accomplish the goal.

No statute of limitations shielded the estate of the "offender" and, on the whole, the Chinese statement sounded as though Peking was prepared to countenance resort to arms vis-à-vis a wider class of border phenomena than the Kremlin, at least judging from the letter of their respective public pronouncements. Generally, in a verbal pattern that had become typical of the Sino-Soviet dialogue, the Chinese leaders set a higher value on violence as a tool to "combat imperialism" and attributed greater danger to the "machinations of the imperialist camp" on the contemporary scene than did their Russian colleagues. Khrushchev's offer thus also fell victim to the ongoing controversy over the correctness of the policy emphasizing peaceful coexistence as compared with a program extolling the virtues of revolutionary militancy.

These are minor points, however, and can hardly account for the vehemence of the Chinese reaction. On most essentials, the document fulfilled the accepted doctrinal criteria. The customary carte blanche was granted the so-called national liberation movements in their drive to shed the few remaining vestiges of former dependency, Chinese contentions to the contrary notwithstanding. All the standard ideological nuances were scrupulously observed, and friend and foe were filed under the by now familiar rubrics. The text likewise eschewed every tangible soupçon of anti-Chinese bias. The sole reference to China unconditionally affirmed the PRC's right to "free" Taiwan by whatever process it pleased; and, in apparent deference to Peking's susceptibilities, the examples of neither Hong Kong nor Macao were presently adduced as comparable experiences.[74] For once, the Soviets even abstained from voicing disparaging remarks about the Sino-Indian border imbroglio, which is quite understandable: If Khrushchev wished to reap maximum support for his initiative, the last thing in the world he could afford to do was put the nonaligned nations in the position of having to commit themselves on such an explosive issue.[75]

74. However, both are mentioned by P. Smolenskii, *Diplomatiya i granitsy* (Diplomacy and frontiers; Moscow: Mezhdunarodnye otnosheniya, 1965), pp. 37–38. This brochure, though, went to print in March 1965 and was written at a time when Soviet official circles had dropped their conciliatory tone and stepped up their denunciation of the Peking regime as a result of the remarks made by Mao in his talk with a group of Japanese Socialists.

75. References to the Sino-Indian border conflict nevertheless appeared in the contemporary Russian literature devoted to an analysis of the legal significance of Khrushchev's circular letter. See, for example, P. Smolenskii, p. 48; S. Molodtsov,

The material contents of the Soviet communication, then, were not calculated to provoke Peking's anger. Yet, the episode certainly did, which suggests that a closer look at the formal aspects of the incident may be in order. Viewed from that angle, Peking's irritation begins to make more sense. The thrust and timing of the Moscow message, for instance, clearly aimed to exploit the emotions aroused by the Himalayan confrontation and, by implication, to condemn the brand of behavior that on this occasion had culminated in blood-letting.[76] Hence, despite the oblique phrasing, no doubt can be entertained that China, because of its role in that affair, was among the principal targets, if not the principal one, of the Soviet stratagem. Further, Khrushchev's proposal was greeted primarily as a legal venture and in home circles was discussed chiefly in that vein,[77] whereas international law was not and is not a Chinese Communist forte and the blatant appeal to its norms by supposed confederates did not, one is morally convinced, sit well with the men running the PRC.

Add to that the fact that the gesture was addressed to every nation on the globe without discriminating between class-kin and enemy and envisaged that relations between all of them, whether they be members of the inner sanctum or neutrals or sworn antagonists, be governed by

Peace to Frontiers! (Moscow: Novosti, 1965), p. 9; B.M. Klimenko, *Gosudarstvennye granitsy—problema mira* (State frontiers—a peace problem; Moscow: Mezhdunarodnye otnosheniya, 1964), p. 86; K. Ivanov, "National Liberation and Territorial Conflicts," *International Affairs*, no. 5:12 (1964); V.A. Zorin, V.L. Israelyan, "The Marxist-Leninist Approach to the Solution of Territorial Disputes," *Kommunist*, no. 2:30 (1964).

76. Invariably, the less specific the reference, the more damning the judgment. Viz., S. Molodtsov, "Frontiers and International Law," *International Affairs*, no. 4:11 (1964): "There have been instances in recent years of attempts to justify armed attacks undertaken with a view to altering existing boundaries by claims that they did not infringe upon the territorial integrity of the country attacked. The attack, it was claimed in such cases, was made to regain 'our own territory' and rectify incorrectly demarcated borders." To the same effect, G. Tunkin, "Mezhdunarodnoe pravo i gosudarstvennye granitsy" (International law and state frontiers), *Izvestia*, Jan. 8, 1964, p. 2: "However, the modern history of international relations knows not a few cases when certain states, attempting to alter by force the existing frontiers, claimed . . . that their forcible actions did not infringe upon the territory of the other state and that they were merely defending their territory and the frontier, well, ran incorrectly."

77. In addition to the items listed in the three previous footnotes, see I. Blishchenko, "International law and the peaceful settlement of disputes," *Novoe vremya* (New times), no. 7:9–11 (1964); B. Dmitriev, "State frontiers and the strengthening of peace," *Mirovaya ekonomika i mezhdunarodnye otnosheniya* (World economy and international relations), no. 3:17–26 (1964); G.P. Zadorozhyi, *Granitsam-mir!* (Peace to frontiers; Moscow: Znanie, 1964); F. Kozhevnikov, A. Piradov, "International law and the question of frontiers," *Kommunist*, no. 2:32–38 (1964).

the same code and it is easy to see why the Chinese should have felt betrayed. To the Peking authorities, the very thought of signing a key political treaty in the company of the pillars of the Western community was anathema. The Russians must have known it and nonetheless tried to maneuver the Chinese into a corner where they either would have to act against what they frankly professed to believe in or reject the bid and so isolate themselves from the mainstream of world opinion. Not the least of Khrushchev's expectations must have been that the Chinese would choose precisely the latter course and enable him to capitalize at will on the wide-spread anti-Chinese sentiment such a decision would infallibly foster.

Finally, while there was no reason to assume that the Sino-Soviet debate over the local boundary issue would ever turn into a serious problem, still, with the sharpened awareness that at some juncture it might conceivably come to a practical test, the knowledge that public sympathies were solidly arrayed against the use of force to redress an alleged wrong in initially fixing the frontier line was bound to give comfort to the Russians and, by the same token, work to handicap their Chinese rivals. The appreciation that, propaganda-wise, the Soviets, perhaps in anticipation of that very contingency, had neatly stacked the deck in their own favor, could not but gall the Chinese comrades. What is more, the prospect that in the event a border crisis between the USSR and China were to erupt, every government on earth would be dragged into the family squabble or could horn in by claiming a valid interest derived from a universal convention of the kind advocated by Khrushchev, again was not prone to mollify the Chinese leaders.

The net impression is that of a successful publicity stunt staged by the Kremlin. Not a shred of evidence can be found to show that the Russians launched the experiment in genuine fear of an imminent Chinese threat to the Soviet Union's territorial integrity or even as a safeguard against the remote possibility of such a situation developing in the years ahead. Indeed, the subsequent fate of the project whose unveiling evoked so much fanfare and which, within a twelve-month period, ended up consigned to oblivion, proves that it was little else than an expendable pawn in a collateral chess-game spun out for the sake of salesmanship alone and with the design to enhance one's image and build up one's credit and undercut the competitor's.

The core theme did not vary. The only novelty was the overt introduction of international law terminology: The audience was different.

As long as the conversation stayed "private," both parties could avoid "juridifying" the exchange; once the polemics had been transferred to open chambers, the topic was general, and employing international law arguments couched at the highest level of abstraction did not then serve to "legalize" the purely Sino-Soviet share of the affair. The scenery was slightly modified, but the lyrics of the central duet were unaffected by the shift.

By this time, the parties probably realized that the rhetorical fusillade had reached a stalemate. The dispute had run as far as it would go without bringing up fresh artillery. All that could be said had been said, and either the original self-imposed limits of the controversy would have to be transcended—and, for the moment at least, the contestants seemed to have no taste for that idea—or a way had to be devised to break the present impasse where each side was determined not to appear to make any concessions to the adversary. So, the next thing we hear about from this sector is that Moscow and Peking had agreed to hold negotiations on the subject of the Sino-Soviet boundary[78] and, on February 23, 1964, "a delegation of Soviet experts on frontier questions" was reported to have "arrived in Peking to discuss certain matters of common interest." The news story, dated February 27, added that already "they have had one meeting with Chinese representatives at which questions of procedure were discussed."[79]

To carry on with the current debate would lead nowhere. The move to the bargaining table offered a logical answer. The two capitals had repeatedly advertised their conviction that the problem should properly be handled through bilateral negotiations—the latest step would prove them both right. Apparently, there were no preliminary arrangements concerning the agenda of the session, and this too facilitated the meeting, for had the opponents had to define their positions previous to the conference, it may never have convened.[80] The reverse danger was equally great: Having failed to establish the order of business, the

78. Edgar Snow's Interview with Chou En-lai, in Conakry, Guinea, January 23, 1964, *The New York Times*, Feb. 3, 1964, pp. 1, 3.

79. Dispatch from Tanjug International Service, Belgrade, February 27, 1964, in Doolin, *Territorial Claims*, p. 37.

80. How aware everybody was of this risk can be gathered from the noncommittal tone of Chou En-lai's statement to Edgar Snow, from which the world initially learned of the impending conclave: asked if the PRC had "any serious border disputes" with the USSR or whether one could "regard existing boundaries as satisfactory to both parties and not subject to future negotiations," his cryptic reply was that "we have reached an agreement with the Soviet Union that negotiations be held on the Sino-Soviet boundary questions."

Russian and Chinese emissaries, once they began exploring each other's views in earnest, might soon discover that they had no uniform frame of reference and therefore were left with no room for a compromise solution.

This, in fact, is what happened. Soviet and Chinese representatives "engaged in consultations in Peking on how best to engage in boundary problems and border questions between the two countries." A contemporary press item captured the ambiance of the occasion and delivered a singularly prophetic judgment on the prospects for the success of the conversations then in progress:

> According to diplomatic sources, the consultations are being conducted at the embassy level and are aimed at determining whether the Russians and Chinese can find common ground for a discussion of the border issues. The ideological dispute between them has grown worse recently and there is substantial doubt here [in Moscow] whether they will be able to agree on a formula for negotiations.
>
> Moreover, the Chinese Communists are understood to demand that the frontier negotiations be regarded as a comprehensive review of frontier disputes. Such an approach may be interpreted as allowing a reexamination of what the Chinese call "unequal" treaties under which czarist Russia obtained large areas of Chinese territory.
>
> Soviet officials are said to insist on a more narrow formula under which the negotiations would be limited to minor boundary "adjustments."
>
> This approach would restrict the talks to such problems as the ownership of islands in the Amur and Ussuri Rivers, which form a large segment of the boundary, the precise site of the shipping channel forming the boundary in these streams, and similar local issues.
>
> The best-known issue is a large, almost uninhabited island situated near the Far Eastern city of Khabarovsk, at the junction of the Ussuri and Amur Rivers.[81]

The Russians clung to their version until the end. On the very eve of the conclave, in his report to a plenary convocation of the Central Committee of the CPSU, Suslov again both criticized the Chinese for their share in precipitating the military confrontation on the Sino-Indian border[82] and repeated the Kremlin's old story about what had meanwhile transpired on the Sino-Soviet frontier. He said:

81. *The New York Times*, Feb. 26, 1964, p. 8. See, too, Colina MacDougall, "Rumanian Failure," *Far Eastern Economic Review*, no. 13:657–658 (1964).

82. Report delivered by Mikhail Suslov to a plenary meeting of the Central Committee on February 14, 1964, *World Communist Unity* (Soviet Booklet No. 3; London, 1964), p. 31. *Plenum Tsentralnogo Komiteta Kommunisticheskoi Partii Sovetskogo Soyuza*, 10–15 fevralva 1964 goda, stenograficheskii otchet (Plenum of the Central Executive Committee of the CPSU, February 10–15, 1964, stenographic report; Moscow: Gospolitizdat, 1964), p. 492.

We also consider it necessary to tell the plenary meeting about the violations of the Soviet-Chinese border, occasioned through the fault of the Chinese side. This has already been mentioned in the documents of the C.P.S.U. and the Soviet government. In 1962 and 1963 violations of the Soviet frontier kept occurring continuously, often assuming the form of crude provocations.

The Soviet government has taken the initiative in proposing that consultations be held in order to specify the frontier line between the U.S.S.R. and China at certain points. We do so in the belief that no territorial issues exist between the U.S.S.R. and the People's Republic of China, that the Soviet-Chinese frontier took shape historically, and that the issue can concern only certain sections of the frontier to make them more precise whenever necessary.[83]

And when, in early March, I.V. Spiridonov, head of a Soviet parliamentary delegation visiting India, revealed to the papers in Delhi that a Sino-Soviet mixed commission had been organized, he still described its function solely in terms of demarcation of the border between the USSR and the PRC "in certain sectors." Asked to explain the principles by which the commission would be guided in its task of demarcating the border, he replied that it was possible that some of the border posts had gotten lost or some other similar developments had taken place.[84] If he knew whereof he spoke, the gap between the Soviet and Chinese interpretations of the job in store could scarcely be wider.

From what little information is available, it sounds as though every effort to draft a mutually agreeable modus operandi immediately foundered on this key point for, after that fleeting debut, the scheme dropped from sight. Much later, in connection with a piece of serious trouble in the mixed Soviet-Chinese commission on shipping in border sectors of the rivers of the Amur basin—the Russians accusing the Chinese of deliberately disrupting the work of its fourteenth session which had met in Harbin on July 11, 1967—a few stray bits of additional data on what had befallen the border agency bobbed to the surface. First, the Soviets protested, "the Chinese side came out with a number of provocative statements and tried to make the Soviet delegation deal with questions of where the border line should pass—a matter not within the competence of the commission [on border shipping]." Discussion of that subject, the Soviet Foreign Ministry's note next recalled, had been instigated in 1964 between government delegations of the two countries "but was not completed through the fault of the Chinese side" which, we now learn,

83. *World Communist Unity*, p. 59; *Plenum*, pp. 516–517. Refer to B.M Klimenko, *Gosudarstvennye granitsy*, pp. 101–102.
84. *Asian Recorder* (1964), p. 5748.

had not yet named a date acceptable to it to continue consultations on a more precise demarcation of the Soviet-Chinese border, although the Soviet side, in its proposal of September 28, 1964, expressed its readiness to continue consultations with the Chinese side in Moscow on October 15, 1964.[85]

Today, of course, thanks to the wave of revelations triggered by the spate of bloody incidents along the Sino-Soviet frontier, a more complete picture of the 1964 affair emerges. While refinements attributable to the wisdom of hindsight pose a constant danger, with due caution one can nevertheless mount a fairly accurate reconstruction of the highlights of the encounter. According to Peking's recollections,

In 1964, the Chinese Government held boundary negotiations with the Soviet Government, during which the Chinese side made it clear that the "Sino-Russian Treaty of Aigun," the "Sino-Russian Treaty of Peking" and other treaties relating to the present Sino-Soviet boundary are all unequal treaties tsarist Russian imperialism imposed on China when power was not in the hands of the peoples of China and Russia. But, prompted by the desire to strengthen the revolutionary friendship between the Chinese and Soviet peoples, the Chinese side was willing to take these treaties as the basis for determining the entire alignment of the boundary line between the two countries and for settling all existing questions relating to the boundary; any side which occupies the territory of the other side in violation of the treaties must, in principle, return it wholly and unconditionally to the other side, but this does not preclude necessary readjustments at individual places on the boundary by both sides on the basis of the treaties and in accordance with the principles of consultation on an equal footing and of mutual understanding and mutual accommodation. However, the Soviet side refused to accept the above-mentioned reasonable proposals of the Chinese side. It refused to recognize the treaties relating to the present Sino-Soviet boundary as unequal treaties and obstinately refused to take these treaties as the basis for settling the boundary question between the two countries in its vain attempt to force China to accept a new unequal treaty and thus to perpetuate in legal form its occupation of the Chinese territory which it seized by crossing the boundary line defined by the unequal treaties. This great-power chauvinist and territorial expansionist stand of the Soviet revisionist renegade clique was severely condemned by the Chinese side. The Chinese side clearly pointed out that if the Soviet side should obdurately insist on such a stand and inexorably refuse to mend its ways, the Chinese side will have to reconsider its position as regards the Sino-Soviet boundary question as a whole.[86]

The account duly confirms what was then suspected concerning Peking's rigid insistence on the proximate redefinition of the full extent

85. *Soviet News*, no. 5402:107 (1967); *Pravda*, Sept. 1 1967, p. 4; *Izvestiya*, Sept. 2, 1967, p. 2.
86. Information Department of the Chinese Foreign Ministry, "Chenpao Island," p. 15.

of the Sino-Soviet boundary line. However, it also sheds added light on the gist of the Chinese position at the talks, the details of which the outer world had not known. For instance, if the above statement is correct, this was the first time in the history of the two-year old debate on the territorial issue that the Chinese formally engaged themselves vis-à-vis the Russians to observe the core formula by virtue of which Tsarist Russia's treaties with imperial China establishing their common frontier would still be accepted, despite their "unequal" character, as "the basis for determining the entire alignment of the boundary line between the two countries and for settling all existing questions relating to the boundary." The Russian delegation might otherwise have welcomed that particular assurance, except that it came coupled with a sine qua non demand for prior official recognition of the "unequal" nature of the operative border agreements and a blanket commitment to replace the latter with an instrument fixing the whole length of the frontier.

Rather unexpected, too, was the disclosure to the effect that the Chinese had already at that early date broached the subject of so-called territorial encroachments beyond the confines set by the corresponding conventions—presumably, the river islands, albeit not explicitly identified yet as a major topic of controversy, fell into this special category. The proposed manner of handling this second item of business again fits the usual pattern favored by the Communist Chinese regime: a preliminary acknowledgment that the Chinese state holds original title to the land at stake in fee simple, followed by a round of negotiations whereby some of the disputed property would be ceded to the other party. This elaborate ritual was destined, in a single move, to corroborate the absolute validity of the Chinese claim to the territory in question, mollify the opponent through an act of formal transfer of a portion of the contested terrain to his name and, *ultima ratio*, cast the Chinese in the enviable role of voluntary donors with the Russians appearing throughout as mere recipients of unique Chinese generosity.

In subsequent reports, the Chinese advocates began to pay greater attention to the job of spelling out the substance of their government's quarrel with the Russians over the matter of the river islands in the context of the 1964 episode. Thus, on the occasion of the nationwide release of the propaganda film, "The New Tsars' Anti-China Atrocities," the local mass media devoted considerable space to comments on a cadre from the movie showing a "map handed to the Chinese side by the Soviet revisionists during the 1964 Sino-Soviet negotiations on the boundary question" as prima facie proof that the Russians had "tampered with the boundary line as they pleased on this map and marked as their territory more than 600 of the over 700 islands on the Chinese side of the central lines of the channels of the Wusuli and Heilung Rivers."[87] Apart from illuminating the magnitude of the problem, the statement managed to convey the impression that even then the PRC authorities endorsed the *thalweg* principle as the proper criterion for charting the boundary line between the two countries where it was pegged to a navigable river. To reinforce that contention, Peking afterwards declared that during the Sino-Soviet boundary negotiations in 1964, the Soviet representative, no less,

> also had to admit that the red line on the map attached to the "Sino-Russian Treaty of Peking" cannot show the precise alignment of the boundary line in the rivers, nor can it possibly determine the ownership of islands; he could not but agree that the central line of the main channel should be taken for determining the boundary line on the rivers and the ownership of islands.[88]

How correct this version of the proceedings is cannot be ascertained at this stage, and only access to the minutes of the conference will provide the final answer. On balance, the claims made in the previously cited passages sound a trifle exaggerated, but not altogether unfounded.

By contrast with the Chinese brief, which ranged far afield, the rival Soviet script in referring to the 1964 events has concentrated exclusively on the theme of "minor border adjustments." This approach is quite understandable, since Moscow wanted to avoid at any cost getting entangled in endless polemics over the juridical respectability of the treaties that shaped the modern profile of the Sino-Soviet frontier and instead sought to narrow the meeting's agenda to an investigation of the prospects for implementing ad hoc "rectifications" of the existing boundary line in spots where technical modifications in the previous modus operandi seemed advisable. But, where Chinese sources paint a tableau of blind Soviet intransigence when asked to surrender a few random bits of "alien" soil, the Soviet official spokesmen's version of the story credits the USSR with taking the initiative at the parley in submitting

87. *PR*, no. 17:3 (1969). *Cf.* Statement of the Government of the People's Republic of China, May 24, 1969, *PR*, no. 22:5 (1969).

88. Statement of the Government of the People's Republic of China, May 24, 1969, *ibid.*, p. 2.

proposals whose adoption would have made it possible within the shortest period to carry out by mutual consent the specification of individual sectors of the Soviet-Chinese border line. The Soviet delegation was guided by the consideration that the successful completion of consultations would be an important contribution to maintaining friendly relations between our peoples and states.

Now the Chinese were blamed for the breakdown of the 1964 negotiations and publicly attacked on the grounds that "the 1964 consultations showed that the Chinese side had no intention of reaching an agreement." Rather,

the PRC delegation attempted to question the state border, which had been historically formed and confirmed by treaties. The Chinese side regarded the idea of the consultations as an opportunity of artificially creating "territorial problems" that would complicate relations between our peoples and countries for many years to come.[89]

For all the impassioned oratory from both quarters, a careful reading of the record still leads one to believe that, in concrete terms, a very small distance separated the opponents and that, with a minimal effort, the remaining gap could easily have been bridged. Indeed, they themselves acknowledged as much, since Peking as well as Moscow has often, as of late, openly said that it would "not have been difficult" to reach a settlement on that occasion, each, of course, interjecting that all that would have been necessary then to ensure the successful outcome of the talks was just the slightest display of inclination on the part of the other to behave sensibly and be willing to make no more than a token compromise. Or, as a recent Soviet communiqué summed it up:

During the consultations in Peking in 1964 the Soviet side expressed its readiness to meet half way the wishes of the Chinese side, which were concerned with the interests of the Chinese population along the banks of the river, and to reach agreement on the demarcation of the frontier line between the USSR and the People's Republic of China along the Rivers Amur and Ussuri on the basis of mutual concessions, on condition that the Chinese side, in its turn, showed a readiness to recognize correspondingly the interests of the Soviet population along particular sections of the frontier. This could have been a reasonable agreement based on a desire on the part of both sides to do away with tension and to maintain tranquillity on the frontier.[90]

89. *Pravda*, Mar. 30, 1969, p. 1; *Izvestiya*, Mar. 30, 1969, pp. 1–2; *USSR Government Statement of March 29, 1969*, p. 13.

90. Statement of the USSR Government of June 13, 1969, *Pravda*, June 14, 1969, pp. 1–2; *Izvestiya*, June 14, 1969, pp. 1, 3; *Soviet News*, no. 5494:139 (1969).

In a nutshell, what apparently torpedoed the 1964 session was not the issue of "territorial accommodations" per se, for both capitals profess, at least in retrospect, to have been prepared at the time to make the requisite sacrifices in order to forge a stable peace on their common frontier, nor is there any solid evidence to indicate that they do not mean what they assert. The mosaic, though fragmentary, thus suggests that the real stumbling block lay in the procedural instead of the substantive sphere and that the contestants might have arrived at a working consensus on the merits of the case without undue trouble had ideological factors not intruded into the conversations and doomed them to failure, namely: Peking's insistence on applying the ex cathedra formula by which all the old treaties relating to the Sino-Russian border first had to be pronounced "unequal," next China's title to the land "beyond the line established by these conventions" which allegedly had been subjected to Soviet "occupation" had to be redeemed, and only then could business-like discussions take place, a scenario to which the Soviets objected as a matter of sheer principle, more for the doctrinal than pragmatic motives. Hence, in the final analysis, the inability to reconcile the competing viewpoints on the question of diplomatic etiquette over the correct manner and suitable style of resolving the problem rather than organic divergence of opinion with respect to the express terms of the settlement proper must be seen as the primary cause of the political impasse which persists to this day.

From all this, one further conclusion recommends itself: the practical impetus for summoning the colloquy stemmed from the Kremlin. The Russians traveled to Peking for that purpose. They subsequently showed interest in keeping the border commission alive, while the Chinese apparently could not care less whether that body functioned or not. Given the past history of the dispute, the present switch in the Soviet attitude can be described only as dramatic. Neither party has ever supplied a formal explanation of these events, but a few conjectures may be ventured that might account for the startling reversal of roles in the marathon diplomatic tournament foreshadowed by this episode.

Looking back, it would seem that Khrushchev had here miscalculated rather badly from the very outset. The decision to inject the territorial theme into the Sino-Soviet dialogue had, on balance, quite obviously boomeranged. True, Peking's reflex to Khrushchev's jibe on its failure to "liberate" Hong Kong and Macao had furnished Moscow with the opportunity to denounce the Chinese as "territorial revisionists" for their pejorative references to the legal status of the Sino-Soviet border, and the fortuitous Himalayan affair added fuel to the flames. In the end, however, the results of the foray had proved disappointing. The Chinese had refused to be stampeded into any rash pronouncements or actions that would lend sustenance to the charge that the PRC regime was bent on physical expansion across its northern perimeter. The dust soon settled on the frontier with India as well, with the Chinese again betraying no desire to annex Indian soil beyond the contested zone, even after its occupation by the PLA.

On the other hand, now that the Soviet leadership had publicly broached the subject, the PRC hierarchy could and did use that lever to exert enough pressure on its ally to annoy and disturb Soviet official circles: Symbolic provocations and demonstrative probes at the border irritated the Russians, and yet no matter how hard Moscow broadcasted these incidents, they sounded too minor in scope and significance to really hurt China's image abroad. Plus, the Kremlin never managed to adduce any concrete evidence that the Chinese behavior in the Siberian and Central Asian border regions was indeed intended to alter by force the configuration of the existing frontier. The desolate river islands might constitute an exception in this respect, but the title to them was sufficiently beclouded for the Soviet charge of Chinese aggressiveness in their sporadic endeavors to exercise rights of possession on these scattered shreds of land to stick. By then, inveighing against the Chinese for having let the Sino-Indian border quarrel degenerate into a shooting war also was like flogging a dead horse: That unpleasantness had blown over, the neighboring countries wanted to forget the upheaval, and the Indians themselves probably preferred not to be reminded that their impotency alone prevented them from recouping their fortunes.

Khrushchev had thus unloosed a Frankenstein and reaped no tangible reward for his efforts; rather he was currently paying a political price out of all proportion to the visible gains. Introducing the territorial issue had undoubtedly aggravated the controversy with the PRC and had come dangerously close to transforming a doctrinal duel into a state confrontation. The ideological conflict between the two capitals had noticeably worsened as of late, and unhappiness with Khrushchev's handling of this situation, among the rest, was beginning to mount at home.

In the light of the above, the pilgrimage to Peking was undertaken, at a guess, in pursuit of one of twin objectives. The primary goal was to put the monster Khrushchev had fathered safely back under wraps with a minimum of advertisement and without undue "loss of face." The trip itself amounted to a placatory gesture; perhaps the Russians planned not to air the matter in advance altogether, for the Chinese proceeded to mention it first. If a satisfactory deal were sealed, Khrushchev would presumably face the domestic opposition with a fait accompli, take personal credit for disposing of a difficult problem, and hope to emerge the victor in the looming intramural struggle for power. If the attempt missed, Khrushchev could still try to salvage his career by launching a full-scale attack on the Communist Chinese for their intransigence and, by identifying his rivals in the Politburo with the Peking faction, seek to portray them as enemies of Russian national interests and so block their bid for control. In either case, the game had to be played with consummate finesse. A positive solution would have to be achieved on terms that could be presented to his disgruntled associates as a vindication of his prior policy line vis-à-vis Peking, and the Chinese would be sure to checkmate any move designed to redeem Khrushchev's prestige at their expense. In the event of a negative outcome, the blame would somehow have to be placed on the shoulders of the mainland regime, and that would not be easy either, considering that the Chinese contribution to the flow of oratory on the Sino-Soviet frontier question had struck throughout a note of remarkable moderation and restraint.

In the end, of course, the gambit failed. One suspects that the Chinese knew of Khrushchev's troubles, for barely had the Soviet and Chinese spokesmen sat down to business than the Central Committee of the Chinese Communist Party saw fit to dispatch a public letter to its Soviet alter ego which spelled out afresh the Chinese views on various aspects of their simmering border feud. The message purveyed a masterly blend of tactfulness-cum-intractability. With an eye to the round of frontier talks that had just opened, the communication began by recalling that

> The Government of the People's Republic of China has consistently held that the question of the boundary between China and the Soviet Union, which is a legacy from the past, can be settled through negotiation between the two Governments. It has also held that, pending such a settlement, the status quo on the border should be maintained.[91]

91. *PR*, no. 19:13 (1964).

On the one hand, the statement was a perfectly accurate description of the official Chinese position on this particular subject up till now, with which nobody could cavil in good faith. On the other, the words plainly implied, as they must have been meant to, that the current discussions fully validated Peking's thesis on this issue.

Not content with this bit of self-congratulation though, the Communist Chinese next tried to pin on the Russian comrades the responsibility for the present crisis in their frontier relations. Insisting that "this is what we have done over the past ten years or more [i.e., maintained the status quo on the border]" and that "had the Soviet Government taken the same attitude, both sides could have lived in amity along the border and preserved tranquility there," Peking then charged,

> With the stepping up of anti-Chinese activities by the leaders of the C.P.S.U. in recent years, the Soviet side has made frequent breaches of the status quo on the border, occupied Chinese territory and provoked border incidents. Still more serious, the Soviet side has flagrantly carried out large-scale subversive activities in Chinese frontier areas, trying to sow discord among China's nationalities by means of the press and wireless, inciting China's minority nationalities to break away from their motherland, and inveigling and coercing tens of thousands of Chinese citizens into going to the Soviet Union. Not only do all these acts violate the principles guiding relations between socialist countries, they are absolutely impermissible even in the relations between countries in general.[92]

The bulk of the Chinese allegations of Soviet meddling in Sinkiang and elsewhere rings true. The rest of the accusations, however, lack credibility. This applies especially to the assertion that the Soviets had "made frequent breaches of the status quo on the border, occupied Chinese territory and provoked border incidents." Not only is there no documented evidence to support this indictment (save perhaps in connection with the midstream islands), but the claim looks suspiciously like a clumsy attempt to tar the Russians with their own brush.

The proposition that the Soviets encouraged China's ethnic minorities to secede from the PRC seems equally far-fetched. More to the point is the fact that the Chinese chose to bring up the topic at this late date and, according to press accounts, the Chinese and Soviet delegates assembled in Peking were expected to deal with it too, for the Russians

92. *Ibid.*

meanwhile were striving to sound as conciliatory as possible on that score. Typical of the new attitude were the contemporary remarks attributed to the Chairman of the Council of Ministers of the Kirghiz S.S.R. who, confirming that many people had entered Kirghizia and Kazakhstan from Sinkiang in the preceding months, amplified on the comment by explaining that "several requests were made to the Chinese to prevent this 'mass flow' of people," that those who had migrated into Russian territory were assigned proper jobs and "economically placed exactly" as Soviet citizens, and that the exodus had since stopped.[93]

The net impression is that the Soviets were trying to wiggle off the hook, as gracefully as circumstances would allow, and the Chinese would have none of it. In similar vein, seeing that Moscow had more than once sought to buttress its case against Peking by invoking the universal norms of international behavior, the latter seized the occasion to reciprocate by promptly adjudging the Kremlin's conduct in this domain to have fallen short of the standards regulating the mode of transaction not merely between "fraternal nations" but between any random pair of countries on earth, whatever their political complexion.

The pattern persists. The Chinese again borrowed a page from Khrushchev's script. The Soviets had freely used the Indian affair to castigate the Chinese and so the Chinese forthwith proceeded to repay them in kind with the cogent observation,

> Among all our neighbors it is only the leaders of the C.P.S.U. and the reactionary nationalists of India who have deliberately created border disputes with China. The Chinese Government has satisfactorily settled complicated boundary questions, which were legacies from the past, both with all its fraternal socialist neighbors except the Soviet Union, and with its nationalist neighbors such as Burma, Nepal, Pakistan and Afghanistan, with the exception of India.[94]

These are telling blows and, in the opinion of many, Peking may well have had the best of the argument. Khrushchev had diligently paraded the example of India in an effort to tarnish China's reputation on the world scene and the Chinese in this instance neatly demonstrated how the Russians could be hoisted with their own petard. Having publicly associated themselves with the Indians in their grievances against the Chinese, the Soviets were now also forced to share with them the dubious distinction of standing virtually alone in bearing

93. *Asian Recorder* (1964), p. 5748.
94. *Ibid.*

that burden when every other state around China's continental rim had already managed to strike a profitable territorial bargain with it. Invidious comparisons can cut both ways. They did here, at any rate, and not to Moscow's great advantage either.

Then came the clincher. After corroborating reports that "the delegations of our two Governments started boundary negotiations in Peking on February 25, 1964," the Communist Chinese let all and sundry know, as they had just finished informing the Russians in camera, that

> Although the old treaties relating to the Sino-Russian boundary are unequal treaties, the Chinese Government is nevertheless willing to respect them and take them as the basis for a reasonable settlement of the Sino-Soviet boundary question. Guided by proletarian internationalism and the principles governing relations between socialist countries, the Chinese Government will conduct friendly negotiations with the Soviet Government in the spirit of consultation on an equal footing and mutual understanding and mutual accommodation. If the Soviet side takes the same attitude as the Chinese Government, the settlement of the Sino-Soviet boundary question, we believe, ought not to be difficult, and the Sino-Soviet boundary will truly become one of lasting friendship.[95]

In short, the Chinese spoke softly, yet on the essentials they refused to yield an inch. As hitherto, what they wanted was a formal clarification of the location of the entire Sino-Soviet boundary line. The Russians either had to accept that cardinal premise or look forward to returning to Moscow empty-handed. Granted, even after the original compromise, they could end up manning a frontier with China more or less identical with the existing one, but for that they would thenceforth be indebted to Peking's magnanimity. An analogous border trace would be the product of special dispensation on the part of the Chinese Communists and not a recognition of the local title purportedly acquired by the Russians by dint of the ancient treaties imposed on China by the Tzarist empire. Moreover, once that Pandora's box was unlocked, who could guarantee the Kremlin that Peking would still not advance further conditions, when the lid could not be snapped shut and after the status quo had been hopelessly jeopardized?

Such an abject psychological surrender and the corporeal risks involved were too much for the Soviets to swallow, no matter how badly they might have wished to put an end to the border "vendetta." For Khrushchev personally, the worst aspect of the whole affair was that

95. *Ibid.*

the Chinese had decisively outmaneuvered him. He had not been able to budge them and, at the same time, their response had been articulated in language so constructive and sensible as to deprive him of an opportunity to cast them persuasively in the role of evildoers. Furthermore, the Russians had been close-mouthed about the conference, and the Chinese had stolen a march on them by releasing their version of the story first, complete with optimistic predictions and a happy solution. Propaganda-wise, Khrushchev had suffered a serious defeat. Lastly, the very sins imputed to him were those he had previously laid at Peking's doorstep, nor could he counter that the Chinese were thus escalating the dispute or spreading lies since earlier he had accused them of the same crimes and had set a precedent by not bothering to furnish evidence to substantiate the charges. Often nothing hurts more than, or is so hard to handle as, a canard coming home to roost. Khrushchev must have found the experience singularly unpalatable.

At this point, the initiative here passed to the Communist Chinese. Mutual recriminations in this area, momentarily interrupted, revived, but the zest was gone. Stock denunciations were traded listlessly, the chorus lapsed into a tired refrain. The Soviet Consul General in Calcutta criticized the Chinese hierarchy for "indulging in adventurism and provoking border incidents with neighboring countries" and recited the staple formula that "the violations of the Soviet border by the Chinese in 1962 and 1963 were a constant occurrence" and that "sometimes this took the form of flagrant provocations."[96] An eminent Soviet international jurist is quoted as having declared that

> no territorial questions exist betwen the USSR and the PRC and that the Soviet-Chinese frontier has taken shape historically. The only question can be one of separate clarifications of the frontier, which are necessary. But the Chinese side has for some time been continually and systematically violating the Soviet-Chinese frontier and, furthermore, frequently in a crude and provocative manner.

The legal expert's conclusion was that this "is in flagrant contradiction of the generally accepted standards of law."[97] The Chinese flailed away

96. Doolin, *Territorial Claims*, pp. 38–39.

97. *Ibid.*, pp. 39–40. Also, *Asian Recorder* (1964), p. 5807. The same theme recurs in *Izvestiya*, May 31, 1964, p. 4; condensed text in English in *Current Digest of the Soviet Press*, no. 23:3–4 (1964): "Observance of sovereignty and equal rights in deeds and not in words means: respect for the laws, practices and traditions that have become established in this or that socialist country; respect for the government and party authorities to whom the people have entrusted the

at recent Soviet tactics in Sinkiang, and the Russians scored the Chinese for conspiring to exploit the proletariat of Hong Kong and of betraying the goals of revolution by bolstering the colony's capitalist economy.[98]

The dialogue led nowhere—a plateau had been reached. This state of suspended animation could, conceivably, have lingered on. Khrushchev had shot his bolt. Having in effect won the match, the Chinese could at this juncture let the subject drop or move to administer the coup de grâce. Mao chose the latter path, and in July 1964, in the course of an interview with a Japanese socialist delegation visiting Peking, the deed was done. But that forms an extra chapter.

CONCLUSION

In sum, a careful analysis of the public record dispels the notion that the territorial element contributed a significant dimension to the Sino-Soviet controversy, at least at the incubating stage. Rather, the foregoing debate over frontiers bears every earmark of an intricate game played for extrinsic political stakes in accordance with a series of well-defined rules. Style is crucial: The parties show keen awareness of what can properly be said, how it should be worded, and that they must observe throughout the exchange the principle of proportionality, lest the fixed limits of the colloquy be transcended and the contest unwittingly take on a riskier character than intended by the opponents. The territorial issue undoubtedly helps inflame the tempers on both sides, nasty enough already, and so aggravates the circumjacent politico-ideological struggle waged by Moscow and Peking, without, however, achieving a raison d'être of its own or gaining a stature sufficiently dominant to steer the overarching conflict into new and uncharted channels.

The role assigned to international law in the process fits the picture just outlined. The weapon of law is used sparingly, and for good cause. Law is rigid, and everybody concerned seeks to maintain maximum flexibility of action. Law deals with right and wrong and ascribes guilt and innocence. Amicable compromise holds out a better promise of attaining success. Law means a collision at a state level, and the

---

administration of the country; and respect for historically evolved state borders. The Chinese authorities are crudely trampling on all these elementary norms of relations between sovereign states."

98. Doolin, *Territorial Claims*, pp. 40–41.

present *malentendu* is, by unanimous vote, pictured as a quarrel between rival teams of dedicated Marxist-Leninists. Law has other defects as well. Arguments drawn from the fund of general international law are ideologically impure and, in any case, probably are out of place in a conversation between "fellow-socialists." And "socialist international law" sheds no light on the matter, for the very phenomenon which now requires a solution is a priori barred as an impossibility under the terms of membership in the "socialist Commonwealth"—hence, the dilemma and the wispy quality of the legal accompaniment to the political solos. Note than even on those rare occasions where, as we have recently learned, genuine international legal formulas were invoked—the *thalweg* rule, for instance, during the 1964 negotiations—the fact was not made public until many years later. Granted, the rationale for citing the principle—the dispute over the status of the river islands—was itself at the time a relatively well-kept secret, but then one wonders if fear of precipitating a legal quarrel or of being caught breaking a doctrinal taboo or exposed for introducing alien standards into a family "debate" was not perhaps a prime motive for maintaining the silence to begin with, since the topic could hardly be discussed intelligently without venturing into the legal sphere.

We can still admire the performance as an impressive piece of orchestration or as a superlative essay in choreography. The trick is not to confuse drama with real life and, a fortiori, a plot's ornamental décor with its essence.

7 / Comparison of the Nationalist and Communist Chinese Views of Unequal Treaties

Hungdah Chiu

INTRODUCTION

On October 10, 1942, the thirty-first national day of the Republic of China, the United States and Great Britain announced that they would relinquish their special rights in China obtained under old treaties. On January 10, 1943, both countries signed treaties for the relinquishment of extraterritorial rights in China. The next day, President Chiang Kai-shek of the Republic of China declared that "today marks a new epoch in China's history and today Britain and America have lighted a new light to guide man's progress on the road to equality and freedom for all peoples."[1] It appeared that from then on, as far as China was concerned, the problem of unequal treaties would become a matter of only historical or academic interest apart from questions such as Kowloon, Hong Kong, and Macao. Subsequent developments did not, however, bear this out.

On August 14, 1945, the Republic of China concluded several agreements with the Soviet Union granting the latter important concessions in China's northeastern provinces (Manchuria). These agreements were later considered "unequal treaties" by Nationalist Chinese scholars.[2] Since the Communist Chinese took over the mainland in 1949, references to "unequal treaties" in Chinese scholarship and official statements

1. Chinese Ministry of Information, ed., *The Collected Wartime Messages of Generalissimo Chiang Kai-shek, 1937–1945* (New York: The John Day Company, 1946), vol. II, p. 734.

2. See Ch'ien T'ai, *Chung-kuo pu-p'ing-teng t'iao-yüeh chih yüan-ch'i chi ch'i fei-ch'u chih ching-kuo* (The origin and abolition of China's unequal treaties; Taipei: Kuo-fang yen-chiu yüan, 1961), pp. 40–44.

have been more frequent. Thus, in January 1950 when the United States tried to invoke the 1943 Sino-American Treaty for the Relinquishment of Extraterritorial Rights in China to protect its consular properties in Peking, Communist Chinese authorities charged the United States with attempting "to procrastinate and resist on the grounds of the unequal treaty."[3] More recently, Communist China (the People's Republic of China) has engaged in a dispute with the Soviet Union over the question of whether or not nineteenth-century treaties delineating the Sino-Soviet boundary are unequal treaties.[4]

These examples suggest that even today there remains a practical need to study the problem of unequal treaties in the light of both Nationalist and Communist theory and practice.

DEVELOPMENT OF THE CONCEPT OF UNEQUAL TREATIES IN INTERNATIONAL LAW

Early in the seventeenth century, Grotius distinguished between "equal" and "unequal" treaties in his famous *De Jure Belli Ac Pacis.* According to him, treaties "which add something beyond the rights based on the law of nature are either on equal or on unequal terms."[5] Another seventeenth-century writer, Pufendorf, made a similar classification of treaties. He defined unequal treaties as those in which "the things promised by the two parties are unequal, or when either party is made inferior to the other."[6] These publicists, however, were silent on the question of the legal validity of those treaties classified as "unequal." Presumably, they considered them legally valid.

In the eighteenth century, the Swiss writer Vattel also distinguished between equal and unequal treaties. His definition of unequal treaties did not differ from that of either Grotius or Pufendorf. Although he did not question the legal validity of unequal treaties, he nevertheless argued that "since Nations are no less bound than individuals to respect

3. See "Peking Military Control Committee Requisitions Foreign Barracks in City," NCNA News Release, in English, no. 261:77–78 (Jan. 19, 1950).

4. See below, pp. 264–265.

5. Hugo Grotius, *De Jure Belli Ac Pacis* (On the law of war and peace), translated by Kelsey from the text of the 1646 ed. (Washington, D.C.: Carnegie Endowment for International Peace, 1925), vol. II, p. 394.

6. Samuel Pufendorf, *De Jure Naturae et Gentium* (On the law of nature and nations), translated by C.H. Oldfather and W.A. Oldfather from the 1688 ed. (Washington, D.C.: Carnegie Endowment for International Peace, 1934), vol. II, p. 1332.

justice, they should make their treaties equal, as far as that is possible."[7] The German writer Wolff in the same period made a lengthy study of the question of equality of treaties.[8] With respect to the legal validity of unequal treaties, however, he concluded that "treaties between nations are valid, if there is no inherent defect in the method of agreement, without consideration of the equity or inequity of the treaty."[9]

In the nineteenth century, Western writers' interest in unequal treaties appeared to decline. Thus, that term is not even mentioned in those standard treatises on international law written by Wheaton, Woolsey, or Phillimore.[10] A few writers such as Calvo[11] and Halleck did make casual reference to this question in connection with their discussion of the problem of classification of treaties. Halleck, however, concluded that "the inequality in the stipulations, or engagements of a treaty, does not, in general, render such engagements any the less binding upon the contracting parties."[12]

Since the beginning of this century, Western treatise writers have generally ignored the problem of unequal treaties.[13] One writer expressed the view in 1901 that the classification of treaties as equal and unequal is "artificial and unfruitful" and should be discarded.[14]

After the 1917 Bolshevik revolution in Russia, the Bolshevik govern-

7. Emerich De Vattel, *Le Droit de gens ou principes de la loi naturelle* (The law of nations or the principles of natural law), translated by Fenwick from the 1758 ed. (Washington, D.C.: Carnegie Endowment for International Peace, 1916), vol. III, p. 165.

8. See Christian von Wolff, *Jus Gentium Methodo Scientifica Pertratatum* (The law of nations treated according to a scientific method), translated by Drake from the 1764 ed. (Washington, D.C.: Carnegie Endowment for International Peace, 1934), vol. II, pp. 204–215.

9. *Ibid.*, p. 214.

10. See Henry Wheaton, *Elements of International Law* (6th ed., Boston: Little, Brown and Company, 1855); Theodore D. Woolsey, *Introduction to the Study of International Law* (3rd ed., New York: Charles Scribner & Co., 1871); Robert Phillimore, *Commentaries upon International Law* (2nd ed., London: Butterworth, 1871). All these books were translated into Chinese in the nineteenth century as *Wan-kuo kung-fa* (Peking: T'ung-wen-kuan, 1864); *Kung-fa pien-lan* (Peking: T'ung-wen-kuan, 1877); and *Ko-kuo chiao-she kung-fa lun* (Shanghai: Hsiao-ts'ang shan-fang, 1896), respectively.

11. See Carlos Calvo, *Le Droit international théorique et pratique* (3rd ed., Paris: A. Rousseau, 1880), pp. 630–631.

12. H.W. Halleck, *International Law* (San Francisco: H.H. Bancroft and Co., 1861), p. 196.

13. The term is not found, in connection with the discussion on treaties, in the treatises of international law written by such famous Western scholars as Brierly, Oppenheim, Hyde, Briggs, Fenwick, Hall, Jessup, Kelsen, and O'Connell.

14. Harris Taylor, *A Treatise on International Public Law* (Chicago: Callaghan & Co., 1901), p. 367.

ment offered to abolish and later did abolish some former Tzarist treaties imposed upon China, Persia, and Turkey;[15] and Soviet writers then began to discuss the question of the validity of those "coercive, predatory, and enslaving" treaties, although the term "unequal treaties" was not widely used until after World War II.[16] This early development in the Soviet Union, however, was generally ignored by Western scholars.

In the 1920s, however, the problem of unequal treaties received world-wide attention when China demanded the abolition of some treaties that it termed unequal. Only then did some Western writers renew interest in the problem. Thus, in 1927 at the annual meeting of the American Society of International Law, a session was devoted to the discussion of China's unequal treaties.[17] With the abolition of what were presumed to be the last of China's unequal treaties in the early 1940s,[18] Western scholars again lost interest in the subject.[19]

With the emergence of many new states in Asia and Africa in the 1960s, the question of unequal treaties again began to attract world-wide attention. When the Draft Articles on the Law of Treaties prepared by the United Nations International Law Commission was sent to UN member states for comment, many states expressed concern about the question of unequal treaties.[20] The 1969 Vienna Conference on the Law of Treaties adopted a declaration "*deploring* the fact that in the past States have sometimes been forced to conclude treaties under pressure exerted in various forms by other States" and "desiring to ensure that in the future no such pressure will be exerted in any form by any State in connection with the conclusion of a treaty."[21]

15. Jan F. Triska and Robert Slusser, *Theory, Law, and Policy of Soviet Treaties* (Stanford, Calif.: Stanford University Press, 1962), pp. 142–143. See also my note 37.

16. *Ibid.*, p. 42.

17. See Frank E. Hinckley, "Consular Authority in China by New Treaty," ASIL *Proceedings*, 22nd annual meeting (1927), pp. 82–87; Albert H. Putney, "The Termination of Unequal Treaties," *ibid.*, pp. 87–90; Raymond L. Buell, "The Termination of Unequal Treaties," *ibid.*, pp. 90–99.

18. See below, p. 256.

19. Fishel made a comprehensive study of the termination of extraterritoriality in China. His approach, however, is historical rather than legal. He did not study the origin and development of the concept of "unequal treaties." See Wesley R. Fishel, *The End of Extraterritoriality in China* (Berkeley and Los Angeles, Calif.: University of California Press, 1952).

20. See comments by Czechoslovakia, Bulgaria, Byelorussian Republic, Colombia, Iraq, and United Arab Republic. Many states also expressed their concern over the use of economic pressure in the process of concluding treaties. See *Yearbook of the International Law Commission, 1966* (UN Doc. A/Cn.4/Ser.A/Add. 1 [1966]), vol. II, pp. 15–20.

21. *International Legal Materials* 8.4:733 (July 1969).

THE DEVELOPMENT OF THE CONCEPT OF UNEQUAL TREATIES IN CHINA

How the concept of unequal treaties came to China is a question that has not yet been systematically studied. In the nineteenth and early twentieth centuries, China was compelled to conclude with many countries treaties that provided for extraterritoriality (also known as consular jurisdiction) for the nationals of those countries in China, restrictive tariff regulations, territorial cessions and leases, the right to station foreign troops in China, and other humiliating infringements on sovereignty. Needless to say, both the Chinese government and the Chinese people resented those treaties, particularly the ones relating to extraterritoriality.

Although the term "unequal treaties" did not seem to be used to describe these treaties until the early 1920s, prior to that period Chinese officials and scholars did express their dissatisfaction with the unequal arrangements in China's treaties with foreign states. Thus, in 1898 the famous Ch'ing reform leader K'ang Yu-wei (1858–1927) stated in his memorial to Emperor Kuang-hsü (1875–1908) that: "Foreigners in China are governed by their own countries and our country [consequently] does not enjoy equal rights [concerning this matter]. This is in fact an extreme national shame."[22]

Chang Chih-tung (1837–1909), who was Governor-General of Hunan and Hupei provinces for eighteen years, stated in his book *Ch'üan-hsüeh-p'ien* (Exhortation to study) written in 1898: "Today . . . the intercourse between China and Western states is different [from the intercourse among Western states]. For instance, the import tax [rate] is decided by the importing state, but China cannot so decide the tax rate. Foreign merchants should be governed by the resident state, but China cannot so govern them. The trade between states can only be carried out in sea ports and not in inland rivers, but [the Chinese case is different]."[23]

22. "Memorial in Response to the Emperor's Edict Calling for Suggestions Concerning the Overall Situation," *Tung-hua hsü-lu* (Supplementary Tung-hua records), chüan 142, pp. 8–12; cited in *Chung-hua min-kuo k'ai-kuo wu-shih-nien wen-hsien* (Documents and materials relating to the 50th anniversary of the Republic of China), 1st series, vol. VII, part I, *Ch'ing-ting chih kai-ke yü fan-tung* (The reform and antireform measures of the Ch'ing government; Taipei: Chung-hua min-kuo k'ai-kuo wu-shih-nien wen-hsien pien-ch'uan wei-yüan-hui, 1965), p. 342.

23. *Chang wen-hsiang kung ch'üan chi* (Collected works of Chang Chih-tung), chüan 203; cited in *Ch'ing-ting chih kai-ke yü fan-tung*, p. 440.

Moreover, the Ch'ing government and the early Republican government (Peking government) repeatedly demanded the revision or abrogation of these treaties. In 1902, the Ch'ing government persuaded Great Britain to recognize in a commercial treaty the impermanence of foreigners' extraterritorial rights in China.

Article 12 of the Sino-British Treaty concerning Commercial Relations of September 5, 1902, provides:

> China having expressed a strong desire to reform her judicial system and to bring it into accord with that of Western nations, Great Britain agrees to give every assistance to such reform, and she will also be prepared to relinquish her extraterritorial rights when she is satisfied that the state of the Chinese laws, the arrangement for their administration, and other considerations warrant her in so doing.[24]

Similar provisions were included in the Sino-Japanese and Sino-American treaties concluded the following year.[25]

Furthermore, on January 1, 1912, when the Republic of China was formally inaugurated, Provisional President Sun Yat-sen issued a declaration which stated in part:

> With the establishment of the Provisional Government we will try our best to carry out the duties of a civilized nation *so as to obtain the rights of a civilized state*. Under the Manchu Government China has been obliged to be under humiliation and bad anti-foreign feeling; but all these should be wiped out, and we should aim at the principle of peace and tranquility, and should also increase our friendship with friendly nations *so as to place China in a respectable place in international society* to follow in the steps of the other Powers of the world. Our foreign policy is based on this point.[26] (Emphasis added.)

This statement clearly indicated that China wanted to enjoy equal status with other civilized states. To achieve that aim, the obvious implication was that existing Chinese treaties incompatible with the sover-

24. Imperial Maritime Customs, *Treaties, Conventions, Etc., between China and Foreign States* (Shanghai: Statistical Department of the Inspectorate General of Customs, 1908), vol. I, p. 365.

25. See *ibid.*, p. 347 (United States); *ibid.*, vol. II, p. 1350 (Japan).

26. *Important Documents Relating to China's Revolution, 1912* (Shanghai: The Commercial Press, Ltd., 1912), pp. 67–68. In December 1911, when Dr. Sun was in Paris, he told a French reporter that he wanted to abolish China's tariff restrictions. On December 25 of the same year he told Chinese and Western reporters that his government would abolish consular jurisdiction after the completion of various reform measures. Wang Shih-chieh and Hu Ching-yü, *Chung-kuo pu-p'ing-teng t'iao-yüeh chih fei-ch'u* (The abolition of China's unequal treaties; Taipei: Chung-yang wen-wu kung-ying-she, 1967), pp. 125–126.

eign rights enjoyed by other civilized states should be revised or abrogated.

On August 14, 1917, China declared war against Germany and Austria-Hungary and abrogated all treaties with them as well as any parts of multilateral treaties that concerned the relations between China and the two countries.[27] Thus, German and Austro-Hungarian extraterritorial rights and other special privileges in China were abrogated.[28] At the 1919 Versailles Peace Conference, China submitted a memorandum concerning the abolition of the following treaty rights in China enjoyed by foreign states:

1. the abolition of spheres of influence;
2. the withdrawal of foreign troops and police;
3. the withdrawal of foreign post offices and agencies for wireless and telegraphic communications;
4. the abolition of consular jurisdiction;
5. the relinquishment of the leased territories;
6. the restoration of foreign concessions and settlements; and
7. the granting of complete tariff autonomy.[29]

While the Versailles Peace Conference did not take any action on the Chinese memorandum, the memorandum clearly indicated the types of treaties that China wanted to revise or abrogate on the ground of their incompatibility with "the structure of a new world based upon the principles of justice, *equality* and respect for the sovereignty of nations."[30] (Emphasis added.) These types of treaties were later referred to by the Chinese government and scholars, among others, as "unequal."

The term "unequal treaties" became a popular one in China after the Kuomintang (the Nationalist Party) began to advocate the abolition of those treaties in the early 1920s. The first reference to "unequal treaties"

27. John V.A. MacMurray, ed., *Treaties and Agreements with and Concerning China, 1894–1919* (New York: Oxford University Press, 1921), vol. II, Republican Period, 1912–1919, p. 1362.

28. The abolition of the German rights and privileges in China was confirmed by a German declaration of May 20, 1921. *League of Nations Treaty Series* 9:283 (1922). The abolition of Austro-Hungarian rights and privileges was confirmed by articles 113–117 of the Saint-Germain Peace Treaty with Austria, September 10, 1919, *British and Foreign State Papers* (London: His Majesty's Stationery Office, 1922), vol. 112, pp. 365–366; and articles 97–101 of the Trianon Peace Treaty with Hungary, June 4, 1920, *British and Foreign State Papers* (London: His Majesty's Stationery Office, 1923), vol. 113, pp. 522–523.

29. For the complete text of the Chinese memorandum, see *Chinese Social and Political Science Review,* vol. 5a, nos. 1, 2:116–161 (Mar. and June 1920).

30. *Ibid.*, p. 116.

in a Nationalist document seems to have appeared in a declaration issued on January 1, 1923. The declaration condemned the imperial Chinese government for concluding many "unequal treaties" which were detrimental to China's national interests. It pledged to "make efforts to rectify [those unequal] treaties so as to restore China's free and equal status on the international level."[31]

The declaration issued by the First National Convention of the Kuomintang on January 31, 1924, four years before it achieved national power, declared that "all unequal treaties . . . should be cancelled and new treaties based upon mutual equality and respect for sovereignty should be reconcluded."[32] Again, the March 11, 1925, will of Dr. Sun Yat-sen, founder of the Chinese Republic and the Kuomintang, stated that "our recent declarations in favor of . . . the abolition of unequal treaties should be carried into effect with the least possible delay."[33]

There does not seem to be any evidence indicating that the Chinese use of the term unequal treaties was suggested by Western sources, as those Western international law treatises translated into Chinese in the nineteenth and twentieth centuries happened to be those which did not even mention the term.[34]

Moreover, even after use of the term became popular in China in the 1920s, few Chinese writers realized the existence of the same term in early Western literature on international law. The only exception I know is Tseng Yu-hao. In his 1933 book, *The Termination of Unequal Treaties in International Law,* he wrote that "the phrase [unequal treaties] was used even when the law of nations was dominated by the principles of

31. *Kuo-fu i-chiao, chien-kuo ta-kang, chung-yao hsüan-yen* (Teaching of the founder of the Republic [of China], outline of national construction [and] important declarations; no date and place of publication), p. 145.

32. *Ibid.,* p. 158.

33. Sun Yat-sen, *San-min chu-i* (The three principles of the people), translated by Price and edited by L. T. Chen (Shanghai: The Commercial Press, Ltd., 1928), p. viii.

34. See treatises cited above at note 10. Oppenheim's *International Law,* one of the most popular Western works used by Chinese scholars and which was translated into Chinese in 1934–1935, did not mention the term "unequal treaties." L. Oppenheim, *International Law,* 3rd ed., Ronald F. Roxburgh, ed. (London: Longmans, Green and Co.), vol. I (1920) translated into Chinese by Ch'en Te-chang, *Ao-pen-hai kuo-chi fa. P'ing-shih* (Shanghai: Shang-wu yin-shu-kuan, 1935); vol. II (1921) translated into Chinese by Ch'en Te-chang, *Ao-pen-hai kuo-chi fa. Chan-cheng yü chung-li* (Shanghai: Shang-wu yin-shu-kuan, 1934). The only part of Phillimore's treatise indirectly related to the problem of unequal treaties is as follows: "Private contracts may be set aside on the ground of the inferences of fraud and unfair dealing arising from their manifest injustice and want of mutual advantage. But no inequality of advantage, no *lésion,* can invalidate a Treaty." *Commentaries upon International Law,* vol. II, p. 72.

the law of nature [and an unequal treaty] was defined by Emerich de Vattel (1714–1767) . . . as [a treaty] which lacks reciprocity."[35] He, however, did not make reference to other early Western writers such as Grotius, Pufendorf, and Wolff, who had also discussed the same subject in their treatises.

No evidence can be found to suggest that the Chinese use of the term "unequal treaties" was suggested by Soviet sources. Both in the 1919 and 1920 Soviet declarations to China, the Soviet government offered to abolish certain treaties which the Tzarist government had imposed upon China, such as those relating to Russian privileges in Manchuria and extraterritoriality. Neither of these declarations nor the Sino-Soviet Agreement on the General Principles for the Settlement of Questions between the Soviet Union and the Republic of China of May 31, 1924, used the term "unequal treaties."[36] In fact, the term has become popular in Soviet scholarship only since World War II.[37]

Similarly, there does not seem to be any evidence that the Nationalist use of the term was suggested by the Chinese Communist Party, as the first Communist Chinese reference to this term appears to have been a declaration issued on July 10, 1925, concerning the May 30th Incident, two years after the first Nationalist use of the term. The declaration called upon the masses to support the Kuomintang in its efforts "to declare the abrogation of all unequal treaties."[38]

35. Tseng Yu-hao, *The Termination of Unequal Treaties in International Law* (Shanghai: The Commercial Press, Ltd., 1933), p. 7.

36. For the text of the declarations, see H.G.W. Woodhead, ed., *The China Year Book 1924–1925* (Tientsin: Tientsin Press, Ltd., 1924), pp. 868–872. Article 3 of the 1924 Sino-Soviet Agreement provides: "The Government of the two Contracting Parties agree to annul at the Conference [to be held one month after the signing of the Agreement] all Conventions, Treaties, Agreements, Protocols, Contracts, etc., concluded between the Government of China and the Tsarist Government and to replace them with new treaties, agreements, etc., on the basis of equality, reciprocity and justice, as well as the spirit of the Declarations of the Soviet Government of the year of 1919 and 1920." *League of Nations Treaty Series* 37:178 (1925).

37. See Triska and Slusser, *Soviet Treaties*, p. 42.

38. *Chung-kuo wen-t'i chih-nan* (Guide to China's problem), vol. II, pp. 64–69; condensed text of the declaration printed in *Kung-fei huo-kuo shih-liao hui-pien* (Collection of historical materials relating to Communist bandits' rebellion; Taipei: Chung-hua min-kuo k'ai-kuo wu-shih-nien wen-hsien pien-ch'uan wei-yüan-hui, 1964), vol. I, pp. 44–46. The May 30th Incident occurred in 1925, when in Shanghai the foreign-controlled police in the International Settlement opened fire on Chinese demonstrators and killed more than ten persons. The May 30th Incident created a fervor of patriotism among Chinese and aroused in them a strong anti-British and anti-Japanese sentiment.

It should be noted that an earlier statement on the current situation issued by

On the official level, the first use of the term "unequal treaties" appears to have been the Peking government's statement issued on November 6, 1926, concerning the termination of the 1865 Sino-Belgian Treaty. The statement referred to "unequal treaties" which "were exacted from China nearly a century ago."[39] When the Nationalist government came to power in 1928, it issued a declaration to foreign countries on June 16, 1928, which stated that "for eighty years China has been under the restrictions of unequal treaties."[40]

The foregoing survey suggests that while the concept of unequal treaties had its origin in Western classical writings, the development of this concept in China was not significantly under Western influence. China's own experience was primarily responsible for the development of the concept of unequal treaties in China.

THE NATIONALIST POSITION ON UNEQUAL TREATIES

The long history of the Nationalist effort to abolish China's unequal treaties has been studied by many scholars.[41] No attempt is made here to duplicate such a study. With respect to the Nationalist position on the problem of unequal treaties, the primary concerns herein are the following:

1. What is the Nationalist concept of unequal treaties?
2. Assuming a treaty is regarded as "unequal," is it legally valid?
3. If an unequal treaty is legally valid, by what process should the aggrieved party revise or abrogate the said treaty?

---

the Central Committee of the Chinese Communist Party on June 15, 1922 advocated the abolition of some treaties imposed upon China, but it did not use the term "unequal treaties." The statement said, inter alia, that one goal of the Party was to "rectify [China's] conventional tariff system, to cancel various extraterritorial rights of major powers in China, and to regain the administration of the Chinese railway by way of repaying all railway loans." Condensed text of the statement in *Chung-kuo wen-t'i chih-nan*, vol. II, pp. 13–31; reprinted in *Kung-fei huo-kuo shih-liao hui-pien*, vol. I, p. 17.

39. *Chinese Social and Political Science Review, Public Documents* (Peking: Chinese Social and Political Science Association, 1927), vol. XI, p. 1. An earlier Presidential Mandate issued by the Peking government on April 28, 1919, stated that "hereafter, all non-treaty countries wishing to enter into treaty relations with China should do so on the basis of *equality*." (Emphasis added.) Cited in *Papers Relating to the Foreign Relations of the United States, 1919* (Washington, D.C.: Government Printing Office, 1934), vol. I, p. 685.

40. *Chinese Social and Political Science Review, Public Documents*, vol. XII, p. 47.

41. See, for example, Ch'ien T'ai; Fishel; and Tseng Yu-hao.

Only in recent years have several Nationalist scholars tried to give a general definition of "unequal treaties."[42] In 1961 Ch'ien T'ai wrote:

> Generally, treaties between states are based on mutual benefit and equality; if only one party undertakes an obligation and the other party does not have a corresponding [obligation], the inequality is obvious. For instance, China allowed other states to enjoy consular jurisdiction in China . . . but other states did not allow China to enjoy the same right in their territories.[43]

Wang Shih-chieh and Hu Ching-yü gave a similar explanation of the term "unequal treaties" in 1967:

> The so-called "unequal treaty" is a term of general usage which does not have a specialized definition. Generally speaking, modern states all insist on the concept of sovereignty and equality; therefore, they try to achieve mutual benefit and equality in treaties concluded by them. If between the contracting states only one party undertakes obligations and the other party enjoys rights, the treaty providing such a relationship is naturally an unequal treaty.[44]

These definitions of unequal treaties do not seem to differ from those given by Western classical writers. However, the Nationalist practice appears to suggest that even if a treaty is unequal in China's favor, the treaty remains an unequal one and should be rejected. Thus, for example, when in 1954 the United States and the Republic of China were negotiating a security treaty, the United States' draft of the treaty contained a territorial clause saying that the treaty should be applicable to the territory under the control of the Republic of China without mentioning any American territory. In other words, the proposed security treaty was in the form of unilateral extension of American protection to the Republic of China. The Nationalist government rejected the draft on the ground that it could not accept any unilateral American protection and the treaty must be made in the form of reciprocity and

42. See Tseng Yu-hao, *The Termination of Unequal Treaties in International Law*, pp. 9–10, where he cites Halleck's definition of unequal treaties. Halleck defined unequal treaties as those by which "the things promised are neither the same nor equally proportioned" between the contracting parties. Halleck, *International Law*, p. 106.

Dr. Sun Yat-sen, founder of the Chinese Republic, called unequal treaties "deeds for selling ourselves." See his speech delivered at Shanghai press conference on November 19, 1924. *Chung-shan ch'üan-shu* (Complete works of Sun Yat-sen; Shanghai: Ta-hua shu-chü, 1927), vol. II, p. 31.

43. Ch'ien T'ai, *Chung-kuo pu-p'ing-teng t'iao-yüeh chih yüan-ch'i chi ch'i fei-ch'u chih ching-kuo*, p. 46.

44. Wang Shih-chieh and Hu Ching-yu, *Chung-kuo pu-p'ing-teng t'iao-yüeh chih fei-ch'u*, p. 45.

equality.[45] As a result, the territorial provisions of the security treaty was made reciprocal. Article 6 of the Sino-American Mutual Defense Treaty of December 2, 1954,[46] provides: For the purposes of articles II and V, the terms "territorial" and "territories" shall mean in respect of the Republic of China, Taiwan and the Pescadores; and in respect of the United States of America, the island territories in the West Pacific under its jurisdiction.

While Nationalist leaders and scholars did not until recent years develop a general definition of unequal treaties, they usually made specific reference to certain treaties as "unequal." Thus, the declaration issued by the First National Convention of the Kuomintang in January 1924, listed as important examples of "unequal treaties" those treaties that provided for any of the following:

> 1. foreign leased territories; 2. consular jurisdiction [extraterritoriality]; 3. administration of customs by foreigners; and 4. Political rights exercised by foreigners that infringe upon the sovereignty of China.[47]

President Chiang Kai-shek analyzed the content of China's unequal treaties and classified them into those that provided for the following items:

1. consular jurisdiction (including the rights to watch trials, to have joint trials, and to establish foreign courts in China);
2. nonreciprocal conventional tariffs;
3. concessions;
4. the right of foreign warships to navigate and to be stationed in Chinese waters;
5. control of the customs administration;
6. the rights of coastal trade (cabotage) and inland navigation;
7. spheres of influence, leased territories, the right to construct railways, railway zones, and the right to work mines;
8. the right to station troops in China;
9. the employment of foreigners on the Chinese postal staff and the setting up of foreign post offices;
10. the right to establish factories in China;
11. the legation quarters;

45. *Kuo-chia chien-she ts'ung-k'an* (National reconstruction series), vol. III, *Wai-chiao yü ch'iao-wu* (Diplomatic relations and overseas Chinese affairs; Taipei: Cheng-chung shu-chü, 1971), p. 155.
46. *UNTS* 248:214 (1955).
47. *Kuo-fu i-chiao, chien-kuo ta-kang, chung-yao hsüan-yen*, p. 158.

12. control of customs revenues and custody of the customs surplus; and

13. improvement of inland waters, employment of foreign pilots, and the construction of light houses, beacons and buoys.[48]

The views of Nationalist scholars are in general the same as Chiang's.[49] Neither Chiang nor Nationalist scholars include the unilateral most-favored-nation clause in their listing of the content of unequal treaties. This is rather puzzling as this item is clearly an unequal arrangement, and they have severely criticized the unilateral most-favored-nation clause in China's unequal treaties.[50] In practice, commercial treaties or agreements concluded by the Nationalist government were all based upon the principle of reciprocity and did not contain any unilateral most-favored-nation arrangement.[51] Moreover, all former Chinese treaties or agreements containing a unilateral most-favored-nation arrangement were abrogated (or replaced by new treaties or agreements) by the Nationalist government in the 1940s.[52] Thus, unilateral most-favored-nation arrangements should also be included in the Nationalist concept of unequal treaties.

It should be noted that while the Nationalists listed many Chinese

48. See his *China's Destiny* (New York: Macmillan, 1947), translated into English by Wang Chung-hui from the 1943 Chinese edition, pp. 28–43.

49. Ch'ien T'ai classified the unequal treaties into the following items: (1) Restriction on China's sovereignty in the political realm—(i) sphere of influence; (ii) leased territories; (iii) concessions [settlements]; (iv) Peking Protocol of 1901 [which provided for the establishment of diplomatic quarters in Peking, stationing of foreign troops along the railway between Peking and Lin-yü, and others]; (v) treaty ports; (vi) foreign police in China; and (vii) right of foreign warships to enter China's ports and inland rivers. (2) Restriction on China's sovereignty in the judicial realm—(i) Right of consular jurisdiction; (ii) right of observing Chinese judicial proceedings; (iii) right of joint trial and mixed courts; and (iv) foreign courts in China. (3) Restriction on China's sovereignty in the administrative realm—(i) Restriction on tariff; (ii) foreign posts and telegraph offices in China; (iii) right of engaging coastal trade [cabotage] and inland navigation by foreigners; (iv) foreign pilots; and (v) [foreigners; control of custom, postal and salt administration]. See Ch'ien T'ai, *Chung-kuo pu-p'ing-teng t'iao-yüeh chih yüan-ch'i chi ch'i fei-ch'u chih ching-kuo*, pp. 46-81. See also Wang Shih-chieh and Hu Ching-yü, *Chung-kuo pu-p'ing-teng t'iao-yüeh chih fei-ch'u*, pp. 46–66.

50. See Chiang Kai-shek, *China's Destiny*, p. 25; Wang Shih-chieh and Hu Ching-yü, *ibid.*, p. 67.

51. For instance, the Sino-American Exchange of Notes of January 11, 1943, provides, inter alia, that "vessels of either country shall enjoy within the territory of the other country with respect to the coast trade and inland navigation treatment as favorable as that accorded to the vessels of any third country." *UNTS* 10:274 (1947).

52. See Wang Shih-chieh and Hu Ching-yü, *Chung-kuo pu-p'ing-teng t'iao-yüeh chih fei-ch'u*, pp. 317–393.

treaties containing territorial cession provisions as unequal treaties, their analysis of the contents of unequal treaties does not include the item of territorial cession. In his book *China's Destiny*,[53] President Chiang referred to the Sino-Russian Treaties of 1858 (ceding Chinese territory north of the Amur River) and 1860 (ceding Chinese territory east of the Ussuri River), the Sino-British Treaty of 1842 (ceding Hong Kong), and the Sino-Japanese Treaty of 1895 (ceding Taiwan), as "unequal treaties," but in his analysis of the content of unequal treaties he did not include territorial cession.

This attitude does not mean that President Chiang and other Nationalist leaders or scholars are not interested in recovering China's territories ceded to other countries through unequal treaties imposed upon China. In *China's Destiny*, Chiang said, "Kowloon [leased to Britain in 1898] and Hong Kong are geographically interdependent and their status must be settled simultaneously,"[54] implying that China would ultimately recover Hong Kong, which was ceded to Britain under the 1842 Treaty. The same book also referred to the Sino-Soviet frontier question and expressed the view that it, among other questions, would be "justly and equitably settled."[55] In an earlier statement of 1938, President Chiang declared that China was determined to recover Taiwan (ceded to Japan by the 1895 Treaty of Shimonoseki) after the conclusion of the Sino-Japanese War.[56]

Despite their intention to recover China's lost territory, the National-

53. Chiang Kai-shek, *China's Destiny*, pp. 28, 29.
54. *Ibid.*, p. 143.
55. *Ibid.*, p. 144. Chiang made reference to the Sino-Soviet Agreement on General Principles for the Settlement of the Questions Between the Republic of China and the Soviet Union, May 31, 1924. *League of Nations Treaty Series* 37:174 (1925). Article 7 of the Agreement provides that the "Contracting Parties agree to redemarcate their national boundaries at the Conference [to be held one month after the signing of the Agreement]. . . ." The conference was not held until August 26, 1925 and after the opening session, the Soviet delegate left for the Soviet Union and never returned. The conference was thus indefinitely postponed. See Wang Shih-chieh and Hu Ching-yü, *Chung-kuo pu-p'ing-teng t'iao-yüeh chih fei-ch'u*, p. 115.
56. President Chiang's speech to the Provisional National Convention of the Kuomintang, April 1, 1938, cited in Huang Shun-ch'ing, Lin Hsiung-hsiang, and Kuo Hai-ming, *T'ai-wan sheng t'ung-chih kao* (Draft history of Taiwan province), vol. X, *Kuang-fu chih* (History of restoration; Taipei: T'ai-wan sheng wen-hsien wei-yüan-hui, 1952), p. 2. Early in 1935, Chiang also referred to the 1895 Sino-Japanese Treaty of Shimonoseki as an unequal treaty. See his preface to Wang Yen-wei and Wang Liang, *Ch'ing-chi wai-chiao shih-liao* (Historical materials on late Ch'ing diplomacy; Peking, Ku-kung po-wu-yüan, 1935), vol. I, p. 7, cited in Wang Shih-chieh and Hu Ching-yü, *Chung-kuo pu-p'ing-teng t'iao-yüeh chih fei-ch'u*, p. 19. Chiang Kai-shek, however, did not include the territorial cessions provisions of these two treaties in his discussions of the content of unequal treaties.

ists clearly understand the diplomatic difficulty they face in attempting to achieve this aim. Therefore, when political reality was not ripe for achieving that aim, they did not raise the question of returning to China the lost territories ceded by unequal treaties. The question of Hong Kong is one example of this cautious approach. After the conclusion of the Sino-British Treaty for the Relinquishment of Extraterritorial Rights in China and the Regulation of Related Matters in 1943,[57] Nationalist leaders and scholars repeatedly raised the question of returning to China the leased territory of Kowloon[58] which was granted to the United Kingdom under the 1898 treaty.[59] They were silent on the question of Hong Kong's cession to the United Kingdom under the 1842 treaty.[60] On the other hand, when political reality appeared fa-

57. *League of Nations Treaty Series* 205:69 (1944–1946).

58. On January 3, 1943, Nationalist Chinese Foreign Minister T. V. Soong said in a press conference that China did raise the question of the leased territory of Kowloon when negotiating the 1943 Sino-British Treaty, but the British government was not prepared to discuss this question. He said that China, however, reserved the right to raise it in the future. See Wang Tieh-yeh, "A General Analysis of the Contents of the New Treaties," *Shih-chieh cheng-chih* (World politics), Special issue on new treaties (Chungking: Chinese Association for the League of Nations, April 30, 1943), reprinted in Pao Tsun-p'eng, Wu Hsiang-hsiang and Li Ting-i, *Chung-kuo chin-tai shih lun ts'ung* (Essays on the modern history of China), 2nd series, vol. I, *Pu-p'ing-teng t'iao-yüeh yü p'ing-teng hsin-yüeh* (The unequal treaties and new equal treaties; Taipei: Cheng-chung shu-chü, 1958), p. 311. Nationalist scholar Wang Sheng-tsu argued that in accordance with the principle of *rebus sic stantibus* and for other reasons, the United Kingdom should return the leased territory of Kowloon to China. See his "The Problem of the Leased Territory of Kowloon," *Shih-chieh cheng-chih* 8.2 (July 30, 1943), reprinted in Pao Tsun-p'eng *et al.*, pp. 328–335.

59. Sino-British Convention respecting an Extension of Hong Kong Territory, June 9, 1898, in *Hertslet's China Treaties* (London: His Majesty's Stationery Office, 1908), vol. I, p. 120.

60. Article 3 of the Sino-British Treaty of Peace, Friendship, Commerce, Indemnity and Others, August 29, 1842, in *ibid.*, p. 8.

In a speech clarifying China's policy toward national minorities at home and neighboring countries delivered to the joint session of the Supreme National Defense Council and the Kuomintang Central Executive Committee on August 24, 1945, President Chiang Kai-shek specifically pointed out that the leased territory of Kowloon should be returned to China, but he made no mention of the problem of returning Hong Kong to China. Chinese Ministry of Information, *Collected Wartime Messages*, p. 859. However, according to Chinese diplomatic records as summarized by Chang Ch'ün and Huang Shao-ku, China did try to restore Hong Kong through negotiation during the Second World War. They wrote: "In early March of 1943, when British Foreign Minister Eden went to the United States to discuss the question of postwar settlement, President Franklin D. Roosevelt told Chinese representative in the United States, Mr. T. V. Soong, that he would make the following proposal to Mr. Eden: Britain should take the initiative to restore Hong Kong to China. At the same time, he would suggest to China that, after the restoration of Hong Kong, China should take the initiative to make Hong Kong and the whole or part of Kowloon as free port area for the purpose of protecting partial interest of British residents. Mr. Soong reported the proposal to

vorable to China, the Nationalists did not hesitate to try to recover China's lost territory ceded by unequal treaties. Thus, in 1941 when China declared war against Japan, the Nationalist government abrogated all Sino-Japanese treaties[61] and, accordingly, China recovered Taiwan from Japan at the end of the war.

The above discussion of practice appears to indicate that the Nationalist concept of unequal treaties should also include treaties ceding territories as a result of coercion.

Despite the fact that the Chinese Nationalists were determined to abolish China's "unequal treaties," they did not argue that such treaties are void or can be abrogated at will. Instead, they favored the revision or abrogation of those treaties through diplomatic negotiations. Such an attitude was clearly stated in a declaration issued by the Nationalist government on June 16, 1928. The pertinent part of that declaration is as follows:

> For eighty years China has been under the restrictions of unequal treaties. These restrictions are a contravention of the principle of mutual respect of sovereignty in international [relations], and are not allowed by any sovereign state. Hence China has asked in various declarations for a sympathetic understanding by friendly nations. We are pleased to note that since the latter part of 1926 the authorities of various friendly nations have expressed their willingness to negotiate new treaties. Now that the unification of China is being consummated, we think the time is ripe for taking further steps and following proper procedures to negotiate new treaties to fulfil the purpose of achieving equality and mutual respect of sovereignty.[62]

This continued to be the position of the Nationalist government even after World War II when China's bargaining position had become

---

President Chiang who immediately submitted the question to the Supreme National Defense Council. The Council decided that if Britain would restore Hong Kong to China, China could take the initiative to declare Hong Kong and the old Kowloon area a custom free port. However, the arrangement for making Hong Kong a free port area must be done through China's own initiative and could not be made a condition for restoring Hong Kong. The Council soon ordered Mr. Soong to inform President Roosevelt of the decision. However, because of the lack of sincerity on the part of Britain, no agreement on the question of Hong Kong was reached." See Chang Ch'ün and Huang Shao-ku, *Chiang tsung-t'ung wei tzu-yu cheng-i yü ho-p'ing fen-tou shu-lüeh* (On President Chiang's fight for freedom, justice and peace; Taipei: Chung-yang wen-wu kung-ying-she, 1968), p. 277.

61. For the text of Chinese declaration of war, see *Contemporary China, A Reference Guide* 1.15:1 (Dec. 15, 1941).

62. Cited in *Chinese Social and Political Science Review, Public Documents*, vol. XII, pp. 47–48. With editorial changes by this author.

much stronger than it had been during the late 1920s and early 1930s. On August 24, 1945, President Chiang said that "our foreign policy is to honor treaties, rely upon law and seek rational readjustments when the requirements of time and actual conditions demand such readjustments." And, in connection with the leased territory of Kowloon, he said that "the present status is regulated by a treaty signed by China and Great Britain [and] changes in the future will be introduced only through friendly negotiations between the two countries."[63]

Although it regarded negotiation as a proper process for terminating China's unequal treaties, the Nationalist government certainly could not tolerate the other contracting parties taking undue advantage of its amicable attitude to prolong their rights under unequal treaties in China. Thus, on the problem of extraterritoriality, after approximately one and a half years of unfruitful negotiation with Western powers, notably the United States, the United Kingdom, and France,[64] the Nationalist government promulgated a mandate on December 28, 1929, as follows:

> For the purpose of restoring her inherent jurisdictional sovereignty, it is hereby decided and declared that on and after the first day of the first month of the nineteenth year of the Republic (January 1, 1930) all foreign nationals in the territory of China who are now enjoying extraterritorial privileges shall abide by the laws, ordinances, and regulations duly promulgated by the Central and Local Governments of China. The Executive *Yüan* and the Judicial *Yüan* are hereby ordered to instruct the Ministries concerned to prepare as soon as possible a plan for the execution of this Mandate and

63. Chinese Ministry of Information, *Collected Wartime Messages*, p. 859. It should be noted that China did not use the opportunity of accepting Japanese surrender in Hong Kong and Kowloon to take over these territories.

64. The Peking government requested the revision of China's unequal treaties at the 1919 Paris Peace Conference and the 1921–1922 Washington Conference. After the establishment of the Nationalist government in 1928, it sent identical notes to the United States, British, and French governments on April 27, 1928, requesting the abolition of extraterritoriality in China.

Some Nationalist scholars suggested that China might invoke the principle of *rebus sic stantibus* to take unilateral action to denounce China's unequal treaties. See., *e.g.*, Wu K'un-wu, *T'iao-yüeh lun* (On treaties; Shanghai: Shang-wu yin-shu-kuan, 1933), pp. 181–182; Wang Fu-yen, *Kuo-chi kung-fa lun* (On the public international law; Shanghai: Fa-hsüeh pien-i-she, 1933), vol. I, pp. 350, 487.

It should be noted that China's restrictive tariff was abolished through negotiations between the Nationalist government and foreign countries in 1928–1930. *E.g.*, see Sino-American Treaty Regulating Tariff Relations, July 25, 1928, *League of Nations Treaty Series* 107:121 (1930–1931). For Nationalist negotiations with other states, such as Belgium, Brazil, Japan, Sweden, Peru and Mexico, on the abolition of unequal treaties, see Fishel, *The End of Extraterritoriality*, pp. 145–149, and Wang Shih-chieh and Hu Ching-yü, *Chung-kuo pu-p'ing-teng t'iao-yüeh chih fei-ch'u*, pp. 238–243.

to submit it to the Legislative *Yüan* for examination and deliberation with a view to its promulgation and enforcement.[65]

On its face, this mandate was a unilateral abrogation of extraterritoriality in China. In fact, the mandate expressed only the determination of the Nationalist government to abolish extraterritoriality in China. After its promulgation, no active steps were taken to compel foreign nationals to comply with Chinese laws or to submit to Chinese jurisdiction, and negotiation with the Western powers continued.[66]

After further fruitless negotiation with the Western powers concerning the abolition of extraterritoriality in China, the Nationalist government finally decided to take unilateral action. On May 4, 1931, it promulgated an act entitled "Regulations Governing the Exercise of Jurisdiction over Foreign Nationals in China."[67] These regulations were to go into force on January 1, 1932. On May 12, 1931, the National People's Conference adopted a resolution supporting the Nationalist government's decision to take the above action. The resolution invoked the principle of *rebus sic stantibus* and article 19 of the Covenant of the League of Nations concerning the reconsideration of treaties that have become inapplicable.[68]

On September 18, 1931, Japan occupied Mukden and soon invaded all China's northeastern provinces (Manchuria). Being occupied with the Manchurian situation, the Nationalist government on December 29, 1931, issued a decree indefinitely postponing the enforcement of the regulations issued on May 4, 1931.[69] Finally, in 1943, the United States and the United Kingdom concluded new treaties with China for the abolition of extraterritoriality and other rights in China.[70] The extraterritoriality and other rights in China of other countries which had not been abolished before 1943 were all liquidated soon after the conclusion of World War II.

Since 1943, the problem of unequal treaties has received very little

65. H. G. W. Woodhead, ed., *The China Year Book 1931* (Shanghai: The North-China Daily News & Herald, Ltd., 1931), p. 487.

66. See Fishel, *The End of Extraterritoriality*, pp. 170–172.

67. H. G. W. Woodhead, ed., *The China Year Book 1932* (Shanghai: The North-China Daily News & Herald, Ltd., 1932), p. 263.

68. For the text of the resolution, see Thomas F. F. Millard, *The End of Extraterritoriality in China* (Shanghai: The A.B.C. Press, 1931), pp. 3–10.

69. Woodhead, *The China Year Book 1931*, p. 264.

70. Sino-American Treaty for the Relinquishment of Extraterritorial Rights in China and the Regulation of Related Matters, January 11, 1943, in *United States Statutes At Large*, vol. 57, p. 676; *UNTS* 10:261 (1947). For British treaty, see *League of Nations Treaty Series* 205:69.

attention from Nationalist leaders and scholars. There have been two exceptions. The first concerned the 1945 Sino-Soviet Treaty of Friendship and Alliance and related agreements.[71] Under the treaty, China granted to the Soviet Union the right of joint administration and possession over the Chinese Eastern Railway, a military base in Port Arthur, special privileges in the port of Dairen, and many other privileges. China also recognized the independence of Outer Mongolia. These agreements would, under the Nationalist concept, be unequal treaties since the Soviet Union did not grant to China any reciprocal privileges in respect to Soviet territory.[72] A Nationalist scholar later specifically pointed out that these agreements are unequal treaties.[73]

The second concerns the 1965 Sino-American Agreement on the Status of United States Armed Forces in the Republic of China.[74] The Agreement granted the United States armed forces the privileges of exemption from visas and taxes, immunity from local jurisdiction over "offenses arising out of any act or omission done in the performance of official duty," the right to establish post offices, and other privileges. Some legislators of the Republic of China regarded this treaty as an unequal treaty.[75] One legislator made a lengthy comment on the unequal nature of this agreement and called upon the United States not to force the Nationalist government to grant such privileges to the United States forces, for to do so would only serve as propaganda material for Communist China's attempts to undermine cooperation between the Republic of China and the United States.[76] The ruling Nationalist Party, however, decided to urge its legislators to ratify the

71. For the texts of the treaty and agreements, see *UNTS* 10:300–369 (1947).

72. For a description of the Soviet pressure on the Nationalist delegation in the course of negotiating the treaty and agreements, see Tang Tsou, *America's Failure in China 1941–1950* (Chicago: University of Chicago Press, 1963), pp. 270–287; see also *Kuo-chia chien-she ts'ung-k'an* (National reconstruction series), vol. III, *Wai-chiao yü ch'iao-wu* (Diplomatic relations and overseas Chinese affairs), pp. 97–115. At the insistence of the Nationalist delegation, the Soviet Union agreed not to use the term "lease" concerning the Soviet base at Port Arthur. See Chiang Ching-kuo, *Fu-chung chih-yüan* (Carrying heavy burdens to a great distance; Taipei: Yu-shih shu-tien, 1963), p. 63.

73. See note 2 above.

74. *United States Treaties and Other International Agreements* (Washington, D.C.: Government Printing Office, 1967), vol. 17, p. 373. *Treaties and Other International Acts Series*, No. 5989.

75. See the discussions at the Nationalist Legislative Yuan meeting held on January 4, 1966. *Li-fa-yüan kung-pao* (Gazette of the Legislative Yüan), 36.8:56–116 (Taipei, Jan. 14, 1966).

76. See Legislator Ch'iao Yi-fan's written opinion to the Legislative Yüan. *Ibid.*, pp. 59–63.

agreement. On January 11, 1966, the Nationalist Legislative Yüan ratified the agreement by a vote of 134 in favor, 22 against; 322 legislators did not participate in the voting.[77] The large number of absentees clearly indicated that the great majority of the Nationalist legislators were not satisfied with the agreement.

Before the abolition of China's unequal treaties in the 1940s, the unequal treaties problem played an important role in Nationalist international relations. But both Nationalist leaders and scholars have always viewed this problem as one that is limited to China's diplomatic situation. They have shown no interest in promoting the concept of unequal treaties as a rule of international law. Nationalist treatises usually do not discuss the problem of unequal treaties.

When the United Nations International Law Commission was codifying the law of treaties, the Nationalist member did not raise the question of unequal treaties. The comment of the Nationalist government upon the Draft Articles on the Law of Treaties did not express any concern about this question although the comments of many other states did.[78] At the 1968 and the 1969 Vienna Conferences on the Law of Treaties, the Nationalist delegation did not play an active role in the adoption of a declaration concerning unequal treaties,[79] although it voted for the declaration.

THE COMMUNIST CHINESE POSITION ON THE PROBLEM OF UNEQUAL TREATIES

The Communist Chinese, though more vocal than the Nationalist Chinese on the question of unequal treaties, have never clearly defined what they mean by this term. A textbook on international trade treaties used by the Peking Foreign Trade Institute states:

> The classical writers of Marxism-Leninism confirmed an important principle concerning international treaties, namely, the genuine sovereign equality between all parties concerned should become the foundation of international treaties. Lenin said: "Negotiation can only be conducted between equals and, therefore, genuine equality between both sides is an essential condition for reaching a genuine agreement."
>
> Consequently, in accordance with Marxism-Leninism, there are equal treaties and unequal treaties, and therefore, progressive mankind takes funda-

77. See *Li-fa-yüan kung-pao* 36.9:26, 46 (Feb. 8, 1966).
78. See note 20 above and the accompanying text.
79. See note 21 above and the accompanying text.

mentally different attitudes towards different kinds of treaties. Equal treaties should be strictly observed. Unequal treaties are in violation of international law and without legal validity.[80]

Similarly a 1958 Chinese article reasons:

Treaties can be classified into equal treaties and unequal treaties and the latter undermine the most fundamental principles of international law—such as the principle of sovereignty; therefore they are illegal and void, and states have the right to abrogate this type of treaty at any time.[81]

These opinions conform generally to the position of most Soviet scholars. Kozhevnikov, for example, states:

Equal treaties are treaties concluded on the basis of equality between the parties; unequal treaties are those which do not fulfill this elementary requirement [and they] . . . are not legally binding.[82]

As to the content of a treaty, Communist Chinese scholars maintain that verbal reciprocity alone does not make a treaty "equal" if important political and economic facts have not been taken into consideration. Wang Yao-t'ien has written that "whether or not a treaty is equal does not depend upon the form and words of various treaty provisions, but depends upon the state character, economic strength, and the substance of correlation of the contracting states."[83] In this respect, several Communist Chinese writers consider the 1946 Sino-American Treaty of Friendship, Commerce, and Navigation,[84] concluded by the Nationalist government, an unequal treaty, despite the fact that the treaty granted, inter alia, reciprocal commercial privileges to each country. One Communist Chinese scholar criticized the treaty in this way:

There was a drastic difference in economic strength between old China and American imperialism; old China was a poor backward country dependent upon the United States, and the Chinese bourgeoisie was extremely weak. How could the Chinese bourgeoisie have had the ability to establish

80. Wang Yao-t'ien, *Kuo-chi mao-i t'iao-yüeh ho hsieh-ting* (International trade treaties and agreements; Peking: Ts'ai-cheng ching-chi ch'u-pan-she, 1958), p. 10. He also wrote (p. 9) that "the international law principle that treaties must be kept does not apply to treaties of an aggressive and enslaving nature."

81. Shih Sung, Yu Ta-hsin, Lu Ying-lui, Tsao K'o, "An Initial Investigation into the Old Law Viewpoint in the Teaching of International Law," *Chiao-hsüeh yü yen-chiu* (Teaching and research), no. 4:14 (Apr. 1958).

82. F. I. Kozhevnikov, ed., *International Law* (Moscow: Foreign Languages Publishing House, 1961), p. 248.

83. Wang Yao-t'ien, *Kuo-chi mao-i t'iao-yüeh ho hsieh-ting*, note 79, p. 31.

84. *UNTS* 25:68 (1949).

factories in the United States, to carry on commerce, and engage in scientific and cultural enterprises in order to realize the rights given to them by the "Sino-American Treaty of Friendship, Commerce and Navigation"? Only the American monopolistic bourgeoisie and its representatives were in a position really to enjoy these rights.[85]

While Communist China charges others with merely verbal reciprocity, its record is not spotless. For instance, a charge of verbal reciprocity in disregard of important political facts could be aimed at the 1960 Sino-Burmese Treaty of Friendship and Mutual Non-Aggression.[86] Article 3 of the Treaty provides that "each Contracting Party undertakes . . . not to take part in any military alliance directed against the other Contracting Party." Communist China, a country with 800 million population and 3 million armed forces, does not need an ally to assist it to invade Burma, a country with 14 million population and 100,000 armed forces. Thus, though equal on its face, the treaty operated in effect to leave Burma unprotected by prohibiting an alliance with the country which could most effectively resist Communist China's expansion, namely, the United States. In fact, an editorial in the *People's Daily* on February 1, 1960, makes it clear that the purpose of this treaty is, inter alia, to thwart United States policy in Southeast Asia.

The following treaties, considered by Communist Chinese leaders or writers to be "unequal," illustrate the range of the Communist Chinese concept of unequal treaties:

1. All treaties imposed on China in the nineteenth and early twentieth centuries (that is, those concerning consular jurisdiction, unilateral most-favored-nation treatment, restrictive tariff regulations, territorial cessions or leases, and other disabilities) are considered unequal treaties.[87] In this aspect, the Communist Chinese position is similar to that of the Chinese Nationalists.

85. Ch'ien Szu, "A Criticism of the Views of Bourgeois International Law on the Question of Population," *Kuo-chi wen-t'i yen-chiu* (Studies in international problems), no. 5:47 (May 1960). Professor Chou Keng-sheng also expressed the same view. He wrote: "Even those treaties which provide mutual benefit in form but, due to the unequal economic position between two contracting parties, in fact yield unilateral benefits to one side and subject the other side only to exploitation, are neither treaties of mutual benefit nor equal international transactions. The most obvious example is the so-called Sino-American Treaty of Commerce concluded in 1946 between American imperialists and the Kuomintang Government." See his "The Principle of Peaceful Coexistence from the Viewpoint of International Law," *Cheng-fa yen-chiu* (Political-legal research), no. 6:41 (Nov. 1955).

86. *PR*, no. 5:12 (Feb. 12, 1960); *British and Foreign State Papers* (London: Her Majesty's Stationery Office, 1967), 164:649.

87. For instance, Mao Tse-tung wrote in December 1939: "The imperialist

2. In 1956, the United States concluded an agreement with Switzerland on cooperation concerning civil uses of atomic energy.[88] The United States agreed to supply 500 kilograms of fissionable materials to Switzerland as well as certain information and equipment. But the United States reserved the right to dispatch personnel to inspect or supervise the use of the materials; it also was granted the right to acquire or use Swiss inventions based on nuclear information supplied by the United States. This agreement was criticized in an article in *People's Daily* as a typical example of an unequal treaty concluded in the name of international cooperation.[89]

3. In 1956, Jordan abolished the 1948 alliance treaty[90] with Britain, which granted Britain two military bases and the right to send troops to Jordan in time of war. *People's Daily* applauded the Jordanian action as abolishing an unequal treaty.[91]

4. The aforementioned 1965 Sino [Nationalist]-American Agreement on the Status of Armed Forces[92] was strongly denounced by the *People's Daily* as an unequal treaty.[93]

5. On July 6, 1946, the United States and the Philippines concluded a trade agreement[94] which provides, inter alia, ceilings for Philippine exports to the United States (article 3) while no restrictions are pro-

---

powers have forced China to sign numerous unequal treaties by which they have acquired the right to station land and sea forces and exercise consular jurisdiction in China, and they have carved up the whole country into imperialist spheres of influence." He went on: "The imperialist powers have gained control of all the important trading ports in China by these unequal treaties and have marked off areas in many of these ports as concessions under their direct administration. They have also gained control of China's customs, foreign trade and communications (sea, land, inland water, and air)." "The Chinese Revolution and the Chinese Communist Party," in *Selected Works of Mao Tse-tung* (Peking: Foreign Languages Press, 1965), vol. II, p. 311. A *People's Daily* editorial listed the following treaties as unequal treaties: the Treaty of Nanking of 1842, the Treaty of Aigun of 1858, the Treaty of Tientsin of 1858, the Treaty of Peking of 1860, the Treaty of Ili of 1881, the Protocol of Lisbon of 1887, the Treaty of Shimonoseki of 1895, the Convention for the Extension of Hong Kong of 1898, the International Protocol of 1901. "A Comment on the Statement of the Communist Party of the U.S.A.," *JMJP* editorial, Mar. 8, 1963, p. 1.

88. *UNTS* 278:41 (1957).

89. Huang Yu, "Such Cooperation," *JMJP*, Dec. 31, 1956, p. 6.

90. *UNTS* 77:77 (1950–1951).

91. Observer, "Jordan Announces the Abrogation of the Anglo-Jordanian Treaty," *JMJP*, Nov. 29, 1956, p. 6.

92. See note 74 above.

93. "U.S.-Chiang Illegally Signed 'Status Agreement' Concerning U.S. Force of Aggression," *JMJP*, Sept. 13, 1965, p. 2; "U.S.-Chiang Kai-shek Illegal 'Status Agreement,' A New Step to Make Taiwan U.S. War Base," *ibid.*, Feb. 14, 1966, p. 2; Commentator, "Another Crime of the U.S.-Chiang Kai-shek Conspiracy," *ibid.*, Feb. 19, 1966, p. 1.

94. *UNTS* 43:136 (1949).

vided for United States exports to the Philippines. It also, in article 5, restricts the freedom of the Philippines to change its currency value in relation to United States dollars or to alter the convertibility of Philippine currency into United States dollars. This agreement was denounced by a Communist writer as an unequal treaty.[95]

6. On August 21, 1968, the armed forces of the Soviet Union, East Germany, Hungary, Poland, and Bulgaria suddenly invaded Czechoslovakia and soon occupied the whole country.[96] The occupation was denounced by a proclamation of the Presidium of the Czechoslovak National Assembly issued on the same day.[97]

However, under Soviet military occupation, Czechoslovakia signed on October 16, 1968, an agreement with the Soviet Union on "the conditions of temporary sojourn of Soviet forces on the territory of the Czechoslovak Socialist Republic."[98] On October 21, 1968, a NCNA news commentary severely criticized the treaty as one that "unscrupulously tramples on Czechoslovak sovereignty and reduces the country to a virtual vassalage of Soviet revisionist social-imperialism."[99]

The examples given above all concern bilateral treaties, but this does not mean that the concept of unequal treaties is inapplicable to multilateral treaties.[100] A recent example of a multilateral treaty that is considered unequal by Communist China is the 1963 Partial Nuclear Test-Ban Treaty.[101] An article in the August 10, 1963, *People's Daily* by

95. C.K. Cheng, "The Philippines: America's Show-Window of Democracy in Asia?" *PR*, no. 6:21 (Feb. 5, 1965). The same article also listed the following US-Philippine treaties as unequal treaties: (1) The 1955 Laurel-Langley Agreement [revising the 1946 trade agreement], *UNTS* 238:264 (1956); (2) The 1947 US-Philippine Military Bases Agreement, *ibid.* 43:271 (1949); (3) The 1947 US-Philippine Military Aid Agreement, *ibid.* 43:47 (1949); (4) The 1951 US-Philippine Mutual Defense Treaty, *ibid.* 177:133 (1953).

96. See "Tass Statement on Soviet Military Intervention," August 21, 1968, reproduced in *International Legal Materials* 7.6:283 (November 1968).

97. Proclamation reproduced in *ibid.*, p. 1286.

98. English text of the treaty translated by W.E. Butler in *ibid.*, pp. 1334–1339.

99. "Diabolical Social-Imperialist Face of the Soviet Revisionist Renegade Clique," *PR*, no. 43:8 (Oct. 25, 1968).

100. Generally speaking, the Nationalist concept of unequal treaties is limited to bilateral treaties only. Recently, Nationalist scholars in Taiwan appear to have expanded this concept to multilateral treaties. Thus, in a seminar on major problems of the United Nations sponsored by the Institute of International Relations at Taipei on September 17, 1968, several participants pointed out that the 1968 Nuclear Non-proliferation Treaty is an unequal treaty. See statements made by Professors Ho Shih and Lei Shun-sheng at the seminar. *Wen-t'i yü yen-chiu* (Issues and studies), 8.1:18, 23 (Oct. 10, 1968).

101. *UNTS* 80:43 (1951).

"Observer,"[102] a pseudonym for a senior Communist Chinese official, severely criticized the treaty because it places the three big nuclear powers—the United States, the United Kingdom, and the Soviet Union —in a privileged position and does not create identical and reciprocal obligations among all contracting parties. The article complained that other countries are induced to undertake an unconditional obligation not to test any nuclear weapons in the atmosphere while the three big powers can continue underground testing. Since the testing of nuclear weapons must begin with atmospheric tests, it would be impossible for other states ever to manufacture nuclear weapons. Thus, states other than the three big powers are relegated to a position of permanent inferiority.

Moreover, the same article commented, the provision for amendment in the treaty also gives the privilege of veto to each of the three big nuclear powers. Thus, no matter how many smaller states accede to the treaty, they are without the right or power to modify it if one of the three big powers disagrees.

Another recent example of a multilateral treaty considered unequal by Communist China is the "Treaty on Non-proliferation of Nuclear Weapons"[103] adopted by the United Nations General Assembly on June 12, 1968.[104] An article in the June 13, 1968, *People's Daily* by "commentator," a pseudonym for a senior official, denounced the treaty as a "thoroughly unequal treaty dished up by the United States imperialists and Soviet revisionists."

The article said:

> Under this treaty, the U.S. imperialists and Soviet revisionists are not only allowed to produce and stockpile nuclear weapons and increase the number of their nuclear bases; they also undertake no commitment whatsoever not to use nuclear weapons against the non-nuclear states. The latter, on the other hand, are totally deprived of their right to develop nuclear weapons for self-defense and are even restricted in their use of atomic energy for peaceful purposes. As the saying goes, "the magistrates are allowed to burn down houses while the common people are forbidden even to light lamps." In reality, this is tantamount to a demand that other countries accept forever the U.S. imperialist and Soviet revisionist position of nuclear monopoly and place themselves at their mercy.[105]

102. Observer, "Why the Tripartite Treaty Does Only Harm and Brings No Benefit?" *JMJP*, Aug. 10, 1963, p. 1; English translation in *PR*, no. 33:20 (Aug. 16, 1963).
103. Text in *International Legal Materials* 7.4:811–817 (July 1968).
104. U.N.Doc. A/RES/2373, XXII (June 18, 1968).
105. Commentator, "A Nuclear Fraud Jointly Hatched by the United States and

It must be pointed out here that the principle suggested by the *People's Daily* of "identical and reciprocal" obligations among all contracting parties under a multilateral treaty is not always followed either by Communist China or its writers. For instance, the United Nations Charter accords special veto power to the big five in the Security Council and in regard to Charter amendment. However, neither government nor scholars has ever maintained that these features of the Charter make it an "unequal treaty." On the contrary, mainland scholars have frequently attacked the alleged attempt of "American imperialism" to eliminate the big five's veto in the United Nations.[106]

Needless to say, the application of the concept of unequal treaties by Communist China is flexible and seems largely determined by political considerations. The following two cases illustrate this point.

1. Communist Chinese leaders or writers have never publicly denounced the above-mentioned 1945 Sino [Nationalist]-Soviet treaty and agreements concerning Manchuria.[107] The record of Communist China's relations with the Soviet Union does, however, amply demonstrate that Communist Chinese leaders were not happy about the 1945 treaty and agreements. In the 1950 agreement between Communist China and the Soviet Union,[108] the latter agreed to hand over to Communist China all Soviet rights over the Chinese Eastern Railway not later than 1952, to evacuate its Port Arthur military base, and to renounce its privileges in the port of Dairen. As for Outer Mongolia, Communist China, in a 1950 exchange of notes with the Soviet Union, recognized Mongolia's independent status.[109] However, Communist China reopened this issue in 1954 when Khrushchev visited China.[110]

2. While Communist Chinese leaders and scholars consider all treaties imposed upon China in the nineteenth and twentieth centuries as unequal treaties, until the 1960s they publicly refrained from classifying the 1858 Aigun Treaty and the 1860 Peking Treaty (by which Tzarist

---

the Soviet Union," *JMJP*, June 13, 1968, p. 5; English translation in *PR*, no. 35:17 (June 21, 1968).

106. *E.g.*, see Kuo Chün, *Lien-ho-kuo* (The United Nations; Peking: Shih-chieh chih-shih ch'u-pan-she, 1956), pp. 101–107.

107. See my note 20.

108. Sino-Soviet Agreement concerning the Chinese Ch'ang Ch'un Railway, Port Arthur and Dairen, Feb. 14, 1950, *UNTS* 226:31 (1956).

109. *Ibid.*, p. 16.

110. "On Mao Tse-tung's Talk with a Group of Japanese Socialists," Editorial, *Pravda*, Sept. 2, 1964; English translation in *International Affairs* (Moscow), no. 10:80 (Oct. 1964).

Russia acquired a large portion of Chinese territory outside the present Chinese Manchuria) as unequal treaties. With the intensification of the Sino-Soviet dispute, however, the Communist Chinese government specifically pointed out these two treaties as unequal treaties.[111] It also cited the writings of Engels, Marx, and Lenin to support its position.[112]

It should be noted that in the Communist Chinese view a treaty once equal or just can become unequal or enslaving as circumstances change. The Communist Chinese attitude toward the Warsaw Treaty is an example.

When the Treaty of Friendship, Cooperation and Mutual Assistance[113] (Warsaw Treaty) was signed on May 14, 1955, Communist China's observer to the drafting conference, General P'eng Teh-huai, said that he was authorized to declare his government's "full support and cooperation" with the treaty.[114] A famous Communist Chinese scholar of international law, Chou Keng-sheng, also wrote an article saying that the Warsaw Treaty, as a collective self-defence arrangement, "is perfectly consistent with the purposes and principles of the United Nations Charter and principles of international law."[115] From 1955 to 1961, Communist China sent an observer to every session of the political consultative committee established under the treaty.[116]

However, its attitude towards the Warsaw Treaty changed with

111. For example, see *JMJP* editorial of March 8, 1963, note 85 above. See also Information Department of the Chinese Foreign Ministry, "Chenpao Island Has Always Been Chinese Territory," *PR*, no. 11:14–15 (Mar. 14, 1969).

112. For example, Communist China's Statement of May 24, 1969 said: "The great teachers of the world proletariat Marx, Engels and Lenin had long made brilliant conclusions on the unequal nature of these treaties. Commenting on the 'Sino-Russian Treaty of Aigun' in 1858, Marx said that '. . . by his second opium war he [John Bull] has helped her [Russia] to the invaluable tract lying between the Gulf of Tartary and Lake Baikal, a region so much coveted by Russia that from Czar Alexey Michaelowitch down to Nicolaus, she has always attempted to get it.' Engels also pointed out in the same year that Russia despoiled 'China of a country as large as France, and Germany put together, and of a river as large as the Danube'. . . . Lenin pointed out that '. . . the European governments (the Russian Government among the very first) have already started to partition China. However, they have not begun this partitioning openly, but stealthily, like thieves' and that 'The policy of the tzarist government in China is a criminal policy.' " *PR*, no. 22:5 (May 30, 1969).

113. *UNTS* 219:3 (1955). The parties to this treaty are: Albania, Bulgaria, Hungary, East Germany, Poland, Rumania, Czechoslovakia and the Soviet Union.

114. *WCC 1954–1955*, vol. III (1958), p. 292.

115. Chou Keng-sheng, "The Warsaw Treaty from [the Viewpoint of] International Law," *Shih-chieh chih-shih* (World knowledge), no. 17:13 (Sept. 5, 1955).

116. See Kazimierz Grzybowski, *The Socialist Commonwealth of Nations* (New Haven, Conn.: Yale University Press, 1964), p. 212.

the deterioration of Sino-Soviet relations, which has characterized the 1960s. A *People's Daily* editorial of September 20, 1968, supporting the Albanian withdrawal from the Warsaw Treaty, said:

> The Warsaw Treaty has long become an instrument for aggression in the hands of the Soviet revisionist renegade clique in pushing ahead with its social-imperialism. By using this treaty, this clique has put the national defense forces of the other member countries into its hands, arbitrarily stationing its own armed forces and holding military exercises in these countries, and it controls, enslaves and plunders them. The Warsaw Treaty controlled by the Soviet revisionist renegade clique is no different from NATO controlled by U.S. imperialism.[117]

With respect to the process of revising or abrogating unequal treaties, several Communist Chinese writers have claimed that these treaties do not have legal validity and can be abrogated at any time.[118] In practice, this principle does not seem to be applicable to China's past unequal treaties relating to boundaries or territorial cession. In 1957, Premier Chou En-lai said in connection with the past Sino-Burmese boundary treaties: "It was the opinion of our government that, on the question of boundary lines, demands made on the basis of formal treaties should be respected according to general international practice."[119] However, he concurrently made it clear that the recognition of the continuing validity of these treaties "by no means excluded the seeking by two friendly countries of settlement fair and reasonable for both sides through peaceful negotiation between their governments."[120]

Similarly, with respect to the 1858 Sino-Russian Aigun Treaty and the 1860 Sino-Russian Peking Treaty, the Chinese Communists have made it clear that "although the old treaties relating to the Sino-Russian boundary are unequal treaties, the Chinese Government is nevertheless willing to respect them and take them as the basis for a reasonable settlement of the Sino-Soviet boundary question."[121]

117. "Courageous and Resolute Revolutionary Action," *JMJP* editorial, Sept. 20, 1968, p. 1; English translation in *PR*, no. 39:9 (Sept. 27, 1968).

118. See note 80 and 81 above, and accompanying text.

119. "Report on the Question of the Boundary Line Between China and Burma to the Fourth Session of the First National People's Congress, July 9, 1957," in Chinese People's Institute of Foreign Affairs, ed., *A Victory for the Five Principles of Peaceful Coexistence* (Peking: Foreign Languages Press, 1960), p. 19.

120. *Ibid.*

121. Letter from the Central Committee of the Chinese Communist Party to the Central Committee of the Soviet Communist Party, Feb. 29, 1964, *PR*, no. 19:13 (May 8, 1964).

CONCLUSION

Although the concept of unequal treaties was discussed by classical Western writers, the development of this concept in China originated primarily from China's own experience. While both the Nationalist and the Communist Chinese denounce those treaties imposed upon China in the nineteenth and twentieth centuries as unequal treaties, their concepts of unequal treaties differ.

The Nationalist concept is specific, limited, and easy to understand. Its leaders and writers did not argue that an unequal treaty is invalid in international law. Nationalist writers, most of whom were trained in the West, usually argued that China's unequal treaties should be revised or abrogated in accordance with the principle of *rebus sic stantibus*, a principle discussed in almost every Western international law treatise. None of them attempted to promote this concept as a rule of the law of treaties. Since the abolition of China's unequal treaties in the mid-1940s, Nationalist writers usually do not even mention the problem of such treaties in their treatises on international law. In view of the foregoing observations, the Nationalist concept of unequal treaties may be reasonably interpreted in light of relevant rules discussed in the writings of Western international law scholars.

The Communist Chinese concept of unequal treaties is flexible and broad. The Communist Chinese consider this concept an important rule of the law of treaties. According to their view, an unequal treaty is invalid in international law. Such a concept of unequal treaties does not seem to have any support in the writings of Western international law scholars.[122]

122. The 1969 Vienna Conference on the Law of Treaties adopted a declaration on the question of unequal treaties (see note 21 above and accompanying text). Thus, in principle, the Communist Chinese position does not seem to differ from that of current Western or non-Communist states. However, there remains the time element for applying the principle contained in the declaration. This declaration is designed to guide all future conduct of the contracting states to the Convention on the Law of Treaties. Communist Chinese theory and practice nevertheless suggests that the PRC considers that the principle contained in the declaration has been a rule of international law and is applicable to all treaties, even those concluded in the past.

8 / The Sino-Indian Dispute over the Internment and Detention of Chinese in India

Jerome Alan Cohen and Shao-chuan Leng

This paper will discuss the Sino-Indian dispute over the internment and detention of persons of Chinese descent in India that resulted from the Sino-Indian border conflict of 1962. Like the other essays in this volume, our inquiry is designed to add to the understanding of Chinese theory and practice of international law. We seek answers to questions such as: Does the governing elite of the People's Republic of China (PRC) appear to perceive and evaluate events in terms of international law? To what extent and in what manner does it invoke international law? Do the views of international law announced by the PRC accord with those of other states? Does the PRC practice what it preaches?

CONDITION OF CHINESE IN INDIA BEFORE 1962

Persons of Chinese descent residing in India have never had the numerical strength or economic power possessed by their counterparts in Southeast Asia. Nor until recently have they been the target of indigenous resentment and governmental restrictions, as have Chinese living in many Southeast Asian countries. The difficulties encountered by Chinese in India in the past decade have resulted mainly from the deterioration of state relations between India and China.

The first group of Chinese to settle in India in modern times came in the middle of the nineteenth century. Initially, the Chinese settlers numbered only a few hundred, most of them supporters of the Taiping Rebellion that had been suppressed in China. As economic and political

NOTE: The authors are grateful to Messrs. Richard R. Baxter, Howard S. Levie, R. Randle Edwards, and Elliot Gewirtz for their valuable criticisms of the manuscript and advice.

discontent spread in China, an increasing number of Chinese were attracted to the Indian subcontinent. By 1931 8,300 Chinese had arrived, and by 1936 there were 14,000. During World War II an influx of Chinese refugees from Southeast Asia further boosted the size of the local Chinese population, which at one point was estimated to be over 40,000.[1]

The end of World War II witnessed a reversal of this trend. Many of the recently displaced Chinese from Southeast Asia decided to return to their homes. Moreover, after India gained independence in 1947, although it continued to allow Tibetan traders considerable freedom of movement along the Sino-Indian border, it began to regulate the entrance of the Chinese more strictly than had the British.

The exact number of Chinese residents in India at the time of the heavy border fighting in 1962 is uncertain. On the basis of Chinese, Indian, and Western sources, a reasonable estimate would be 20,000.[2] In addition, there were approximately 20,000 Tibetans in India, many of whom had fled Tibet following the Communist suppression of the Tibetan revolt in early 1959.[3]

About 80 percent of the Chinese resided in Calcutta, and the rest were scattered in Bombay, Assam, Kalimpong, and other places. Among the economic activities in which the Chinese were primarily engaged were tanning, shoe manufacturing, retail trades, carpentry, and the restaurant business. As in the Southeast Asian countries, the overseas

1. For a short historical survey of the overseas Chinese in India, see Commission for Compiling Overseas Chinese Records, comp., *Yin-tu hua-ch'iao chih* (Record of the overseas Chinese in India; Taipei: Bennett, Coleman, 1962), pp. 28–29, 34–35, and "Brief Survey of the Overseas Chinese in India," *Ch'iao-wu pao* (Journal of overseas Chinese affairs; Peking) 6:10 (Dec. 1962).

2. A Nationalist Chinese publication estimates the number of Chinese residents in India at 23,000. *Yin-tu hua-ch'iao chih*, pp. 25–27, 38. A Communist Chinese source, on the other hand, gives a figure of 16,000. "Brief Survey of the Overseas Chinese in India," p. 10. *The Times of India, Directory and Yearbook 1958–59* (Bombay, 1959), p. 8, reports the number of Chinese residents to be 23,481, but the same publication of 1960–1961 gives a much lower figure without any explanation. In an Indian parliamentary debate on November 19, 1962, A.C. Guha of the House estimated the number of Chinese residents in India at between 20,000 and 30,000. *Lok Sabha Debates*, 3rd Ser./3rd Sess. 9:2261 (1962). According to an American newspaper, there were over 20,000 Chinese living in India at the time the Sino-Indian border war broke out in 1962. Joseph Lelyveld, "Curbs on Chinese Retained in India," *The New York Times*, Sept. 4, 1967, p. 12.

3. Both Chinese sources cited in note 2 estimate the number of Tibetans living in India to be over 20,000, while the Indian source gives a figure of less than 15,000. It should be noted that after the unsuccessful Lhasa revolt in early 1959, some 13,000 Tibetans reportedly escaped to India. UP, New Delhi, May 12, 1959, in *Yin-tu hua-ch'iao chih*, p. 36.

Chinese in India organized themselves into various cultural groups, occupational guilds, chambers of commerce, welfare societies, religious groups, youth organizations, and dialect associations. After Peking's establishment of diplomatic relations with New Delhi in January 1950, these Chinese groups, along with a dozen Chinese grade schools and high schools in India, became areas of contest between pro-Nationalist and pro-Communist forces in the overseas Chinese community.

On the whole, the Indian government gave Chinese the same treatment as other foreigners, except that citizens of Commonwealth countries were accorded certain privileges.[4] The Communist-Nationalist rivalry, however, made New Delhi's policy toward Chinese residents take on a distinctive hue, the shade of which at any given time reflected the current state of Sino-Indian relations.

During the 1950–1959 period, when the Nehru government enjoyed generally good relations with China's new rulers, New Delhi was quite accommodating toward Peking in regard to Chinese living in India. It has even been reported that pressure from the Indian government caused many Chinese residents formally to adopt the citizenship of the People's Republic.[5] Most of those who refused to do so became "stateless" in the eyes of their host, but were allowed to stay in India. In accordance with article 5 of the Constitution of India and the Citizenship Act of 1955,[6] almost nine hundred Chinese acquired Indian citizenship either by birth or by naturalization.

During this period, the PRC resorted to "carrot and stick" tactics to

4. For instance, the Foreigners Laws (Amendment) Act 1957 inserted a new Section 3A exempting citizens of Commonwealth countries from application of the Act in certain cases. See the *Gazette of India, Extraordinary*, Pt. II, Sec. 1, No. 9, dated April 3, 1957.

5. This was claimed by some Chinese residents in India. See Joseph Lelyveld, "Curbs on Chinese Retained in India."

6. Article 5 of the Constitution stipulates that at the commencement of the Constitution, anyone who had domicile in India and: (a) who was born in India; or (b) either of whose parents was born in India; or (c) who had been ordinarily a resident in India for not less than five years is to be considered a citizen of India. The Citizenship Act of 1955 provides for citizenship by birth (born in India on or after January 26, 1950), by descent, by registration, by naturalization, and by incorporation of territory. For the text of this Act, see Indian Ministry of Law, *Acts of Parliament, 1955* (New Delhi: Government of India Press, 1956), pp. 307–317. Speaking before the Parliament in November 1962, Mr. Datar (Minister of State in the Ministry of Home Affairs) estimated the number of Indian citizens of Chinese origin to be 871 at the time the border war broke out in 1962. According to him, "Under Article 5 of the Constitution, the total number of Chinese who obtained Indian citizenship or who were treated as Indians were 430. Subsequently, a few persons of Chinese origin have become Indian citizens either by naturalization or by registration. The total there is about 441." *Lok Sabha Debates*, 3rd Ser./3rd Sess. 9:2268 (1962).

combat Nationalist Chinese influence and to secure support in the overseas Chinese community. As inducements, the Chinese embassy and the Bank of China often offered "subsidies" or "loans" to Chinese business and cultural establishments in India. Resistance to Communist "persuasion" invited violent reprisals at times. In 1952, for instance, a group of pro-Peking Chinese attacked the offices of the pro-Nationalist *Chinese Journal of India* and manhandled its publisher; an unsuccessful attempt was also made to seize by force Chenkuo School, a Nationalist-supported institution in Calcutta.[7] Nevertheless, during his visit to India in late 1956, Premier Chou En-lai told Chinese residents in Calcutta that they should respect local laws and customs and that regardless of political differences among themselves they should unite under the banner of patriotism.[8]

Under diplomatic prodding from Peking, New Delhi occasionally took steps to curb the political activity of pro-Nationalist Chinese residents. They were prohibited from displaying the Nationalist flag in celebrating the October 10th anniversary of the founding of the Republic of China. The *Chinese Journal of India* was ordered to use the term "Chinese Communists" instead of "Communist bandits" in its publication.[9] Following Chou En-lai's first visit to India in August 1954, the Indian government expelled some prominent Nationalist Chinese figures, including the publisher of the *Chinese Journal of India*.[10] Surprisingly, as late as December 5, 1959, India issued instructions to prevent all future pro-Nationalist meetings and demonstrations, threatened to expel foreigners who indulged in such "objectionable activities," and promised not to permit "any activities designed to promote the idea of two Chinas."[11]

The outbreak of the Tibetan revolt and the flare-up of the Sino-

7. *Yin-tu hua-ch'iao chih*, pp. 57–58, 112.

8. "Premier Chou Receives Overseas Chinese," NCNA, Dec. 10, 1956, in *SCMP*, no. 1430:32 (Dec. 13, 1956).

9. *Yin-tu hua-ch'iao chih*, p. 117.

10. *Ibid.*, p. 113; Overseas Publisher, comp., *Ch'iao-wu erh-shih-wu nien* (Twenty-five years of overseas Chinese affairs; Taipei: Government of China Press, 1957), p. 67.

11. Ministry of External Affairs Note, December 5, 1959, in Ministry of External Affairs, Government of India, ed., *Notes, Memoranda and Letters Exchanged Between the Governments of India and China, White Paper*, vol. III, p. 110. For cogent criticism of this short-lived position of the Indian government as "obviously undemocratic and not warranted by International Law either, which merely forbids tolerance by a government of subversive activity against foreign governments," see T.S. Rama Rao, "The Sino-Indian White Papers and Some Incidental Questions of International Law," *Indian Year Book of International Affairs* 13:191, 235 (1964).

Indian border dispute in 1959 initiated a reversal of India's policy toward persons of Chinese descent. Shortly thereafter, New Delhi began to take measures against pro-Communist elements, ordering the registration and classification of all persons of Chinese descent in India and tightening the requirements for residential permits for those who were not Indian citizens.[12] And it soon became more tolerant of pro-Nationalist activities in the Chinese community.[13]

Between 1959 and the outbreak of large-scale Sino-Indian hostilities in October 1962, India's "ill-treatment" of ordinary Chinese nationals as well as official and semiofficial Chinese representatives became a constant subject of dispute between Peking and New Delhi.[14] According to an editorial of a major Communist journal on overseas Chinese affairs, in 1959 the Indian authorities "colluded" with secret agents of Chiang Kai-shek's "gang" to make out a black list for "premeditated persecution" of the overseas Chinese.[15] Whatever the truth of this allegation, India did begin to detain and to deport "subversive" Chinese in 1959; Chinese sources claim that by October 1962 some 200 Chinese had been deported to mainland China. Among them were merchants, storekeepers, senior staff members of the *China Review* (a pro-PRC paper published in Calcutta), and a number of principals and teachers of Chinese schools in India. The deportation of this last-mentioned group compelled many Peking-oriented schools to close.[16]

12. *Yin-tu hua-ch'iao chih*, p. 116; also Shih P'eng, "The Indian Government's Atrocious Acts of Persecuting Overseas Chinese," *Shih-chieh chih-shih* (World knowledge) 9:17 (May 10, 1963). Restrictions on Chinese nationals in India were based on the Foreigners Act of 1946 (Act No. 31) and the subsequent regulations made in pursuance of this Act.

13. For instance, China complained that the *Chinese Journal of India* in Calcutta slandered the head of the People's Republic and that the "Chiang Kai-shek clique elements" and Tibetan rebels in Kalimpong and Calcutta were allowed to celebrate the "National day of the Republic of China." Counsellor of India in China Note, Oct. 29, 1959, *White Paper*, vol. III, p. 109. In another protest, the Chinese Foreign Ministry charged that "the Indian government has gone back upon its promise and allowed and permitted Chiang Kai-shek clique elements and Tibetan rebels to carry out flagrant political activities in India against the People's Republic of China." Ministry of Foreign Affairs Note, Mar. 6, 1962, *ibid.*, vol. VI, p. 164.

14. Communications between India and China over these charges are in volumes III to VII of the *White Paper*. For an able Indian scholar's discussion of the legal questions involved, see generally T.S. Rama Rao, "The Sino-Indian White Papers."

15. "The Indian Government Must Stop Persecuting Overseas Chinese at Once," *Ch'iao-wu pao* 1:7 (Feb. 1963).

16. Shih P'eng, "The Indian Government's Atrocious Acts," p. 17; "The Overseas Chinese in India Subject to Barbarous Persecution," *Ch'iao-wu pao* 6:9 (Dec. 1962).

In its frequent communications with New Delhi, Peking called the Indian treatment of these "law-abiding" Chinese "unreasonable" and "unjustified" and demanded an end to India's "discriminatory" and "unfriendly" acts. India, on the other hand, usually insisted that the measures taken were within its sovereign right to defend itself against foreigners who were engaged in activities "prejudicial to Indian national interest and security."[17] In interviews and at public meetings held in China, the overseas Chinese who had returned from India vigorously protested their innocence and condemned the "persecution" and "anti-China" campaign conducted by Nehru. Ma Tsu-ts'ai, a seventy-two-year-old overseas Chinese, became the center of this publicity, and his "sufferings" were played up to exemplify India's "inhumane treatment" of Chinese nationals.[18]

INTERNMENT, DETENTION AND RELATED MEASURES TAKEN BY INDIA IN 1962–1963

After the Sino-Indian border dispute escalated into a large-scale armed conflict in the fall of 1962, Chinese residents in India were subjected to extensive control and regulation.[19] Following his proclamation of national emergency on October 26, President Radhakrishnan of India issued the Defense of India Ordinance, which suspended the exercise of certain individual rights during the emergency. Promulgated under this ordinance and its successor, the Defense of India Act, were the Defense of India Rules, which provided for the restriction of movement and detention of suspected persons, both citizens and aliens.[20]

Besides these special emergency powers, the Indian government in-

17. For some typical arguments put forth by China and India, see *White Paper*, vol. V, pp. 100–123.

18. "Returned Chinese Condemned Nehru," NCNA-English, Dec. 10, 1961 in *SCMP*, no. 2641:29–30 (Dec. 18, 1961); "The Truth of India's Anti-China Campaign," *JMJP* editorial, Dec. 7, 1961, p. 1; Liu Hsüan, "A Visit with Mr. Ma Tsu-ts'ai, a Returned Overseas Chinese from India," *Ch'iao-wu pao* 3:28–29 (June 1962).

19. A detailed examination of the various acts, rules, and orders which were applied to the Chinese community in India is available in Robert N. Hornick, "Restrictions on Chinese Nationals in India Following the Sino-Indian Border Conflict of 1962," unpublished paper, Harvard Law School, 1969.

20. The text of the Defense Ordinance is in *The Current Indian Statutes, 1962*, A.M. Suri, ed. (Chandigarh: Printed and published by L. Anand Mohan at The Punjab Law Reporter Press, 1963), Pt. III, pp. 5–20; the text of the Defense Act is in *The Current Indian Statutes, 1963*, Pt. II, pp. 18–41; the text of the Defense Rules, G.S.R. 1465, published in *Gazette of India, Extraordinary*, Pt. II, Sec. 3 (1), dated November 5, 1962.

voked the Foreigners Act of 1946[21] to issue a number of far-reaching orders that regulated the Chinese community during the crisis. These orders authorized restrictions on movement, deprivation of certain basic rights of Indian citizenship, and arrest followed by either internment in camps or detention in prison.

There were two major orders restricting the movement of Chinese nationals. The Foreigners (Restriction of Chinese Nationals) Order, October 25, 1962, prohibited a Chinese national from leaving the limits of his city or village or absenting himself from his registered address for longer than twenty-four hours without prior written permission from his registration officer, who was authorized to impose whatever conditions he deemed appropriate to the granting of permission. It also prohibited a Chinese national from leaving India except in accordance with such conditions, which were to be recorded in a permit specifying, among other things, the route, time, and place of departure; there were to be no air or sea departures except from Bombay, Calcutta, Madras, and New Delhi.[22] The Foreigners (Restricted Areas) Order, January 14, 1963, prohibited all Chinese nationals and all persons of Chinese origin from entering or remaining in designated restricted areas (the state of Assam and some districts of West Bengal, Uttar Pradesh, and Punjab) without a permit, even if they were Indian citizens and residents of those areas.[23]

President Radhakrishnan promulgated on October 30, 1962, the Foreigners Law (Application and Amendment) Ordinance, which made the Registration of Foreigners Act of 1939,[24] the Foreigners Act of 1946, and all rules and orders issued thereunder, applicable to "any person not of Indian origin who was at birth a citizen or subject of any country at war with, or committing external aggression against, India."[25] Another order issued on the same day suspended for the duration of the emergency the right of such persons, as well as foreigners, to move any court for the enforcement of basic constitutional protections against the

21. Act No. 31, 1946, text in Ministry of Law, Government of India, *General Statutory Rules and Orders* (Delhi: Manager of Publications, 1961), II, 230–241.
22. Text of this Order is in *The Current Indian Statutes, 1963*, Pt. I, p. 122.
23. Text of this Order is in *The Current Indian Statutes, 1963*, Pt. I, pp. 113–114.
24. Act No. 16, 1939, in *The Current Indian Statutes, 1939*, Pt. III, pp. 175–177.
25. Text of this Ordinance is in *The Current Indian Statutes, 1962*, Pt. III, pp. 20–21. This Ordinance was replaced by the Foreigners Law (Application and Amendment) Act, 1962 (Nov. 24, 1962), in *Acts of Parliament, 1962*, pp. 231–232.

arbitrary deprivation of life or liberty.[26] In order to effectuate the Indian government's intention to subject all Indian citizens of Chinese origin to both of the October 30 measures, their definition of "person" was soon broadened to make the regulatory scheme applicable to "any person who, or either of whose parents, or any of whose grandparents was at any time a citizen or subject of any country at war with, or committing external aggression against, India."[27] This became the definition of "person of Chinese origin" as that term was used in subsequent measures, such as the Foreigners (Restricted Areas) Order, 1963, mentioned above. The effect of these measures was to deny the almost 900 Indian citizens of Chinese origin the benefits of citizenship and to subject them to the same restrictions and controls as Chinese aliens.

Substantially the same formula—"any foreigner who is, and any person who (or any of whose parents or grandparents) was at any time," etc.—was used to designate those persons who without cause were subject to arrest and "internment" in camps under the Foreigners (Internment) Order of November 3, 1962. The order also authorized the arrest without warrant and the detention of any foreigner who is reasonably suspected of "having acted, of acting, or being about to act, with intent to assist a country at war with or committing external aggression against India, or in a manner prejudicial to the public safety or to the safety of any building or machinery."[28]

There is no question that India was profoundly shaken by the Chinese border conflict and the military reverses that it suffered in 1962. As one Indian scholar observes, shock, humiliation, frustration, and anger characterized the response of the entire country.[29] The sweeping restrictive measures against persons of Chinese descent were an obvious manifestation of this Indian national sentiment, which also found expression in occasional anti-Chinese demonstrations and attacks on Chinese shops and nationals.[30]

In the face of this difficult situation, many members of the local

26. G.S.R. 1418 in *The Current Indian Statutes, 1962,* Pt. I, p. 123.

27. The language quoted is from The Foreigners Law (Application and Amendment) Act, 1962 (Nov. 24, 1962), note 25.

28. G.S.R. 1463 (amended by G.S.R. 1595 on Nov. 16, 1962) in *The Current Indian Statutes, 1962,* Pt. I, pp. 124–125.

29. V.P. Dutt, "India and China: Betrayal, Humiliation, Reappraisal," in A.M. Halpern, ed., *Politics Toward China: Views from Six Continents* (New York: McGraw-Hill, 1965), p 217.

30. For instance, student demonstrators on November 1, 1962, raided six Chinese shops and stoned a Chinese restaurant in New Delhi. *Times of India,* Nov. 2, 1962, p. 1.

Chinese community went out of their way to show their friendship and solidarity with the Indian people. During the months of October and November 1962, Chinese residents in various parts of India, such as Kanpur, Kalimpong, Calcutta, and Bombay, condemned Communist China's "aggression," pledged their loyalty to India, and contributed to the Defense Fund.[31] In Bombay, a group of Chinese even publicized their sympathies with Taipei and disassociated themselves from the "pro-Peking" elements in the local Chinese community.[32] In Calcutta, the Overseas Chinese Association, with a claimed membership of 20,000, not only expressed support for the Indian government but also urged it not to accept Peking's "dirty" offer of a cease-fire in November.[33]

All these efforts, however, failed to allay the Indians' suspicion of the Chinese. This mistrust was very much in evidence during the Parliamentary debates in November 1962. To be sure, Prime Minister Nehru told Parliament on November 14:

> We have nothing against the Chinese people. We regret many things that their government has done. . . Anyhow, we must always distinguish between the people of any country . . . and its government and not transfer somehow our anger and bitterness at what has been done by the governmental action to the people as a whole. Therefore, I have not liked some poor Chinese shopkeepers, some restaurant-keepers, being attacked in Delhi or elsewhere as if they were the symbols of the attack on us.[34]

But the prevailing view in the Parliament was expressed by such members as H.V. Kamath and U.M. Trivedi. Urging the government to impose restrictions on the movement and activities of Chinese residents in India, Mr. Kamath suggested that there were reasons to believe that the much publicized pro-Indian gestures by these Chinese might be a mere camouflage.[35] In discussing the loyalty of Indian citizens of Chinese origin, Mr. Trivedi said: "The whole question is, even if he becomes a citizen of India, if his parents or grandparents belong to a country which is at war with me, I have no faith in such a person."[36]

The only member in the House of the People (Lok Sabha) who

31. *Ibid.*, Oct. 26, 1962, p. 1; Oct. 27, 1962, p. 10; Oct. 29, 1962, p. 9; Oct. 31, 1962, p. 5.
32. *Ibid.*, Oct. 31, 1962, p. 5.
33. *Ibid.*, Nov. 26, 1962, p. 9.
34. *Lok Sabha Debates*, 3rd Ser./3rd Sess. 9:1648–1649 (1962).
35. *Ibid.*, p. 1454; also "Strict Action Against 'Security Risks,'" *Times of India*, Nov. 15, 1962, p. 8.
36. *Lok Sabha Debates*, 3rd Ser./3rd Sess. 9:2266 (1962).

expressed reservations about the bill to declare Indian citizens of Chinese origin "foreigners" was Indragi Gupta of Calcutta, who commented:

> If the definition of "foreigner" is extended to them . . . they can also be deported. I think that is a very strange thing. I do not know whether such a law exists in any other country whereby a national of a country can be deported. I would like the government . . . to see whether it is likely to have any undesirable repercussions on Indians who are residents, either as citizens or, maybe, as stateless persons, in very large numbers in some other countries.[37]

Mr. Gupta's concern notwithstanding, the emotions running against China and the Chinese were such that the bill in question quickly passed.

It was against this background of anti-Chinese hysteria that persons of Chinese descent came to bear the brunt of India's restrictive measures. Following the promulgation of the Foreigners (Internment) Order of November 3, 1962, Indian authorities in Assam and certain districts of West Bengal arrested all residents of Chinese descent and took them to the permanent internment camp at Deoli, Rajasthan; and elsewhere in India certain other Chinese, who were suspected of "anti-Indian activities," were arrested and either sent to Deoli for internment or detained in various jails.[38] These persons included not only aliens but also citizens. By February 18, 1963, according to the Indian government's account, there were 2,165 Chinese interned at Deoli and an additional 143 detained in local jails.[39] Inasmuch as persons of Chinese descent, whether Indian citizens or aliens, were precluded from seeking judicial enforcement of their constitutional protection against arbitrary deprivation of liberty,[40] it is not surprising that no Chinese seem to have challenged the internment order in the courts. Although on January 23, 1963, Mr. Datar of the Home Ministry mentioned the "prosecution" of 32 Chinese out of 2,162 who had thus far been arrested, there is no indication that any Chinese were actually brought to trial upon espionage or other charges.[41]

37. *Ibid.*, pp. 2251–2252.
38. See text at notes 86, 89, and 93 to 96.
39. *Lok Sabha Debates*, 3rd Ser./4th Sess. 13:1141 (1963).
40. Recall text at note 26.
41. The figures were contained in Mr. Datar's table of persons arrested, interned, detained, and prosecuted. *Lok Sabha Debates*, 3rd Ser./3rd Sess. 12:5943–5944 (1963). However, on February 27, 1963, Home Minister L.B. Shastri told the Parliament that there was no plan to bring internees to trial for espionage charges. *Lok Sabha Debates*, 3rd Ser./4th Sess. 13:1143 (1963).

On the outbreak of hostilities between China and India the International Committee of the Red Cross (ICRC) had offered its humanitarian services to the national Red Cross Societies of both countries. The Indian government had immediately accepted the offer and, after interning persons of Chinese descent, granted the request of the ICRC delegate in New Delhi to visit the internment camp at Deoli. Three times, on December 12, 1962, June 25, 1963, and March 10, 1966, ICRC delegates visited the camp. China, on the other hand, although it had captured several thousand Indian military personnel, had refused to permit an ICRC visit to the prisoners of war, insisting that all problems concerning prisoners should be settled between the two countries. Despite the fact that diplomatic relations were not broken off between the countries, Indian diplomats in China were not permitted to visit the Indian prisoners, nor were Chinese diplomats in Delhi allowed to visit the internment camp at Deoli or to see other detained persons. Nevertheless, neither China nor India attempted to appoint a Protecting Power to protect the interests of nationals confined by the other state.[42]

The large number of Chinese residents in India who were not interned or detained suffered a variety of other disabilities. Those who resided in the "restricted" areas were forced to move their homes. Many had to give up their businesses. Chinese employees and workers were dismissed from their positions in Indian firms and factories. Chinese seamen and ship repairmen were barred from harbors, docks, and shipyards. The fact that Chinese were forbidden to leave their residential area for longer than twenty-four hours without a permit handicapped them in their work and adversely affected their children's schooling. At the height of the crisis Chinese restaurants in some Indian cities even found it prudent to use Japanese names.[43]

42. See International Committee of the Red Cross, *Annual Report, 1962* (Geneva: ICRC, 1963), pp. 22–23; *Annual Report, 1963* (Geneva: ICRC, 1964), pp. 26–27; *International Review of the Red Cross* (Geneva), no. 22:15 (Jan. 1963) and no. 24:149 (Mar. 1963); the ICRC's published reports do not note the 1966 visit to interned Chinese nor the failure of the parties to appoint protecting powers.

43. This account is based on the following sources: Joseph Lelyveld, "Curbs on Chinese Retained in India"; comments from some overseas Chinese on conditions in India published in "Views from Overseas Chinese," *Chung-yang jih-pao* (Central daily news; Taipei), Dec. 13, 1968, p. 1 and Jan. 21, 1969, p. 1; personal interviews with former Chinese residents in India now living in the United States. For Communist Chinese sources on the "persecution" of the overseas Chinese in India, see "Maltreatment of Chinese Continues in Indian Concentration Camps," *JMJP*, June 4, 1963, p. 3; "India Obstructs Chinese Nationals from Returning to China," *JMJP*, June 5, 1963, p. 3; "Victimized Chinese Bereft of Relatives by Indian Persecution," *ibid.*, June 6, 1963, p. 4; "Continued Indian Persecution of Chinese Na-

REPATRIATION OF INTERNED CHINESE AND DEPENDENTS

On November 8, 1962, the Peking government officially protested against India's Foreigners Law (Application and Amendment) Ordinance and urged the Indian government to stop its "persecution" of Chinese nationals and release all the Chinese "unjustifiably" arrested.[44] This was followed by an extensive exchange of charges and countercharges between the two countries.[45] In a note dated December 18, 1962, Peking proposed to send ships to India to bring back all interned Chinese nationals, and the Indian reply on the 31st offered to repatriate those who "wish to return to China of their own free will."[46] After some prolonged negotiations the two sides concluded on April 9, 1963, a six-point agreement on repatriation arrangements.[47] As a result, three groups of Chinese repatriates left India by ship during 1963, one each in the months of April, May, and July.

Even as the Chinese internees were being repatriated, controversy arose over India's alleged violation of the repatriation agreement. Among other things, the PRC accused Indian authorities of mistreating the first group of repatriates during their trip from Deoli to Madras, of confiscating many of their personal belongings, and of separating some repatriates from their families. New Delhi sought to refute these charges and labeled them "wild and unsubstantiated."[48] In an effort to avoid further charges, the Indian government gave a great deal of publicity to the elaborate arrangements that it made for transporting the second group of Chinese repatriates to Madras with a special train that included hospital, kitchen, canteen, and water storage cars.[49]

The total number of Chinese repatriated in 1963 was 2,395, of whom

---

tionals Exposed," NCNA-English, Aug. 12, 1963, in *SCMP*, no. 3041:24–25 (Aug. 16, 1963); "Persecution of Chinese in India," *Ch'iao-wu pao* 3:1–14 (June 1963) and 4:17–21 (Aug. 1969).

44. The Chinese note also complained about attacks on Chinese nationals and stores by "Indian ruffians."

45. See Part V of this chapter.

46. See Ministry of Foreign Affairs Note, Dec. 18, 1962, *White Paper*, vol. VIII, p. 105, and Ministry of External Affairs Note, Dec. 31, 1962, *ibid.*, p. 111.

47. See Exchange of Letters between the Chinese Embassy and the Indian Ministry of External Affairs, Apr. 9, 1963, *White Paper*, vol. IX, pp. 116, 117.

48. Chinese Embassy Memorandum, Apr. 27, 1963, *ibid.*, p. 125; and Ministry of External Affairs Memorandum, May 16, 1963, *ibid.*, p. 134. For a statement made on Apr. 27, 1963, by a spokesman for Peking's Overseas Chinese Affairs Commission, see *WCC 1963*, vol. X (1965), pp. 77–81.

49. "Second Batch to Leave Today: Chinese Repatriates," *Times of India*, May 25, 1963, p. 5.

1,665 were internees and 730 were their dependents.[50] The group that left India in April numbered 908, the May group about 650, and the July group more than 800.[51] When the PRC offered to send another ship to repatriate a fourth batch, India refused on the ground that none of the remaining internees wished to go back to China.[52]

According to a statement made on August 14, 1963, by the spokesman for the Indian Home Ministry, 594 Chinese internees preferred confinement in India to repatriation (they were never asked to give their reasons); the spokesman went on to say that all but "those whose presence at liberty is considered prejudicial to security" would be allowed eventually to resettle in India.[53] Very gradually, the Indian government released these remaining internees. In February 1964, the number of Chinese still interned was reported to be 566.[54] Eight months later the number had decreased by 100.[55] The last inmates at Deoli were not released until some time in 1967.[56]

Aside from those who were subjected to repatriation or deportation to China, between 1962 and 1967 some 7,500 other persons of Chinese origin left India for China, Hong Kong, Canada, Pakistan, Taiwan, and other places.[57] For the remaining group of approximately 10,000, life has not been easy. As late as the fall of 1967, five years after the Sino-Indian border conflict, curbs on Chinese were reportedly still in force. As of that time only four persons of Chinese descent enjoyed full rights as Indian citizens: two leaders of the Indian Overseas Chinese Association, a pro-Chinese Nationalist group, and their wives. From time to time leaders of the Chinese community obtained promises from New Delhi to relax restrictions, but local officials consistently ignored instructions to that effect from the central government.[58]

There are signs, however, that conditions may be improving for the overseas Chinese in India. For one thing, development of unofficial

50. Ministry of External Affairs Note, Sept. 3, 1963, *White Paper*, vol. X, pp. 64, 65.

51. "Internees Go Aboard China's Ships," *Times of India*, April 14, 1963, p. 1; "Another Batch Goes to Madras: Chinese Internees," *Times of India*, May 22, 1963, p. 5; "Chinese to Leave India," *The New York Times*, May 22, 1963, p. 3; "Third Group of Chinese Victims from India Arrive in South China Port," NCNA-English, Aug. 12, 1963, in *SCMP*, no. 3041:25–26 (Aug. 16, 1963).

52. *White Paper*, vol. X, pp. 59, 60.

53. *Lok Sabha Debates*, 3rd Ser./5th Sess. 14:368 (1963).

54. *Lok Sabha Debates*, 3rd Ser./7th Sess. 25:279 (1964).

55. *Rajya Sabha Debates* 49:4141 (1964).

56. J. Lelyveld, "Curbs on Chinese Retained in India," p. 12.

57. *Ibid.*

58. *Ibid.*

contacts between India and Nationalist China may soften the strong feeling generally held by Indians against Chinese.[59] For another, the termination on January 10, 1968, of the state of emergency that had been proclaimed at the time of the border hostilities brought an end to those controls that were based upon the special emergency powers.[60] But the measures taken under the Foreigners Act of 1946, as amended, are apparently deemed to be of permanent duration. Thus, persons of Chinese descent remaining in India can hardly expect to regain the rights and status accorded to them before 1962. They are confronted with the bleak prospect of living under continuing restrictions and either being regarded with suspicion as nationals of the PRC or being treated as stateless persons, with the disadvantages which that status implies.

CHINA'S INVOCATION OF INTERNATIONAL LAW

The foregoing account makes clear that, unlike the governments that ruled China until the latter part of the nineteenth century, the People's Republic did not ignore the tribulations of Chinese living abroad but sought to alleviate their suffering.[61] Yet, unlike some other powerful nation-states that have moved vigorously to protect their nationals abroad, the PRC did not resort to military intervention. Apart from sending ships to repatriate its nationals, the PRC, like its predecessors the Republic of China and the imperial Chinese government during the last decades of the Manchu dynasty (1644–1912), confined itself to verbal interventions and to an assortment of diplomatic pressures and sanctions. In seeking to protect persons of Chinese descent in India,

59. Taipei's official newspaper, for instance, has reported the advocacy by certain members of the Indian Parliament of diplomatic ties with Nationalist China and the presence of some prominent Indian figures at the meetings sponsored by pro-KMT overseas Chinese. "Dr. Sun's Birth Commemorated by Overseas Chinese in India," *Chung-yang jih-pao,* Nov. 12, 1968, p. 2; "Chinese in Calcutta Entertain India MPs," *ibid.,* Feb. 8, 1969, p. 2; "Indian MPs Advocated Ties with Taipei," *ibid.,* Apr. 17, 1969, p. 1.

60. The Presidential order of January 10 revoking emergency rules meant the release of 770 persons, most of them Mizo tribesmen, who had been held without trial in the northeastern state of Assam and the restoration of certain fundamental rights guaranteed by the Constitution but suspended by the Presidential Proclamation of Emergency in 1962. Joseph Lelyveld, "India to End Emergency Rules," *The New York Times,* Jan. 2, 1968, p. 8; "India Ends Emergency Dating from '62 War," *The New York Times,* Jan. 11, 1968, p. 74.

61. For discussion of the changes in the attitude of the Chinese government toward the protection of the overseas Chinese, see H.F. MacNair, *The Chinese Abroad* (Shanghai: Commercial Press, 1933), pp. 268–311, and Lea E. Williams, *The Future of the Overseas Chinese in Southeast Asia* (New York: McGraw-Hill, 1966), pp. 51–71.

China simply assumed that even those who had acquired Indian nationality were Chinese nationals, and its claims for protection made no distinction between dual nationals and persons who enjoyed only Chinese nationality.

The nature of the PRC's verbal efforts to protect its nationals in India changed over time. Despite the fact that, as early as 1959, the PRC articulated its position with respect to the Sino-Indian boundary in terms of international law, the record of official Sino-Indian communications pertaining to disputes over Chinese nationals in India from 1960 until 1962 fails to reflect any explicit references to international law. To be sure, there were occasional allusions that may be interpreted as implicit references to international legal standards. When, for example, in 1960 Indian authorities detained the manager of the Bank of China in Calcutta, China protested against "such an unruly action as violates human rights" and "such discriminative measures as violate . . . personal freedom."[62] And when in 1961 India arrested and deported certain Chinese nationals, the Chinese embassy in New Delhi requested the Indian government to "respect the proper and legitimate rights of the Chinese nationals and immediately stop measures of persecution against Chinese nationals."[63] But, apart from such vague allusions, the tenor of the Chinese notes and memoranda was one of injured friendship that expressed regret at both India's actions and its allegedly distorted reporting of its actions. India's conduct was characterized as "extraordinary,"[64] "unfriendly,"[65] "unreasonable,"[66] "inhumane,"[67] or creating "a serious political incident."[68] Emphasis was placed on "upholding the friendly relations between the peoples of the two countries" by attaining a "reasonable settlement."[69] To the extent that the Chinese communications contained specific references to law, these consisted of allegations that Indian authorities had violated Indian law[70] and that accused Chinese nationals had not violated Indian law.[71]

As the Sino-Indian dispute over the overseas Chinese intensified dur-

62. Chinese Embassy Note, Dec. 6, 1960, *White Paper*, vol. V, p. 104.
63. Chinese Embassy Memorandum, Dec. 4, 1961, *ibid.*, vol. VI, p. 147.
64. Ministry of Foreign Affairs Note, March 13, 1961, *ibid.*, vol. V, p. 119.
65. Chinese Embassy Note, Jan. 3, 1961, *ibid.*, p. 109.
66. Chinese Embassy Note, Feb. 25, 1961, *ibid.*, p. 115.
67. Consulate General of China, Calcutta, Memorandum to the Government of West Bengal, Nov. 28, 1961, *ibid.*, vol. VI, p. 145.
68. Chinese Embassy Note, Jan. 23, 1963, *ibid.*, p. 159.
69. Chinese Embassy Note, Jan. 3, 1961, *White Paper*, vol. V, p. 109.
70. Chinese Embassy Note, Feb. 25, 1961, *White Paper*, vol. V, p. 115.
71. Chinese Embassy Note, Jan. 3, 1961, *White Paper*, vol. V, p. 109.

ing 1962, China's communications came to reflect more explicit awareness of international law. In rejecting India's claim that a Chinese embassy protest against the deportation of Chinese nationals constituted interference in internal affairs, in March 1962 the Ministry of Foreign Affairs in Peking stated:

> As for protecting the proper rights and interests of its nationals abroad and making reasonable representations to the government of the host country when they suffer unwarranted persecution there, this is the legitimate right as well as bounden duty of the Embassy and Consulate-General of every country, as is internationally acknowledged.[72]

And a few months later, when India charged that the Chinese consulate-general in Calcutta had violated "well-recognized principles of customary international law" by authorizing the Chinese Trade Agent in Kalimpong to take over the property of an overseas Chinese school there, Peking responded that this "was an exercise of the normal functions and powers of the Chinese Consulate-General, and was fully in accord with international practice." India's charges, the PRC claimed, were slanderous fabrications that constituted "an expression of contempt for the well-recognized and customary principles of international law."[73]

Thus, prior to the outbreak of serious hostilities in October 1962, China had been slow to invoke international law in behalf of its nationals in India and finally did so only in response to legal arguments advanced by India. The outbreak of hostilities and the severity of the measures that India consequently took against Chinese nationals—especially their internment—led to a marked increase in the extent to which the PRC invoked international law. For example, shortly after the October 31, 1962, promulgation of the Foreigners Law (Application and Amendment) Ordinance, 1962, a note from Peking's Ministry of Foreign Affairs charged that the Indian government had "violated openly the acknowledged principles of international law and practice."[74] A few days later, after India announced that Chinese nationals would be allowed to leave the country only from four specified ports and to leave their residence for a period exceeding twenty-four hours only with

72. Ministry of Foreign Affairs Note, March 6, 1962, *White Paper*, vol. VI, pp. 163, 165.

73. For the Indian accusation, see Ministry of External Affairs Note, June 26, 1962, *ibid.*, p. 184. For China's response, see Ministry of Foreign Affairs Note, Aug. 7, 1962, *ibid.*, vol. VII, p. 155.

74. Ministry of Foreign Affairs Note, Nov. 8, 1962, *ibid.*, vol. VIII, p. 93.

the prior permission of their registration officer, the PRC branded these actions as "not only discriminative and special restrictions imposed on Chinese nationals, but violations of acknowledged international practice."[75] And subsequent statements were sprinkled with references to "the accepted norms of international law,"[76] "the principles of international law,"[77] and the "code of conduct in international relations."[78]

Yet invariably these references merely constituted flat assertions that certain conduct by India violated international law. The PRC made no attempt to demonstrate the validity of these assertions by identifying the sources of the applicable principles of law or by articulating the rationale of those principles. Peking's protests sometimes even left in doubt the precise actions that allegedly violated international law, lumping together a variety of activities as "unlawful."[79] Even the claim by India that its refusal to permit the Chinese embassy the ordinary peacetime right to protect nationals was consistent with the 1949 Geneva Convention Relative to the Protection of Civilian Persons in Time of War (hereafter the Civilian Convention)[80] elicited not a reasoned official argument in rebuttal, but simply the *ipse dixit* that "the Chinese Government hereby points out to the Indian Government once again that, while normal diplomatic relations are maintained between China and India, it is an acknowledged practice in accordance with the principles of international law that the Chinese Embassy should exercise its right to protect its nationals."[81] And the PRC made no distinction between persons of Chinese descent in India who were dual nationals and those who were only Chinese nationals, nor did it clarify the basis for determining Chinese nationality.

Although some Chinese interpretations of India's duties under international law seem extravagant, Peking's failure to develop underlying support for its claims does not always appear attributable to the absence of such support. With respect to certain aspects of India's treat-

75. Ministry of Foreign Affairs Note, Nov. 13, 1962, *ibid.*, vol. IX, p. 94.
76. Ministry of Foreign Affairs Note, Feb. 23, 1963, *ibid.*, p. 98.
77. Chinese Embassy Note, March 14, 1963, *ibid.*, pp. 104, 105.
78. Chinese Embassy Memorandum, Dec. 25, 1962, *ibid.*, pp. 84, 85.
79. Ministry of Foreign Affairs Note, Nov. 8, 1962, *White Paper*, vol. VIII, p. 93.
80. *U.S. Treaties* 6:3516; *UNTS* 75:289 (1950); *American Journal of International Law* Supplement 50:724 (1956). India deposited its ratification with the Swiss Federal Council on November 9, 1950. *UNTS* 78:368 (1951). The instrument of ratification (actually an accession) of the People's Republic of China was deposited on December 28, 1956, *UNTS* 260:444 (1957).
81. Ministry of Foreign Affairs Note, Jan. 19, 1963, *White Paper*, vol. IX, pp. 90, 91.

ment of Chinese nationals, Peking's arguments were easier to muster than New Delhi's. For example, in the spring of 1963, while China persisted in its unsuccessful efforts to learn the identity of all Chinese nationals interned or imprisoned by India and to obtain the rights to visit and correspond with them, the Vienna Convention on Consular Relations was signed, guaranteeing consular officers these rights of communication and contact with nationals of their state.[82] Despite the fact that the People's Republic of China had not been invited to the United Nations Conference that adopted the Consular Convention, Peking might well have cited the convention as further evidence of the generally acknowledged existence of these rights. Yet the People's Republic permitted the event to go unmentioned. India, on the other hand, displayed somewhat more of a taste than China for the elaboration of legal argument, when it sought to have its consular officials visit an Indian national imprisoned on a criminal charge in China, attend the trial and arrange legal representation; even though it had failed to sign the convention after participating in the conference, it pointed to article 36 of the Consular Convention as evidence that "these rights have always been recognized in the law and practice of all states."[83] Characteristically, the PRC's response to India's claim cryptically labeled it an appeal "to so-called international law and practice," ignored the Consular Convention, and stated that China's handling of the case was "in full conformity with international practice."[84]

This demonstrated reluctance to articulate the intellectual bases for claims to protect Chinese nationals in India does not reflect a reluctance of the Chinese Communist elite to engage in detailed argumentation. Indeed, the diplomatic correspondence reveals a Chinese zest for factual disputation that is fully equal to India's. Nor does the lack of legal amplification in the correspondence necessarily suggest utter disdain for the skills of the international lawyer. The *People's Daily*, the official newspaper of the Chinese Communist Party, occasionally carried long articles by Chinese scholars buttressing their government's claims to protect nationals in India.[85] These essays referred not only to specific

82. See Article 36. For the text of this Vienna Convention, UN Doc. A/CONF. 25/12, April 23, 1963; *AJIL* 57:995 (1963).

83. Ministry of External Affairs Note, March 2, 1964, *White Paper*, vol. XI, pp. 50, 52.

84. Ministry of Foreign Affairs Note, Sept. 15, 1965, *ibid.*, vol. XII, pp. 118, 119.

85. See Chou Keng-sheng, "The Persecution of Chinese Nationals and Infringement of the Right of China to Protect Chinese Nationals Are Serious Internationally Illegal Acts," *JMJP*, Jan. 22, 1963, p. 5; Ni Cheng-ao "Introduction to the 1949

provisions of international conventions but also to the works of "bourgeois" authorities on international law. Articles that were similar in content but written in a less legalistic vein appeared in other newspapers and journals.[86] Moreover, editorials in the *People's Daily* and the *Journal of Overseas Chinese Affairs* occasionally referred to international law.[87] To a modest extent these semiofficial materials elucidate the bases of the PRC's claims. With the aid of these materials as well as the diplomatic correspondence, we will analyze China's principal claims relating to the internment and detention of its nationals.

INDIA'S RIGHT TO INTERN AND DETAIN

Internment

The essential Chinese position on internment was first set forth in the Ministry of Foreign Affairs' protest of November 24, 1962:

> The Ministry has been informed that the Indian Government issued on November 20 an order to arrest and intern all the Chinese nationals and those of Chinese descent in Assam State and five districts of West Bengal. This unprecedentedly cruel persecution constitutes a serious violation of international law and the standard of international relations. . . .
>
> There had been reports even earlier that the Indian Government was prepared to arrest Chinese nationals on mass [sic] and that concentration camps had been set up for them. Now the Indian Government does come out with its mass arrest of Chinese nationals . . . Chinese nationals in India have not only suffered serious encroachment on their personal liberty but have been deprived of the minimum right to a normal living. Such arbitrary and unwarranted arrests and internments of large numbers of innocent foreigners by the Indian Government constitute outrages rarely seen in international relations.[88]

Two weeks later the Ministry indirectly called attention to the fact that, despite the border hostilities, war had not been declared between India and China; ignoring a good deal of state practice during wartime, it stated, with respect to internment as well as actions taken against Chinese diplomatic and consular staff: "Such abnormal treat-

---

Geneva Convention Relating to the Protection of Civilian Persons in Time of War," *JMJP*, Jan. 22, 1963, p. 5; and Fu Chu, "The Persecution of Chinese Nationals by the Indian Government Is a Serious Violation of International Law," *JMJP*, Nov. 30, 1962, p. 3.

86. See our note 16.

87. See our notes 15 and 18.

88. Ministry of Foreign Affairs Note, Nov. 24, 1962, *White Paper*, vol. VIII, p. 99.

ment meted out to the Chinese in India . . . is rarely seen even when a war has been formally declared between two countries."[89]

The Indian government's reply opened with the truism "that the established practices of international law require foreign nationals living in the territory of another State to respect the laws and regulations of that State. The maintenance of law and order and public security assumes greater significance when the country concerned has been subjected to external aggression."[90] India maintained that the basic governmental authorization for the sanctions of which China complained—the Foreigners Law (Application and Amendment) Ordinance, 1962—was, like the measures taken against Indian nationals under the Defense of India Regulations, designed "to safeguard the security of the country endangered by massive Chinese invasion" and that "promulgation of this Ordinance is a matter solely within the sovereign jurisdiction of the Government of India." The internment of all Chinese nationals in Assam and West Bengal that elicited Peking's protest occurred, according to New Delhi's Ministry of External Affairs, because "it became necessary for the Government of India to remove all Chinese nationals from that region along with others who were security risks when Chinese aggressors had been moving threateningly toward these areas."[91]

Peking's note of December 18, 1962, claimed that New Delhi's reply had "deliberately evaded matters of substance and made denials in hollow and vague terms in a futile attempt to absolve itself of the guilt of cruel persecution of Chinese nationals."[92] Security considerations were merely a pretext for India's actions, it said; India had aggressively provoked the border conflict. Moreover, the PRC emphasized, India's action consisted of "wholesale indiscriminate arrests of law-abiding peaceable Chinese nationals, both man and woman, old and young." The arrested persons were allegedly "thrown into concentration camps, cut off from their families and deprived of their personal liberty and property" and "subjected to all kinds of inhuman treatment." The PRC rejected as "completely untenable" the assertion that India's action was within its sovereign jurisdiction; "according to international practice, the country of residence has the obligation to respect the human rights and fundamental freedoms of foreign residents and to protect the safety

89. Ministry of Foreign Affairs Note, Dec. 8, 1962, *ibid.*, p. 123. See also Ministry of Foreign Affairs Note, May 18, 1963, *ibid.*, vol. IX, p. 160.
90. Ministry of External Affairs Note, Dec. 13, 1962, *ibid.*, vol. VIII, p. 104.
91. *Ibid.*
92. Ministry of Foreign Affairs Note, Dec. 18, 1962, *ibid.*, vol. VIII, p. 105.

of their person and property." India's failure to meet that obligation constituted "a serious international delinquency." Peking contrasted India's conduct with its own "protection for law-abiding Indian nationals in China" and pointed out that "not a single Indian national had been interned on account of the border conflict."[93]

Subsequent Indian notes sought to bolster its security argument. India at one point characterized the action as "the minimum that any Government would take under similar circumstances."[94] Although the bulk of the Chinese interned were "from the sensitive border areas, from where they have had to be removed in the interest of national security,"[95] some Chinese from other areas were also interned, and India sought to justify this action on a nominally more individualized, but equally vague, basis. For example, a Chinese protest against the internment of certain named nationals from various places[96] elicited the answer that the action had been taken "under the Defense of India Rules because of their prejudicial and anti-Indian activities." Although India failed to specify the nature of these activities, it maintained that "there were very clear reasons for their arrest";[97] it repeatedly denied that law abiding Chinese nationals were subjected to any persecution.[98] As the debate wore on, India attempted to lend color, if not particularity, to its defense. It claimed that prior to the outbreak of hostilities, China had "built up a network of espionage and agents-provocateurs, using mainly for this purpose, persons of Chinese origin in India," and that at the time of "the Chinese invasion" certain of these persons had "to be taken into camp" in order "(i) to prevent acts of subversion and sabotage; (ii) to prevent fifth-column activities; and (iii) to protect enemy agents from the wrath of the people."[99]

China, of course, had other explanations of India's conduct. Internment was not motivated by a concern for defense, Peking alleged, but was solely a retaliatory action.[100] At one point, China claimed that Indian authorities adopted these "frenzied measures" because they were "enraged by shame."[101] More frequently, however, the PRC asserted

93. *Ibid.*
94. Ministry of External Affairs Memorandum, Jan. 8, 1963, *ibid.*, p. 114.
95. Ministry of External Affairs Note, Dec. 31, 1962, *ibid.*, p. 111.
96. Chinese Embassy Memorandum, Dec. 25, 1962, *ibid.*, vol. IX, p. 84.
97. Ministry of External Affairs Memorandum, Feb. 8, 1963, *ibid.*, p. 97.
98. See Ministry of External Affairs Note, May 14, 1963, *ibid.*, p. 133.
99. Ministry of External Affairs Note, June 10, 1963, *ibid.*, pp. 145, 146.
100. Ministry of Foreign Affairs Note, April 27, 1963, *ibid.*, p. 122.
101. Ministry of Foreign Affairs Note, May 18, 1963, *ibid.*, pp. 160, 162.

that its interned nationals were being held as hostages to blackmail China. This, Peking suggested, was why India had announced its willingness to provide information about internees only on a reciprocal basis in exchange for information about the Indian soldiers who had been taken prisoner by China.[102] And this, according to Peking, was the significance of India's statements that the cases of internees would be reviewed from time to time so that "only those who constitute serious risk to national security will continue under detention," and that India would in the first instance repatriate only holders of PRC passports against whom no complaints were pending rather than all Chinese who wished repatriation.[103] India was merely manufacturing pretexts to retain large numbers of Chinese as hostages.[104]

India hurled the hostage charge back at China: "If there is any question of anyone holding hostages," the Ministry of External Affairs argued, "it is the Chinese Government who are still holding as hostages over 3,000 Indians who had been unscrupulously captured."[105] That India had not sought to link the fate of the Chinese internees to that of the Indian prisoners of war should have been clear, the Ministry stated, from the fact that India had announced its intention to repatriate willing Chinese nationals on December 31, 1962, while China had not announced its intention to release the Indian prisoners of war until April 2, 1963.[106] China, of course, rejoined not only that India was willing to repatriate only a limited number of Chinese but also that China had begun to release sick and wounded prisoners of war before India's repatriation decision was announced.[107] And it might have pointed out that neither the six-point agreement on repatriation arrangements nor any actual repatriation by India occurred until after China had announced its intention to release all its prisoners of war.[108]

When challenging the validity of India's internment of Chinese nationals, the PRC studiously avoided reference to the Geneva Civilian Convention. But Professor Chou Keng-sheng, writing in the *People's Daily* of January 22, 1963, invoked specific provisions of the Convention

102. See our note 92.
103. See our note 95.
104. Ministry of Foreign Affairs Note, Jan. 19, 1963, *ibid.*, pp. 90, 91.
105. Ministry of External Affairs Note, March 26, 1963, *ibid.*, p. 109.
106. Ministry of External Affairs Note, May 17, 1963, *ibid.*, pp. 137, 138.
107. Chinese Embassy Note, March 14, 1963, *ibid.*, pp. 104, 105; Ministry of Foreign Affairs Note, April 25, 1963, *ibid.*, p. 120.
108. Recall text at our note 47.

to support his government's challenge to the internment.[109] After repeating the allegation that the interned Chinese were being held as hostages, he pointed out that article 34 of the convention expressly prohibited the taking of hostages. He also claimed that "one can hardly find any basis in the Geneva Convention for carrying out the so-called 'differentiation' among peaceful and law-abiding interned civilians" whereby the Indian government proposed to distinguish between those who constituted a serious risk to national security and would continue to be detained and those who would be released. India's position, of course, was based on the assumption that not all internees were "peaceful and law-abiding," and its proposed "differentiation" was apparently guided by article 43 of the convention, which requires periodic reconsideration of the cases of interned persons "with a view to the favorable amendment of the initial decision, if circumstances permit."[110]

Professor Chou asserted that the internment was inconsistent with the convention on other grounds as well. Although some of the interned Chinese nationals were arrested because they were, in the words of article 5 of the convention, "definitely suspected of or engaged in activities hostile to the security of the State," according to India the bulk of the internees were acted against en masse solely by virtue of their residence in "sensitive areas," under that provision of the Foreigners (Internment) Order which authorized internment "without cause."[111] It was apparently this factual situation that led Professor Chou to argue:

> According to article 5 of the convention, only an individual protected person "who is definitely suspected of or engaged in activities hostile to the security of the State" shall lose the rights and privileges under the convention. According to article 42, the internment or placing in assigned residence of protected persons may be ordered only if the security of the detaining power makes it "absolutely necessary." India has placed a large number of innocent, peaceful, and law-abiding Chinese nationals in internment and such an extreme measure has been taken during a limited border conflict. Where is the "absolute necessity"? Moreover, after the Chinese government has on its own initiative declared a cease-fire and withdrawn its border forces, the Indian government continues to intern and persecute Chinese nationals. Where are the similarities between India's acts and the provisions of the Geneva Convention?[112]

It is not clear whether Professor Chou was arguing that the combination of articles 5 and 42 prohibits all mass internments without regard

109. See Chou, "The Persecution of Chinese Nationals."
110. See our note 80.
111. Recall the text paragraph concluding with note 28 and also the text at note 95.
112. Chou, "The Persecution of Chinese Nationals."

to individual behavior or that India had simply failed to demonstrate why this particular mass internment was "absolutely necessary" to its security. On its face the convention does not prohibit all mass internment but only the mass application of measures more severe than internment. Under article 5, more severe measures than internment may be applied only to "an individual protected person" who, because his conduct is definitely suspected of infringing national security, loses the protection of the convention to the extent that security requires. Article 42 lays down no similar restriction but speaks of the internment of "protected persons," implying that mass internment is permissible if "absolutely necessary." Indeed, after long discussion, the Geneva conference refused to adopt an amendment that would have required that each decision to intern or to place in assigned residence "should be taken individually." The amendment was rejected out of recognition that situations might exist, as for example when a state is threatened by invasion, that might require a government to move quickly to prevent hostile acts by confining categories of persons before being able to examine individual cases. The periodic reconsideration provided in article 43 was deemed sufficient guaranty against the risks of arbitrary decision.[113]

If, as seems likely, Professor Chou was actually arguing not that all mass internments were prohibited but that this particular one was, he might have strengthened his argument. He could have pointed out that the *Commentary* on the convention published by a group of experts of the International Committee of the Red Cross (ICRC), after emphasizing that article 42 gives states a large measure of discretion in determining whether threats to their security necessitate internment, equally emphatically asserts that:

> The mere fact that a person is a subject of an enemy Power can not be considered as threatening the security of the country where he is living; it is not therefore a valid reason for interning him or placing him in assigned residence. To justify recourse to such measures the State must have good reason to think that the person concerned, by his activities, knowledge or qualifications, represents a real threat to its present or future security.[114]

Even if we take into account the broad discretion accorded to the interning power by the convention and the fact that India limited its mass internment to persons of Chinese descent living in certain

113. Jean S. Pictet, ed., *Commentary on the Geneva Convention Relative to the Protection of Civilian Persons in Time of War* (Geneva: ICRC, 1958), p. 256.
114. *Ibid.*, p. 258.

areas which, because of geography, might understandably be regarded as "sensitive," it nevertheless remains difficult to justify the internment of all such persons from those areas; they appear to have been interned not because of their "activities, knowledge or qualifications" but because they were nationals of an enemy power. Indeed, Home Minister L. B. Shastri told the Indian Parliament that the Chinese "have not been arrested for any overt action they took. They have been detained because they are foreigners."[115] Furthermore, even if, as India maintained, it was necessary to remove all Chinese nationals from the sensitive areas, it hardly follows that it was also necessary to intern them rather than to impose less severe methods of control, such as assigned residence.[116]

One may wish to grant India the benefit of the doubt and characterize the initial mass internment as the action of a state that perceived a threat of invasion and a consequent need to move quickly to prevent hostile acts by interning a potentially dangerous category of persons before individual cases could be examined.[117] But it is surely more difficult to state a respectable defense under the convention for India's continuing internment of large numbers of persons of Chinese descent long after the crisis had passed. Professor Chou's mention of this failure to release the internees after the cessation of hostilities implicitly invoked not only article 43's provision for periodic reconsideration of the need for internment but also many other provisions: article 46, which requires that "restrictive measures taken regarding protected persons shall be cancelled as soon as possible after the close of hostilities"; article 132, which requires the release of each interned person "as soon as the reasons which necessitated his internment no longer exist"; article 133, which states that "internment shall cease as soon as possible after the close of hostilities"; article 134, which obligates the parties to "endeavour, upon the close of hostilities . . . , to ensure the return of all internees to their last place

115. *Lok Sabha Debates*, 3rd Ser./4th Sess. 13:302 (1963).

116. Pictet *et al.* recognize that, generally, placing foreign nationals in assigned residences is a less severe sanction than internment. Pictet, ed., *Commentary on Geneva Convention*, p. 256. Moreover, assigned residence is a recognized method of moving enemy aliens away from a restricted area.

117. For an Indian scholar's assertion that the internment met the standards of the Civilian Convention, see T. S. Rama Rao, "International Law as Practiced by India, China and Pakistan in Their Relations with One Another," Second Conference of the Indian Society of International Law *Proceedings*, 1963 (New Delhi, 1964), pp. 30, 48–49.

of residence, or to facilitate their repatriation"; and article 6, which provides that, "in territory of Parties to the conflict, the application of the present Convention shall cease on the general close of military operations," also provides that after that date protected persons are to continue to benefit from the convention until their release.

The preparatory work on article 6 plainly revealed the policy of the convention toward internment continuing beyond the period of hostilities. Although the draft convention had stipulated that the convention would not cease to apply on territory of parties to the conflict until one year after the general close of military operations, the one-year provision was stricken by the conference out of fear that it might legitimate the prolongation of security measures, particularly internment or placing in assigned residence, which were thought to be justified only by the existence of an armed struggle.[118] This did not mean, of course, that it was thought that internment could always be brought to an end shortly after the end of active hostilities, for "the disorganization caused by war may quite possibly involve some delay before the return to normal."[119] What the convention sought to avoid was the indefinite prolongation of internment under one pretext or another.

This point gained force with the passage of time, as China repeatedly reminded India. A Chinese note of January 12, 1966, for example, stated that, more than three years after the brief border conflict, "several hundred innocent Chinese nationals are still being detained in the concentration camp and the jails in various places of India . . . These crimes which grossly trample upon the principles of international law are rare in the history of international relations."[120]

Thus, the PRC's invocation of international law to invalidate the internment of its nationals seems to have rested on solid, if unarticulated, grounds. Even though, as the PRC had pointed out, neither party to the brief Sino-Indian conflict had declared war, Peking did not seem to base its challenge on the assumption that India's conduct should be measured by the standards applicable to the regulation of aliens in ordinary time of peace. Rather, it argued that "such atrocities are absolutely impermissible even when two countries are formally at

118. See Pictet, ed., *Commentary on the Geneva Convention Relative to the Protection of Civilian Persons*, p. 61.
119. *Ibid.*, p. 515.
120. Ministry of Foreign Affairs Note, Jan. 12, 1966, *White Paper*, vol. XIII, p. 27.

war."[121] Nevertheless, although it plainly recognized that hostilities had taken place, the PRC did not affirmatively assert the applicability of the Civilian Convention, and carefully avoided reference to it regarding the validity of the internment. Instead, it simply assigned to its publicists the task of elucidating the argument that internment violated the convention. In elliptical fashion, Professor Chou Keng-sheng fulfilled that task with respect to the internment of the "large number of innocent, peaceful, and law-abiding Chinese nationals" who were arrested en masse rather than because of their behavior as individuals. In addition, he made clear that, whatever might be the justification for the initial internment of any Chinese nationals during the period of hostilities and immediately thereafter, there could be none under the convention once the threat had obviously passed.

Detention

We have already noted that a small number of Chinese nationals were arrested and interned on an individual basis because of allegedly "prejudicial and anti-Indian activities."[122] It should also be recalled that, for similarly vague reasons, by early 1963 Indian authorities had arrested and detained in local jails 143 other Chinese.[123] The Home Ministry mentioned the "prosecution" of some of the latter group, but none appear to have been brought to trial upon espionage or other charges relating to national security.[124] The distinction between those detained and those interned on an individual basis was never made clear in the diplomatic correspondence and was ignored in the writings of publicists.

China's protests against detentions in local jails usually branded them as "unjustifiable," "unreasonable," and "cruel" persecution on the ground that the detained persons were innocent and had not infringed India's national security.[125] But Peking's attacks upon detentions generally did not reflect the same degree of outrage as

121. Ministry of Foreign Affairs Note, May 18, 1963, *ibid.*, vol. IX, pp. 160, 162; and recall text at our note 89. See also scholar Fu Chu's statement, note 85, that "it is worthwhile to note that the current violent acts and measures toward Chinese nationals adopted by the Indian Government are not permissible even in the case of the treatment of enemy nationals by belligerents."
122. Recall text at our notes 96 to 98.
123. Recall text at our note 39.
124. Recall text at our note 41.
125. See, for instance, Chinese Embassy Note, May 25, 1967, *White Paper,* vol. XIV, p. 28.

its protests against the wholesale internment, and its publicists focused on the latter, which was not only more important statistically and more novel but which was also easier to attack on legal grounds. As we have seen, article 5 of the Civilian Convention plainly contemplated detention—a more severe measure of control than either internment or placing in assigned residence—if in the judgment of the detaining power a resident national of another party to the conflict is "definitely suspected of or engaged in activities hostile to the security of the State." While India offered no evidence to support its allegations that detained persons had engaged in activities prejudicial to its security, the Civilian Convention does not require that the detaining power make any showing of the reasonableness of its action but instead allocates the decision to its discretion. Nevertheless, although the initial detentions were not readily susceptible to legal challenge, it is difficult to find that their continuation years after the termination of the conflict complies with the requirement of article 5 that the rights of protected persons under the convention be granted to detainees "at the earliest date consistent with the security of the State." Although neither the PRC nor Chinese scholars spelled out this argument in terms of the convention, it appeared to underlie the PRC's persistent protests against the continuing detentions.

CHINA'S CLAIM TO INFORMATION AND ACCESS

Prior to the outbreak of the border conflict in 1962 China's right to information about and access to its nationals detained by India did not constitute a significant issue in the Sino-Indian diplomatic exchanges. To be sure, following the 1960 arrest on criminal charges of Ma Tsu-ts'ai, whose case subsequently became a cause célèbre, the PRC claimed that the local authorities in Kalimpong had failed to comply with China's requests for reasons and evidence justifying the arrest, for an opportunity to discuss the case with the authorities, and for access to the accused.[126] But two months later, India reported that Chinese consular officials had been permitted an interview with the accused,[127] and Peking's attention subsequently fastened on other aspects of the case.

126. Statement made by the Vice-Minister for Foreign Affairs for China to the Indian Ambassador, Oct. 21, 1960, *ibid.*, vol. V, p. 100.
127. Enclosure to the Government of India Note, Dec. 20, 1960, *ibid.*, p. 107.

Information and access became a major issue, however, after India's large-scale internment, for India persistently rejected the repeated requests of the Chinese embassy and the Chinese consulates-general to exercise what Peking termed "the universally acknowledged right of protecting their own nationals" by visiting the arrested nationals and obtaining relevant information about them.[128] India took the position that:

> The Chinese nationals, whom the Government of India have been compelled to intern for reasons of security, are being well looked after. This fact has also found confirmation in the report of the officially accredited representatives of the International Committee of the Red Cross in India. The facilities accorded to these internees are in full conformity with acknowledged international practice. All relevant information pertaining to the internment has been provided to the International Red Cross in keeping with the Geneva Convention of 1949 to which the Chinese Government are also a signatory. In the circumstances, there is no need to inform the Chinese Government specifically of actions which are within the sovereign jurisdiction of India.[129]

India apparently indicated that it "was willing to exchange information concerning the internees only on a reciprocal basis and through the medium of the International Committee of the Red Cross."[130] China's response was that:

> While diplomatic relations are still maintained between China and India, it is the indisputable diplomatic privilege of the Chinese Embassy in protecting its nationals to request the Indian Government to provide information concerning the unwarrantedly arrested Chinese nationals and to arrange visits. By dragging in the International Committee of the Red Cross, the Indian Government is attempting to deprive the Chinese Embassy of its legitimate right and cover up India's crime of persecuting Chinese nationals. The Chinese Government absolutely will not agree to this.[131]

Peking insisted that India "immediately supply the number, name list and places of detention of the arrested Chinese nationals and afford facilities for the realization of visits and other reasonable requests made by the Chinese Embassy."[132] It spurned India's offer to exchange information about prisoners on a reciprocal basis:

128. Ministry of Foreign Affairs Note, Dec. 18, 1962, *ibid.*, vol. VIII, pp. 105, 106.
129. Ministry of External Affairs Memorandum, Jan. 8, 1963, *ibid.*, pp. 114, 115.
130. See our note 128.
131. *Ibid.*, p. 107.
132. *Ibid.*, p. 108.

Everyone knows that the Chinese nationals persecuted in India and Indian military personnel captured on the battle-field belong to totally different categories. Yet out of ulterior motives the Indian Government insist on confusing the two, and in December, 1962 proposed China and India on a so-called reciprocal basis exchange information about prisoners through the International Committee of the Red Cross. The Chinese Government of course absolutely could not accept such an unreasonable demand.[133]

China claimed that, as part of the "most lenient and amicable treatment" that it accorded Indian prisoners of war, it provided them with facilities to correspond by mail and cable with their families. Moreover, it contended that the Red Cross Society of China had "all along maintained normal contacts with the Indian Red Cross Society and has successively provided it with name lists of the captured Indian military personnel and information about them."[134] Peking also claimed that it had "done its best to satisfy other demands raised by the Indian Red Cross Society," a claim that flew in the face of the facts that for months Peking had failed to answer the requests of the Indian Red Cross Society for permission to visit Indian prisoners[135] and Peking never did permit such a visit.[136] With respect to the suggestion that the ICRC obtain information about the prisoners of war and visit them, the PRC stated:

Since diplomatic relations are still being maintained between China and India and the Red Cross Society of China has already made direct contacts and cooperated in concrete matters with the Indian Red Cross Society there is of course no need to introduce a third party into the matter. Therefore an unequivocal answer was long [sic] given by the Red Cross Society of China and the Chinese authorities concerned to the requests made by the International Committee of the Red Cross.[137]

India charged that "the Chinese Government expressly violated the Geneva Convention [Relative to the Treatment of Prisoners of War] when it refused to allow a representative of the International Red Cross to visit the prisoners camp where Indian personnel were kept."[138]

Professor Chou Keng-sheng conveniently ignored China's refusal

133. Ministry of Foreign Affairs Note, April 25, 1963, *White Paper*, vol. IX, p. 120. India's offer to exchange information about internees for information about prisoners may have reflected its understanding of article 140 of the Civilian Convention, which authorizes the establishment of a single Central Information Bureau that can convey information about internees and prisoners.
134. Ministry of Foreign Affairs Note, May 18, 1963, *ibid.*, p. 160.
135. Ministry of External Affairs Note, March 29, 1963, *ibid.*, p. 158.
136. Ministry of External Affairs Note, June 1, 1963, *ibid.*, pp. 162, 163.
137. See note 134, pp. 160–161.
138. See note 136.

to permit either the ICRC, the Indian Red Cross, or Indian diplomats to visit Indian prisoners and the question whether this violated the Prisoner of War Convention. Instead, he concentrated on supporting his government's claim that India's refusal to grant it information about and contact with its interned nationals violated international law and that the ICRC's inspection of the internment camp did not satisfy India's international obligations and indeed violated the provisions of the Civilian Convention. Professor Chou cited both Oppenheim's treatise on international law and the 1961 Vienna Convention on Diplomatic Relations for the proposition that one of the rights of diplomatic envoys is to protect their nationals in the state to which they are accredited.[139] Nothing in the Civilian Convention negates that right, he argued; as article 13 made clear, the fundamental purpose of the convention is to protect peaceful residents from mistreatment in time of war by requiring that any measures taken against them be consistent with humanitarianism. In general, he maintained, the provisions of the convention that entrust the nationals of one state residing in a second state to the protection of a third state or to a humanitarian organization come into play only when the first and second states are at war and diplomatic relations are severed. Diplomatic relations were not severed during the Sino-Indian border conflict, and there was thus no basis for substituting a visit by the ICRC for a visit by the Chinese embassy. Moreover, Professor Chou contended, article 10 of the convention required the protective activities undertaken by the ICRC to be "subject to the consent of the Parties to the conflict concerned," and China had never consented to the visit of the ICRC to the internment camp.

A leading Indian scholar has rejected the contention that, because diplomatic relations were not broken off, the Chinese embassy should have been allowed its normal right of affording protection to its nationals. After suggesting that "it hardly lies in the mouth of the Chinese to protest against India's action, in view of the fact that the Chinese did not permit the Indian as well as the International Red Cross to visit the Prisoner of War camps maintained by them," Professor T.S. Rama Rao has written:

> The Conventions are applicable even to cases of non-war hostilities, i.e. cases where diplomatic relations between the parties have not been severed.

139. Chou, "The Persecution of Chinese Nationals."

Still the Conventions, including Convention IV [regarding civilians], confer powers of supervision only on the "Protecting Powers" and international organizations like the Red Cross. It follows that the other authorities including diplomatic envoys do not enjoy these powers or rights. This is but natural, considering the strained relations between the parties and the consequent distrust about the unbiased character of the "enemy" embassy. That is why the powers of supervision were conferred on impartial neutral parties.[140]

Professor Rao in effect argued that the convention reflected a conscious recognition of the fact that where diplomatic relations continued to exist between enemy parties to the conflict they could not be relied upon to carry out the protective functions of the convention and that the ordinary right to protect nationals was suspended by the conflict even in the absence of a declaration of war. Professor Chou appeared to argue that the convention normally contemplated operation in a time of war, when diplomatic relations were severed, and that, so long as relations were maintained during a conflict, for the protection of enemy nationals the convention relied upon the ordinary right to protect nationals directly rather than through the aid of third parties.

Actually, despite their obvious attempt in article 2 to make the convention applicable to hostilities of any kind, even if the state of war is not recognized,[141] the draftsmen of the convention seem to have assumed that normal diplomatic relations would never be maintained between enemy parties to a conflict.[142] "War," as the ICRC *Commentary* put it, "is accompanied by the breaking off of diplomatic relations between the belligerents."[143] The convention therefore made no provision for the unusual Sino-Indian type of situation in which neither side moved to break off relations and neither sought to appoint a "protecting power" to supervise the application of the Geneva Conventions by

140. Rao, "International Law," pp. 49–50.

141. Somewhat cryptically, article 2 provides that "the present Convention shall apply to all cases of declared war or of any other armed conflict which may arise between two or more of the High Contracting Parties, even if the state of war is not recognized by one of them."

142. This is why, for example, article 136 requires each party to a conflict to establish an Information Bureau, and Article 137 provides that the Bureau "shall immediately forward information concerning protected persons . . . through the intermediary of the Protecting Powers and likewise through the Central Agency" to be established as a clearing house for information. The possibility that normal diplomatic relations might persist between belligerents is not entertained.

143. Pictet, ed., *Commentary on the Geneva Convention Relative to the Protection of Civilian Persons*, p. 65. It should be noted, however, that while this is generally true, there have nevertheless been many cases in which diplomatic relations have not been broken off despite the outbreak of war. See Fritz Grob, *The Relativity of War and Peace* (New Haven, Conn.: Yale University Press, 1949), pp. 275–278.

the other side.[144] In these circumstances, the question arises whether the Chinese position—that the continuation of diplomatic relations between belligerents precludes third party supervision of the application of the convention and requires observance of the peacetime obligations to permit diplomatic protection—or the Indian position—that the continuation of diplomatic relations does not affect the ordinary application of the convention—is more likely to effectuate the purposes that the convention was designed to serve.

Interestingly, neither Professor Chou nor Professor Rao referred to relevant materials that, while not explicitly dispositive of the question, nevertheless afford guidance as to the better view. The text of the convention indicates that the draftsmen did not overlook the situation created by the continuation of diplomatic relations between belligerent and neutral powers or between belligerents and their co-belligerents. Article 4 provides:

> Nationals of a neutral State who find themselves in the territory of a belligerent State, and nationals of a co-belligerent State, shall not be regarded as protected persons while the State of which they are nationals has normal diplomatic representation in the State in whose hands they are.

Professor Chou might have argued (a) that this provision reveals a policy of excluding from the purview of the convention all persons who are nationals of a state that has normal diplomatic representation in the state in which they reside and of relying on ordinary diplomatic channels for their protection; and (b) that, if the draftsmen had foreseen the possibility that diplomatic relations might continue between enemy parties to the conflict, they would have applied the above policy to this situation as well as to those specified in article 4.

That Professor Chou failed to make such an argument is undoubtedly due to more than the persuasive effect of the maxim "inclusio unius est exclusio alterius." First of all, the argument would clearly prove too much, for it would deny Chinese nationals the substantive protections of the convention, protections that Chou was not loath to

144. Professor Rao comments: "Curiously enough, neither India nor China seems to have attempted to secure the selection of . . . a Protecting Power . . ." Rao, "International Law," p. 44. The Sino-Indian conflict is not the only recent case in which diplomatic relations have been maintained and no protecting power has been appointed. A similar situation occurred in the conflict between India and Pakistan in 1965. In that situation, however, both belligerents permitted the ICRC to work in favor of prisoners of war and persons arrested or interned as a result of the conflict.

invoke against India. Moreover, it would result in a curious situation in which nationals of the belligerents in each other's territory would not be protected persons but nationals of neutral states or of co-belligerents would be, if they found themselves in the territory of a belligerent with which their state did not maintain normal diplomatic relations.

Professor Chou might have extracted some support from the report of the committee that was charged by the Geneva Conference with the responsibility of examining the draft convention, which defined "normal diplomatic representation" as "that which functions in peace time, comprising at least one diplomatic representative accredited to a Ministry of Foreign Affairs."[145] Chinese representatives, of course, continued to be accredited to India's Ministry of External Affairs throughout the border conflict. But the authoritative ICRC *Commentary* on the convention expressed dissatisfaction with this formulation, characterizing it as useful but insufficient. It is necessary, at a minimum, the *Commentary* states, to give the words "accredited to" the widest meaning, "as implying that the representations made by the diplomatic representative will be followed by results and that satisfactory replies will be given to him"; moreover, the diplomats must have "sufficient liberty of action and liberty of movement to be able to visit their fellow-countrymen and come to their help when circumstances so require."[146] Otherwise their nationals would require protection under the convention.

Since by no stretch of the imagination could it be said that Chinese diplomats in India during the conflict and its aftermath were able to operate effectively and freely and to visit and aid their nationals as the circumstances demanded, it seems clear that under the *Commentary's* interpretation, even if the existence of "normal diplomatic representation" between belligerents had been included within article 4 as a criterion for denying their nationals protection under the convention, in the Sino-Indian case that criterion could not be deemed to have been satisfied.[147] In any event, a state is never under an

145. Quoted in Pictet, ed., *Commentary on the Geneva Convention Relative to the Protection of Civilian Persons*, p. 49.

146. *Ibid.*

147. Indeed, a Chinese note of December 8, 1962, after pointing out a number of Indian restrictions upon the freedom of action of Chinese diplomats and consuls regarding other functions in addition to the protection of nationals, specifically charged that "the Chinese Embassy and consulates . . . have been unable to carry out their normal diplomatic functions." *White Paper*, vol. VIII, pp. 123–124.

obligation to maintain diplomatic relations with other states, and article 4 plainly takes account of the fact that a belligerent need not allow normal diplomatic representation or any kind of diplomatic relations between itself and neutrals or co-belligerents, not to mention its enemies. This is the raison d'être of resort to protecting powers, the ICRC or other third party assistance. Given the enmity that generally prevails between parties to even an undeclared conflict and given the importance to them of security considerations, an interpretation that required them, if they maintained diplomatic relations, to grant each other the ordinary peacetime right to protect nationals would appear unrealistic and would surely diminish the already minimal incentives for them to maintain relations.

If during the Sino-Indian conflict, for example, the maintenance of diplomatic relations had obligated India to permit Chinese embassy personnel to travel to the internment camp and places of detention to see nationals, it is quite possible that India might have broken off relations. This would have increased tensions, and both parties would then have lost the use of diplomatic facilities that constituted a convenient channel not only for peace negotiations but also for a limited amount of protection of nationals during the conflict.[148] The world community should wish to encourage continuing relations between the parties to an undeclared conflict. It would appear wise not to burden them with protection of their nationals unless they can agree on the extent to which such protection should supplement or substitute for the protection of third parties provided by the convention. Thus Chinese insistence upon the ordinary diplomatic right to protect nationals during the conflict seems misplaced, but it certainly cannot be considered frivolous.

Although China was unpersuasive in contending that, during the conflict, it was entitled to exercise peacetime diplomatic protection, India's restrictions upon the Chinese embassy's ordinary right to obtain direct information about and access to the confined Chinese nationals could be justified only for the duration of the conflict and perhaps a

148. One should note that to some extent India did respond directly to certain demands for information made by the PRC and its embassy. When, for example, China requested details on an outbreak of violence that occurred in the internment camp on March 29, 1963, India did provide an explanation of the events but did not report the names and injuries of arrested internees. Compare Chinese Embassy Note, April 1, 1963, with Ministry of External Affairs Note, April 23, 1963, *White Paper*, vol. IX, pp. 114, 118.

brief period thereafter. Just as it is difficult to defend India's continuing internment and detention of persons of Chinese descent years after hostilities had ended, it is also difficult to defend India's corresponding delay in restoring the PRC's normal capacity for diplomatic protection.[149] China protested, for example, that on February 19, 1966, India "went so far as to arbitrarily prevent the Chinese Embassy from exercising its right of protecting Chinese nationals and refuse to let the Embassy send its personnel to Calcutta to visit the persecuted Chinese nationals in prison."[150] And as late as May 25, 1967, the PRC bitterly complained about India's repeated rejection of requests for embassy access to a Chinese national who had been detained under the Defense of India Rules since January 1, 1964.[151]

It is interesting to compare India's national security rationale for continuing to deny China diplomatic protection of its confined nationals with China's rationale for its 1963–1964 refusal to permit the Indian embassy to visit an Indian national during the period that he was held in prison pending conclusion of his trial. Instead of attributing its refusal to the existence of the Sino-Indian conflict or to India's refusal to permit China access to interned or detained Chinese nationals, China simply explained its conduct in terms of legal principles applicable to ordinary peacetime conditions: "According to the regulations of the Chinese authorities concerned, visits to prisoners are allowed after they have been sentenced."[152] This, Peking asserted, was "in full conformity with international practice." Following an appellate court's affirmance of the original sentence in the case in question, the PRC permitted Indian embassy officials and relatives of the convicted person to visit him on a number of occasions, although India expressed strong dissatisfaction at the conditions in which the visits took place.[153] Peking failed to note, of course, that its interpretation of what constitutes ordinary peacetime access proved to be narrower in the case of India's demand for access to its national detained in China than it was in the case of Peking's demand for access to its nationals detained in India.

149. Recall text at note 120.

150. Ministry of Foreign Affairs Note, Sept. 21, 1966, *White Paper*, vol. XIII, p. 29.

151. Chinese Embassy Note, May 25, 1967, *ibid.*, vol. XIV, pp. 28–29.

152. Ministry of Foreign Affairs Note, Sept. 15, 1965, *ibid.*, vol. XII, pp. 118, 119. Recall text at note 83, 84.

153. Ministry of External Affairs Note, Nov. 2, 1965, *ibid.*, vol. XII, pp. 120–121.

VALIDITY OF ICRC INSPECTION

There was, it should be remembered, a second aspect to the problem of who was authorized to protect the interned Chinese nationals. The PRC had not only protested against India's refusal to allow the Chinese embassy to extend ordinary diplomatic protection but it had also protested against the Indian government's "dragging in the International Committee of the Red Cross . . . to deprive the Chinese Embassy of its legitimate right and cover up India's crime of persecuting Chinese nationals."[154] Professor Chou had supported this complaint against "substituting a visit by the ICRC for a visit by the Chinese Embassy," contending that article 10 of the Civilian Convention required the protective activities of the ICRC to be undertaken "subject to the consent of the Parties to the conflict concerned," and that China had never consented to the intervention of the ICRC.[155]

This Chinese contention appears to have been based on misapprehensions of both fact and law. Factually, when the ICRC offered its humanitarian services to the Indian government and, upon obtaining India's consent, visited the interned Chinese nationals, it had not purported to do so in behalf of China as a substitute either for the Chinese embassy or for a protecting power that the PRC might have chosen to protect its nationals. Rather, it had acted on its own initiative in behalf of the world community to fulfill its traditional independent role of endeavoring to aid interned civilians, prisoners of war, and other enemy detainees.[156] In the ordinary case, where no protecting power has been appointed, in addition to carrying out its traditional humanitarian functions, the ICRC, under article 11 of the Civilian Convention, has also undertaken the humanitarian functions of a protecting power.[157] In the Sino-Indian case, however, this

154. Recall text at note 131.
155. Recall the fourth sentence of the text following note 139.
156. See ICRC, *Annual Report, 1962*, p. 22.
157. Article 11, ¶2 provides that when persons protected by the Convention do not benefit, "no matter for what reason," from the activities of a protecting power or an organization which the parties to the conflict have agreed should be entrusted with the duties of a protecting power, "the Detaining Power shall request a neutral State, or such an organization to undertake the functions performed under the present Convention by a Protecting Power designated by the Parties to a conflict." Article 11, ¶3 then provides: "If protection cannot be arranged accordingly [i.e., under the preceding paragraph], the Detaining Power shall request or shall accept . . . the offer of the services of a humanitarian organization, such as the International Committee of the Red Cross, to assume the humanitarian functions performed by Protecting Powers under the present Convention."

would have been inappropriate because of a reservation that the PRC had filed to article 11 when it ratified the convention, a reservation that required the PRC's consent before the ICRC could act in its behalf.[158]

The independent humanitarian role of the ICRC is recognized by many provisions of the convention, especially articles 10 and 143. Article 10 provides:

> The provisions of the present Convention constitute no obstacle to the humanitarian activities which the International Committee, the Red Cross or any other impartial humanitarian organization may, subject to the consent of the Parties to the conflict concerned, undertake for the protection of civilian persons and for their relief.

Article 143, after stating that "representatives or delegates of the Protecting Powers shall have permission to go to all places where protected persons are, particularly to places of internment, detention and work" and specifying the conditions of such visits, goes on to provide:

> The delegates of the International Committee of the Red Cross shall also enjoy the above prerogatives. The appointment of such delegates shall be submitted to the approval of the Power governing the territories where they will carry out their duties.

The PRC did not file a reservation to either of these provisions.

Although article 143 plainly requires that, prior to visiting internment camps, ICRC delegates need only have the approval of "the Power governing the territories where they will carry out their duties," article 10 restricts such humanitarian ICRC activity by the vaguer phrase "subject to the consent of the Parties to the conflict concerned." And it is this proviso that Professor Chou invoked in behalf of the contention that the consent of the PRC as well as that of India was prerequisite to legitimate ICRC inspection of the camp at Deoli.

Professor Chou's assumption was that China was one of "the Parties to the conflict concerned" as that term of art is used in the conven-

158. The reservation stated: "Regarding Article 11, the People's Republic of China will not recognize as valid a request by a Detaining Power of protected persons to a neutral State or to a humanitarian organization, to undertake the functions which should be performed by a Protecting Power, unless the consent has been obtained of the government of the State of which the protected persons are nationals." The Chinese filed a counterpart reservation to the Prisoner of War Convention also. See *UNTS* 260:442 (1957).

tion. Yet this assumption appears to be erroneous. First of all, it should be noted that article 10, unlike articles 9, 11, and many other provisions of the convention, does not simply refer to "the Parties to the conflict" but tacks on the qualifying adjective "concerned." Although not wholly free from ambiguity, the ICRC *Commentary* on the convention indicates that the "Parties . . . concerned" does not mean all parties to the conflict but

> must be taken to mean those upon which the possibility of carrying out the action contemplated depends. For example, when consignments of relief are forwarded, it is necessary to obtain the consent not only of the State to which they are being sent, but also of the State from which they come, of the countries through which they pass in transit and, if they have to pass through a blockade, of the Powers which control the blockade.[159]

This need to obtain the consent of all parties whose cooperation is essential to carrying out any particular action among the entire range of possible actions contemplated under article 10 undoubtedly explains why it employs a broader phrase than does article 143, which deals with the specific problem of visits to protected persons and can therefore confine itself to the approval of the power governing the territories where the visits will take place. Yet the typical situation envisaged by the ICRC *Commentary* under article 10 is one in which the ICRC enters into the territory of a belligerent and therefore requires that belligerent's consent, for "a belligerent Power can obviously not be obligated to tolerate in its territory activities of any kind by any foreign organization. That would be out of the question."[160]

Nothing at all is said in the *Commentary* about the need to obtain the consent of the power of origin of the protected persons. That this omission was not accidental was made clear, in the same year that the *Commentary* was published, by M. Claude Pilloud, one of its authors and then head of the legal department of the ICRC. In distinguishing between the situation where the ICRC performs its traditional humanitarian functions in behalf of the world community and that where, in addition to those functions, it assumes under article 11 the humanitarian tasks incumbent upon a protecting power in behalf of the power of origin of the persons to whom it brings relief, M. Pilloud points out that only in the latter situation is it necessary

159. Pictet, ed., *Commentary on the Geneva Convention*, p. 98.
160. *Ibid.*

for the ICRC to obtain the prior approval of the power of origin.[161]

This interpretation is firmly grounded in long-standing practice prior to adoption of the 1949 conventions, according to which the ICRC's humanitarian activities regarding persons detained in various countries were predicated solely upon specific agreements concluded with the detaining power and not with the power of origin.[162] Indeed, article 10 is merely a broader reformulation of article 88 of the 1929 Geneva Prisoners of War Convention, which was careful to state that that convention did not constitute any obstacle to the ICRC's humanitarian work in behalf of prisoners of war "with the consent of the belligerents concerned."[163] And this phraseology in turn reflected ICRC activities that had been undertaken in behalf of prisoners of war—solely with the permission of the detaining authorities—extending back as far as 1864.[164]

Moreover, no valid public policy would appear to be served by departing from past practice and interpreting article 10 to require consent of the power of origin before the ICRC can act to aid interned persons. Such an interpretation would leave foreign nationals without third-party assistance of any kind during a conflict between their state of residence and the state whose nationals they are—even when the former is willing to permit third-party assistance—so long as the power of origin unsuccessfully insists on exercising its peacetime right to diplomatic protection during the conflict and persistently refrains from appointing a protecting power or consenting to the activities of a humanitarian organization. This would contradict both the spirit of the Geneva Conventions, which were "drawn up first and foremost to protect individuals, and not to serve state interests,"[165] and the general humanitarian principles of international law.

One can only speculate whether, at the time that it ratified the Civilian Convention and filed a reservation to article 11, the PRC ever focused on the important difference between articles 10 and 11. The PRC's reservation was expressly designed to prevent the detaining

161. Claude Pilloud, "Reservations to the 1949 Geneva Conventions (II)," *International Review of the Red Cross*, no. 7, Supp.:155 (July 1958).

162. This was recognized, for example, by the report of the Conference of Government Experts that met in 1947 to draft a new set of Geneva Conventions. See *Government Experts, Preliminary Documents*, II, 215, 217.

163. The text of Article 88 of the 1929 Geneva Prisoner Convention may be found in *League of Nations Treaty Series* 118: 343, 393.

164. See Pictet, ed., *Commentary on the Geneva Convention*, p. 570.

165. *Ibid.*, p. 21.

power from appointing a neutral state or humanitarian organization to undertake the functions of a protecting power without obtaining the consent of the power of origin. This was also the motivation behind the USSR reservation to article 11, which constituted the model for the reservations of the PRC and other Communist states.[166] Yet the record of the diplomatic conference that adopted the convention indicates that, despite its objection to article 11, the USSR had no objection to the ICRC continuing to offer its humanitarian services under article 10,[167] and this may account for its failure to file a reservation to articles 10 and 143.

On the other hand, it may be that the phrase "the Parties to the conflict concerned" misled the Soviet Union, China, and others into assuming that no reservation to article 10 was necessary because the consent of all parties to the conflict, including the power of origin, would be prerequisite to any independent action by the ICRC. But, as the foregoing discussion suggests, there was no basis for such an assumption. In light of the dispute with India on this point, it will be interesting to see whether, during the forthcoming efforts to revise the 1949 conventions to take account of subsequent experience, the PRC will move to alter articles 10 and 143 so as to require the power of origin's consent to independent ICRC activity and, failing this, will file a reservation to those provisions. In view of the profound mistrust that Peking has displayed toward international organizations in general and toward the ICRC in particular, such a move would come as no surprise.[168]

LEGAL ASPECTS OF REPATRIATION

The People's Republic made numerous charges that its interned nationals were subjected to "inhuman" treatment in what it called

166. For the arguments that the Soviet delegation advanced against article 11, see *Final Record of the Diplomatic Conference of Geneva of 1949* (Berne, Switzerland: Federal Political Department, 1950–1951), vol. II-B, pp. 29, 351. The Soviet reservation to article 11 may be found in *ibid.*, vol. I, p. 356.

167. See *ibid.*, vol. II-B, p. 67.

168. For an example of the Chinese Communist view that "the imperialists have done their best to enhance the status of international organizations . . . in order to establish world dominance through them," see K'ung Meng, "A Criticism of the Bourgeois International Law Theory on Subjects of International Law and the Recognition of States," *Kuo-chi wen-t'i yen-chiu* (Studies in international problems), no. 2:50 (Feb. 1960). For the PRC's view of the ICRC as a tool of American imperialism during the Korean conflict, see "Acheson's Absurd Statement on Red Cross Investigation Sternly Refuted by NCNA," *SCMP*, no. 301:2–4 (1952).

"Indian concentration camps [that] are a very hell on earth."[169] Although Peking did not take the initiative in invoking the provisions of the Civilian Convention that relate to conditions of internment, preferring in the first instance to rely on general principles, a note from its Ministry of Foreign Affairs responded to an Indian claim of compliance with the convention by detailing allegations of maltreatment made by the earliest repatriated internees and then rhetorically asking: "Is this what you meant when asserting that the treatment given to victimized Chinese nationals was 'in full conformity with the scales of the Geneva conventions of 1949'?"[170] And Professor Chou followed this up with a recitation of all the provisions of the Civilian Convention that India was accused of having violated.[171] Professor Rao, on the other hand, claimed that the allegations were baseless, credited Indian reports that the internees had received "sumptuous rations," and noted Home Minister Shastri's statement that the ICRC had found camp conditions to be "very satisfactory" and that India had made certain improvements in the camp at the ICRC's suggestion.[172] Amid the exaggerated claims of both sides, it would be difficult to determine the actual situation of the internment camps. The important point for our purposes is that the treatment of the internees gave rise to disputes over facts rather than law.

Much the same can be said about most of China's challenges to the manner in which India carried out repatriation of the interned persons. For example, Peking's detailed assertions that India had in many respects violated the six-point agreement and other agreements on concrete arrangements and that Indian authorities had forcibly seized the Chinese passports of some of the repatriates "in grave violation of [the] code of conduct in international relations"[173] were flatly denied by New Delhi as factually "baseless" and "absurd."[174] And India's announcement that Chinese nationals returning to China would be allowed to take back with them proceeds from the sale of their property, in accordance with Indian regulations, was factually disputed

169. Ministry of Foreign Affairs Note, April 27, 1963, *White Paper*, vol. IX, pp. 122, 123.
170. *Ibid.*, p. 123.
171. Chou, "The Persecution of Chinese Nationals," note 83.
172. Rao, "International Law," p. 49.
173. Chinese Embassy Memorandum, April 27, 1963, *White Paper*, vol. IX, pp. 125–126.
174. Ministry of External Affairs Memorandum, May 16, 1964, *ibid.*, vol. IX, pp. 134–136. Recall text at notes 47–49.

on the ground that the Maharashtra state government had "openly ordered the requisition of property of Chinese nationals . . . completely in violation of international law."[175]

On several occasions, the PRC distorted the documentary record in order to score a debater's point about repatriation. After the PRC stated that it would send ships to bring home its interned nationals who wished to go to China and asked India's cooperation, India replied that it was willing to cooperate and that its facilities would, "in the first instance, be limited to holders of passports issued by the Government of the People's Republic of China who have no criminal or civil complaints pending against them."[176] Yet China's rejoinder claimed that India's reply had not said a word about cooperation; and then, by ignoring the phrase "in the first instance," Peking also sought to give the impression that India would allow only the repatriation of passport-holders and would detain other nationals as hostages.[177] Similarly, although the six-point agreement called for the repatriation on the same ship of interned persons and members of their families "who desire to come back to China,"[178] Peking's protest against the failure of certain family members to accompany a repatriated internee omitted reference to the crucial requirement of voluntariness.[179]

Despite this propaganda ploy, China plainly agreed to the principle of voluntary repatriation of civilian internees. Unlike the situation with respect to prisoners of war in the Korean conflict, where the PRC accepted the principle of nonforcible repatriation only after a long, harsh dispute and after it had been threatened with nuclear devastation if it prolonged the stalemate,[180] from the outset of the Sino-Indian discussion of the repatriation of interned civilians Peking asked merely that New Delhi "ensure the freedom of departure of Chinese nationals wishing to return to their motherland."[181]

175. Ministry of Foreign Affairs Note, Jan. 19, 1963, *ibid.*, vol. IX, pp. 90, 92.

176. Ministry of External Affairs Note, Dec. 31, 1962, *ibid.*, vol. VIII, pp. 111, 112.

177. See note 175, at p. 91.

178. See note 47.

179. Ministry of Foreign Affairs Note, June 13, 1963, *White Paper,* vol. IX, pp. 148, 149.

180. See Roscoe Drummond and Gaston Coblentz, *Duel at the Brink* (Garden City, N.Y.: Doubleday, 1961), p. 113; Dwight D. Eisenhower, *Mandate for Change* (Garden City, N.Y.: Doubleday, 1963), pp. 95, 179–181.

181. Ministry of Foreign Affairs Note, Dec. 18, 1962, *White Paper,* vol. VIII, pp. 105, 108.

Peking's ready acceptance of the voluntary repatriation of civilian internees does not imply a retreat from its original position with respect to prisoners of war in Korea but reflects its perception of relevant differences between the Civilian and the Prisoner of War Conventions. In Peking's view, the text of the latter makes clear that all prisoners are to be repatriated, without exception, at the cessation of active hostilities; moreover, the PRC emphasizes the fact that the diplomatic conference overwhelmingly rejected an Austrian amendment that would have authorized prisoners, instead of being repatriated, to apply for transfer to any other country that is ready to accept them, some delegations being "concerned lest prisoners of war might not be able to express themselves with complete freedom while in captivity."[182] The Civilian Convention, by contrast, although not ideally explicit, suggests that both transfer of custody and repatriation are to take place on a voluntary basis. Article 45 states that "in no circumstances shall a protected person be transferred to a country where he or she may have reason to fear persecution for his or her political opinions or religious beliefs"; and, in allocating responsibility for expenses, article 135 provides for the contingency where "the internee elects to return to his country." The preparatory work leaves no doubt that the Civilian Convention "implicitly recognizes the internee's right to choose between return to his residence or repatriation."[183]

There does appear to be doubt, however, whether the internee is free to make a wholly unfettered choice based upon any factors that suit his fancy or whether he must accept repatriation—at least when ordered to do so by his government—unless he has reason to fear political or religious persecution. The Indian government seems to have believed that the latter interpretation might receive support in some quarters. When, on the floor of Parliament, Home Minister Shastri was asked whether those internees who had declined repatriation had told the authorities that living conditions in India were more favorable than in China, he is reported to have replied: "The

182. For discussion of the pertinent provisions of the Prisoner of War Convention and the preparatory work and for citation to the secondary sources on the Korean dispute, see Jean de Preux, in Pictet, ed., *Commentary on the Geneva Convention Relative to the Treatment of Prisoners of War* (Geneva: International Committee of the Red Cross, 1960), vol. III, pp. 540–546.

183. Pictet, ed., *Commentary on the Geneva Convention Relative to the Protection of Civilian Persons*, p. 519. See also de Preux in *ibid.*, pp. 513–514.

mere fact that conditions of living are more favorable in India may not be a sufficient reason for refusing repatriation, if the Chinese Government demanded it, unless the detenus feared persecution also."[184]

Whether China approves this interpretation is unclear. Because India refused to provide China with a list of all internees through the diplomatic channel and because China refused to exchange information on a reciprocal basis through the ICRC, China never received a list of all internees and thus never had an opportunity formally to order identified persons to come home. Moreover, because India refused to permit the Chinese embassy to interview the internees and because China did not seek to have a third party conduct such interviews, there was no opportunity for China to ascertain the reasons why some internees chose to remain in India; and India was careful not to ask those internees who decided to reject repatriation to give reasons for their decision. Yet, to the extent one can judge from the formulations China employed in the diplomatic correspondence, it is probable that China shares what seems to be the Indian view—that internees may make an unfettered choice.

As has already been suggested, where the two countries differed sharply was over how the principle of voluntary repatriation was to be effectuated. This difference of interpretation of the convention was not a simple reflection of the disagreement we have previously canvassed over whether the maintenance of diplomatic relations during the conflict required the parties to continue to grant each other the ordinary peacetime rights of diplomatic protection of nationals and precluded third-party protection under the convention. For, unlike its position with respect to conditions at the internment camp, which permitted the inspection of a humanitarian organization such as the ICRC, India's position on repatriation assigned the detaining power exclusive responsibility for verifying the wishes of the internees.

Thus, when the PRC pressed for "arrangements for the Embassy to send its personnel to the concentration camps and other places of detention to visit the arrested Chinese nationals and undertake registration with regard to their return to China,"[185] India replied:

184. Rao, "International Law," p. 50. It is interesting that, although the ICRC *Commentary* on the Civilian Convention recognizes that an internee is free to disobey his government's order to return if he fears political or religious persecution, it does not specify whether he may disobey the order on other grounds as well.

185. Chinese Embassy Memorandum, Jan. 22, 1963, *White Paper*, vol. IX, p. 92.

The views of Chinese nationals detained under the Foreigner's Law (Application and Amendment) Ordinance 1962, on the offer of the Government of the People's Republic of China to arrange facilities for their repatriation to China are being ascertained. As soon as a list is compiled, discussions will be initiated with the Chinese Embassy in New Delhi for finalizing their departure procedures.[186]

The Ministry of External Affairs subsequently informed the Chinese embassy that approximately 1,450 Chinese internees expressed their desire to go to China and that those internees claimed that about 900 of their dependents living outside the camp wanted to accompany them. The Ministry stated that "the wishes of these dependents are being ascertained independently by the Indian local authorities."[187]

China protested that the Indian government had "only provided a figure which it unilaterally considered represented the number of Chinese nationals wishing to return to China." The PRC went on to assert:

While diplomatic relations are maintained between China and India, the Chinese Embassy's sending of persons to contact the victimized nationals and compile a list of Chinese nationals wishing to return to China is an indisputable power of the Embassy in carrying out its diplomatic function of affording protection to its nationals. Nobody has the right to obstruct the Embassy from exercising this power or fact [sic] in its stead. Moreover, being interned by the Indian Government, the Chinese nationals are in no position to express their wishes freely.[188]

Unlike the situation in the Korean conflict, where concern for the inability of the prisoners to make a free choice while in the hands of their captors led the Communist side—once it had been forced to accede to the principle of voluntary repatriation—to demand an opportunity to have explanatory conferences with unwilling prisoners while they were in neutral custody,[189] the PRC did not seek to have its civilian internees placed in neutral custody or to have a protecting power, the ICRC or any other organization, verify the internees' choice.

Despite its displeasure over India's refusal to permit the Chinese embassy to verify the internees' choice, "in order to save at the earliest

186. Ministry of External Affairs Note, Jan. 25, 1963, *ibid.*, pp. 94, 95.
187. Ministry of External Affairs Note, March 7, 1963, *ibid.*, p. 101.
188. Chinese Embassy Note, March 14, 1963, *ibid.*, pp. 104, 105–106.
189. The PRC had sought these conferences with prisoners "to eliminate their apprehensions and to inform them of all matters related to their return to their homeland, particularly of their full right to return home to lead a peaceful life." *The New York Times*, April 27, 1953, p. 3. "Text on Foe's Plan on Prisoners, official text of the Communist proposal yesterday to settle the dispute over prisoners of war in Korea."

possible date the Chinese nationals who have suffered long in Indian concentration camps and prison," Peking agreed to repatriate the groups that had signified their desire to go to China, and it characterized this as "yet another major effort by China for a settlement of the question of Chinese nationals."[190] Nevertheless, during negotiations to arrange the return of those groups, Peking continued to demand the list of all interned Chinese including those who, according to India, had clearly expressed their desire to remain in India. When India claimed that this request "exceeded the terms of reference of the meeting and amounted to a gross interference in the internal sovereign jurisdiction of the Indian Government," China persisted in what India termed "an equally unreasonable demand" for "an omnibus list of all internees and dependents who had expressed their desire to leave for China." All that India would do was to provide, shortly before departure, lists of those repatriates who were scheduled to board a particular ship.[191]

Not surprisingly in these circumstances, as the time for the beginning of repatriation drew near, the People's Republic charged India with coercing and retaliating against internees who wished to go to China and

> creating various pretexts alleging that victimized Chinese nationals have changed their minds and are no longer willing to return to China or [using] all kinds of intrigues to detain those Chinese who desire to return or even unscrupulously kill them lest they reveal the facts of the atrocious maltreatment of Chinese nationals.[192]

Chinese accusations of a "deliberate attempt to forcibly detain" the remaining internees and their dependents reached a peak after India rejected China's request to send a ship to repatriate a fourth batch on the ground that no others wished to leave.[193] The PRC branded India's statement "an utterly baseless assertion":

> According to verified information available to the Chinese Government and revelations made by the third batch of returned Chinese, a large number of peaceable law-abiding Chinese nationals are still interned in the Indian concentration camp and prisons. In the Deoli concentration camp alone, their number totals as many as six hundred. "Interrogation chambers" and "dark cells" have been set up in the concentration camp for the purpose of

190. Chinese Embassy Note, March 14, 1963, *White Paper*, vol. IX, p. 106.
191. Ministry of External Affairs Note, March 26, 1963, *ibid.*, pp. 109–110.
192. Ministry of Foreign Affairs Note, April 27, 1963, *ibid.*, pp. 122, 124.
193. Chinese Embassy Note, July 31, 1963, *ibid.*, vol. X, p. 56; Ministry of External Affairs Note, Aug. 10, 1963, *ibid.*, p. 59.

coercing the Chinese nationals into expressing their "desire" to remain in India and their "unwillingness to go back to China."[194]

The obvious legal question in these circumstances was one that China, of course, had no political or legal interest in asking—whether, in the absence of agreement upon a state or an international organization to fulfill the functions of a protecting power, India was under an obligation to arrange, without China's consent, for a humanitarian organization to verify the internees' choice with respect to repatriation. As we have seen, the Chinese took the position that India was under no such obligation and indeed was legally precluded from doing so.[195] India's reasons for not arranging for ICRC verification are unknown. It is highly unlikely that India deemed itself legally precluded from requesting ICRC verification, and it is clear that India did not regard itself as bound to make such a request. Possibly India did not regard verification as among the ICRC's traditional humanitarian activities. Yet at the time of the Sino-Indian conflict, the ICRC maintained a large delegation in Japan for the purpose of verifying whether Korean nationals who had come to Japan from North Korea and who decided to return to the Democratic Republic of Korea had made that choice freely. In the Japanese case, it should be noted, the initiative had not come from the ICRC but from the Japanese Red Cross, which in 1959 had requested the assistance of the ICRC.[196] In the Sino-Indian case, too, the ICRC did not request permission to monitor the repatriation process. Had the ICRC done so, India might well have granted permission, but India probably saw no need to take the initiative in this matter. In any event, neither the Geneva Conventions nor any principle of customary international law require third-party verification, although, as we have previously suggested concerning ICRC inspection of camp conditions, India was surely authorized to cooperate with the ICRC if it wished.[197]

194. Chinese Embassy Note, Aug. 26, 1963, *ibid.*, pp. 61–62.

195. Recall text at notes 131, 154, and 155.

196. See *International Review of the Red Cross* (Geneva), no. 4:85 (Apr. 1958) and no. 8:152 (Aug. 1959).

197. On its face, the Civilian Convention does not indicate any intention upon the part of its draftsmen to have third party verification of the internees' free choice concerning repatriation, and neither the preparatory work to the Civilian Convention nor the ICRC *Commentary* suggests this. It may have been assumed, however, as it apparently was with respect to the repatriation provisions of the Prisoner Convention, that the protecting power, the ICRC or some other body would make regular visits to the place of internment and would thus be able to

CONCLUSION

Plainly enough, it is not possible to generalize about Chinese views of international law solely from this case study of the principal international legal questions involved in the internment and detention of Chinese nationals in India. Nevertheless, the conclusions that emerge from this study may be of assistance in formulating generalizations that are based on a much broader range of experience.

The documentary record suggests that the governing elite of the People's Republic perceived and evaluated India's actions in terms of international law as it is understood in Peking. Yet China was slow to invoke international law in its efforts to protect the overseas Chinese in India. In the initial stages of the dispute, it preferred to conduct the diplomatic correspondence in terms of maintaining Sino-Indian friendship. When in 1962, however, the intensification of Indian sanctions against Chinese nationals culminated in mass internment, Peking shifted to the level of international law. As is common in diplomatic practice, China's repeated invocation of international law was largely limited to flat assertions that its actions and claims were consistent with international law and the code of conduct of international relations and that the actions and claims of India were not. Although the PRC displayed a considerable penchant for detailed disputation of India's factual allegations and sometimes indulged in exaggerated, picayune, or frivolous factual allegations of its own in order to score propaganda points, it shied away from any careful articulation of its position on legal questions. Throughout the dispute, China simply assumed that all persons of Chinese descent in India—even those who had acquired Indian nationality—were Chinese nationals, and its claims for protection made no distinction between dual nationals and persons who maintained only Chinese nationality.

To a modest extent, Peking relied on the writings of its legal scholars, published in the official newspaper of the Chinese Communist Party, to support its claims. A major article by Professor Chou Keng-sheng was particularly important, elucidating the Chinese case in terms of accepted

---

receive complaints, dispense information and make certain that the internees could in fact exercise a free choice. See de Preux, in Pictet, ed., *Commentary on the Geneva Convention Relative to the Treatment of Prisoners of War*, pp. 548–549, and article 30 of the Civilian Convention, which contemplates "within the bounds set by military or security considerations," relatively easy access on the part of humanitarian organizations.

sources of international law such as treaties, customary rules, and, as evidence of those rules, the works of bourgeois legal scholars. Yet, even the long essay by Professor Chou was not as comprehensive, clear, and persuasive an exposition of the Chinese position as one might have expected, given the frequently high quality of Chinese scholarly argumentation on major issues of international law affecting the PRC.[198] One would have welcomed not only closer analysis of the Geneva Civilian Convention itself but also references to the preparatory work of that convention and the ICRC *Commentary* that provides a guide to the convention's understanding.

Because the dispute over internment and detention raised questions of first impression under the convention, questions that were not anticipated by its draftsmen, we have not been able precisely to measure the extent to which China's views on these questions coincide with those of other states. We have, however, appraised the Chinese position on each issue according to what we believe to be the most enlightened interpretation of the convention, and we have also indicated whether China's position, if different from our interpretation, at least represents a responsible rather than a frivolous resort to international law.

Whether, as China claimed, the mass internment of all Chinese nationals residing in Assam and certain districts of West Bengal was inconsistent with the convention seems to us to present a close question. India selected this large group solely on the basis of its nationality, an act that the convention appears to prohibit. On the other hand, in view of the border conflict, it is understandable that India regarded the area in which these Chinese resided as a sensitive one and believed that some of them, by virtue of residing in that area, would have knowledge or qualifications that might prove of use to the enemy. Yet there were undoubtedly many elderly and ill Chinese residents of the area, as well as children, who could not remotely have been thought to threaten security, and surely their inclusion in the category of persons interned seems, on balance, to be inconsistent with the underlying humanitarian purposes of the convention. Thus, in the long-run interest of the international community, the restrictive application of the convention implicitly advocated by China seems more desirable than India's

198. See, *e.g.*, Shao Chin-fu, "The Absurd Theory of 'Two Chinas' and Principles of International Law," translated in *Oppose the New U.S. Plots to Create "Two Chinas"* (Peking: Foreign Languages Press, 1962), pp. 85–97; Ch'en T'i-ch'iang, "Unconditional Repatriation—An Inviolable Principle of the Geneva Convention," *People's China*, no. 2:26–28 (Jan. 16, 1953).

more expansive interpretation of what was "absolutely necessary" to its security. In any event, India's contention that internment was justified because all Chinese had to be removed from the sensitive area seems inadequate, for those who represented no threat to security could have been placed in an assigned residence instead of being subjected to the harsher sanction of internment. Moreover, even if the initial mass internment is regarded as consistent with the convention, the same cannot be said of India's continuing internment of a large number of unrepatriated Chinese several years after hostilities had ceased.

Peking's claim that the maintenance of diplomatic relations requires the parties to an undeclared conflict to grant each other's diplomats the same degree of information about and access to confined nationals as they would enjoy in peacetime, although certainly not frivolous, seems contrary to the basic assumptions of the convention: that armed conflict precludes normal diplomatic representation (indeed, usually any diplomatic relations), that no rule of international law demands otherwise, and that the convention therefore must provide alternative modes of protecting civilians through third parties. China's view would have the effect of further reducing the already minimal incentives for the parties to a conflict to maintain diplomatic relations, and it therefore runs counter to the community interest in fostering such contacts in the hope of terminating or moderating the conflict. Of course, just as India's defense of internment and detention weakened with the passage of time after hostilities ceased, so too did its justification of its refusal to permit China ordinary diplomatic protection of its nationals.

China's challenge to the ICRC's visits to the internment camp without China's consent appears to reflect a misunderstanding of the important difference between the ICRC's traditional independent activities undertaken in behalf of humanity, as recognized by article 10 of the convention, and the additional activities that the ICRC might undertake under article 11 as a substitute for a protecting power. Moreover, the Chinese view rests upon a misinterpretation of the qualification, "subject to the consent of the Parties to the conflict concerned," that article 10 imposes upon the ICRC's independent activities, the PRC implicitly asserting that this phrase includes all parties to the conflict including the power of origin of protected persons. Here again the effect of the Chinese position would be unfortunate—in this instance, denying any protection to the nationals of a party to the conflict so long as their government fruitlessly insisted on exercising normal diplomatic protection during the conflict and refused to agree to the appointment of a protecting power or humanitarian organization.

The PRC's recognition of the right of interned civilians to voluntary repatriation accords with the expectations of the signatories to the Civilian Convention. Although few states would quibble with the accuracy of Peking's observation that internees cannot freely exercise this right while in the hands of the detaining power, it is unlikely that many states would share the Chinese view that the power of origin has the right, at least when diplomatic relations are maintained during a conflict, to have its diplomats interview interned nationals in order to verify the voluntariness of their decision. There might well be considerable support for a rule that required verification by a protecting power or humanitarian organization, but such a rule is not embodied in the convention. The issue was never sharply presented in this case because China did not seek third-party assistance in any respect, and it therefore did not raise the matter of third-party verification. Nor did the ICRC request permission to verify the choice of the interned persons.

What emerges from this survey is the conclusion that the Chinese position regarding mass internment of civilian nationals and the principle of their voluntary repatriation coincides with what appears to be the most enlightened interpretation of the Civilian Convention. With respect to diplomatic protection of nationals during a conflict and ICRC humanitarian inspection of internment conditions without the consent of the country whose nationals are interned, China's views, although understandable from the perspective of China's national interest, seem plainly at odds with the system of protection prescribed by the convention.

Finally, did China take its own legal claims seriously? Did it practice what it preached? Although China's national security was never threatened by the conflict, India's actions against Chinese nationals presented an obvious temptation for Peking to take similar measures against Indian civilians in China. Such measures might have been rationalized not as reprisals, which are prohibited by article 33 of the Civilian Convention, but on vague grounds similar to those invoked by India in defense of its actions. Yet the PRC did not resort to internment of Indian civilians, nor is there any indication in the diplomatic correspondence that it detained any Indian civilians on grounds relating to the conflict.

When in 1963, Peking did detain an Indian national on a rape charge and India, despite its refusal to permit China the usual peacetime rights of consular access to Chinese nationals detained in India, insisted that China grant those rights to India, Peking did not claim that its refusal to permit preconviction access to the defendant was justified because of its hostile relations with New Delhi. Instead, it claimed that its refusal was consistent with the very peacetime standard upon which New Delhi insisted. What Peking failed to note was that it defined that standard more restrictively in response to India's demand than it did when making its demand upon India for access to its own nationals; in the latter case, Peking never manifested a belief that under international law access to detained nationals may be denied until they are convicted of the charges on which they are held.

The PRC's position regarding access to captured Indian military personnel revealed a similar effort to make its views as a detaining power appear consistent with its claims for access to Chinese nationals interned in India. The principle upon which China insisted was that, while diplomatic relations existed during a conflict, both detained prisoners and interned civilians were to be protected by the diplomatic representatives and the national Red Cross Societies of their countries. But, again, China applied the principle more restrictively in practice when responding to India's demands than when making demands of its own. Although it bitterly protested against India's refusal to permit the Chinese embassy to visit interned Chinese nationals and although it claimed to be cooperating with Indian efforts to protect detained prisoners of war, Peking did not permit Indian representatives to visit the prisoners. As so often occurs in world politics, in this case the Chinese Communist elite adopted a "do as I say, not as I do" approach to international law.

9 / Some Conditions of Peking's Participation in International Organizations

Byron S. J. Weng

THE RECORD OF PEKING'S PARTICIPATION IN INTERNATIONAL ORGANIZATIONS

The record of a nation's participation in international organizations is not the only index of that nation's international status. Nor is it the most important. But it is certainly one of the more significant of such indices. Today, all nations of the world belong to international organizations, both because they are provided with services and facilities otherwise unavailable to them and because acceptance in international organizations brings prestige. Indeed, it may well be more than mere speculation that the more international organizations a nation belongs to, the better is that nation accepted in the family of nations. Conversely, the more "established" a nation is, the more international organizations it is likely to become associated with. It is no wonder, therefore, that the elites of most newly independent nations consider the application for membership in the United Nations as primary business.

When the People's Republic of China (PRC) was established in 1949, the new Peking government followed this pattern of behavior, although it requested recognition of its right to represent China rather than submitting an application for membership.[1] However, after 22 years of

NOTE: The author is grateful to George Ginsburgs for his helpful comments on an earlier version of this paper, which was read at the regional conference of the American Society of International Law, cosponsored by the Graduate Faculty of Political and Social Science of the New School for Social Research on February 8, 1969.

1. For an account of Peking's first actions regarding China's representation in the UN, see Hungdah Chiu and R.R. Edwards, "Communist China's Attitude Toward the United Nations: A Legal Analysis," *AJIL* 62.1:20–50 (Jan. 1968), particularly note 6.

existence, the PRC has just now been allowed to participate in the proceedings of the UN and its related special agencies. It is still not deeply involved in the other international organizations, either intergovernmental (IGO) or nongovernmental (NGO).

Three sets of simple statistics can be used to illustrate the PRC's position. First, according to the *Worldmark Encyclopedia of Nations,*[2] as of December 1966, there were 193 IGOs, aside from the UN and its related agencies. Of these, the PRC is a member of only two and participates in one other as an observer. When compared with the records of participation of other countries, these statistics clearly indicate the very limited scope of the PRC's involvement in the process of international organization. (See Table 9.1.) The PRC's participation not

Table 9.1. Participation of selected countries in IGOs other than the UN family, December 1966

Country	Membership	Associate Membership	Observer	Corresponding
France	91			
UK	77		1	1
West Germany	73			
USA	51	1	3	
Japan	37	1		
USSR	29			
South Korea	17			
ROC (Taiwan)	15		1	
South Vietnam	15			
East Germany	5			
PRC	2		1	
North Korea	2		1	
North Vietnam	2		1	

only lagged far behind that of every other major power but also that of most of the other independent nations of the world. With the exception of a handful of the microstates that have become independent recently, only North Korea and North Vietnam share this meager record with the PRC.

Second, in regard to the NGOs, the *Yearbook of International Organi-*

2. John D. Balcomb, ed., "The United Nations," *Worldmark Encyclopedia of the Nations* (3rd ed., N.Y.: Worldmark Press, 1967), vol. I, pp. 249–269.

zations[3] listed no fewer than 2,188 that were operative in December 1968. Participation by groups and/or individuals from China in these NGOs is indicated in Table 9.2. Here "China" and "Taiwan" refer to the

Table 9.2. Number of NGOs in which Chinese groups and/or individuals participated, December 1968

Participants from "China"	141
Participants from "China" and "Taiwan"	8
Participants from "Taiwan"	117
Total NGOs with "Chinese" participants	266

PRC and the Republic of China (ROC) respectively. In the first category, however, "China" actually could designate either the PRC or the ROC or both. The Nationalists have often insisted that their delegations to international organizations or conferences be designated "China" rather than Taiwan and are so listed in many official rosters. A closer examination of the first category results in the adjusted Table 9.3.[4]

From Table 9.3, we obtain the following figures: NGOs with participants from the PRC 42 (minimum) to 122 (maximum); NGOs with participants from the ROC 152 (minimum) to 232 (maximum). Thus comparing the two Chinese governments, the PRC is much more limited

Table 9.3. Number of NGOs in which Chinese groups and/or individuals participated, December 1968

Participants from "China"		141
From PRC only	34	
From ROC only	27	
From either PRC or ROC or both	80	
Participants from "China" and "Taiwan"		8
Participants from "Taiwan"		117
Total NGOs with "Chinese" participants		266

3. Eyvind S. Tew, ed., *Yearbook of International Organizations, 1968–1969* (12th ed., Brussels: Union of International Associations).

4. Only those clearly identifiable as associated with one or the other are adjusted. For instance, it is clear that the PRC does not participate in the International Confederation of Free Trade Unions (Brussels) and the ROC does not take part in the World Federation of Trade Unions (Prague). It is also clear that the "China" participating in the International Olympic Committee is the ROC and not the PRC, since the latter withdrew from the IOC in 1957.

in its involvement in NGOs than the ROC. In fact, the PRC's own inventory[5] shows that in 1957, Peking was a participant in 64 international organizations, including both IGOs and NGOs. Since then, it has withdrawn from at least 11 of these.[6] It may not be too far from fact to estimate Peking's participation in the NGOs at 60 out of a total of 2,188.

Third, the same *Yearbook*'s listing of addresses for the headquarters and regional offices of all international organizations, including both IGOs and NGOs, has only two entries under Peking. Again, in comparison with other countries, particularly the better established Western nations, the PRC is far behind. (See Table 9.4.)

The reasons for Peking's meager record of involvement in international organizations are many and complicated. Much is due to the Cold War policies of the United States and its allies. There is no doubt that the PRC has been relatively isolated. But it is also true that Peking's own policy choices have had a great deal to do with this situation.

Table 9.4. Number of international organizations' addresses in selected countries, December 1968

Country	Number of addresses
France	649
UK	412
USA	314
West Germany	169
Japan	33
USSR	10
East Germany	3
South Korea	3
PRC	2
ROC	2
South Vietnam	1
North Vietnam	0
North Korea	0

5. *Shih-chieh chih-shih nien-chien* (World knowledge yearbook, 1957; Peking: Shih-chieh chih-shih ch'u pan she, 1957), pp. 1058–1061.

6. These are: International Amateur Swimming Federation, International Amateur Basketball Federation, Table Tennis Federation of Asia, International Amateur Wrestling Federation, Union Cycliste Internationale, International Amateur Athletic Federation, International Shooting Union, International Weightlifting Federation, International Olympic Committee, International Astronomical Union, Comité Special de l'Année Geophysique Internationale. The International Red Cross Conference from which the PRC also withdrew in 1957 was not included in the list of 64.

PROBABLE CONDITIONS OF PEKING'S PARTICIPATION IN INTERNATIONAL ORGANIZATIONS

For analytical purposes, four conditions that appear to determine Peking's participation in international organizations are identified and discussed in the following pages.

"Correct" Ideological Orientation

The first is that the international organization in which the PRC participates as a member must have a "correct" ideological orientation. This condition involves two stipulations: The objectives of the international organization must not be antagonistic to anti-imperialist struggles, and its membership policy must be nondiscriminatory with respect to the PRC and those adhering to Peking's ideological pronouncements.

In a somewhat arbitrary fashion, all operative international organizations may be classified under three broad categories on the basis of this condition: those with "correct" orientation, those with "incorrect" orientation, and those that are more or less "neutral."

The first category is at once prosocialist and anti-imperialist. It includes (1) the international organizations of the "fraternal" socialist countries such as the Warsaw Treaty Organization (WTO), the Council for Mutual Economic Assistance (COMECON), the Joint Nuclear Research Institute (JNRI) at Dubna, the Organization for the Collaboration of Railways (OCR), the Organization for Cooperation in Telecommunications and Postal Services Among Socialist States (OCTP), and the Fisheries Research Commission for the Western Pacific (FRCWP); (2) the Communist-directed nongovernmental organizations such as the World Council for Peace (WCP), the World Federation of Trade Unions (WFTU), the World Federation of Democratic Youth (WFDY), the World Federation of Scientific Workers (WFSW), Women's International Democratic Federation (WIDF), the International Organization of Journalists (IOJ), the International Union of Students (IUS), and the International Association of Democratic Lawyers (IADL); and (3) Left-oriented nongovernmental organizations of the Afro-Asian nations such as the Afro-Asian People's Solidarity Organization (AAPSO) and the Games of the Newly Emerging Nations (GANEFO).

During the 1950s, the PRC was relatively active in the socialist international organizations.[7] It was a founding member of the four IGOs: the JNRI (1956), the FRCWP (1956), the OCR (1957), and the OCTP (1957); and an "observer" of two: the WTO (1955) and the COMECON (1956). As a result of the Sino-Soviet dispute, however, the PRC gradually severed its ties with these organizations during the 1960s. Peking did not send observers to the WTO and the COMECON after 1961. In the case of the COMECON, it went on record in opposition to the Council's specialization policy, and openly cast the organization as "a tool of Soviet revisionist social-imperialism for controlling the financial and economic lifelines of several East European countries and plundering and exploiting their people."[8] Peking's association with the JNRI also terminated in July 1966.[9] Whether its membership in the remaining three IGOs will also be withdrawn is, at this writing, a moot question.

The PRC has also been an important participant in the formation and/or operation of the NGOs of the Left, both within the socialist bloc and among the Afro-Asian nations. However, here too, Peking's role has been drastically influenced by the Sino-Soviet dispute. In the World Council for Peace, for instance, Peking tried to press its hard line anti-imperialist approach upon the December 1963 Budapest conference. After failing, it declared that the Council had been usurped by the Soviets to carry on the erroneous line of peaceful coexistence with the "imperialists." In April 1964, the Peking delegation not only did not gain the majority support of the members of the WCP's presidium but also found it necessary to denounce the "discriminatory and inglorious" decision not to grant full recognition to the South Vietnamese National Liberation Front.[10]

The PRC was originally one of the most enthusiastic supporters of the AAPSO. Peking was successful in its struggle against the Soviet Union

7. See Hungdah Chiu, "Peiping's Role in Communist Inter-Governmental Organizations," *Issues and Studies* 3:33–35 (1967); Z.K. Brzezinski, "The Organization of the Communist Camp," *World Politics* 13:175–209 (1960–1961); and K. Grzybowski, *The Socialist Commonwealth of Nations* (New Haven: Yale University Press, 1964), pp. 71, 130–135, 143–150, 164–166, 210–213. The author is grateful to Professor George Ginsburgs for bringing to his attention the relevant information concerning the OCTP.

8. "How Soviet Revisionists Use the 'CMEA' to Plunder and Exploit East European People," *PR*, no. 48:24–26 (Nov. 29, 1968).

9. Douglas M. Johnston and Hungdah Chiu, eds., *Agreements of the People's Republic of China, 1949–1967* (Cambridge, Mass.: Harvard University Press, 1968), p. 52.

10. *JMJP*, Dec. 4, 1963, p. 3; and May 6, 1964, p. 3.

at the Moshe (Tanganyika) conference of the organization in February 1963, and the Accra (Ghana) conference in 1965.[11] At the fourth conference, Peking pushed through a resolution, despite the opposition of the Soviet, Mongolian, and Indian delegations, to hold the fifth conference in Peking in 1967. However, China's Great Proletarian Cultural Revolution made this impossible, and, in February, the Cairo-based Secretariat voted to hold the conference in Algiers instead. At the same time, the Secretariat also rejected membership applications from four pro-Chinese African groups. On March 18, 1967, it was reported that the PRC was severing all ties with AAPSO's Secretariat since it had "fallen to the Soviet revisionists."[12]

These practices would suggest that, when an international organization's ideological orientation changes from "correct" to "incorrect", Peking withdraws from or, at least, curbs temporarily its participation in that organization.

The second category—those organizations with "incorrect" ideologies—includes all political and military organizations of the Western allies. The best example among them is SEATO. SEATO's objectives are clearly antagonistic to Peking, and its membership is confined to Peking's enemies. Needless to say, Peking could not and would not ever become a participant in this type of international organization. By necessity, such organizations are targets of Peking's propaganda attacks. When the Manila Pact was being negotiated, Peking sought to demonstrate that any Asian country that participated in that alliance would be linked with the United States' policy of "aggression against China" and its "interference" in China's internal affairs, i.e., its support for the Nationalist Chinese government.[13] After the formation of SEATO, Peking cautiously avoided any overt and direct threat to SEATO members that might draw the United States into a military confrontation with China, but consistently gave unofficial aid to armed struggles in Southeast Asia. Similar treatment has been accorded the NGOs belonging to this category, e.g., the International Federation of Free Trade Unions.[14]

11. See "Afro-Asian Conference Success," *PR*, no. 7:5 (Feb. 15, 1963), and "Success of the Fourth Afro-Asian People's Solidarity Conference," *PR*, no. 22:13 (May 28, 1965).

12. K. Cooley, "Red China Quits Afro-Asian Group," *Christian Science Monitor*, Mar. 30, 1967, p. 11.

13. R. Gavin Boyd, "Communist China and SEATO," in George Modelski, ed., *SEATO: Six Studies* (Vancouver: Publication Center of the University of British Columbia, 1962), pp. 167–201.

14. *Shih-chieh chih-shih nien-chien 1957*, pp. 1023–1026.

In the third category may be included all the international organizations not covered in the first two categories. The various universal organizations, including the UN and its related agencies, are the notable examples. In a broad sense, such organizations are not "correctly oriented" in Peking's view, for they are invariably oriented toward stability and order if not the intolerable status quo. It can be argued that since Peking sees itself as the champion of world revolution, it has a vested interest in change, perhaps even disruption of international order. Myres S. McDougal and Richard M. Goodman totally discredit Peking's verbal support for the principles and purposes of the UN Charter and take the position that Communist China is not only a self-proclaimed "new state" but, by its own words and deeds, "explicitly promises ill for the United Nations."[15] However, this generalization, which ignores Peking's changing attitudes toward the UN, is obviously too sweeping. It may well be that an "anti-system regime," as Leon Lipson calls Peking,[16] is not prone to participating in the evolutionary process of international organization. Still, Alexander Dallin[17] and Alvin Rubinstein,[18] among others, have shown how the Soviet Union opted to become involved in the UN even during the Stalinist era. Implications are that the socialist countries are not blind to the functional utility of universal international organizations. Peking too might pursue a more flexible policy toward international organizations that aspire to universal concerns and subscribe to universal membership. We must, therefore, look into other conditions that explain in further detail the behavior of Peking toward international organizations with "neutral" orientation.

Nonparticipation of the Republic of China (Taiwan)

In October 1960, Edgar Snow asked Chou En-lai: "Would China refuse to sit in the UN as long as any kind of Taiwan government was allowed to represent Taiwan separately there?" The Premier replied:

This question is relatively simple. If the so-called "Taiwan Clique" is to appear in the United Nations, under whatever form and in whatever name—

15. Myres S. McDougal and Richard M. Goodman, "Chinese Participation in the United Nations," *AJIL* 60.4:671–727 (Oct. 1966).
16. ASIL *Proceedings* (1967), p. 108.
17. Alexander Dallin, *The Soviet Union at the United Nations: An Inquiry into Soviet Motives and Objectives* (N.Y.: Praeger, 1962).
18. Alvin Z. Rubinstein, *The Soviets in International Organizations: Changing Policy Toward Developing Countries, 1953–1963* (Princeton, N.J.: Princeton University Press, 1964).

be it the Chiang Kai-shek clique or some other clique—we shall definitely refuse to take part in the United Nations and sit together with them, so as not to create a situation of "two Chinas." This applies also to our participation in other international organizations and conferences.[19]

Peking's legal position on the question of Taiwan has always been rather rigid. It argues that the PRC is already a member of a number of international agencies by virtue of assuming the government of China. The official name of China has been changed to read "the People's Republic of China" instead of "the Republic of China" but that, they say, is a prerogative of any sovereign state and the international organizations have no right to meddle in such internal affairs but have the obligation to accept the change. Taiwan is an integral part of China. As such, Peking welcomes the participation of loyal citizens residing in Taiwan as members of China's delegations to international organizations, but Peking will never tolerate a separate delegation from Taiwan by any name.

The Universal Postal Union (UPU), at its 1950 Montreux session, passed a resolution, which, "leaving all political considerations aside," decided "to admit to the present session of the Executive Committee as the only qualified representative of China the delegate of the Chinese popular republic."[20] Consequently, a Peking delegation, headed by Su Yu-nung, took part in the May 1950 session of the Executive and Liaison Committee of the UPU. Peking's delegate demanded that the name "China" on the UPU membership roster be changed to "the PRC" but this claim was denied by a vote of 10 to 3. This caused no difficulty for Peking's continued participation, however. In December 1950, Peking notified the UPU of its decision to adhere to the 1947 Convention of the UPU and four other specific postal agreements and in January 1951, took part in a joint meeting between the same UPU committee and the International Air Transport Association (IATA).[21] However, at its 1951 session, after Chinese intervention in the Korean War, the UPU reversed its earlier decision and accepted the postal administration of the ROC as the representative of China on the basis of a referendum among all of its members.[22] Peking protested to no avail.

19. Edgar Snow, *China, Russia and the U.S.A.: Changing Relations in a Changing World* (New York: Marzani & Munsell, 1962), p. 760.
20. See M.A.K. Menon, "Universal Postal Union," *International Conciliation,* no. 552:26 (Mar. 1965).
21. See *Shih-chieh chih-shih nien-chien 1957,* pp. 928–929.
22. Menon, "Universal Postal Union," pp. 26–27.

During the 1950s, the United States attempted to create a "two Chinas" solution to the question of Chinese representation in several nonpolitical and nongovernmental international organizations. In each case, the PRC started off as an enthused participant but withdrew when a concurrent invitation was sent to the countergroup representing the ROC.

The case of the International Geophysical Year (IGY)[23] is most revealing. In 1952, the Comité Special de l'Année Geophysique Internationale (CSAGI) sent invitations to both the PRC and ROC governments. For three years, there was no reply from either. On September 12, 1955, the president of CSAGI reported that the vice-president of Peking's Academia Sinica, Dr. Chu K'o-chen, had notified him that the PRC would participate in the IGY on the sole condition that the Nationalist Chinese would not be accepted. A delegation of scientists from Peking then took part in the IGY regional conference for eastern Europe and Asia, held in Moscow from August 20 to 25, 1956, and a month later, in the Barcelona conference of the CSAGI.

In November of that year, the ROC suddenly notified the CSAGI's president, Dr. Chapman, of its intention to join the IGY and demanded the deletion of the PRC from the official list of IGY participants. In early 1957, Taipei requested an invitation to the Western Pacific regional conference to be held in late February. In an effort to arrive at an acceptable compromise for all parties concerned, the reply to Taipei's request was delayed. A week before the conference was to open, Peking reiterated its condition of participation in the IGY. On the opening day, Taipei asked to participate as observer and was politely refused by Dr. Chapman. In April 1957, Dr. Chu sent two letters from Peking to the officials of CSAGI, one of which stated that Peking would contribute to the budget of that committee US$7,500 in gold for each of the next three years, while the other further explained Peking's position. Among other things, it said:

> We realize that the IGY will accept all bona fide participants to the enterprise it has launched, irrespective of their political creeds; but is it not true that a man of science, as well as a person in any other profession, cannot very well disregard the national consciousness of his own countrymen?

23. Discussion of the case of the IGY in this section is largely based on Walter Sullivan, "The International Geophysical Year," *International Conciliation,* no. 521 (Jan. 1959). See also *Oppose U.S. Occupation of Taiwan and "Two Chinas" Plot* (Peking: Foreign Languages Press, 1958), pp. 77–78.

It noted that Peking would not object to scientists from Taiwan coming to the IGY gatherings as long as they agreed to the stipulation, implicitly or explicitly, that there is only one China, the PRC.

In June of that year, pressured by both Chinese groups and the USA, which had now intervened on behalf of the Taipei group, CSAGI decided that henceforth no IGY committees would be listed in its documents as "national." At the same time, notifications were given to the contending groups that in the list of participating IGY committees, two consecutive entries would be included to read: (1) Chinese IGY Committee: Peking and (2) Chinese IGY Committee: Taipei. Peking replied on June 29, 1957, that until the acceptance of Taipei was revoked Peking was withdrawing from CSAGI and all its activities.

Similar situations occurred with regard to the International Olympic Committee and its several affiliates[24] and the Commission on Asian and Far Eastern Affairs of the International Chamber of Commerce[25] in 1956, the International Red Cross Conference in 1957,[26] and the International Astronomical Union in 1960.[27]

It may be argued that Peking's ad hoc participation in the UN in November 1950 represents an exception to the condition that the ROC not be concurrently present. In 1950, Peking had lodged a formal complaint against US "aggression in the Taiwan Strait" according to the procedures of the UN Security Council. In connection with this complaint, which was placed on the agenda of the Council and of the First Committee of the General Assembly, Peking cabled the appropriate authorities of the UN several times and asked for invitations to take part in the deliberations of the relevant UN organs on the grounds that, as the sole legal government representing the Chinese people, and being the accuser in the case, it had the right and necessity to present its case directly. As a result, an ad hoc delegation led by General Wu Hsiu-ch'uan was sent to Lake Success where it participated in the proceedings of the Security Council and the Assembly's

24. For statements of the Chinese Olympic Committee (Peking) on the International Olympic Committee during 1956 and 1957, see *Oppose U.S. Occupation of Taiwan and "Two Chinas" Plot*, pp. 87–104. The International Olympic Committee has since been characterized as "a tool manipulated by U.S. imperialism." See *PR*, no. 12:33 (Mar. 22, 1968).

25. See *Shih-chieh chih-shih nien-chien 1957*, pp. 965–966; also *JMJP*, Apr. 7, 1956.

26. See statements by Li Te-ch'üan and Pan Tzu-li in *Oppose U.S. Occupation of Taiwan and "Two Chinas" Plot*, pp. 79–86.

27. See *Ta-kung pao* (Hong Kong), Feb. 7, 1960, p. 1.

First Committee.[28] The invitations to Peking were legally dubious.[29] Peking, nevertheless, accepted the invitations without insisting that the representatives of the ROC first be expelled from the UN. In effect, the ad hoc delegation from Peking sat in the same meeting chambers with Taipei's delegation in those instances.

This temporary ambiguity does not appear to have been due to Peking's willingness to yield on the claim that the Taipei regime "represents nobody," but rather to the naïveté of Peking's policy in the early years. It seems that, in its eagerness to present its case, the decision-makers of Peking felt impelled to come to the UN and for a time thus ignored the PRC's own precondition for participation. This was not repeated. In 1955, Peking was invited to discuss a New Zealand proposal concerning the hostilities between the two Chinas over the offshore islands.[30] Premier Chou replied that the New Zealand proposal was a violation of the UN Charter because it suggested interference in China's domestic affairs and that Peking would take part in Security Council activities only after the representative of the PRC had been seated in the name of China and the other occupant of China's seat had been expelled.[31] In short, Peking would not again take part in UN activities on the ad hoc and ambiguous basis that it did in 1950.

In his mid-1956 report to the National People's Congress, Chou En-lai said:[32]

> Those who vainly seek to create "two Chinas" recognize that it is becoming more and more difficult to continue to exclude the PRC from international organizations and conferences. Therefore they are attempting to create beforehand a state of "two Chinas" in international organizations and conferences. The Chinese people long ago saw through this plot. It is futile to hope that China will fall into this trap. International organizations and conferences are only one means of effecting international exchanges and contacts. China will not find it any more difficult to expand its contacts and connections with other countries because of its being excluded from international organizations and conferences. Only one China exists in the world. Only the Government of the PRC can represent the Chinese people. We believe that sooner

28. See *China Accuses!* (Peking: Foreign Languages Press, 1951).
29. See Chiu and Edwards, "Communist China's Attitude Toward the United Nations," pp. 38–40.
30. UN Doc. S/P.V. 690.
31. UN Doc. S/3358.
32. "Premier Chou En-lai's Speech on Present International Situation, China's Foreign Policy, and the Liberation of Taiwan Delivered at the Third Session of the First National People's Congress, June 28, 1956."

or later this fact will receive general recognition in the world. The sooner this day arrives, the sooner will normal international relations be restored.

This statement leaves little doubt that Chou was setting forth Peking's determination not to compromise on this condition of participation.

"Favorable" Political Climate

Another condition which plays a role in Peking's decisions about participation has to do with the political climate of international organizations. Peking will not subject itself to the process of international organization—to be forced to take stands on ticklish issues, to defend its position and behavior—if the political climate is clearly unfavorable. For instance, in 1961, after Sino-Soviet relations had become badly tarnished and Sino-Indian relations had deteriorated, Peking realized that if it were in the UN, it would be struggling at one and the same time not only against the "imperialists" but also against the Soviet "revisionists" and the Indian "reactionaries." At that time, an article in the top secret military bulletin, *Kung-tso t'ung-hsun,* said:[33]

> If our country joins the United Nations, we cannot have a majority in voting; formally the difficult situation may be moderated to some extent, but actually the struggle that arises will be more violent and we shall lose our present freedom of action. Though standing outside of the United Nations, we could still participate in the Bandung Conference. We made tremendous achievements in that conference. Last year we signed treaties of friendship with five countries (Cambodia, Nepal, Afghanistan, Yemen and Guinea), and settled problems about the boundary lines between China and Burma and between China and Nepal just because the United States had no chance to join in the negotiation or to exert pressure . . . Outside of the United Nations, we have enjoyed a peaceful co-existence with the countries in Asia, Africa and Latin America, and the peaceful area is being enlarged.

It further stated, "some wished to limit the development of China by dragging it into the United Nations in order to harness it," and then warned its select readership that "the world is like a chessboard, and 'one careless step will cause the loss of the whole game.' "[34]

On the other hand, in 1955, Peking's National People's Congress

33. *Kung-tso t'ung-hsun* (Bulletin of activities), no. 17 (Apr. 25, 1961); English translation in J. Chester Cheng et al, eds., *The Politics of the Chinese Red Army: A Translation of the Bulletin of Activities of the PLA* (Stanford, Calif.: The Hoover Institute on War, Revolution and Peace, 1966), p. 480.
34. *Ibid.,* p. 481.

"studied" the constitution of the Inter-Parliamentary Union (IPU), passed a resolution to send a Chinese delegation, elected a 61-man special committee, enacted a law for that purpose, and formally notified the IPU of Peking's readiness to participate in the forthcoming conference at Helsinki, Finland.[35] It turned out that during the previous year, the IPU had passed a resolution recommending that the PRC's rights in the UN be restored. The political climate was favorable. Peking's quest was thwarted, however, because the Executive Committee of the IPU decided to postpone consideration of Peking's application. The following year, the Executive Committee of the IPU reversed its position, accepted Peking, and rejected Taipei. But the General Council overruled the report of the Executive Committee and adopted a Thai resolution to postpone the question again until the UN reached a solution to the Chinese question. Correspondingly, Peking's interest in the IPU waned.[36]

These two examples indicate that Peking was willing to take a chance if the political climate was not clearly unfavorable, but would postpone participation if the political atmosphere was hostile to it.

It would be a mistake to assume that Peking has been idly and passively waiting for a "favorable" political climate to develop. Since many of the existing international organizations are not friendly, Peking has turned to the logical alternative by calling an international conference of the Asian and Pacific regions. As a result, a Peace Liaison Committee of the Asian and Pacific Regions was established with its headquarters in Peking.[37] From 1962 to 1965, the PRC attempted to court the Afro-Asians in order to create a substitute for the UN. This was the period when Peking was most active in Afro-Asian international gatherings such as the AAPSO and the GANEFO. In 1965, it formally protested against the attendance of a UN ECA representative at an Afro-Asian Economic Seminar held in Algeria[38] and against U Thant's participation in the preparatory meeting of the Second Afro-Asian Conference.[39]

During 1969, public opinion in the General Assembly showed a clear change in favor of the PRC after three consecutive years of reversals.

35. See *JMJP*, July 31, 1955, p. 1.
36. See *JMJP*, Aug. 30, 1955, p. 3. See also *Ta-kung pao* (Tientsin), Aug. 30, 1955, editorial; and *JMJP*, Apr. 12, 1956, p. 1, Observer's comments.
37. *Shih-chieh chih-shih nien-chien 1957*, p. 978.
38. See *PR*, no. 11:18 (Mar. 12, 1965).
39. See *PR*, no. 41:7, 10 (Sept. 29, 1965).

This was due partly to Peking's conciliatory policies toward the outside world following the Ninth Party Congress. It soon became clear that Peking's leaders were actively seeking the earliest possible entrance into the UN as well. Whether the PRC would have modified its conditions of participation had the political climate in the UN continued to be unfavorable, we will probably never know. At any rate, support for Peking's claim to China's seat increased steadily, and the General Assembly finally accepted Peking's terms of participation with a vote of seventy-six in favor to thirty-five against (with seventeen abstentions) at its twenty-sixth session.

Institutional Safeguards

Still another condition of Peking's participation in international organizations relates to institutional safeguards. Alexander Dallin has pointed out that the Soviet Union considers its veto power in the Security Council to be indispensable so long as the socialist countries remain a "permanent minority" within the UN.[40] Similarly, Wojciech Morawiecki, a distinguished Polish scholar on international organizations, observed that socialist states more than other states are sensitive to matters of institutional safeguards such as voting methods, budget control, seating distribution in limited membership councils and administrative organs; that they more than other states are in favor of limiting the powers of intergovernmental organizations.[41] There is little quarrel that Peking shares these concerns. The PRC should find few objections, if any at all, to the voting procedures in the Security Council of the UN. We can expect Peking to hold on to the veto power allocated to the permanent members of the council. Hungdah Chiu and R. Randle Edwards have observed that Peking's commentators have insisted on the unanimity of the five big powers while rejecting the special status conferred upon the three nuclear powers—the US, the USSR, the UK—by the UN endorsement of the Partial Test-Ban Treaty of 1963.[42]

In other organs of the UN and other universal international organizations, the story may be somewhat different. On occasion, Peking has

40. Dallin, *Soviet Union at the UN*, pp. 50–54.
41. Wojciech Morawiecki, "Institutional and Political Conditions of Participation of Socialist States in International Organizations: A Polish View," *International Organization* 22.2:494–507 (Spring 1968).
42. Chiu and Edwards, "Communist China's Attitude Toward the United Nations," p. 31.

referred to what it called "the US voting machine in the UN."[43] Delegates from the PRC have sought "unanimity through consultation" at various multinational conferences.[44] This is so because the PRC still insists that "in international affairs, all countries should have equal rights."[45] However, most universal international organizations no longer require unanimous votes for passage of resolutions. Under such circumstances, Peking's best bet seems to be a sort of "collective veto." To some degree, this interpretation has been consistent with Peking's practical behavior. At the 1964 Conference of the Presidium of the World Council for Peace, Peking was unable to prevent the adoption of several resolutions which it charged were "a surrender policy imposed by the Soviet revisionists." So it declared that it would not be restricted by such resolutions.[46] In other words, there is a possibility that when its vital interests are involved, Peking will selectively and unilaterally declare resolutions passed by such organizations over the "collective opposition" of Peking's own group as not legally binding.

Along this line, Chiu and Edwards have also observed that the criteria which Peking employs to measure the validity of resolutions include:

> one, whether the resolution conflicts with the UN Charter (as interpreted by Communist China); two, whether the total population of the states voting in favor of the resolution exceeds the sum of populations of the states voting against the resolution or abstaining; . . . three, whether the resolution is simply "unjust." A resolution failing even one of these tests is declared void.[47]

On the distribution of seats on executive councils, special committees, the secretariat, and other administrative organs of universal

43. For instance, "the development of history is not determined by the main UN voting machines . . . This United States voting machine in the UN is becoming less efficient." Editorial, *JMJP*, Oct. 19, 1960.

44. Harold C. Hinton, *Communist China in World Politics* (Boston: Houghton Mifflin, 1966), pp. 98–99. Also McDougal and Goodman, "Chinese Participation in the United Nations," p. 717, notes 237 and 238.

45. Observer, "The More He Tries to Cover Up, the More He Exposes—on Adlai Stevenson's UN Speech," *PR*, no. 12:13 (Feb. 5, 1965). See also Yang Hsin and Ch'en Chien, "Exposing and Criticizing the Fallacious Reasoning of Imperialists on Questions Concerning National Sovereignty," *Cheng-fa yen-chiu* (Political-legal research), no. 4:6–11 (1964); English translation in *Chinese Law and Government: A Journal of Translations* 1.2:12–26 (Summer 1968).

46. See *JMJP*, May 6, 1964, p. 3. A similar situation occurred in the International Association of Democratic Lawyers. See "Focus of the Struggle," *PR*, no. 16:14–16 (Apr. 17, 1964).

47. Chiu and Edwards, "Communist China's Attitude Toward the United Nations," p. 31.

international organizations, Peking might demand proportionate representation for not only the Communist bloc but also for the pro-Peking Afro-Asians. In 1963, Peking argued for broader representation of the Afro-Asians in the Security Council and ECOSOC on the grounds that those countries represented more than a half of the UN membership and more than two thirds of the world's population.[48] As to China's own seat in these organs, it is doubtful whether Peking would tolerate the recent humiliating experience of the ROC in the UN with comparable equanimity; for the ROC has become the only permanent member of the Security Council not elected to the limited membership organs in most cases unless it is a member by Charter provision.[49]

Peking clearly favors restricting the powers of international organizations. The UN, for instance, is not a "world government" superior to states;[50] nor is it "comparable to a state which possesses sovereignty."[51] The various international organizations are merely means of exchanges and contacts. Peking will be less inclined to join an international organization that has powers to penetrate the shield of state sovereignty. It will be prone to adhere to the view that the powers of international organizations are not legally binding but rather recommendatory. Likewise, Peking might follow the Soviet and French example in refusing to pay for operations of international organizations to which it did not agree.

Institutional safeguards, as Wojciech Morawiecki put it, "can prevent the total disintegration of an organization when the dangers against which they have been erected begin to materialize."[52] He noted that in the early 1950s the socialist states remained in the UN because, among other reasons, the Soviet Union's veto power in the Security Council prevented the transformation of the UN into a mere political tool of the West. On the other hand, they resigned from such organizations as FAO, WHO, and UNESCO because these organizations lacked institutional safeguards. It stands to reason that Peking too will con-

48. See *PR*, no. 52:14–16 (Dec. 27, 1963).

49. See, for example, membership chart of the UN bodies in *International Organization* 22.3:689–691 (Summer 1968).

50. *Hsien-tai Ying-Mei kuo-chi-fa ti ssu-hsiang tung-hsiang* (Trends in the thought of modern Anglo-American international law; Peking, 1963), p. 66.

51. K'ung Meng, "A Criticism of the Bourgeois International Law Theory on Subjects of International Law and the Recognition of States," *Kuo-chi wen-t'i yen-chiu* (Studies in international problems), no. 2:44, 50 (1960).

52. Morawiecki, "Institutional and Political Conditions of Participation of Socialist States in International Organizations," p. 502.

sider institutional safeguards to be relevant conditions of its participation in international organizations.

CH'EN YI'S SEPTEMBER 1965 STATEMENT ON THE UN[53]

In September 1965, Foreign Minister Ch'en Yi made several stiff demands upon the UN at a press conference. He said:

> How can China be expected to take part in an international organization which calls her an aggressor? Calling China an aggressor and then asking the aggressor to join, would not the United Nations be slapping its own face? The question now is how to reform the UN in accordance with the purposes and principles of its Charter and to free it from the control of the United States and other big powers. If the task of reforming the UN cannot be accomplished, conditions will no doubt gradually ripen for the establishment of a revolutionary United Nations. . . . The United Nations must rectify its mistakes and undergo a thorough reorganization and reform. It must admit and correct all its past mistakes. Among other things, it should cancel its resolution condemning China and the Democratic People's Republic of Korea as aggressors and adopt a resolution condemning the United States as the aggressor; the UN Charter must be reviewed and revised jointly by all countries, big and small; all independent states should be included in the United Nations; and all imperialist puppets should be expelled.[54]

There have been various interpretations of these demands. Some American observers have concluded that Peking has challenged the right of the UN to exist as a world organization,[55] while others viewed Ch'en's words as signs of Peking's abandonment of the Charter prin-

53. Both Ch'en Yi and Chou En-lai made pronouncements expressing such demands upon the UN in late 1965. Among Peking's leading personalities, these two men have been generally considered relatively more knowledgeable about the outside world and more realistic in their approach. That they might have been under domestic pressure to make such demands on the eve of the Cultural Revolution is a suggestion that deserves our attention.

According to a semiofficial source in Taiwan, when the Red Guards turned their spearhead on Ch'en Yi in February 1967, Ch'en reportedly wrote a sarcastic and bitter but frank and bold "confession." See Chinese Information Service (New York), "Missing Ambassadors A Mystery—Peiping's Foreign Affairs Drift on Without Direction," *Report on Mainland China*, no. 18:8 (Jan. 27, 1969). A Hong Kong account of Ch'en's self-criticism does not include such passages. See *Tsu kuo*, no. 76:33–35 (July 1970). According to the Hong Kong account, Ch'en submitted his confession on January 24 rather than in February. It is not known whether Ch'en actually made more than one confession.

54. The full text of this important press conference is in *PR*, no. 41:7–14 (Oct. 8, 1965). Also see an earlier speech by Chou En-lai in *PR*, no. 5:5 (Jan. 29, 1965).

55. McDougal and Goodman, "Chinese Participation in the United Nations," p. 703.

ciples.[56] In retrospect, it seems quite probable that this statement expressed Peking's lack of interest in the UN at that time rather than the necessary conditions of its participation in the organization. The Indonesian withdrawal from the UN in January 1965, followed by Cambodia's withdrawal from the UN special committee on decolonization,[57] seems to have led Peking's decision-makers to mistake their own wishful thinking for a realistic hope that a substitute for the UN was not out of reach. Peking decided to accelerate its cultivation of the Afro-Asian Conference and the Newly Emerging Forces (NEFO), where it intended to stage and direct its own drama of world politics. Perhaps a decision was reached in Peking that the cautious approach prior to 1965 should be abandoned in favor of a more aggressive and frontal one that would discredit the UN and promote Afro-Asian solidarity at the same time. If such was the case, it is understandable that Peking's utterances during and after 1965 turned openly hostile toward the UN and the special agencies.[58] The Ch'en Yi statement of September 1965 can thus be deemed to contain a set of internationally impossible conditions for Peking's participation in the UN. Prior to 1965 and at the time of Assembly acceptance of the PRC in 1971,[59] the only condition for Peking's participation in the UN was the expulsion of the Nationalist representatives and the complete restoration to the PRC of China's legal rights.

If we keep in mind that Ch'en Yi was intentionally stating impossible conditions and consider the reasons behind the words, we may be able to analyze his statement meaningfully.

Logically, the statement contained three conditions: (1) the UN should condemn the US as "an aggressor"; (2) the UN must "admit and correct all its past mistakes"; and (3) the UN must undergo a

56. Chiu and Edwards, "Communist China's Attitude Toward the United Nations," p. 23.

57. For a Chinese account of the "September 30 Movement" in Indonesia, see *PR*, no. 43:7 (Oct. 22, 1965). For Peking's reaction to Indonesia's withdrawal from the UN, see *PR*, no. 3:5 (Jan. 15, 1965). For Peking's reaction to Cambodia's withdrawal from the UN special committee on decolonization, see *PR*, no. 40:15–16 (Oct. 1, 1965).

58. See Byron S.J. Weng, "Communist China's Changing Attitudes Toward the United Nations," *International Organization* 20.4:694–700 (Autumn 1966). See also Nan Han-ch'en's speech at the Afro-Asian Economic Seminar in *PR*, no. 10:16–26 (Mar. 5, 1965).

59. Chou En-lai told a visiting Japanese Komeito group in the summer of 1971 that Peking would participate in UN activities if the legal position of the PRC were restored and Chiang Kai-shek driven out of that body, and "that is all that needs to be done." See *The New York Times*, July 1, 1971, pp. 1, 22.

thorough reform and reorganization in order "to free itself from the control of the United States and other big powers."

The first condition, if realized, would be tantamount to the UN's self-destruction. It is entirely unrealistic. Obviously, as long as Peking held on to this condition, it was not really interested in joining the UN.

With regard to the second condition, Peking had in mind the cancellation of the earlier Security Council resolutions which condemned the PRC and North Korea as "aggressors" and imposed embargoes upon them. As the representative of a self-portrayed "New China," Peking has been jealous of its prestige; it has been "face-conscious." Whether or not the relevant Security Council resolutions actually constitute a "mistake," it may be pertinent to observe here that, until now, the PRC and North Korea have been the only governments officially condemned by the UN as "aggressors," even though serious offenses by other actors have not been lacking.[60] The nullification of the said resolutions, in effect, would not lead to further complications and might even inject a new sense of fairness into the world organization. Even so, Peking understands the difficulties involved in nullifying any resolution. Having made the point, the matter was not raised again in 1971 at the time of Peking's entry.

As to the numerous "other mistakes" of the UN, they need not be dwelt upon here. Peking's insistence would perhaps only have indicated its lack of interest.

The third condition is more complicated. It states that the UN must be thoroughly reformed and reorganized in accordance with the purposes and principles of its Charter. But Peking did not support this broad and abstract demand with any specifics, so we have merely empty words. Peking actually has five different concepts of the UN: the UN of the Charter, the UN controlled by the United States, the UN of parliamentary diplomacy, the UN of US-USSR collaboration, and the "revolutionary" UN.[61] The second and the fourth are the UN in operation, which Peking has opposed. Peking has always expressed its support for the first and the third and talked openly about the fifth only after the Indonesian withdrawal from the UN in 1965.

That Peking has always supported the Charter can be considered

60. The Soviet invasion in Hungary, 1956, in Czechoslovakia, 1968, and American intervention in the Dominican Republic in 1965 come to mind as possible examples.

61. See Byron S. J. Weng, *Peking's UN Policy: Continuity and Change* (New York: Praeger Publishers, 1972), pp. 182–183, 207–212.

a propaganda gimmick designed to woo the Asian-African nations. But, more than that, the Charter also represents a hope for Peking. For, according to the Charter, the PRC can aspire to play the role of an equal with the other big four nations in the world arena. If the Charter is faithfully adhered to, the veto power will serve to safeguard Peking's vital interests, as it has for the Soviet Union. In 1963, when Peking gave its support to the Afro-Asian quest for greater representation in the Security Council and the ECOSOC, it also painstakingly suggested a readjustment in the distribution of seats in the two organs rather than a revision of the Charter. To be sure, Peking did not argue against a revision of the Charter, but it certainly showed reluctance to support any revision of the Charter without its participation.[62]

In short, the UN as it has been operating is no longer the UN of the Charter, but has often become the UN under American control or the UN where the two superpowers conspire to maintain their dominating position at the expense of countries like the PRC. Hence, the demand that the UN must "free itself from the control of the US and other big powers," so that it may "better reflect the balance of forces in the world and present international realities."[63]

The expansion of Afro-Asian representation alone is not enough to free the UN; for it has "by no means brought any fundamental change."[64] Peking suggests further that all "independent states" be included and all "imperialist puppets" excluded. However, it has never identified those it considered to be "imperialist puppets." Broadly interpreted, this may mean all UN members who follow the lead of the US, including all the Latin American countries other than Cuba and Chile. It is hard to believe that this is what Peking wants. Narrowly interpreted, we can identify only the ROC, South Korea, and South

62. See *PR*, no. 52:14–16 (Dec. 27, 1963). In 1961, Peking also argued that "revision of the Charter needs the PRC" but that the question of Chinese representation and the question of broadening the membership of the two Councils "are of [an] entirely different nature: one procedural, one substantial." McDougal and Goodman seem to be mistaken in asserting that Peking had made the seating of the PRC a precondition to enlargement of the two Councils. Cf. Chou Keng-sheng, "China's Legitimate Rights in the UN Must Be Restored," *JMJP*, Dec. 5, 1961, the English translation of which is in *SCMP*, no. 2637:38–40 (Dec. 12, 1961) and McDougal and Goodman, "Chinese Participation in the United Nations," p. 710, note 197.

63. In the China-Pakistan Joint Communiqué of March 7, 1965, the reorganization of the UN was advocated with these words. See *PR*, no. 11:10 (Mar. 12, 1965). A similar statement appeared in the Sino-Burmese Joint Communiqué. See *PR*, no. 32:30 (Aug. 6, 1965).

64. *JMJP* editorial, Jan. 10, 1965. See *PR*, no. 3:6–9 (Jan. 15, 1965).

Vietnam as the "imperialist puppets" that Peking will not consider to be states. North Korea, North Vietnam, and the two Germanies, on the other hand, are considered to be "independent states."[65] If Peking insists on excluding the former and including the latter, a stalemate may result with respect to the representation of the divided Korean and Vietnamese states at the UN.

In sum, these conditions in Ch'en's 1965 statement, some simply impossible and some difficult and improbable, were no more than Peking's calculated strategic demands as of that date.

CONCLUSIONS

Commenting on Chinese attitudes toward international law, Jerome Alan Cohen has observed: "Any government strong enough to rule the China mainland will be ardently nationalistic for some time to come and unwilling to promote world order on other people's terms."[66]

This statement keynotes the present essay, for Peking has tried to promote world order on its own terms. In doing so, however, it has imposed conditions that have severely limited its involvement in the processes of international organization during the last two decades. Even before Ch'en Yi's 1965 statement, its rigid ideological position, its refusal to accept any form of "two Chinas" solution, and its calculated policy of nonparticipation in international organizations when a clearly "unfavorable" political climate prevailed, shut the PRC off from most of the universal international organizations that have been dominated by the United States—more recently, in conjunction with the Soviet Union. Only a few international organizations have met Peking's conditions of participation.

The world is constantly changing, however. Now that the PRC has become an active member of the UN, China's seats in other interna-

65. According to Peking's spokesman, the splitting of Germany represents a situation different from that of China. While the former was divided on the basis of international agreements growing out of World War II, the latter has been entirely a domestic affair, albeit involving foreign intervention. See Shao Chin-fu, "The Absurd Theory of 'Two Chinas' and Principles of International Law," in *Oppose the New U.S. Plots to Create "Two Chinas"* (Peking: Foreign Languages Press, 1962), pp. 82–85. In fact, Peking has long been ready to recognize "two Germanys." This was one of the three principles that Chou En-lai and Marshal Montgomery agreed upon in 1961 in order to ease tension in the international situation. See *JMJP*, Sept. 23, 1961, p. 1.

66. Jerome A. Cohen, "Chinese Attitudes Toward International Law—And Our Own," ASIL *Proceedings* (1967), p. 111.

tional agencies, formerly held by the ROC government, will soon pass over to the PRC. Both internal and external factors will no doubt function to redefine the conditions discussed in this paper and, consequently, facilitate Peking's expanded participation in many more international organizations, public and private, existing now or to be created.

10 / The People's Republic of China and the Red Cross

G. I. A. D. Draper, O.B.E.

The purpose of this study is to subject to legal analysis the published transactions, available in the West, between the People's Republic of China (PRC) and the Chinese National Red Cross Society, on the one hand, and the two main organs of the International Red Cross movement, namely, the International Committee of the Red Cross (ICRC) and the League of Red Cross, Red Crescent, and Red Lion and Sun Societies, on the other.[1]

1. The documentary materials used herein may be grouped conveniently under seven main heads: 1. *Recueil de documents; Le Comite international de la croix rouge et le conflit de Corée* (Geneva: Le Comite International de la Croix Rouge, 1952), Vol. I (June 26, 1950–December 31, 1951), Vol. II (January 1–June 30, 1952); 2. The transactions of the eighteenth, nineteenth, twentieth, and twenty-first International Conferences of the Red Cross, prepared by the International Committee of the Red Cross (ICRC), Geneva. These four conferences were held in Toronto, 1952, New Delhi, 1957, Vienna, 1965, and Istanbul, 1969, respectively; 3. The transactions of the Centenary Congress of the International Red Cross held as a meeting of the Council of Delegates in Geneva in 1963; 4. The transactions of the Executive Committee of the League of Red Cross, etc., Societies held in Geneva in 1966; 5. The *Annual Reports* published by the ICRC from 1949 to 1969; 6. Miscellaneous materials such as *Information Notes* and the *International Review of the Red Cross* published by the ICRC in Geneva; and 7. Selected translated extracts from the Chinese press.

The sources for this study, then, are not well balanced, for there is a marked lack of original Chinese material about the relations of the PRC and its Red Cross Society with the International Red Cross movement. Furthermore, the main organ of the Red Cross which has had the greatest amount of communication with the PRC and the National Red Cross Society of China is the ICRC. This organ is entrusted with extensive humanitarian functions in times of armed conflict between states. Much of the work done by the ICRC is in the form of reports and communications with governments engaged in armed conflicts; these confidential reports are not published. The political, if not the juridical, basis of such activities of the ICRC is such that maximum confidence must prevail between it and governments. Without that confidence governments are either reluctant or

THE INTERNATIONAL RED CROSS: STRUCTURE AND FUNCTIONS

The constitutional structure of the International Red Cross movement is complex. From its beginnings as a modest committee called "The International Standing Committee for Aid to Wounded Soldiers" established on February 17, 1863, in Geneva,[2] it has now become a nongovernmental international organization with an elaborate constitution and a number of different organs. The two main organs are the International Committee of the Red Cross operating pursuant to its own statutes (dated March 10, 1921 and last amended on September 25, 1952)[3] and the League of Red Cross Societies (under a constitution of 1950).[4] The ICRC, governed by and enjoying legal personality under article 60 *et seq.* of the Swiss Civil Code, is therefore a creation and entity of Swiss municipal law. It also is an international legal entity. Article 71 of the United Nations Charter accords it consultative status, Class B. However, its more significant status as an international organization derives from its recognition as such in the various Geneva Conventions that have been concluded from 1864 to 1949 and from the series of international conferences of the Red Cross held from 1864 to 1965. At these conferences, states that are parties to any of the Geneva Conventions from 1864 to 1949 participate as of right. The ICRC has its headquarters at Geneva and is limited to twenty-five members all of whom must, under article 6 of its statutes, be Swiss citizens.[5] This gives the ICRC a unique character among other nongovernmental international organizations and one which has played a part in coloring the relations between that body and the PRC.

The special role of the ICRC is "to maintain the fundamental and permanent principles of the Red Cross, namely: impartiality, action independent of any racial, political, religious or economic considera-

averse to allowing an ICRC presence on their territory or in the areas in which their armed forces are engaged or in territories under military occupation.

Finally, the published accounts of the transactions of the various international conferences of the Red Cross are limited to those of the plenary sessions. They exclude the detailed debate and arguments conducted in the various commissions into which such conferences are fragmented, and we are left with a distorted image of what occurred at such conferences.

2. J. Pictet, ed., *Commentary on the Geneva Conventions of August 12, 1949*, 4 vols. (Geneva: ICRC, 1952), vol. I, p. 9.

3. *Handbook of the International Red Cross*, 10th ed. (Geneva: ICRC, 1953), pp. 321–324.

4. *Ibid.*, pp. 325–335.

5. *Ibid.*, p. 322.

tions, the universality of the Red Cross and the equality of the National Red Cross Societies."[6] Article 4(b) provides that it shall be the role of the ICRC "to recognize any newly established or reconstituted National Red Cross Society which fulfills the conditions for recognition in force, and to notify other National Societies of such recognition."[7] It is this role which has of recent years placed the ICRC in a position of considerable difficulty. This article must be read with the Conditions for the Recognition of National Red Cross Societies approved by the Seventeenth International Red Cross Conference, 1948,[8] and article 2 of the Regulations for the Admission of New Societies to the League of Red Cross Societies, approved by the Board of Governors of the League in 1948.[9] Regulation 2 provides: "Any Applicant National Red Cross or Red Crescent Society must belong to a country where no other Red Cross or Red Crescent Society is yet in existence, and should embrace in its sphere of activity, its entire country and its dependencies." Acting under these instruments of its constitution, the organs of the International Red Cross accepted the National Red Cross Society of the PRC in October 1950. Thus, at the next international conference of the Red Cross in 1952 in Toronto, the PRC sent a government delegation and a National Red Cross Society delegation. The Republic of China (ROC) sent a government delegation, but the representative of its Red Cross Society had the status only of an "observer" present by invitation. That representation was strictly in conformity with the constitutional instruments of the International Red Cross (Rules of Procedure of the International Red Cross, article 3).[10]

6. Article 4 (a), *ibid.*, p. 321.
7. *Ibid.*, p. 322.
8. *Ibid.*, pp. 319–320.
9. *Ibid.*, pp. 349–350.
10. *Ibid.*, p. 313. The view taken by the Eighteenth International Red Cross Conference held at Toronto in 1952 seems to have been that the PRC Red Cross Society had been accepted by the League of Red Cross Societies since, at least, October 1950; see p. 351 below. As there can be only one National Red Cross Society in respect of the territory of an independent state in which any of the relevant Geneva Conventions (1864, 1906, 1929, and 1949) are in force (Conditions 1 and 2 for the Recognition of New National Red Cross Societies; see *Handbook*, pp. 319 and 320) and there being no dispute that the conventions of 1864 and 1929 applied on the mainland of China, the conference accepted the delegation of the PRC Red Cross Society as a member of the conference with the right to speak and vote. (Article 1 of the Rules of Procedure of the Conference; *Handbook*, p. 312.) Accordingly, the conference and the standing commission which convened it (statutes, article 111; *Handbook*, p. 306) were not able to recognize the ROC Red Cross Society, the delegation of which could be present

The "International Red Cross," in constitutional terms, comprises (a) the National Red Cross Societies, recognized in the manner indicated above, (b) the ICRC, and (c) the League of Red Cross Societies.[11] The League is the "international federation of National Red Cross Societies . . . having the status of a corporate body."[12] "National Red Cross Societies" include the Red Crescent Societies (of Moslem countries) and the Red Lion and Sun Society of Iran. In spite of attempts to secure the recognition of a Star of David Society (Magen David Adom) for Israel, this has so far failed as a result of objections by Arab states. Inclusion of the Star of David as the emblem and distinctive sign of the Israeli armed forces' medical services would

---

at a conference only by invitation and as an observer (article 3 of the Rules of Procedure; *Handbook*, p. 313.)

As to the governmental delegations of the PRC and the ROC, the conference seems to have taken the view that the statutes prevailing at the opening of the Toronto conference, July 1952, did not preclude the attendance and participation of either of them. This view may be challenged outside the forum of a conference. During a conference it is itself entrusted with exclusive interpretative competence by the statutes; article 11 (4). (*Handbook*, p. 306.) In the view of the conference, the facts that the PRC government had neither signed nor ratified the Geneva Sick and Wounded Convention, 1949, that the ROC government had so signed, but not ratified, and that the government of the PRC had purported to recognize the signing of the relevant convention by the ROC government were not controlling. See statement of Chou En-lai of July 13, 1952, reported in *People's China*, no. 15:33 (1952). The conference relied upon the existing statutes and rules of procedure governing the conference. Various governments of China may have signed or ratified the relevant Geneva Conventions, or some of them, but the state of China had been the party to such conventions, as a result of such signatures and ratifications. The conference, in spite of allegations to the contrary, never attempted to assert the existence of "two Chinas." It was confronted with a situation in which two delegations claimed to represent one state, China, a party to two of the four relevant Geneva Conventions, viz., 1864 and 1929. The conference may be seen to have refused to adjudicate on the claims of either delegation, as a matter outside its competence, or to have interpreted the statutes in favor of maximum inclusion and minimum exclusion, so far as governmental delegations were concerned, particularly bearing in mind the objects of the Red Cross and the purposes of the Geneva Conventions, 1864 to 1949. Quite other considerations applied to the seating and participation of National Society delegations at the conference. There the Red Cross organization had its own system of recognition, applied it, and in the result never denied the full participation of the PRC Red Cross Society or the observer status of the ROC Red Cross Society. Not surprisingly, the debates at the conference concentrated upon the right to participate of the PRC and ROC governmental delegations. Each denied that right to the other. The conference accepted neither contention but allowed the right of both. Any argument to exclude both was not before the conference. Doubtless, other views are possible, but it is not easy to argue that the solution of the conference is excluded by the relevant statutes and rules of procedure.

11. Statutes, article 1 (1), *ibid.*, p. 305.

12. Article 1 of the Constitution of the League of Red Cross Societies, *ibid.*, p. 325.

require a revision of article 38 of the Geneva Sick and Wounded Convention of 1949.

The organ of the International Red Cross that has the main burden of contact with governments in time of armed conflicts is without doubt the ICRC. It is inevitably committed in the international political arena by reason of its international constitutional nexus with states and governments. The statutes of the ICRC make this clear. Article 4 numerates the special roles of the ICRC. One of these is "to undertake the tasks incumbent on it under the Geneva Conventions, to work for the faithful application of these Conventions, and to take cognizance of any complaints regarding alleged breaches of the humanitarian Conventions."[13] This is a heavy and wide-ranging task in that the Geneva Conventions of 1949 now bind 129 states and contain some 417 detailed provisions. Under these conventions the ICRC has elaborate and detailed humanitarian functions, varying from visiting places where prisoners of war and civilian detainees are held in time of armed conflicts to assuming the humanitarian functions of a Protecting Power, when no such Power is functioning. Article 4(d) of its statutes requires the ICRC "to take action in its capacity as a neutral institution, especially in case of war, civil war or internal strife, to endeavour to ensure at all times that the military and civilian victims of such conflicts and of their results receive protection and assistance, and to serve, in humanitarian matters, as an intermediary between the parties."[14] This task is a great deal broader than those conferred upon the ICRC by international law and provides a fertile breeding ground for disputes with governments, authorities not universally recognized, and insurgent organizations.

In each of the four Geneva Conventions of 1949, there is one common article—the third—which deals with the role of the ICRC "in armed conflicts not of an international character, occurring in the territory of one of the High Contracting Parties. . . ." It provides: "An impartial humanitarian body, such as the ICRC, may offer its services to the Parties to the conflict."[15] That is the sole legal initiative allowed by these conventions to the ICRC in an internal conflict in the absence of functions accorded to it by agreement of all the parties to any such internal conflict. It is not surprising that this article proved the most difficult of all the articles of the Geneva Conventions upon which

13. Article 4 (c) of the ICRC Statutes, *ibid.*, p. 322.
14. *Ibid.*, p. 322.
15. *UNTS* 75:32, 86, 136, and 288 (1950).

to secure the agreement of states at the diplomatic conference held in 1949 at Geneva. It is generally felt that to secure any amending protocol aimed at extending the article's terms will prove no easy task. For any extended role of the ICRC in an internal conflict there must be, as the law now stands, the agreement of the parties to the conflict to bring to bear all or some of the relevant provisions of the conventions. Where the status of belligerency has been accorded to the insurgent party to an internal conflict, those functions of the ICRC which are accepted by customary international law, a debatable matter, will apply. Thus, the role of the ICRC in the numerous internal conflicts that have occurred since the Geneva Conventions came into force on October 21, 1950, has been meager. Its precise juridical limitations are open to some debate.

The third main role of the ICRC—article 4(f) of the statutes—is "to work for the continual improvement of humanitarian international law and for the better understanding and diffusion of the Geneva Conventions and to prepare for their possible extension."[16] This appears to give the ICRC a foothold in the development of international law, a position that it has not been slow to explore and exploit. Its main achievement in this area has been the preparation of the draft texts of the four Geneva Conventions of 1949 submitted to the diplomatic conference held in Geneva in 1949 and at which the conventions were concluded and signed. Since that date the ICRC has labored hard but without success to procure the acceptance, by Red Cross conferences and by governments, of draft international law texts designed to govern the combat law, as opposed to the law governing the treatment of war victims.

In practice, the ICRC is the active and decisive international organ of the International Red Cross movement for the recognition of new National Societies. It also plays a prominent part in the preparation for, and work at, the international conferences of the Red Cross. These conferences are now governed by statutes adopted at the Hague in 1928 and revised at Toronto in 1952. Such conferences are the sole bodies competent to amend the statutes in their present form.[17] The conference is "the supreme deliberative body of the International Red Cross."[18] It is to meet normally every four years. In the interim, according to article 10, the body known as the Standing Commission[19]

16. *Ibid.*, p. 322.
17. Article 11(4), *ibid.*, p. 306.
18. Statutes, article 1(2), *ibid.*, p. 305.
19. Article 10(2), *ibid.*, p. 310.

"shall take any measures which circumstances demand" but "subject, where necessary, to final decision by the (international) Conference."[20]

THE PRC AND THE STATUTES

The provision in the statutes of the conference that has been of central interest to the PRC and its National Society has been article 1(2) controlling the composition of the conference. It is in the meaning and application of this provision that the main difficulties have arisen between the International Red Cross movement and the PRC. This provision states: "The International Conference of the Red Cross shall be composed of delegations of duly recognized National Red Cross, Red Crescent, and Red Lion and Sun Societies, delegations of the States parties to the (*participant aux*) Geneva Conventions and delegations of the ICRC and of the League of Red Cross Societies."[21] The rules of procedure of the conference, which are subordinate instruments, slightly expand article 1(2) of the conference statutes in one direction and slightly contract them in another. The legal effect of either operation is open to doubt. The rules of procedure, article 1, refer to "the right to take part in all discussions and to vote" at a conference of, inter alia, "the delegates of the States parties to the Geneva Convention for the Amelioration of the Condition of the Wounded and Sick in Armed Forces in the Field (1864, 1906, 1929 or 1949)."[22]

It is around these provisions that the debates about the designation, presence, and participation of the PRC and the Republic of China at Red Cross international conferences have centered. The obscurity of the language employed and the uncertainty involved in the relationship of the statutes of the conference to the rules of procedure have done little to reduce the acrimony of debates heightened by those political considerations which the statutes required to be excluded from the work of a conference. Article 1(5) of the statutes stipulates: "It [the conference] may not deal with political matters nor serve as a forum for political debate."[23] It is the misfortune of the International Red Cross movement, which is committed to the exclusion of political considerations, that the statutes governing its supreme body, the Inter-

20. *Ibid.*, p. 310.
21. *Ibid.*, p. 305.
22. *Ibid.*, p. 312.
23. *Ibid.*, 306.

national Conference, are so framed that, in the context of China, those political issues come into play *in limine*. Determining the right to participate in such a conference requires an initial decision by the conference that gives rise to political disagreement. The matter is not eased by the constitutional position that the statutes of the conference may be amended only by a two-thirds majority of the members of the conference, present and voting.[24] The difficulty is thus circuitous and lends itself to no cure beyond that of goodwill, which heretofore has not been conspicuous.

The first international conference of the Red Cross in which the PRC participated was the eighteenth, at Toronto in 1952. It was during this conference that the statutes and rules of procedure for the conference that are now in force were established at a joint session of the Council of Delegates and the Board of Governors of the League. At such sessions, governments are not represented. Thus the Chinese Red Cross Society was able to take part in the debates that settled the part of the statutes and rules of procedure that controlled participation in, and composition of, the international conference. Although the statutes of the International Red Cross control the functions and composition of the international conference, governments, though participants as of right at such conferences, had no say in the revision of the statutes which conferred that right upon them. On the other hand, in the revision of the statutes as they now stand, governments are entitled to debate and to vote.

The time factor has played an important part in the relations between the PRC and the Red Cross. During the closing months of the armed struggle between the Kuomintang and the Communist forces of Mao Tse-tung in the first half of 1949, the diplomatic conference in Geneva, which established the texts of the four Geneva Conventions, was in progress. At that conference, a delegate of the Nationalist Chinese participated and, on August 12, 1949, signed the conventions on behalf of his government. The government of the PRC was established on October 1, 1949. The four Geneva Conventions were ratified by the PRC on December 28, 1956, subject to the identical reservations made by the USSR and other Communist states upon signature of the conventions on August 12, 1949.

The Korean conflict began on June 25, 1950, at a time when the Geneva Conventions of 1949 had not yet come into operation. By the

24. Article 13(2), *ibid.*, p. 311.

date of the Panmunjom Armistice Agreement of July 27, 1953, to which the commander of the Chinese People's Volunteers was a party, the PRC had not ratified the four Geneva Conventions of 1949, which the previous Chinese government had signed. Thus, when the Chinese People's Volunteers were taking part in the Korean conflict—from November 5, 1950, to July 1953—the Geneva Conventions of 1949 were not de jure applicable, whatever may have been the de facto position by virtue of various declarations made by the parties to that conflict.[25] This legal situation was quite apart from the questions whether the PRC was a party to the Korean conflict, and the nature of that conflict. However, it is apparent that sometime between April 28 and November 8, 1950, the PRC National Red Cross Society had been accepted as the only National Red Cross Society of China, both by the ICRC and the League of Red Cross Societies.

It would seem that the original recognition of a Chinese National Red Cross Society in 1912 remained unaffected by all the catastrophic events in China which occurred between 1912 and 1949. All that happened after 1949 was that the Chinese National Red Cross was able to convince the ICRC and the League of Red Cross Societies that it had changed its personnel after October 1, 1949, and was able to function as the one National Red Cross Society in China. Certainly, for all international Red Cross transactions, whether with the ICRC or the league or international conferences of the Red Cross, the PRC National Red Cross Society was accepted as the sole Chinese Red Cross Society organized and functioning in a manner that met the requirements of the International Red Cross regulations dealing with recognition of National Societies.

The first recorded international meeting of a Red Cross organ in which the PRC National Society participated would appear to be a meeting of the League of Red Cross Societies' Board of Governors, which met at Monte Carlo October 16–20, 1950. At that meeting, Madame Li Te-ch'üan represented the PRC National Red Cross Society and introduced that organization as "the Red Cross of New China."[26]

25. The Democratic Republic of Korea "recognized" the Geneva Prisoner of War (POW) Convention, 1949, as applicable to the Korean conflict, *The New York Times* (July 14, 1950), p. 1. The PRC did the same, but considerably later, *The New York Times* (July 17, 1952), p. 1. The UN Command so declared at the outset of the hostilities; U.N. Doc. S/1834, p. 5.

26. Board of Governors of the League of Red Cross Societies *Proceedings*, 21st Meeting (Monte Carlo, October 16–20, 1950), p. 15.

Its recognition may be said to have been beyond challenge from that time.

RELATIONS BETWEEN THE INTERNATIONAL RED CROSS AND THE PRC AND ITS NATIONAL SOCIETY

According to article 5(1) of its statutes, the ICRC is supposed "to maintain close relations with the National Red Cross Societies. . ."[27] The ICRC seems to have been punctilious in the discharge of this obligation. In its *Report on General Activities* for the year 1949, it stated: "The former London Delegate (of the ICRC) . . . was instructed to make contact with the two Chinese Governments. On his arrival at Hong Kong in January, 1949, he conferred with the Director of the Press Agency of the PRC."[28] He was reported cooperating with the then Chinese Red Cross of the Nationalist government and distributing relief to various hospitals in the territory of the Chinese People's Government. Manifestly at that time, there was no National Red Cross Society of China other than that depending on and operating in the territory of the Nationalist government. The principle of impartiality controlling all Red Cross humanitarian relief activities was shown in that "relief sent in response to a Chinese Red Cross appeal at the beginning of 1949, to the League of Red Cross Societies, has been distributed equally by the ICRC between the two parties in conflict."[29] In August 1949, the diplomatic conference at Geneva came to a successful conclusion with the formulation of the four Geneva Conventions of 1949, probably the most important landmark in the development of international humanitarian law since 1929. In this work, the PRC and its National Society had no part, as neither had been established at that time. It was unfortunate that the first major contact between the PRC and the ICRC occurred during the Korean conflict. By the time that the Chinese People's Volunteers had become a party to that conflict in the fall of 1950, the states of the world had already been divided in their recognition or nonrecognition of the government of the PRC. The Geneva Conventions of 1949 had not yet become binding upon any state with armed forces participating in that conflict. The United Nations Organization had not then, and has not since, acceded to these conventions.

27. *Handbook*, p. 322.
28. *Ibid.*, p. 91.
29. *Ibid.*, p. 91.

The UN "presence" in the Korean conflict, whatever its legal bases, accentuated the difficulties of the ICRC in seeking to carry out its international humanitarian role for the benefit of the victims of that conflict. The failure of the PRC to secure the seating of its representatives in any organ of the United Nations must be seen as the controlling factor behind most of the difficulties experienced by the ICRC in its dealings with the PRC both at the time of the Korean conflict and thereafter. Although the ICRC is a nongovernmental international organization, it has been an inevitable, albeit indirect, casualty, in terms of its humanitarian tasks and relationships, of the failure of the PRC to secure seating in the organs of the UN and its specialized agencies. Professor Hungdah Chiu has shown that the initial enthusiasm of the Chinese Communists for UN participation expressed through Mao Tse-tung met a severe rebuff when their attempts to dislodge the Nationalist delegates in Taiwan proved abortive.[30] Through the ensuing years, 1950 to 1952, the Peking government addressed communications to a number of specialized agencies demanding the expulsion of the Nationalist delegates and the seating of the PRC delegates. Among the organizations so addressed was the ICRC, on April 28, 1950, i.e., before the outbreak of the Korean conflict. On that date, Chou En-lai, the Foreign Minister of the PRC, addressed the following cable to the ICRC:

> The Central Government of the PRC is the sole legal Government representing the Chinese People. On behalf of the PRC's Central Government I now notify you no longer to accord formal recognition to the so-called "representatives" of the KMT reactionary clique, who are completely without qualification to participate in the ICRC or to be present at its various discussions. I would be grateful if you would immediately expel them from the ICRC and communicate this to the organs of the ICRC and related bodies.[31]

It is reasonably apparent from the text of this cable, in spite of its indifferent translation, that the PRC government had only a limited understanding and appreciation of the elaborate structure of the International Red Cross. It looks as if the Chinese leaders shared the common error of equating the ICRC with the International Red Cross—the ICRC is but a part of it. There could be no participation by the

30. Hungdah Chiu, "Communist China's Attitude towards the U.N.," *AJIL* 62:20 (1968).
31. *WCC 1949–1950*, vol. I (1957), p. 113, cited in Chiu, "Communist China's Attitude," p. 23, n. 6.

delegates of any government in the functions of the ICRC itself, a non-governmental body confined by its statutes to a membership of not more than twenty-five Swiss nationals. More probably Chou En-lai meant the International Red Cross comprising the ICRC, the League, and the National Societies.

The Korean Conflict

On the day after the Korean hostilities began on June 25, 1950, the ICRC addressed cables to the North and South Korean governments in which it offered its humanitarian services on strictly neutral and non-political terms.[32] Article 3, common to all the Geneva Conventions of 1949, provided expressly for such an offer. The fact that the conventions were not in force did not inhibit the ICRC in this regard. Indeed, it pointed this out in its cables. Somewhat hopefully, as events transpired, the ICRC expressed the view that the fact that Korea was not a party to the Geneva Conventions in no way inhibited the de facto application of their humanitarian principles to the victims of the conflict. Accordingly, the ICRC declared itself ready to send delegates to each government with a view to examining the conditions under which the principles of the conventions could be given practical effect. This act may be considered optimistic when two factors are recalled. First, the conventions were not yet in operation among any states. Second, the common article 3 in the Geneva Conventions was the first attempt in the long series of conventions governing the law of war, including the Geneva Conventions from 1864 onward, to regulate in any way the conduct of internal hostilities. Not surprisingly, it proved the most difficult of all the provisions in the Geneva Conventions of 1949 upon which to secure agreement. Some twenty-five meetings of the relevant committee of the diplomatic conference at Geneva were needed to establish the article in the form in which we now have it.[33] The acceptance by governments of international legal restrictions binding upon them in their handling of rebellions is an extremely sensitive matter. Moreover, the ambitious endeavor to impose legal humanitarian obligations upon the insurgent party, not a party to the conventions and not even in existence at the time of their conclusion, is exceeded

32. *Recueil,* I, 4 and 6, nos. 1 and 3.

33. For a summary of the transactions leading to the establishment of the common article 3, see *Commentary* I: 43–48.

only by the practical difficulties in securing the observance of such a provision.

The participation of the United Nations, by the device of placing national contingents under a United Nations unified command entrusted to the US, may have lifted the conflict out of the possible ambit of the article 3 internal conflict envisaged in the Geneva Conventions. The ICRC seems, in the main, to have treated the Korean conflict as an international conflict in which the various states providing armed forces, whether to the UN unified command or by way of the Chinese People's Volunteers assisting the North Korean forces as from the fall of 1950, were de facto required to apply the Geneva Conventions of 1949. This demand also was ambitious in that the various states concerned made separate and conflicting unilateral declarations about the applicability and application of the Geneva Conventions of 1949.

The initial transaction between the ICRC and the PRC was a long and protracted endeavor by the ICRC to secure the passage of its delegate to North Korea through Chinese territory.[34] In the main, the transaction consists of a series of telegrams from the ICRC to the Peking government requesting a transit visa for the ICRC delegate and permission for him to enter and cross Chinese territory into North Korea. The initial Chinese attitude was that such permission could not be granted without the consent of the North Korean government. As a result of the good offices of the government of India, the ICRC delegate was able to arrive at Tientsin from Hong Kong on August 10, 1950, but the permission to enter North Korea was not forthcoming, and the ICRC delegate left Chinese territory because permission to stay there had a strict time limit. No delegate of the ICRC was able to secure a presence on North Korean territory at any time during the Korean conflict.[35]

In the specific endeavor of the ICRC to secure the presence of its delegate on North Korean territory, entering by way of China, the

34. The ICRC has published the documents of this transaction in the *Recueil*, volume I, numbers 119–150. The decision to publish was the outcome of ICRC frustration and of the marked failure of North Korea and the PRC to cooperate with it.

35. The fact that the ICRC was unable to go to North Korea during the conflict, combined with the scale of the hostilities and the extent of the suffering, led the ICRC to inform the various governments and other authorities concerned of its intention to publish the documents comprised in the two volumes of the *Recueil*. See the *Recueil* Introduction.

PRC, though dilatory and procrastinating in the granting of the transit visa, did eventually grant that permission. The eventual expiration of the transit visa issued by the PRC was attributed by its government to the refusal of the North Korean government to allow the delegate to enter Korean territory. In the absence of proof of lack of good faith by the Chinese government, e.g., in urging the North Korean government to deny access to the ICRC delegate, it is impossible to condemn the PRC authorities for more than delaying conduct. As a matter of law, they were not obliged to allow the ICRC delegate to enter or traverse their territory. They were fully entitled to decide the length of his visit. The communications that passed between the North Korean and PRC authorities, if they exist, are not available.[36]

The more serious engagement between the ICRC and the PRC arose after the participation of the Chinese People's Volunteers in the conflict. During this participation, the PRC was not bound by the Geneva Conventions of 1949. Moreover, the PRC government had no hand in the diplomatic conference at Geneva in 1949 or in the signing of the conventions there concluded. However, there is nothing anomalous in a state's changing government between the dates of signing and ratifying a treaty. In the phase of the Korean conflict before the entry of the Chinese People's Volunteers, the relationship between the PRC and the ICRC was marked by gross discourtesy and almost complete refusal to cooperate on the part of the Chinese government, rather than by conduct that could properly be considered a violation of international law. Following the entry of Chinese forces, the legal situation may have become different in that the PRC, under the guise of sending Chinese People's Volunteers to assist the North Korean armed forces in the conflict, had become a party to that conflict.

On July 3, 1951, the ICRC sent a telegram to the commanders of all forces engaged in the conflict, including the commander of the Chinese People's Volunteers, expressing the hope that it would be allowed to carry out its humanitarian tasks under the Geneva Conventions, particularly visiting prisoner of war (POW) and civilian detention camps on both sides and delivering necessary medicaments

36. For a summary of the lengthy and abortive transactions designed to secure the transit of the ICRC delegate through the territory of the PRC into North Korea, see Report of ICRC on General Activities, Jan. 1 to Dec. 31, 1950, pp. 80–84.

that had been stored in Hong Kong for some time.[37] No reply came from the PRC.

On August 6, 1951, a further and longer telegram was despatched by the ICRC to the commanders of the North Korean and Chinese Volunteer forces. This cable recapitulated the frustration experienced by the ICRC at the hands of those commanders. It recited, inter alia:

> During the 13 months of the Korean war and up to now we have been able under the Third Geneva (POW) Convention to forward to the North Korean Government names of some 163,559 prisoners held by the U.N. Forces, this figure comprising names of 14,347 Chinese volunteers, while only 110 U.N. prisoners held by the Forces of the People's Democratic Republic of Korea have been officially notified to Geneva . . . The ICRC has constantly offered to contact regularly through its delegates all POW. Whilst able to work in this respect in South Korea it regretfully states that it has not been enabled to do so in respect of POW held by the North Korean authorities who have not so far admitted our impartial delegates. Moreover, all our endeavours to convey medical supplies for sick and wounded of the forces, for prisoners and civilian war victims in North Korea have so far failed, but we recall that the stocks earmarked for such purposes and part of which are in Hong Kong remain available, as well as food parcels for POW. For this we have been pleading for a year in the spirit of the Red Cross . . . Therefore, whatever delay the settlement of other issues may involve, we hope no further obstacles will be opposed to the establishment of necessary personal contacts in the spirit of the Third (POW) Geneva Convention between our delegates and the prisoners whom they have been so far debarred from visiting.[38]

This cable was typical of the stream of communications that passed from the ICRC to the commanders of the North Korean forces and of the Chinese Volunteers and to the two governments concerned. The ICRC's appeal was not accepted, and its frustration mounted. Such obstruction by silence and disregard as occurred in the years 1951–1952 was, for the organization, a relative novelty in its traditional humanitarian service in time of armed conflict. In the years that have intervened since the Korean conflict, this negative response to the ICRC's humanitarian appeal can, regrettably, no longer be considered either novel or exceptional.

The published correspondence of the ICRC in the early months of 1951 shows repeated humanitarian appeals to the PRC government and its Red Cross Society for the admission of ICRC delegates to visit camps and distribute relief and for the return of information

37. *Recueil*, I, 41, no. 53.
38. *Ibid.*, p. 42, no. 55.

about POWs and civilian detainees in the hands of the Chinese and North Korean authorities. In a reply to the repeated demands of the ICRC to secure the transit passage of its delegate through Chinese territory to North Korea, the PRC Foreign Minister, Chou En-lai, stated on January 15, 1951: "The . . . Government of the PRC is in no position to give any consideration to the question of the transit of your mission through China to the Korean . . . Republic before the said mission has secured the consent and authorization of the Korean . . . Republic regarding its entry into Korea."[39] Attempts by the ICRC to secure the delivery of medicine received no better response from the PRC Red Cross Society. On April 1951, Madame Li Te-ch'üan, president of that society, cabled the ICRC: "Before ICRC and the Red Cross of the Korean . . . Republic reach an agreement we are not in a position to consider forwarding your medical consignments."[40]

Relations between the ICRC and the PRC Red Cross Society seem to have deteriorated rapidly during the second half of 1951. The ICRC had sought to secure the services of the PRC Red Cross Society in Korea, by reason of the noncooperation of the Korean authorities, both governmental and Red Cross. The ICRC, perhaps prematurely, had assumed that the PRC Red Cross would be willing to undertake that role. This led to an angry denial by the PRC Red Cross on July 11, 1951, and a demand that this denial be published in the ICRC *Review* and *Bulletin*.[41] The ICRC's July 27, 1951, reply to the PRC Red Cross, after repeating the evidence upon which the ICRC had relied for the offer of cooperation by the PRC Red Cross, contained the following passage:

> I cannot therefore refrain from expressing our great disappointment. Nevertheless the ICRC still hopes and expects that in accordance with the Geneva Conventions, ways and means will at last be found, even though only after more than a year of warfare, to convey the required assistance provided for under the Geneva Conventions, to the victims of hostilities in North Korea, among whom there are also wounded Chinese Volunteers. According to your wish your statement will be published, together with my reply, in the *Review* . . . as soon as you have confirmed your agreement to this procedure. I take this opportunity of informing you furthermore that the ICRC feels the time has come to publish shortly a volume containing a full record of the steps taken, and the cables and memoranda sent to the belligerent Powers engaged in the Korean conflict.[42]

39. *Ibid.*, p. 60, no. 78.
40. *Ibid.*, p. 65, no. 85.
41. *Ibid.*, p. 68, no. 90.
42. *Ibid.*, p. 69, no. 91.

The ICRC's patience, which the correspondence shows to have been extraordinary, was reaching the point of exhaustion. No reply seems to have been received to the last cited ICRC communication, and in due course the two volumes of communications were published by the ICRC.

On November 23, 1951, acting on information received from the US Consul-General in Geneva on November 16, the ICRC sent a telegram to the PRC Red Cross Society. The telegram referred to broadcasts in English from Peking stating "the Red Cross Society of China has lodged a strong protest against the bombing of POW camps by an American plane in North Korea on 13th October." The ICRC asked for locations of POW camps and their identification marks, as required by article 23(3) and (4) of the Geneva (POW) Convention of 1949.[43] No reply was received.

On December 10, 1951, the ICRC informed the PRC Red Cross that it had at its disposal quantities of food and medicine parcels prepared by the American Red Cross for American POW in Korea. The ICRC asked the PRC Red Cross, as requested by the American Red Cross, "to investigate means of having these parcels distributed to their addresses . . . (and) for any advice it may be able to give on this subject."[44] No answer was received.

In the year 1952, relations between the ICRC and the PRC Red Cross deteriorated still further. The posture of the PRC Red Cross shifted from procrastination and failures to reply to direct attacks on the good faith and integrity of the ICRC. The ICRC had taken certain initiatives, through its delegate, to approach the Chinese and North Korean commanders about the manner in which the ICRC might assist after the armistice in the arrangements for the repatriation of POW. The proposal made by the North Korean commanders was that once the armistice had been signed, joint delegations composed of the ICRC, North Korean, and PRC Red Cross personnel should visit POW camps on both sides to collaborate in repatriation activities.[45] To this the ICRC replied that it was prepared to help before and after the signing of the armistice provided that the joint commissions of the Red Cross Societies had representatives of all parties to the conflict.[46] This proposal of the ICRC never received a reply.

43. *Ibid.*, p. 175, nos. 235 and 236.
44. *Ibid.*, p. 210, no. 290.
45. *Recueil*, II, 9, no. 318.
46. *Ibid.*, p. 11, no. 320.

In the New China News Agency release of January 19, 1952, it was stated, inter alia, that Dr. Lehner, the ICRC delegate entrusted with the approach to the commanders of the North Korean and Chinese Volunteers about repatriation,

> spent war years in Berlin and lent his service to Hitler by visiting Theresienstadt Concentration Camp . . . After this his Red Cross issued a scandalous report describing pleasures and benefits of life in Hitler's concentration camps. Lehner is now here for what he describes as "non-political" motives which seem to coincide sufficiently with those of Americans for them to provide helicopters and other facilities and break the neutrality agreement [by bringing him into the Panmunjom neutral area]. His assistance to Hitler was also "non-political."

The ICRC defended its delegate in a communication of February 5, 1952, to the president of the PRC Red Cross Society:

> We were extremely surprised at the comments made about the head of our Delegation in Korea by Mr. Winnington and broadcast by Radio Peking . . . The insinuation that Dr. Lehner failed to observe absolute impartiality while on mission in Germany is completely unfounded. In his capacity as Delegate of the ICRC in Berlin during the Second World War Dr. Lehner's essential task was to protect war victims and especially allied POW. To throw doubt on the impartiality with which he carried out this duty is not only to accuse him unjustly, but also to do real harm to the Red Cross movement throughout the world as a whole, since its action can only be effective if its impartiality is recognized. It is realized that the Radio and Press are free in all democratic countries. Nevertheless, in the present instance, we should be obliged if you would kindly draw the attention of those in charge of Radio Peking to the grievous mistake which has been made . . . We know that you will not fail to give us your help and support in this matter and so defend a cause which is not so much that of the International Committee as of the Red Cross movement as a whole.[47]

On March 5, 1952, the ICRC found it necessary to remind the two Communist commanders in North Korea that their apparent confusion of the ICRC with the UN was erroneous. It took the occasion, while

47. *Ibid.*, p. 10, no. 319. The ICRC recited the New China News Agency release dated January 19, 1952, published in Hong Kong, in their letter to the PRC Red Cross of Feb. 5, 1952. No reply has ever been received by the ICRC to their letter. Mr. Winnington, a UK national, was the correspondent of the UK daily newspaper, *The Daily Worker*, at the time of the Korean conflict. He was particularly active at this time in North Korea, being one of the few correspondents who was in a position to procure details of British POW held by the Democratic Republic of Korea. This information, not available to the ICRC, considerably increased the circulation of *The Daily Worker* in the UK. Mr. Winnington's activities in Korea attracted considerable interest in Parliament and were the subject matter of parliamentary questions to Ministers of the Crown.

pointing out the distinction, to give a brief excursus into the history of the ICRC and its functions and to try to convince the two commanders that the role of the ICRC between two belligerents was as impartial during the current events in Korea as it was in 1870 and thereafter. It asked the two commanders to reconsider their attitude to the ICRC and to allow it to carry out its humanitarian functions in their territory.[48]

By March 11, 1952, it would appear that Mr. Winnington, the pro-Communist propagandist, had been active again. He was reported as stating: "As far as this side [North Korea and the PRC] is concerned, if the International Red Cross is willing to allow 44,000 names it compiled as POWs to be wiped off its own lists by Americans without raising any protests, they are not regarded as entirely reliable to protect the interests of this side's POWs without some other check." This serious allegation was categorically denied by the ICRC in its reply to the president of the PRC Red Cross on March 11, 1952: "Accordingly, there has never been any question of the International Committee eliminating the names of 44,000 POW from lists."[49] Apparently Mr. Winnington was no better informed of the activities of the ICRC than he was of its structure and functions. However, his activities must not be dismissed as of no importance. The systematic attack upon the impartiality and trustworthiness of the ICRC played a role in undermining the mission of that body to a degree to which it is still the victim. Doubtless Mr. Winnington realized that if he could spread doubts about the impartiality and good faith of the ICRC it would be rendered inoperative not only in the Korean conflict but elsewhere. His work was not badly done.

Earlier, on December 12, 1951, the PRC Red Cross had taken a fresh initiative by informing the ICRC of atrocities alleged to have been committed by the American armed forces in Korea. The PRC Red Cross Society had first moved these allegations at a meeting of the executive committee of the League of Red Cross Societies held on December 6. At that meeting, the general allegation, of which the president of the PRC Red Cross gave details in support, was that "the US armed forces in Korea are bombing and shelling day and night indiscriminately cities and villages, which have no military objectives at all, slaughtering the peaceful inhabitants, including women, chil-

48. *Ibid.*, p. 13, no. 322.
49. *Ibid.*, p. 15, no. 325.

dren, the aged and invalids, massacring the POW on a large scale, and successively resorting to the use of poisonous gas." This allegation was followed by a demand from the PRC Red Cross that "the ICRC will adopt effective measures to halt these atrocities which are seriously against the Red Cross principles of peace and humanitarianism." In the list of actions by the International Red Cross movement that the PRC Red Cross considered appropriate there was one omission. In the same speech before the executive committee of the League, the president of the PRC Red Cross Society accused the US armed forces of using poisonous gas shells in Korea, repeating the text of a telegram dated August 11, 1951. She concluded her allegations with the following remarks: "But the most unpardonable inhuman crime is that the American Armed Forces is going to use more than 1000 POW in the experiment of atomic bombs. This is indeed the atrocity unprecedented in the human history."[50] There was at no time any suggestion that an impartial body should investigate the truth of these allegations and report to the Red Cross or governments, or both, the outcome of their findings.

When the American armed forces were accused of using chemical weapons against their opponents, they categorically denied the allegation and asked the ICRC to open an inquiry into it.[51] The ICRC had on November 23, 1951, reminded all governments and National Red Cross Societies that its powers to hold such an inquiry must, as a matter of law and good sense, stem either from a convention or from an agreed mandate from the parties concerned.[52] On March 12, 1952, the ICRC informed the North Korean and Chinese Volunteers commanders that it proposed to set up a commission under its direction composed of people with the requisite integrity and scientific knowledge to investigate the Chinese allegations.[53] The proposal was accepted by the US government on March 14, two days after it was made.[54] No response was made to this proposal by the Chinese or North Korean authorities at any time and the project necessarily was aborted. Preparations already made for the commission were abandoned. Such response as there was took the then standard pattern: abuse of the ICRC. On March 28, 1952, the ICRC informed the PRC

50. *Ibid.*, p. 79, no. 394.
51. *Ibid.*, p. 89, no. 406.
52. *Recueil*, I, 222, no. 315.
53. *Recueil*, II, 89–91, nos. 407, 408.
54. *Ibid.*, p. 96, no. 418.

Red Cross by telegram: "Radio Peking . . . has once again launched violently offensive attacks against the ICRC. Moreover position attributed to ICRC absolutely contrary to facts . . . Now in view of these new and unjustifiable attacks I request you again as President Chinese Red Cross to take steps to have . . . Radio Peking rectify errors and cease attacks which are outrage to ICRC and injure work of whole Red Cross."[55] Getting no response, on March 31, 1952, the ICRC repeated to the PRC Legation in Geneva its request for a rejection of attacks upon itself by Chinese agencies.[56] It received the following reply from that legation, dated April 3, 1952: "We regret to inform you that we are not in a position to transmit the copy of the telegram annexed to your letter of 31st March . . . We therefore return herewith the said copy."[57]

The remaining transactions of importance between the ICRC and the PRC and its Red Cross were those concerning the repatriation of POW. The long negotiations that led up to the eventual signing of the armistice at Panmunjom on July 27, 1953, were chiefly concerned with the bitterly contested issue of the repatriation of the large numbers of North Korean POW in the hands of the UN "unified command." In fact, those North Korean POW were detained by the US armed forces. Article 111 of the Armistice Agreement of July 27, 1953, dealt with "arrangements relating to prisoners of war." The role to be carried out by the Red Cross under this provision was entrusted to the National Red Cross Societies of those states contributing forces to the UN command and to the North Korean and PRC Red Cross Societies, and, in the case of certain special roles concerning the Neutral Nations Repatriation Commission, to the Indian Red Cross Society.[58] The ICRC is not mentioned in any provision of the Armistice Agreement.

The negotiations for the armistice exposed certain defects in article 118 of the Geneva (POW) Convention of 1949,[59] which failed to cover the Korean situation in which large numbers of North Korean POW refused to be repatriated to North Korea. Forcible repatriation was out of the question as an acceptable interpretation of a humanitarian convention. To the extent that the convention was silent or ambiguous

55. *Ibid.*, p. 102, no. 426.
56. *Ibid.*, p. 103, no. 428.
57. *Ibid.*, p. 104, no. 429.
58. The Korean Armistice Agreement, U.N. Doc. S/3079, August 7, 1953.
59. This article provided that POW should be "released and repatriated without delay after the cessation of active hostilities," and that, failing such a provision in the armistice, each Detaining Power must establish and execute without delay a unilateral plan of repatriation. *UNTS* 75:224 (1950).

about compulsory repatriation, the customary law based on belligerent practice came into play. This did not sanction compulsory repatriation of POW.[60] Rather than look to the ICRC for a solution, the Neutral Nations Repatriation Commission was created. In the light of the published transactions between the ICRC and the PRC and the Chinese Red Cross Society during the years of the conflict, it is not surprising that the ICRC had no role to play under the terms of the armistice that ultimately brought that conflict to a close.

The Tibetan Struggle, 1958–1959

The activities of the International Red Cross in relation to the Tibetan situation have, due to the nature of the situation, been minimal. Tibet never had a National Red Cross Society. Under the "17-Point" Agreement of May 23, 1951, between the Central People's Government of the PRC and the local government of Tibet, Tibet was stated to be an integral part of the state territory of China enjoying "national regional autonomy under the unified leadership of the Central People's Government."[61]

Documentary evidence of the transactions between the ICRC and the PRC relating to Tibet is not available. What is known is that from time to time the ICRC has offered its humanitarian services on the basis that an internal conflict, as defined in article 3 of the four Geneva Conventions of 1949, is in progress in Tibet. It is understood that the replies of the PRC are not couched in diplomatic language, deny the existence of any such conflict, and claim that the PRC government is dealing with criminal elements that are not within the protection of the Geneva Conventions and are not the concern of the ICRC.

The Sino-Indian Conflict, 1962–1963

Almost immediately after the armed conflict in the Himalayas broke out in October 1962 between India and the PRC, the ICRC sent cables

60. In spite of the literal wording of the provision the UN considered that forcible repatriation of POW could not be considered mandatory under a humanitarian convention. Further, the sequence of the words "released and repatriated" was not consistent with forcible repatriation in that once a POW was released he was not available for compulsory movement in any direction. For a useful collection of articles written on this subject, see H. Levie, *AJIL* 50:897 (1956), and R. Baxter, *BYBIL* 30:489–498 (1953).

61. *The Question of Tibet and the Rule of Law* (Geneva: International Commission of Jurists, 1959), p. 139, Doc. No. 10.

to New Delhi and Peking offering its humanitarian services to the National Red Cross Societies of both countries. By then both states were parties to the Geneva Conventions of 1949 and the conflict was international in character, for the purposes of article 2 of those conventions.

The Indian government allowed the ICRC delegation to function at once on Indian territory. The PRC Red Cross Society sent a number of food and clothing parcels for the benefit of the Chinese civilians detained in India, and these were transmitted to their destination through the ICRC.

A different situation arose with regard to the approximately 4,000 Indian POW in the hands of the PRC authorities. The ICRC requested permission from the Chinese government to send a delegate to visit Indian POW, in accordance with the provisions of the Geneva (POW) Convention of 1949.[62] The Chinese reply was not favorable; it urged that such ICRC action was unnecessary since the two countries in conflict maintained normal diplomatic relations. It is not altogether clear what the PRC had in mind in this reply. It is probable that their attention had been directed to the reservation, made on their ratification, to article 10 of the POW Convention. This reservation indicated that the PRC "would not recognize as valid a request by the Detaining Power of POW to a neutral state or to a humanitarian organization, to undertake the functions which should be performed by a Protecting Power, unless the consent has been obtained of the Government of the State of which the POW are nationals." The PRC took the view that the existence of diplomatic relations between itself and India rendered the activities of a Protecting Power unnecessary. In its view, article 126 of the Geneva (POW) Convention, 1949, pertaining to visits to POW did not apply to the ICRC. That article stipulates that the appointment of ICRC delegates must be submitted to the approval of the power detaining the POW to be visited. It is clear that the PRC was not prepared to accept the presence of ICRC delegates on Chinese soil in any circumstances. In this refusal, the PRC has been consistent until the present time.

The ICRC asked the Chinese Foreign Minister, Ch'en Yi, to allow an ICRC delegate to visit the Indian POW in China in accordance with the Geneva (POW) Convention. On February 18, 1963, the Foreign Minister replied, informing the ICRC of the various measures of

62. *ICRC Annual Report* (1962), pp. 22, 23.

good treatment accorded the Indian prisoners by Chinese authorities. He protested against the internment of Chinese civilians in India and stated that all questions about the Indian POW could be settle directly between the two countries. The maintenance of diplomatic relations, however, did not in fact enable Indian embassy officials in Peking to visit the Indian POW. India at the same time barred Chinese embassy officials in India from visiting interned Chinese civilians. Finally, on April 2, 1963, the ICRC was told by the PRC Red Cross that repatriation of all Indian POW held by the Chinese authorities was imminent. The repatriation was carried out in stages. The ICRC delegate did visit Chinese civilians detained in India,[63] as the contribution to this volume by Professors Cohen and Leng makes clear.

It would appear from the evidence available that the PRC was determined that no ICRC delegate should be allowed on Chinese soil. It must be appreciated that by that time, 1963, the PRC and its Red Cross Society had attended two international conferences of the Red Cross, the eighteenth at Toronto in 1952 and the nineteenth at New Delhi in 1957. Neither of these occasions improved relations between the ICRC or the League and the PRC. Indeed, the PRC has not attended another Red Cross international conference since the one in New Delhi, although it participated in the centenary congress of the Council of Delegates in 1963 and in the meeting of the executive committee of the League of Red Cross Societies in October 1966.

THE EIGHTEENTH INTERNATIONAL CONFERENCE OF THE RED CROSS, TORONTO, 1952

The Eighteenth International Conference, the first of such conferences in which the PRC and its Red Cross Society participated, took place during the Korean conflict. That fact was hardly propitious. The exchanges that had taken place between the ICRC and the PRC and its Red Cross Society mentioned above did not assist in making the conference a practical expression to the world of Red Cross principles in action. The factor that proved the most decisive in debate was the presence of the governmental delegation from Nationalist China. That presence in itself spelled out the clear rejection of the application made by Chou En-lai to the ICRC in his telegram of April 28, 1950, which had demanded the expulsion of the Chinese Nationalists.[64]

63. *ICRC Annual Report* (1963), pp. 26, 27.
64. See n. 31, above.

Also germane to the difficulties that were experienced at the conference was the fact that the statutes governing the conference were themselves under revision at that conference. The failure to revise the operative article 1(2) at the Toronto conference had a direct and disastrous impact at the next international conference held at New Delhi in 1957. The text of the controlling article 1(2) of the statutes of the International Red Cross emerged untouched from the revision of the statutes carried out by a legal subcommittee of the general commission and adopted at a joint meeting of the League and the Board of Governors during the Toronto conference. Article 1(2) read, and still reads: "The International Conference of the Red Cross shall be composed of delegations of duly recognized Red Cross, etc., Societies, delegations of the States parties to the Geneva Conventions."[65] It was therefore a text which the PRC and its Red Cross Society had the opportunity to express their views and to vote in the general commission of the conference. The PRC governmental delegation would not have been entitled to participate in the joint session of the League and of the Board of Governors, as states are not members of these two international Red Cross organs. However, the PRC delegation had participated in the debates and voting in the general commission.

The record of the plenary session of the international conference makes it clear that the PRC Red Cross was much opposed to the text of the statutes as it emerged from the revision. Its objection, not expressed in the record of the plenary session, is not difficult to discern. The phrase "delegations of the states parties to," found in article 1(2) of those statutes, enabled both Chinese (PRC and Nationalist) governmental delegations to participate at the international conference as of right unless the conference was to adjudicate upon the issue whether one or both of the two delegations physically before it were delegations of China. The method of convening the conference effectively precluded any such determination. It was not possible to exclude either party

65. *Handbook*, p. 305. The previous article of the pre-1952 statutes of the International Red Cross was identical. However adequate for the situation prevailing in 1928, when the previous statutes had been formulated, it was not a provision which resolved the difficult question of participation of the governmental delegations of the PRC and the ROC in the post-1949 period. In retrospect, those entrusted with the revision of the 1928 statutes in 1952 were not percipient of the difficulties that would be encountered at the very first International Red Cross Conference after 1949, when both the PRC and the ROC would probably send delegations. In the result, since 1957, such conferences take place without the participation of the governmental and Red Cross delegations of the PRC. Their presence is not denied by the conveners, but they decline to attend.

without doing violence to the language of the controlling provision. This meant that an international conference of the Red Cross is always to be confronted at the outset by the "two Chinas" situation unless either government elects to be absent.

This situation remains unchanged as of 1972, and, indeed, cannot be remedied without a revision of those same statutes. The provision for their amendment is contained in article 13: "The Conference, following the same procedure," i.e., a two-thirds majority of the members of the Conference present and voting, "may amend the present Statutes." Notice of any such proposed amendments must be given six months ahead of a conference.[66] In any revision of the statutes, including the offending article 1(2), governments cannot be denied participation. Thus the statutes of the International Red Cross have ingested the "two Chinas" situation into the supreme organ of the Red Cross, the international conference.

The International Red Cross movement has been able to solve the delicate question of recognition of National Red Cross Societies in a manner that is relatively immune from challenge. But by the unfortunate wording of the relevant article of the statute retained at Toronto in 1952 when there was an opportunity to revise it, it is now saddled with a virtually insoluble question as to the participation of the governmental delegations of the "two Chinas" at an international conference. Thereby the Red Cross movement has imported many of the diplomatic and international law difficulties over recognition of the government of China. An attempt to resolve the question by allowing both Chinese governmental delegations to take part is an illusion. If both delegations avail themselves of their right to participate, then there is a bitter political dispute between the two delegations that goes far to disrupt the conference, obstructs genuine Red Cross business, and displays political arguments in a forum from which they are prohibited by those same statutes. Such political debate creates a public impression wholly alien to the best interests of the Red Cross movement and its principles.

In every way, the crucial article 1(2) of the statutes, when it involves the "two Chinas" situation, has had an unfortunate outcome. Since the New Delhi conference of 1957 the PRC has ceased to participate at such conferences, an absence which is regretted the more by reason of

66. *Handbook*, p. 311.

the scale of the population no longer represented in the paramount deliberations of the International Red Cross movement. As long as the PRC absents itself from such gatherings, there can be no proper implementation of the Red Cross principle of "universality." Needless to say the injection of the "two Chinas" situation into the Red Cross forum also puts the Red Cross principles of "impartiality" and "neutrality" at risk.

The limping solution of the voluntary absence of the PRC means a breakdown of any dialogue between the ICRC and the PRC and its National Society. Much thought has been devoted to resolving this predicament. To date it remains without solution. It means in practice that the ICRC has found that its performance of solely humanitarian tasks has been systematically prohibited, since no ICRC delegate has as yet been allowed to set foot on any PRC, North Korean, or North Vietnamese territory (other than in transit in the PRC). This in its turn means that the supervision of the enforcement of the many practical humanitarian provisions in the Geneva Conventions of 1949 has been rendered impossible in those areas.

The statements of the PRC delegates at the Toronto conference display with repetitive clarity the attitude of the PRC to the Red Cross movement as a whole and to the ICRC in particular. Most of what emerges from such public statements by the PRC also represents the thinking and policies of the governments of North Korea and North Vietnam. The presence of the PRC National Red Cross Society at an international conference of the Red Cross enables a double presentation of Chinese views about the Red Cross. In Communist states, the general pattern is that the National Society is very closely identified with the organs of government and of the Communist Party. It is not unusual, as in the case of the Chinese Red Cross Society, for the president of the society to be, or to have been, a former minister of public health. Madame Li Te-ch'üan, the president of the PRC National Society, served in that capacity. One person can appear as leader of the governmental or the National Society delegation or of both with equal facility. This, however, is not unique to Communist states. For reasons of economy or convenience, some states attending a Red Cross conference have one delegate, a member of their diplomatic staff, representing both his government and the National Society of his state.

The opening words of the PRC delegate, Mr. Su Ching-kuan, place the attitude of the PRC to the Toronto conference beyond any doubt:

In the name of the Governmental delegation of the PRC I wish to present at once a motion demanding that the remnants of the Chinese Kuomintang, now refugees in Formosa who are pretending to represent the Government and Red Cross of China be immediately excluded from the Conference . . . only the Central Government of the PRC has the right to participate in . . . the international conference of the Red Cross . . . In spite of the opposition of the Chinese people the permanent Commission of the International Red Cross [i.e., the Standing Commission, a small body which exercises specified control over the International Red Cross between international conferences, convenes and arranges such conferences, and in practice ceases to function during the existence of such conferences] invited the remnants of the Chinese Kuomintang in Formosa who pretend to represent the Chinese Government, to participate in this Conference, and more, the Commission is just about to confer on them a status equal to that of the PRC. [It is thought that he had in mind the offending article 1(2) of the statutes relating to the right to participate and which would allow delegates of the "two Chinas" to be seated.] . . . In so doing it has made a serious attack on the position and prestige of the Eighteenth International Conference.

He then proceeded to remind the conference that since 1950 the PRC National Society had been recognized as the sole Chinese Red Cross Society, in accordance with the recognition regulations, and that it had operated within the League on that basis since that time. His charge that the standing commission invited the Chinese (Nationalist) Red Cross Society to the conference overlooked the fact that it was present not as a society but as an observer capable of participating in the debates only with the consent of the chairman of the conference but with no right to vote (conference rules of procedure, article 3). However, his strictures were well based to the extent that the (Nationalist) Red Cross Society was present only by invitation of the standing commission of the Red Cross. He concluded this part of his address thus: "To maintain the principles of the Red Cross organization and to allow the Conference to carry out its work properly and normally I propose then that the Conference immediately excludes the remnants of the Chinese Kuomintang."[67] It is not difficult to see that the Red Cross Conference had got itself "between the hammer and the forge."

Subsequently, there was a joint session of the Council of Delegates and the Board of Governors of the League at which the revision of the conference statutes was debated. This revision had been entrusted to a legal subcommittee of the general commission of the conference. At the

67. *Proceedings of the Eighteenth International Conference of the Red Cross, Toronto* (Geneva: ICRC, 1952), 1st Plenary Session, p. 49.

joint session, the main argument seems to have centered around the status and functions of the ICRC in relation to the other international Red Cross organs, particularly the League.

The main movement against the revised text of the statutes emanated from the Soviet Union Red Cross Society. It complained that the ICRC was not a truly international body, being composed of Swiss; was committed politically, as demonstrated in the Korean conflict; and, compared with the League, had a preeminence that was disproportionate, especially since the League purported to be a federal association of all the Red Cross societies in the world.[68] No attack appears to have been made against the unrevised rule in article 1(2) determining the composition of an international conference.

Madame Li Te-ch'üan, president of the PRC Red Cross, supported the Soviet attack on the ICRC at the joint session:

> With regard to the position of the ICRC in the centre of the International Red Cross, I wish to say once again that this institution is not a universal institution as its name indicates. It is an institution of Swiss citizens which has not been elected according to democratic principles. That is why it cannot control the activities at the centre of the International Red Cross. What is more, the actions of this institution since the Second World War until the Korean war have not been based on the principles of the Geneva Conventions, and that is why I cannot accept its privileged place at the centre of the International Red Cross movement. The Chinese delegation supports the motion of the Soviet Union.[69]

The PRC's distrust of the ICRC, generated during the Korean War, influenced the conduct of the PRC and its Red Cross delegation throughout the Toronto conference. Considering that the Korean conflict was still in progress, it is hardly surprising that a public confrontation between the PRC, its National Society, and the ICRC occurred.

The outcome of the dispute about the revision of the statutes was that the joint session of the Board of Governors and the Council of Delegates approved them in the revised form in which they now stand and to which the PRC and the Soviet Union had taken such strong exception. The expressed distrust of, and attack upon, the ICRC by the PRC and its society led to one of the resolutions of the conference (no. 22): "having heard with regret the attacks directed against the ICRC and having heard the explanations of this Committee, *declares* its confidence

68. *Ibid.*, p. 35.
69. *Ibid.*, p. 38.

in the ICRC."[70] In retrospect, it is difficult to envisage any amendment to the statutes that would have dissipated the PRC hostility to the ICRC, a hostility that at that time commanded the active support of the Soviet Union and the other Soviet states.

The following day, in plenary session of the conference, Li Te-ch'üan again charged:

> The so-called International Committee of the Red Cross is not an international institution. The activities of that institution in no way conform to the humanitarian principles, particularly in the war in Korea. It is quite clear that this institution cannot be considered neutral or impartial; it is even reduced to the role of an instrument of a Western Power. The Chinese people disapprove of such an institution.[71]

The PRC and its National Society then moved to the question that had been debated in the commission, namely, the allegation of US atrocities in the Korean conflict. The PRC and its National Society had declined to produce evidence before, or participate in any way in, an inquiry that had been proposed by the ICRC in Korea. The US had accepted this inquiry, but no response was forthcoming from the PRC.[72] Then the PRC had sought to introduce evidence before the commission supporting its charges of atrocities, particularly in the alleged use of bacteriological weapons by US aircraft in Korea. Apparently, for there is no record of the commission debates, the PRC delegation had been called to order for embarking upon political matters. Dr. Su Ching-kuan, the PRC government delegate, spoke in the fifth plenary session on this topic:

> When the facts of such violation [of the Geneva Conventions] are produced and put forward at this Conference, that touches exactly the point of application of these Conventions, and one cannot call the speaker to order simply on the insupportable pretext that the item under debate is called "Ratification, dissemination and application of the Geneva Conventions." It is even less plausible to avoid the question on the pretext of political propaganda. [He was interrupted at this point by the President of the Conference.] If humanitarianism is truly in the hearts of the delegates present here . . . they must accord us serious attention to these facts in an impartial spirit and bearing in mind their responsibilities to humanity.[73]

The final word rested with Li Te-ch'üan: "The Conference must . . . examine the evidence in our possession in support of the allegations

70. *Ibid.*, p. 137.
71. *Ibid.*, p. 104.
72. See p. 363 above.
73. *Ibid.*, p. 108.

contained in our draft resolution."[74] The evidence consisted of foliage alleged to show the effects of bacteriological agents released by US aircraft in Korea. She continued, "However, for obvious reasons, the Chinese delegations are certain that the Chinese people would be opposed to any inquiry conducted by . . . an organization such as the so-called ICRC."[75]

On this note, the PRC and its National Society concluded their part in the Eighteenth International Red Cross Conference. The PRC's objection to the role of the ICRC and its place in the Red Cross movement, together with its even stronger objection to the presence of the Chinese (Nationalist) delegation, combined to make the Toronto conference an unfortunate occasion which did little to advance the interests of the International Red Cross movement.

By the time of the next conference, held in New Delhi in 1957, the Panmunjom Armistice had been signed more than four years. Although that conference proved nearly as frustrating and harmful to the International Red Cross movement as the previous one, the pattern of disruption was different. This time the main complainant was the Nationalist Chinese government, whose cause was espoused by the US government delegation.

THE NINETEENTH INTERNATIONAL CONFERENCE OF THE RED CROSS, NEW DELHI, 1957

By 1957, the PRC had found itself excluded from the organs of the UN for eight years. The PRC's determination to contest any suggestion of the existence of "two Chinas" had hardened. The main target of its political anathema was the US, which had secured the exclusion of the PRC from the UN and had firmly supported the Nationalist Chinese government on Formosa. The effective exclusion of the PRC from the UN and its specialized agencies afforded little opportunity for confrontation in an international forum between the PRC and its political opponents. Unfortunately, the international conference of the Red Cross provided one of such rare forums. The statutes of the International Red Cross afforded grounds for the presence of the Nationalist Chinese, the US, the ICRC, and the PRC, if they all wished to be present. The experiences of the Toronto conference of 1952 made those entrusted with

74. *Ibid.*, p. 110.
75. *Ibid.*, p. 111.

the arrangements for the New Delhi conference extremely concerned about a repetition that would further damage the International Red Cross movement.

Besides, the substantive Red Cross business that was to be transacted at New Delhi was a consideration of the "Draft Rules for Limitation of the Dangers Incurred by the Civilian Population in Time of War,"[76] a politically sensitive issue. These rules had been prepared over a number of years by the ICRC, aided by various groups of experts, and were a serious attempt by the ICRC to achieve that measure of progress in the law of armed combat that had been secured in the law governing the protection of war victims in the four Geneva Conventions of 1949. It was an ambitious task, genuinely humanitarian in character and purpose, but subjected to numerous political, military, and juridical difficulties. The Hague Convention No. IV of 1907 and more contemporary conventions were manifestly anachronistic and bore only a modest relationship to the war technology of the 1950s. As if to emphasize this fact, during the New Delhi conference, the USSR achieved a pioneer technological feat in outer space with the orbiting of "Sputnik 1." The worthy purpose of the ICRC was to modernize and humanize the "Hague stream" of the law of war. Few could deny that such an effort was urgently needed but few could be sanguine about the outcome.

The draft rules purported to prohibit direct attacks against civilian populations, and, as a necessary corollary, to define exhaustively lawful targets for armed attack. The rules stipulated certain precautions in carrying out attacks on accepted targets, with a view to the maximum exclusion of civilians from the effects of such attacks. More specifically, these sought to prohibit the use of weapons with harmful effects that could not be controlled in space or time. This prohibition was aimed at nuclear, chemical, and biological (bacteriological) weaponry. The converse obligation was laid upon states—that of keeping their civilian population away from the vicinity of military targets.

The draft rules were rough hewn and clearly demanded a great deal more technical attention before they could be brought to the serious attention of governments. If the draft rules received the favorable reception of the New Delhi conference, the ICRC then hoped for a mandate that would enable it to submit the rules to governments with the ultimate purpose of convening a diplomatic conference, wherein the

76. *Draft Rules for the Limitation of the Dangers to the Civilian Population in Time of War* (Geneva: ICRC, 1956).

rules could be translated into a multilateral law-making convention.

The reception of the draft rules by the three nuclear powers, the US, the UK, and the USSR, was not enthusiastic. This factor, combined with (i) the PRC/ICRC estrangement, (ii) the Toronto confrontation of the "two Chinas" and the ICRC, and (iii) the divisive issue of nuclear weapons accentuating the already bad relations between the PRC and the US, made the prospects of the New Delhi Red Cross Conference look poor. Furthermore, this was the period of John Foster Dulles' ascendancy in the US State Department, the "containment of communism," and the "hard policy" toward Communist China. It is difficult to conceive of a period and place less likely to be propitious for humanitarian law-making projects.

The preliminary arrangements for the conference virtually ensured that the disastrous concatenation of circumstances should lose none of its destructive potential. The series of diplomatic faux pas that preceded the opening of the conference and accompanied its actual proceedings border upon the incredible, but their factual occurrence is now part of the history of diplomatic error. The unfortunate victim of this interlude of misfortune was the International Red Cross movement as a whole and the ICRC in particular. It is still too early to say whether the ICRC has recovered its international, impartial standing as it existed before the New Delhi conference of 1957. It is now necessary to trace the detailed steps of this doleful story.

Under article 3 of the statutes of the International Red Cross, the standing commission is one of the bodies empowered to convene an International Red Cross conference.[77] Under article 10, the standing commission is required to establish the agenda of, and to make the arrangements for, such a conference. These activities it carries out in conjunction with the host Red Cross Society.[78] Article 1 provides that "the International Red Cross Conference shall be composed of delegates of duly recognized Red Cross, Red Crescent, and Red Lion and Sun Societies, delegations of the States Parties to the Geneva Conventions. . . ." In article 1 of the rules of procedure of such conferences, it is provided:

> The following shall be members of the International Conference with the right to take part in discussions and to vote:
> a. the delegates of National Red Cross Societies . . .

77. *Handbook*, p. 206.
78. *Ibid.*, p. 310.

b. the delegates of States parties to the Geneva Convention for the Amelioration of the Condition of the Wounded and Sick in Armed Forces in the Field (1864, 1906, 1929, or 1949)
c. the delegates of the ICRC and those of the League of Red Cross Societies.

At this point, it will be recalled that the government of the Republic of China (ROC) had signed the Geneva Conventions of 1949 at the conclusion of the diplomatic conference in August 1949. The PRC government ratified the Geneva Conventions of 1949 in 1956. The Geneva Sick and Wounded Convention of 1864 had been ratified by the Imperial (Manchu) Chinese government in 1904. The Geneva Sick and Wounded Convention of 1906 was neither ratified nor acceded to by any government of China. The Geneva Sick and Wounded Convention of 1929 was ratified by the Chinese (Republican) government in 1935. Thus, no strong basis could be invoked for excluding the delegates either of the PRC or of the ROC. The fact that only the Red Cross Society of the PRC had been recognized by the appropriate organ (the ICRC) of the International Red Cross was in no way decisive as to the right of government delegates to participate at a conference.

As a matter of Red Cross practice, the host Red Cross Society issues a formal letter of invitation to the National Red Cross, etc., Societies and to the Ministers of Foreign Affairs of the governments (states) that are parties to the relevant Geneva Conventions. Strictly, these letters are notices of the date and place of the conference and of courteous welcome rather than formal invitations. Invitations are not the legal basis of the presence of delegates at an International Red Cross conference. Such delegates are present as of right if they meet the requirements of the statutes and rules of procedure cited above.

The standing commission had extended its letter of invitation to the ROC government under the style of "the government of Taiwan, at Taipei." This letter was dated March 26, 1957, and received a normal reply from the ROC government on May 14, 1957. The reply did not complain about the style of address and contained a list of the Nationalist Chinese delegates who would be attending the conference. However, on October 5, three weeks before the opening of the conference, the authorities in Taiwan sent a letter to the Indian Red Cross complaining that the use of the incorrect style of address had abused them and they would not attend the conference. For this situation they blamed the Indian Red Cross Society. The standing commission had already received protests from the PRC and its Red Cross Society against the invitation to the Taiwan authorities.[79]

Thus the stage was set for one of those diplomatic irritants that do much to accentuate bad relations and little for the promotion of the business of a conference. Whatever the rights and wrongs of the unfortunate letter of invitation to "Taiwan," one thing was clear: Neither the government of India nor its Red Cross Society was in any way at fault. Nevertheless, it was the host government and host society of the conference that received the full force of the diplomatic explosion at the conference. The Indians were the victims of complaints from the PRC, the US, and the ROC, not to mention other states.

In fact, the mischief had started at the instance of the standing commission, a body that in practice does not function during the holding of the conference. The handling of the complaints and countercomplaints at the conference devolved upon the chairman of the conference, Princess Amrit Kaur, who was also the chairman of the Indian Red Cross Society and a member of the standing commission. It remains a mystery why the Taiwan authorities declined to complain at the receipt of the original misstyling in March and did not consider themselves abused thereby until October, some seven months later and less than a month before the opening of the conference. The evidence is inconclusive.

Knowing that the PRC had already protested at the proposal of the standing commission to extend an invitation to the Nationalist Chinese and that the states of the world were divided on the recognition of the PRC government at Peking, the misstyling of the authorities in Taiwan by the standing commission was a singular exercise in diplomatic ineptitude. This dispute over a misstyling in a document that had no legal import or efficacy seriously distracted the attention of the conference from the draft rules upon which the ICRC had devoted many years of patient preparation. Further, the misstyling worsened the already impaired relations between the PRC and the International Red Cross.

In accordance with its stated intention, the Nationalist Chinese delegation was not present when the conference opened. The PRC delegation promptly launched an attack on the standing commission for extending an invitation to the Taiwan authorities, which in turn led to an intervention on the part of the US delegation complaining that the

79. See *Proceedings of the Nineteenth International Conference of the Red Cross, New Delhi* (Geneva: ICRC, 1957), pp. 45–50, for a summary account of the events preceding the conference.

absence of the Taiwan authorities was the direct result of the insult they had sustained by the misstyling, in breach of Red Cross principles. The chairman of the conference, Princess Amrit Kaur, saw in the US complaint a censuring of the Indian government and Red Cross Society.

After the formal speeches of welcome and introduction by the President and Prime Minister of India on October 28, the PRC Red Cross delegate, Li Te-ch'üan, set the tone for the ensuing debate in these words:

> The chairman of the Standing Commission, M. Francois-Poincet, under the direction of the United States delegation . . . has gone so far as to rob the name of the Standing Commission to send of his own will, a telegram to the so-called Minister of Foreign Affairs of the Government of the Republic of the Chiang Kai-shek clique entrenched as the Republic of China, Taiwan, to send delegates speedily to attend the Conference. The delegates of the Chiang Kai-shek clique are on their way to the Conference . . . M. Francois-Poincet as chairman of an international organization has the audacity to misuse his authority to serve the cause of the US in creating two Chinas and disrupt the Conference. This is a provocation against the Conference and it is intolerable to the Chinese delegation as to all fair minded people.

She then proposed a resolution that the conference condemn the US delegation for its "sinister political plot" and "the illegal act of M. Francois-Poincet" and forbid Nationalist Chinese participation at the conference. "The Chinese people and the Chinese Government resolutely oppose the creation of two Chinas," she said, and "would have absolutely nothing to do with any international conference in which the elements of Chiang Kai-shek's clique attend and take part."[80]

To this M. Francois-Poincet made the following rejoinder:

> It has been asked why the Standing Commission sent a letter of invitation to the Government of Formosa and not to the Government of the Republic of China, and some have seen in this designation a political intention. . . . I wish to solemnly declare here that the Standing Commission was moved by no political considerations. The day is not purer than our intentions. It considered that the two terms "Republic of China" and the "People's Republic of China" would lead to confusion and that Formosa was clear. That was the sole reason. Has that been a mistake? . . . The International Red Cross is not a legal authority, still less a political authority, and it has no special authority to create any precedents. The incident may therefore be regarded as closed, and I ask you to put an end to it. It has led us very far from our normal preoccupations, far from the subjects for which we have gathered here.[81]

80. *Ibid.*, p. 41.
81. *Ibid.*, p. 48

The incident was far from closed. The standing commission, by the use of the term "Taiwan" (Formosa), had started a dispute that lasted for the greater part of the conference, detracted from its main business, and resulted in a series of incidents which were no less unfortunate in their short term, than they were in their long term, consequences. Few were convinced that the expression "Taiwan" was used for the purpose of avoiding confusion. In point of fact it caused much serious confusion. The PRC has not attended an International Red Cross conference since this incident.

In the course of the many and various exchanges that took place on the issue of this misstyling, it is possible to deduce those criteria which controlled the attitudes of the PRC to the International Red Cross as a whole.

On the morning of October 29, Princess Amrit Kaur reminded the plenary meeting of the conference that "the Red Cross is not competent to deal with political matters." She expressed the hope that "all delegates . . . will not impute motives to each other and will not attack personalities."[82] It was a vain hope. Many of the ensuing speeches did precisely that. Li Te-ch'üan lost no time in stating the PRC position. She rejected M. Francois-Poincet's explanation *in limine*. She stated that although he again and again emphasized that the International Red Cross organization should be "outside of politics," a great part of his report dealt with China's internal affairs, attempting to create at the conference a situation of "two Chinas." Everyone knows, she said, that recently certain forces inimical to China with the United States at their head have been actively engaged in the plot of creating "two Chinas"; M. Francois-Poincet's activities are a part of these sinister activities of the United States. Everyone knows, she continued, that the PRC is a state party to the Geneva Conventions and that the government of the PRC is the only legal government representing China, and that the Red Cross Society of China, the sole Chinese Red Cross organization, is also a member of the League of Red Cross Societies. Mme. Li asked: "If the invitation to elements of the Chiang Kai-shek clique on Taiwan to attend the Conference is not deliberately intended to split China and interfere in China's internal affairs, then what is it?"[83]

The government delegate of the PRC (P'an Tzu-li) took up the theme on November 5:

82. *Ibid.*, p. 51.
83. *Ibid.*, p. 51.

The regrettable thing is that not the delegations of all the countries have come to this Conference in a spirit of friendly co-operation, and with the aim of furthering the cause of humanitarianism. Some delegations intend to utilize this Conference to achieve . . . ulterior motives. This is clearly not in conformity [interrupted by Chairman]. The US delegate asserts that the so-called "Government of the Republic of China" is a party of [sic] several Red Cross Conventions, and therefore is fully qualified to participate in this Conference by the by-laws of the International Red Cross. True, the so-called "Government of the Republic of China" was a state party to the 1929 Geneva Convention and also signed on [sic] the 1949 Geneva Convention. But that was when it was not yet overthrown by the Chinese people. Everyone knows that in any country after its old regime has been overthrown its international rights are inherited by the new government. This is a world recognized principle of international law. The former Manchu Government of China was also a State party to the 1864 Geneva Convention, and according to the logic of the US delegate can it be that remnants of the Manchu Government should also be invited to the present session of our Conference? The attempt of the US delegate to use the pretext that because the so-called "Government of the Republic of China" was a State party to the Geneva Convention, or signed its name to the Convention, and therefore advocates that the Chiang Kai-shek [words expunged by order of the chairman] on Taiwan is qualified to take part in this Conference is totally untenable . . . Our Swiss colleagues advocate that invitations to the International Red Cross Conference should include all Governments exercising authority over territory where the Geneva Conventions are applicable. We find that this proposition is also untenable . . . Whether calling the Chiang Kai-shek [words ordered expunged by the chairman] on Taiwan as the so-called "Government of the Republic of China" or as the so-called "Government of Formosa," it is all the creation of a situation of "two Chinas" on China's territory. Taiwan is an inalienable part of China's territory . . . We hold that the correct draft resolution of the Chinese delegation in defence of the Statutes of the International Red Cross should be discussed and adopted at this Conference. This is the Resolution:

> Considering that in accordance with the provisions of Article 1, paragraph 2 of the "Statutes of the International Red Cross" and the second paragraph of the "Conditions for the Recognition of National Red Cross Societies," the local authorities and local Red Cross Organization of any State are not entitled to take part in the International Red Cross Conference.
>
> Resolves that the authorities exercising authority in the Taiwan province of China and the Red Cross organizations there are not allowed to take part under whatever name in the Nineteenth International Red Cross Conference.[84]

This draft resolution misfired in that the Red Cross organization on Taiwan was not present at the conference, had never been invited, and no question arose as to its nonrecognition by the appropriate organ of

84. *Ibid.*, pp. 65–68.

the International Red Cross, namely, the ICRC. As to the representation of the Republic of China, the statutes and rules of procedure applicable did not exclude the participation of delegates either of the PRC or of the ROC. In accordance with those statutes both had been invited, although no invitation was needed. Unfortunately, in the nonprerequisite invitation, the ROC had been misstyled. Needless to say, the PRC's draft resolution received no voting support at the conference except from the Communist bloc. In the event, shortly before the close of the conference, the PRC delegation voted with its feet, walking out of the conference once the rival US resolution had been adopted, without waiting for the PRC resolution to be put to the conference.

As to the substantive matter of the draft rules, P'an Tzu-li expressed himself thus:

> As a humanitarian organization the Red Cross has a responsibility not only to alleviate the suffering of mankind but also to try its utmost to prevent all possible sufferings. The prohibition of atomic and hydrogen weapons is not only necessary for protecting the health of our generation and the next generation from suffering from the harmful effects of radioactivity but is also an important step in defending world peace. Therefore the Red Cross Societies have the responsibility of urging their respective Governments to stop or suspend the testing of such weapons.[85]

This position was reiterated by Li Te-ch'üan of the PRC Red Cross, who concluded by expressing the Chinese attitude to the work of the International Red Cross in these terms:

> The Chinese Red Cross Society considers that the League of Red Cross Societies and the ICRC have done much work which is beneficial to friendly co-operation among peoples. The past experiences have proved that the International Conferences of the Red Cross and the co-operation in the daily work of the National Red Cross Societies are helpful to the understanding and friendship of the peoples of all nations. This would help to achieve greater unity of action among the National Red Cross Societies in the humanitarian cause, thereby making greater contributions to the defence of world peace.[86]

Unfortunately these harmonious and praiseworthy sentiments did not control the conduct of the PRC and its Red Cross delegations at the conclusion of the conference. On its closing day, November 7, 1957, the US resolution on misstyling was put to the conference and adopted by

85. *Ibid.*, p. 107.
86. *Ibid.*, p. 135

62–44–16, a majority of 18. The adopted resolution stated that "in accordance with the traditional principles of the Red Cross . . . it is the sense of the Conference that all parties invited to attend the Conference be addressed according to their official titles."[87]

The vote was carried out by secret ballot as provided in the rules of procedure (article 18) when so requested by ten delegations. No reference to "governments" appeared in the text of the US resolution as finally adopted by the conference—there were too many states represented that recognized the Peking government as the de jure government of China to make the inclusion of the word "governments" prudent if the narrow supporting majority was not to be in jeopardy. The adoption of this resolution had a number of immediate effects at the conference, all of which were disastrous for the Red Cross movement in general and the conference in particular. First, the PRC delegate announced immediately upon the count being declared: "And now we declare that we withdraw from the Nineteenth International Red Cross Conference."[88] They did so. Second, the response of the chairman of the conference and of the Indian National Red Cross Society, Princess Amrit Kaur, was no less immediate:

> I cannot help but protest that it was not given to the host Society of the Red Cross to have any choice in the matter of issuing invitations by the designation that has now been accepted by the Conference . . . I consider that the way that this Resolution has been introduced at the last minute, is—if I may say so in all humility—grave discourtesy to the Indian Red Cross Society. The only protest I can make is to leave this Conference Hall. I do not do it in any spirit of antipathy or antagonism to the Red Cross movement. Of that I have been a soldier all my life and I shall continue to be that soldier . . . I will ask now Prince de Mérode [of the Belgian Red Cross] to take the Chair in my place.[89]

Princess Amrit Kaur and the delegates of the Indian Red Cross Society then left the conference. Her departure was followed by the delegations of the USSR, Czechoslovakia, Rumania, Bulgaria, Hungary, East Germany, North Korea, North Vietnam, Poland, Yugoslavia, Indonesia, and Egypt. The Egyptian delegate nearly got left behind in the movement for withdrawal. Before he had announced his intention to leave the conference a bizarre incident occurred. Two individuals entered the conference hall and took the places recently vacated by

87. *Ibid.*, pp. 139–141.
88. *Ibid.*, p. 141.
89. *Ibid.*, p. 141.

the delegates of the PRC. The designation board of the latter was then removed and replaced by one bearing the designation, "Republic of China." Thus there was no time in the life of the conference when the delegates of the PRC and of the Republic of China were both present. The Indian government delegate, Mr. Karmarkar, moved that the newly arrived Chinese delegates should have awaited a telegram of invitation addressed to them in accordance with the resolution just adopted. On a vote (51–31–18), the conference resolved that the delegates of the Republic of China should remain in their seats.[90] These delegates took no part during the few remaining minutes of the conference.

As to the draft rules prepared by the ICRC, the resolution adopted by the conference reflected a harmless compromise between humanitarian aspirations and the reality of nuclear weapons. It urged "the ICRC to continue its efforts for the protection of the civilian population against the evils of war" and requested "the ICRC on behalf of the Nineteenth International Conference to transmit the Draft Rules . . . to the Governments for their consideration."[91]

Thus concluded the conference. The Draft Rules were duly transmitted to all governments and a few of them responded by acknowledging their receipt. That is the sole progress that has been made in relation to them. The PRC has never attended another international conference of the Red Cross, although it has participated in two later international meetings of organs of the Red Cross. No further international conference of the Red Cross was held until 1965. During the centenary year of the Red Cross movement, 1963, the memory of the Delhi conference was considered too recent and too painful for the holding of a Centenary International Red Cross Conference.

The scars of the Delhi conference debacle still mar the International Red Cross and have proved a serious obstacle to the proper discharge of the humanitarian functions of the ICRC in the major armed conflicts that have disturbed the world since 1957. Neither in North Vietnam nor in Nigeria has the ICRC been able to carry out its proper humanitarian role. Since the start of the conflict in Vietnam, no ICRC delegate has ever been allowed to set foot in North Vietnam. Likewise, no ICRC delegate has ever been allowed to enter Tibet at any stage during the internal armed conflict that flickers there from time to time.

90. *Ibid.*, p. 146.
91. Resolution XIII, *ibid.*, p. 153.

At the twentieth and twenty-first International Red Cross conferences, held in Vienna and Istanbul in 1965 and 1969, respectively, neither the PRC nor the PRC Red Cross was present.

THE CENTENARY MEETING OF THE COUNCIL OF DELEGATES, GENEVA, 1963

The statutes of the International Red Cross provide in article 2 that "the International Conference shall normally meet every four years."[92] By 1961, the standing commission felt that another conference would serve no useful purpose. However, in view of the fact that the year 1963 marked the centenary of the International Red Cross, a meeting of the Council of Delegates was deemed appropriate. The council is composed of all the recognized National Red Cross, etc., Societies, and representatives of the ICRC and the League. Governments are not participants. Accordingly, neither the ROC government nor Red Cross Society was represented at the meeting.

The meeting of the Council of Delegates was harmonious. The PRC Red Cross participated and spoke on the resolutions on peace and the relation of the ICRC to the Cuban missile incident of 1962, during which the Secretary General of the UN had proposed an ICRC role. The PRC Red Cross delegate, Li Shou-pao, had this to say on the Cuban affair:

> In considering the ICRC intervention we think that two decisive factors must not be overlooked. First, the ICRC should always guard against being utilized to serve the political ends of a few Great Powers. Secondly, the sovereignty of the country involved should always be respected. The ICRC adopted a cautious attitude when its assistance was called upon during the Caribbean crisis. It has stressed the four categorical requirements for intervention in major conflicts, including the requirement that the ICRC must first seek the agreement of all the interested parties before intervention is to be undertaken. It has also expressed its insistence on the principle of non-interference in political matters . . . If these aspects are not well handled, the prestige of the ICRC will not be enhanced but will be impaired.[93]

The PRC Red Cross withheld its support from the resolution approving the action taken by the ICRC in the Cuban incident, but expressed

92. *Handbook*, p. 306.

93. *Proceedings of the Centenary Congress of the Council of Delegates* (Geneva: ICRC, 1963), p. 95. For the text of the resolution adopted see *ibid.*, p. 120.

its views with moderation and caution. It appears to have been anxious to make a good impression and to avoid controversial matters during the centenary year meeting. It was not difficult to avoid controversial matters because the Cuban missile confrontation had passed without armed conflict and the ICRC had not intervened.

MEETING OF THE EXECUTIVE COMMITTEE OF THE LEAGUE, GENEVA, 1966

Under article 10 of the Constitution of the League of Red Cross Societies, the League's Board of Governors is composed of a governor appointed by each National Society. Provision is made in article 16 for an executive committee on which sit one representative of each of the National Societies to which the chairman and vice-chairman of the Board of Governors belong, and representatives of twelve other member Societies elected by the board of governors for two years.

The Board of Governors carries out the objectives of the League, and the executive committee exercises the bulk of the powers of the Board when the Board is not sitting.[94] The PRC Red Cross Society representative was a member of the executive committee in 1966 and, participating at its meeting at Geneva on the first day, October 4, 1966, made a brief intervention. The delegate, Wang Min, objected to the presence of an observer from the South Vietnam Red Cross. When the body failed to expel the South Vietnam observer, Wang left the meeting.[95]

Two reasons may be advanced for this somewhat abrasive relationship of the PRC Red Cross with an organ of the International Red Cross. First, the Vietnam conflict was escalating, and the PRC saw the US presence in Vietnam as aggression and the ICRC as associated with the aggressor. Second, part of the agenda of the executive committee related to the question of arrears of financial contributions by National Societies to the League. The PRC Red Cross Society's arrears were small, some 15,000 Swiss francs. Nevertheless, the PRC Red Cross Society had appealed against this determination. Its appeal was disallowed.[96] It is apparent that the PRC Red Cross Society had no intention of taking a serious part in this committee meeting other than to protest against the presence of a Red Cross observer from South Vietnam.

94. *Handbook*, p. 329.
95. *Proceedings of the Eighty-sixth Session of the Executive Committee of the League of Red Cross Societies* (Geneva: ICRC, 1966), p. 4.
96. *Ibid.*, Annex III, p. 4, and Annex IX, resolution no. 4.

THE MOST RECENT INTERNATIONAL RED CROSS CONFERENCES

The Vienna conference of October 2–9, 1965, which met prior to the 1966 meeting of the executive committee of the League, was the first international conference of the Red Cross which the PRC and its Red Cross Society declined to attend. The deterioration of relations between the PRC and most of the other Communist states could be detected. At New Delhi, in 1957, there had been solidarity among all the Communist states. At Vienna, eight years later, the USSR delegate made only a token protest about the absence of the PRC. When, at the opening plenary session of the Vienna conference, the USSR delegate, Professor Miterev, asked the chairman of the conference why the PRC and North Vietnam were not represented, the chairman of the conference and of the Austrian National Red Cross Society, Dr. Lauta, replied that "Peking's reason for deciding not to come is solely due to the fact that the Government of the Republic of China—we will say Formosa—is on the list of Governments which are entitled to attend this conference. I regret this absence, Professor Miterev, just as you do, perhaps even more so . . . I deplore this decision because it is contrary to the fundamental principles of Red Cross unity and universality." Professor Miterev thanked the chairman for this explanation and expressed his "deep regret" that the representatives of the PRC were not present. "Certainly," he said, "it complicates our work and . . . to some degree it is to the damage of the Standing Commission of the International Red Cross which has taken such decisions." His government, said Miterev, supported the PRC and North Vietnam positions.[97] Poland, North Korea, Mongolia, Albania, Hungary, East Germany, Bulgaria, Czechoslovakia, and Cuba all deplored the absence of the PRC. In the main this was done with moderation except on the part of the Albanian Red Cross delegate, who was eventually silenced by the chairman. Apart from a reply from the ROC, the conference was not disturbed further by the question of the "two Chinas."

At the last International Red Cross conference held at Istanbul in September 1969, the PRC and its Red Cross Society were not present and no delegate drew attention to the fact. The realities of inter-Communist relationships had removed one polemical, political issue from Red Cross conferences, swiftly to be replaced by others not relevant to this study.

97. *Report of the Twentieth International Conference of the Red Cross, Vienna* (Geneva: ICRC, 1965), pp. 39 and 40.

CONCLUSION

One must be cautious in assessing PRC attitudes toward the International Red Cross. Caution is even more necessary in arriving at condemnatory judgments of those attitudes. From the written record, the PRC might appear as a state unable to accommodate its policies and actions to the principles of the International Red Cross movement. These principles, now solemnly proclaimed as a prelude at International Red Cross conferences, are humanity, impartiality, neutrality, independence, voluntary service, unity, and universality.[98] To the extent that the principles guiding the policies of the PRC since 1949 are to be found in the writings of Chairman Mao Tse-tung and the public statements of the organs of the government and of the press, a case can readily be made that there is little room for cooperation between the PRC and the International Red Cross. We can also assume that the PRC National Red Cross Society is an emanation of the PRC and that no area of independence of thought or of action is allowed to that society by the Peking government.

It must not be too swiftly assumed that in the events leading to the virtual severance of relations between the PRC and the ICRC, the former was wholly at fault. It may be that the attempt to attribute fault in this context is both irrelevant and unrewarding. It is possible, however, to analyze the steps leading to this severance and the principles and conduct that have led to that result.

Perhaps the *fons et origo* of the disenchantment of the PRC with intergovernmental organizations stems from the exclusion of the PRC from representation in the organs of the United Nations. The state of China is a founding member of the United Nations and has been a permanent member of the Security Council since the birth of the organization in 1945. In the twenty-one years of the history of the PRC, from 1949 to 1970, not one delegate of the PRC has ever sat in the place marked "China" in the organs of the UN. Although the tactics of the PRC in seeking participation in the UN were not diplomatic or accommodating, the PRC's exclusion for 20 years does not redound to the credit of the organization or of those states which have assiduously used the full thrust of their state power to preserve that exclusion.

As a matter of international law, recognition of a government of an existing state is not controlling as to membership or participation in the UN. However, in terms of voting policies, recognition does determine

98. *Ibid.*, prefatory page.

the vote in the General Assembly on the acceptance of individual delegates' credentials. Without such acceptance, there can be no participation in the activities of UN organs. The PRC has been a victim of the unsatisfactory nature of the legal device of recognition in the international sphere. As long as recognition is seen as a political act and not a determination of legal consequence deduced from bona fide appraisal of a factual situation, namely, the exercise of effective authority and control over the territory of a state, so long will the PRC be the victim of policies that take their legal bases from within the citadel of state sovereignty. The PRC has not done much to reduce the opposition to its UN "presence" and sees no reason why it should seek participation as a concession or reward. Rather, it claims participation as a matter of right. When it failed to vindicate that claim, it began to condemn the organization which excluded its delegates.

The relationship between the PRC and the UN in large part colored the relationships between the PRC and the International Red Cross. At conferences of the International Red Cross can be seen just that confrontation with the Formosan authorities and the "two Chinas" situation which the PRC had refused to countenance in the UN. Like the UN, the ICRC asserted its neutrality and impartiality, but, to the PRC, how could it be sincere about either principle when the Red Cross movement allowed the delegates of Formosa to attend Red Cross conferences and refused to exclude them on demand? If the sole Chinese Red Cross Society was that of the mainland and no such society from Formosa was recognized by the ICRC, how then could the Formosan government be allowed to participate in such conferences? Again, the Red Cross conferences purported to exclude political matters from their transactions. Why, then, did the standing commission allow "the two Chinas" situation to be highlighted at Red Cross conferences by inviting the Formosan delegates to be present? Was that not the very essence of a political, nonneutral, highly partial act? The ICRC, in particular, suffered from the same vices as the UN; it was neither neutral nor nonpolitical. It sought to make demands of the Chinese People's Volunteers during the Korean conflict that were unacceptable to the PRC's conception of state sovereignty. Moreover, the ICRC sought to be active during the Korean "aggression" carried out by the US masquerading under the UN flag—the UN was a mask for the US and both were a protective screen for the ICRC. Such was the current of PRC arguments.

The PRC not only denied the neutrailty and impartiality of the ICRC, but it also denied that the ICRC was even "international." In the language of the PRC, the ICRC "is not a universal institution as its name suggests. It is an institution of Swiss citizens not elected according to democratic principles."[99] On another occasion, the PRC stated that "the so-called international committee is not an international institution. It is quite clear that this insitution can be considered as neither neutral nor impartial."[100] It thus had the vices of the Holy Roman Empire, being neither Holy, Roman, nor an Empire. It was apparent from the constitution of the ICRC, from its own statutes, that it was limited exclusively to Swiss nationals. That rendered it the opposite of "international." The members of the ICRC, it was said by the PRC, are elected by the other Swiss on the ICRC. There are no other members. Here, in the PRC view, is a large international movement, the Red Cross, one of whose key organs, the one most active in dealings with governments in interstate armed conflicts, the ICRC, is a body not elected by the members of the National Red Cross, etc., Societies all over the world nor even by the organs of the League of Red Cross Societies but by its own members from the nationals of one state, Switzerland. In terms of real world political cleavages, Switzerland is far from neutral. It is a highly successful bourgeois, capitalist society. It is idle to pretend that its citizens, however distinguished, can be dissociated from the principles upon which their state is organized. Such is the pattern of attack mounted by the PRC.

Nothing that has happened in the Vietnam conflict has reduced the incompatibility between the policies of the PRC and those principles of the ICRC which form its raison d'etre. Although the PRC accuses the ICRC of partiality and political involvement,[101] the element of insincerity in such accusations is transparent. In the first place, the PRC ideology has no respect, and only contempt, for neutrality. The statements of Chairman Mao allow no room for neutrality in the great struggle of the Chinese masses against the imperialist plot of the US and the USSR. If the ICRC were, in the PRC view, genuinely neutral and impartial and eschewed politics, then to that extent the ICRC would be a class enemy and contemptible. For the PRC to accuse the ICRC of lack of neutrality and of political commitment comes well

99. *Proceedings of the Eighteenth International Conference of the Red Cross, Toronto* (Geneva: ICRC, 1952), p. 38.
100. *Ibid.*, p. 104.
101. *Ibid.*, pp. 38 and 104.

within the classical Voltairean definition of hypocrisy—"the tribute that vice pays to virtue."

The ICRC purports to make no distinction between peoples of different races, creeds, religions, and colors. It seeks to relieve the suffering of all mankind, whether from natural or man-made tragedies, whether from tidal waves or the Vietnam conflict. It seeks to uphold a belief of man in man, whoever is the aggressor and whoever is the victim. The ICRC is, in modern terms, seeking to secure the observance of human rights even in time of armed conflicts. It makes no judgments about the just or unjust nature of participation in armed conflicts, whether international or internal. It can readily be seen that in terms of orthodox Chinese Maoist thinking such ideas are, by definition, repugnant.

The ICRC assumes that, in securing the relief of all suffering combatants, irrespective of the nature of the cause for which they are engaged in the conflict, it has only one loyalty—to mankind. Its formula to describe the human victims of armed conflicts is that they are "the victims of events." Such an approach is anathema to orthodox Chinese Communist thinking. Those who are not totally loyal to Chinese Communism are "class enemies" who must be humiliated and maltreated until they confess their errors. So-called neutrals are disguised "class enemies," more insidious for their neutral cover. Further, there is a strain of thinking that, in conformity with a tradition older than Chinese communism, does not accept that non-Chinese peoples stand in parity with the Chinese, either in human, social, political, or cultural evaluation. To assume that the cause of the Chinese People's Volunteers during the Korean conflict, or of the North Vietnamese in the current Vietnam conflict, can be treated, for the purposes of the Geneva Conventions of 1949, as lying under the same prohibitions and restraints that govern other peoples, is totally unacceptable. The cause of the Chinese and North Vietnamese masses in expelling the US aggressor criminals cannot, for any purpose, be equated with that of the latter.

There is such a total cleavage between the principles which inspire PRC policies and those which control and guide the ICRC that it would indeed be anomalous if the relations between the two could be other than they are. There is a small area in which purely humanitarian actions by the ICRC are accepted by the PRC without acerbity. Chinese fishermen who get stranded by weather conditions on non-Chinese coasts are from time to time repatriated to the PRC under arrangements made by the ICRC with the involuntary host government, whether of Hong Kong, Macao, or even Formosa. However, these activities are quite different from those in which the ICRC purports to remind the PRC of its obligations under the Geneva Conventions of 1949 in an international conflict such as that in Korea or on the Indian border, and certainly in an internal conflict such as that which flickers into life spasmodically in Tibet, an autonomous region of China.

In juridical terms, the conduct of the commander of the Chinese People's Volunteers of the PRC in the Korean conflict was not manifestly contrary to the Geneva Conventions in that those instruments were applicable only ad hoc, and to the extent that they were made applicable by unilateral declarations of the participants. Delay in allowing the ICRC delegates to travel through Chinese territory to get to North Korea may have been obstructive but was hardly an illegality. The making of unsubstantiated allegations of bacteriological warfare against the United States in Korea and then declining to participate in a neutral inquiry commission was obstructive and not in good faith, but not illegal.

Refusal to allow ICRC delegates to enter Tibet during the insurrections there was not a violation of the Geneva Conventions of 1949. In internal conflicts the ICRC has no legal right to a presence in the territory concerned. It has the right, with other impartial humanitarian organizations, to offer its services, but it cannot demand their acceptance.

As to the role of the ICRC during the Sino-Indian border conflict, the matter was curious in that diplomatic relations were not severed between the two states. It is arguable that as long as those relations subsist the machinery of the protecting power provided in the Geneva Conventions of 1949 is not operative. To the extent that the PRC declined to give full lists of POW held by it to the Indian diplomatic missions this may have been in breach of the Geneva POW Convention, 1949, as it applied to the two states but it was not a breach of the convention as to which the ICRC had any *locus standi*. In any event, the PRC repatriated the Indian POW shortly after the demands by the Indian government for lists of all the POW that it held. To the extent that the Indian POW were repatriated, the call for lists of those held by the PRC was superseded.

The abuse directed by the PRC against the ICRC during the Korean conflict was unpleasant, discourteous, and untrue—but does not brand the PRC conduct with the stigma of illegality. It did, however, lead to a serious and acrimonious confrontation with the ICRC and the International Red Cross as a whole at the Toronto and New Delhi conferences of 1952 and 1957, respectively. In the former the PRC delegates behaved badly. However, that being said, their reaction to the presence of the Formosan delegation and the highlighting of the "two Chinas" situation was predictable and not entirely reprehensible. In the light of the Korean war and the conflict between the principles of the International Red Cross and those of Chinese communism, the debacle at the Toronto conference should have caused no surprise.

Indeed, it may be postulated that if the standing commission of the Red Cross and the ICRC thought that such a confrontation could be rendered innocuous, they were naïve. Admittedly, in 1957 the statutes of the International Red Cross made it impossible to exclude either governmental delegation of the "two Chinas" from International Red Cross conferences. The PRC persisted in arguing that if the rule were that a territory could not have a National Red Cross Society recognized by the ICRC under its statutes unless it were "the only National Red Cross Society of the . . . State,"[102] and if the ICRC had in fact recognized the Red Cross Society of the mainland and no such society in Taiwan, then the ROC governmental delegates had no right to a presence at the conference.[103] On the merits there was much in the PRC's point. However, the statutes governing participation at international conferences purported to let in all "State parties" to any of the Geneva Sick and Wounded Conventions, 1864 to 1949. It is arguable that such a formula excluded the delegates from Taiwan; although the Nationalist government had signed the Geneva Conventions of 1949 at the diplomatic conference in Geneva in August when its governmental position was undisputed, mere signature did not make it a "party" to these conventions, which expressly required ratification before any signatory was bound by them. The ratification was carried out by the Peking (PRC) government in 1956. Switzerland, the depository, has never accepted any such ratification by the Taiwan authorities.

As to the argument that the Nationalist government of China on Taiwan was the successor to the ratification by Chinese governments

102. Condition No. 2; see *Handbook*, p. 319.
103. *Proceedings of the Nineteenth International Conference of the Red Cross, New Delhi* (Geneva: ICRC, 1957), p. 51.

of the earlier Geneva Sick and Wounded Conventions of 1929, 1906 and 1864, the PRC delegates failed to make their best point, either at Toronto or at New Delhi. They put forward the argument that if the ROC delegates' contention was sound then the survivors of the Manchu government were entitled to be present. That point had some oratorical value but little legal merit. What the PRC delegates failed to point out was that the Geneva Sick and Wounded Convention of 1949, article 59, provided that: "The present Convention (1949) replaces the Conventions of . . . 1864, 1906 and 1929, in relations between the High Contracting Parties." The ROC had been a party to the 1929 Geneva Convention, which had in its turn replaced the two earlier Geneva Conventions of 1906 and 1864. The Manchu Empire of China had been a party to the latter, but not to the former. It is a viable contention that upon the PRC's ratification of the 1949 Geneva Convention in 1956 it (i) became a party thereto, (ii) the ROC never became a party thereto, being a signatory only, and (iii) the 1929 and 1864 Geneva Conventions became no longer operative, so far as China and the other parties were concerned, from the date of ratification of the 1949 Convention by the PRC government. The Convention of 1906 was not in point in that the Manchus had never been a party to it.

What is surprising is that the delegates of governments and National Red Cross Societies present at Toronto in 1952, alerted to the gathering storm clouds over relations between the PRC and the International Red Cross, did not take clarifying or palliative measures in the revision of their statutes. One of the items of business at the Toronto conference was that revision, which resulted in the present form of the statutes but left the crucial article 1, on participation, untouched. This merely postponed the more dramatic and final rupture between the PRC and the International Red Cross at the New Delhi conference in 1957.

It can be said in mitigation of this unfortunate failure to revise article 1 of the statutes so that the "two Chinas" situation would cease to disrupt the Red Cross movement, that the Red Cross principles operate in favor of inclusion, universality, unity, and generosity, and conversely, against exclusion and purely legal considerations. There may have been a strong desire by the standing commission, charged with the arrangements for the Delhi conference, not to antagonize the Taiwan authorities or the United States and to avoid the type of painful scenes that had done much to disorganize and frustrate the Toronto conference. It was doubtless felt that the International Red

Cross would suffer great harm if the disruptive "two Chinas" issue continued to be a feature of future Red Cross conferences. No doubt that was true, but the method adopted to avoid this threat was neither apt nor skilled. The statutes governing composition of Red Cross conferences remain laden with obscurities. The statutes could be further revised only at a conference when, by definition, the "two Chinas" issue would be in the forefront of the transactions. The curious ambivalence displayed by the Red Cross, in this instance by the standing commission, was to let the statutes stand in favor of the inclusion of both "Chinas" at conferences, and at the same time to be responsible for invitations to the Taiwan authorities for the Delhi conference, misstyling them as the "Government of Taiwan, at Taipei." Nothing could have been more disastrous either for the solution of the very real difficulty confronting the standing commission, or for the harmonious functioning of Red Cross conferences, or for the crucial diplomatic role of the ICRC in armed conflicts. The damage was done.

In the end, the New Delhi conference was a multiple disaster and a setback to the role of the ICRC at a time when it was crucial for the world and mankind that it should function according to the Geneva Conventions of 1949 and with the good will of all states. In January 1972, relations between the ICRC and the PRC are virtually nonexistent. The PRC no longer attends Red Cross conferences or meetings of the other organs of the International Red Cross such as the League, the Board of Governors, or the executive committee of the League.

What then is to be done to mend the relations between the PRC and the International Red Cross, and, more immediately, those with the ICRC? Nothing can be done in this area in a hurry. It must be a patient and careful process. Much will depend on the PRC's future role in the UN.[104] It is too early to assess what changes in the relationship between the PRC and the ICRC will occur as a result of the PRC influence in all the organs of the UN. The Twenty-second International Red Cross Conference, proposed for 1973, will be an indicator.

The absence of the PRC and its National Red Cross Society does weaken the proper functioning of the Red Cross movement and is alien to Red Cross principles. The absence of any representatives of the government and National Red Cross Society of the state with the

104. The PRC's delegation took their seats in the UN General Assembly on November 15, 1971, and its representative was seated in the Security Council on November 23, 1971, pursuant to Resolution 2578 (XXVI), October 25, 1971.

largest population in the world makes the Red Cross claims for universality a little hollow. Given the PRC's unyielding position that the juridical implications of state sovereignty should be stressed to their outer limit, the vital humanitarian role of the ICRC is frustrated virtually to the level of impotence.

For its part, the ICRC has a traditional tenacity and devotion to the cause of suffering humanity that will never accept defeat. At the same time it knows from other armed conflict situations that its nineteenth-century standing of unchallenged neutrality and impartiality, associated with the permanent neutrality of Switzerland, means very little to Communist states and states born in the post-1945 era. In a world of swiftly changing values, humanitarianism is stronger than neutrality. The ICRC is immensely persuasive in its rightful claim of guardian of the humanitarian ideal. It stands on weaker ground in relation to universal neutrality, not because it is a key organ of the International Red Cross movement, but because of its exclusively Swiss composition and self-perpetuating election system. One can suggest, with caution, that some amendment of the statutes of the ICRC, allowing that body to have a truly international composition, elected by a genuinely democratic system within the League of Red Cross, etc., Societies of the world, may, as a measure for the future, be more rewarding than attempting to amend or to interpret the statutes of the International Red Cross conferences so that the "two Chinas" dilemma is avoided. The heroic and humanitarian role of the International Red Cross is far too precious to be expended and dissipated in conference squabbles and in denial or limitation of the essential role of the ICRC in armed conflicts.

The question remains whether out of the sorry tale of deteriorating relationships between the PRC and the ICRC something positive and beneficent may be attempted in the future. The measures suggested above need patient preparation and negotiations. It must be stressed that the present location, staffing, and financing of the ICRC have many practical advantages not lightly to be jettisoned. Members of the ICRC, all Swiss nationals, perform their great services to mankind for no remuneration. They are dedicated men and women who give their lives and energies to the task of relieving the suffering of mankind, primarily in armed conflicts. They are based permanently in Geneva, they work closely together, and achieve an esprit de corps, not to mention an élan, that might well be the envy of other voluntary organizations dedicated to relief work. They are available in Geneva for instant call and collective consultation all hours of every day of the year. The ICRC has amassed, over more than a century, a considerable treasury of experience in humanitarian activities in time of armed conflicts. Its members speak the same language. Then can call upon numbers of devoted compatriots to act as ICRC delegates in dangerous and remote areas of the world, in circumstances of the greatest difficulty and delicacy. The ICRC is also the recipient of considerable funds placed at its disposal by the generous government of the Swiss Federation.

All of these factors constitute very solid advantages in maintaining the present structure and composition of the ICRC, as established in the statutes of 1921 and amended down to 1952. Nothing in the experiences sustained by the ICRC at the hands of the PRC can derogate from the cogency of such factors. Nevertheless, this must not inhibit a bona fide inquiry whether the existing functions of the ICRC ought not to be extended and whether such extension might not be furthered by a change in the composition and structure of that body. It may not be entirely in disregard of the existing evidence and of the pattern of contemporary international developments to suggest that the time for such changes may have arrived. These changes, introduced gradually and with caution, might take the form of "internationalizing" the ICRC by making it more truly representative of the whole Red Cross movement throughout the world. The method of electing members might be "opened" so that, through the machinery of the League, National Red Cross, etc., Societies elect the ICRC of the future. Thus each National Society might put forward two candidates upon which the Board of Governors of the League[105] might vote to fill the places on the proposed international committee with stipulated majorities. The existing "Swiss" ICRC would certainly continue to function but as a form of permanent executive committee in Geneva, answerable to the new "international" committee elected through the League. There are a number of possibilities.

What is suggested here is that such proposals might take their proper place in forthcoming international conferences of the Red Cross for discussion and resolution by Red Cross and governmental delegations there present. The work of the International Red Cross movement is far too precious to be lost in the interstices of the international power pressures of our time. At the same time, the Red Cross movement is

105. *Handbook*, pp. 327–329.

not exempt from the changes made necessary by the passage of time and the essentially dynamic and shifting character of international affairs. Sober, patient, skilled, and honest inquiry may now be timely to consider the proposals ventured, in very general terms, in this paper.

Such proposals are not the less cogent because they derive, immediately, from the harsh experience sustained by the Red Cross movement at the hands of the PRC and its National Society. Transcending all other considerations, the PRC and its National Red Cross Society are, and must remain, a vital part of the International Red Cross movement. The millions of individuals who comprise the population of the PRC are part of mankind. The International Red Cross movement, for its part, is dedicated to the proper treatment of man by man, everywhere and at all times. The solution implicit in these two situations is compelling and irresistible.

Chinese and Japanese Language Titles and Glossary

Notes on Contributors

Index

CHINESE AND JAPANESE
LANGUAGE TITLES AND GLOSSARY

Asahi shimbun 朝日新聞.

Chang Ch'ün 張羣 and Huang Shao-ku 黃少谷. *Chiang tsung-t'ung wei tzu-yu cheng-i yü ho-p'ing fen-tou shu-lüeh* 蔣總統爲自由正義與和平奮鬪述略. Taipei, Chung-yang wen-wu kung-ying-she 中央文物供應社, 1968.

Chang wen-hsiang kung ch'üan chi 張文襄公全集. Peking, Ch'u-hsüeh ching-lu 楚學精廬, 1937.

Ch'en Te-chang 岑德彰. *Ao-pen-hai kuo-chi fa* 奥本海国際法. *P'ing-shih* 平時. Shanghai, Shang-wu yin-shu-kuan 商務印書館, 1935.

——— *Ao-pen-hai kuo-chi fa. Chan-cheng yü chung-li* 奥本海國際法戰爭與中立. Shanghai, Shang-wu yin-shu-kuan, 1934.

Cheng-fa yen-chiu 政法研究.

Chiang Ching-kuo 蔣經國. *Fu-chung chih-yüan* 負重致遠. Taipei, Yu-shih shu-tien 幼獅書店, 1963.

Chiao-hsüeh yü yen-chiu 教學與研究.

Ch'iao-wu erh-shih-wu nien 僑務廿五年. Taipei, 1957.

Ch'iao-wu pao 僑務報.

Ch'ien T'ai 錢泰. *Chung-kuo pu-p'ing-teng t'iao-yüeh chih yüan-ch'i chi ch'i fei-ch'u chih ching-kuo* 中國不平等條約之緣起及其廢除之經過. Taipei, Kuo-fang yen-chiu yüan 國防研究院, 1961.

Chung-hua jen-min kung-ho-kuo fa-kuei hui-pien 中華人民共和國法規彙編. Kuo-wu-yüan fa-chih-chü 國務院法制局. Peking, Fa-lü ch'u-pan-she 法律出版社.

Chung-hua jen-min kung-ho-kuo min-fa chi-pen wen-t'i 中華人民共和國民法基本問題. Chung-yang cheng-fa kan-pu hsüeh-hsiao 中央政法幹部學校. Peking, Fa-lü ch'u-pan-she, 1958.

Chung-hua jen-min kung-ho-kuo t'iao-yüeh chi 中華人民共和國條約集. Chung-hua jen-min kung-ho-kuo wai-chiao-pu 中華人民共和國外交部. Peking, vols. I–X, Fa-lü ch'u-pan-she, 1957–1962; vols. XI–XIII, Shih-chieh chih-shih ch'u-pan-she 世界智識出版社, 1963–1965.

Chung-hua jen-min kung-ho-kuo tui-wai kuan-hsi wen-chien chi 中華人民共和國對外關係文件集. Peking, Shih-chieh chih-shih ch'u-pan-she.

Chung-hua min-kuo k'ai-kuo wu-shih-nien wen-hsien pien-chuan wei-yüan-hui 中華民國開國五十年文獻編纂委員會, ed. *Chung-hua min-kuo k'ai-kuo wu-shih-nien wen-hsien* 中華民國開國五十年文獻. *Ch'ing-ting chih kai-ke yü fan-tung* 清廷之改革與反動. Taipei, 1965.

———, ed. *Kung-fei huo-kuo shih-liao hui-pien* 共匪禍國史料彙編. Taipei, 1964.

Chung-kuo wen-t'i chih-nan 中國問題指南.

Chung-shan ch'üan-shu 中山全書. Shanghai, Ta-hua shu-chü 大華書局, 1927.

Chung-yang jih-pao 中央日報.

Hsien-tai Ying-Mei kuo-chi-fa ti ssu-hsiang tung-hsiang 現代英美國際法的思想動向. Peking, Shih-chieh chih-shih Ch'u-pan-she, 1963.

Huang Shun-ch'ing 黃純青, Lin Hsiung-hsiang 林熊祥, and Kuo Hai-ming 郭海鳴. *T'ai-wan sheng t'ung-chih kao* 臺灣省通志稿. *Kuang-fu chih* 光復志. Taipei, T'ai-wan sheng wen-hsien wei-yüan-hui 臺灣省文獻委員會, 1952.

Jen-min jih-pao 人民日報.
Jih-pen wen-t'i wen-chien chi 日本問題文件集. Peking, Shih-chieh chih-shih ch'u-pan-she.

Ko-kuo chiao-she kung-fa lun 各國交涉公法論. Shanghai, Hsiao-ts'ang shan-fang 小倉山房, 1896.
Kung-fa pien-lan 公法便覽. Peking, T'ung-wen-kuan 同文館, 1877.
Kung-tso t'ung-hsun 工作通訊.
Kuo-chi wen-t'i yen-chiu 國際問題研究.
Kuo-chia chien-she ts'ung-k'an 國家建設叢刊. *Wai-chiao yü ch'iao-wu* 外交與僑務. Taipei, Cheng-chung shu-chü 正中書局, 1971.
Kuo Chün 郭郡. *Lien-ho-kuo* 聯合國. Peking, Shih-chieh chih-shih ch'u-pan-she, 1956.
Kuo-fu i-chiao, chien-kuo ta-kang, chung-yao hsüan-yen 國父遺敎, 建國大綱, 重要宣言.

Li-fa-yüan kung-pao 立法院公報.

Nichu kankei shiryo shu 日中關係資料集.

Pao Tsun-p'eng 包遵彭, Wu Hsiang-hsiang 吳相湘, and Li Ting-i 李定一. *Chung-kuo chin-tai shih lun ts'ung* 中國近代史論叢. *Pu-p'ing-teng t'iao-yüeh yü p'ing-teng hsin-yüeh* 不平等條約與平等新約. Taipei, Cheng-chung shu-chü, 1958.

Sekai shūhō 世界週報.
Shih-chieh cheng-chih 世界政治.
Shih-chieh chih-shih 世界知識.
Shih-chieh chih-shih nien-chien 世界知識年鑑. Peking, Shih-chieh chih-shih ch'u-pan-she.
Sun Yat-sen 孫逸先. *San-min chu-i* 三民主義. Shanghai, 1928.

Ta-kung pao 大公報.
Tsu kuo 祖國.
Tung-hua hsü-lu 東華續錄.

Wan-kuo kung-fa 萬國公法. Peking, T'ung-wen-kuan, 1864.
Wang Fu-yen 汪馥炎. *Kuo-chi kung-fa lun* 國際公法論. Shanghai, Fa-hsüeh pien-i-she 法學編譯社, 1933.
Wang Shih-chieh 王世杰 and Hu Ching-yü 胡慶育. *Chung-kuo pu-p'ing-teng t'iao-yüeh chih fei-ch'u* 中國不平等條約之廢除. Taipei, Chung-yang wen-wu kung-ying-she 中央文物供應社, 1967.
Wang Yao-t'ien 汪堯田. *Kuo-chi mao-i t'iao-yüeh ho hsieh-ting* 國際貿易條約和協定. Peking, Ts'ai-cheng ching-chi ch'u-pan-she 財政經濟出版社, 1958.
Wang Yen-wei 王彥威 and Wang Liang 王亮. *Ch'ing-chi wai-chiao shih-liao* 淸季外交

史料. Peking, Ku-kung po-wu-yüan 政宮博物院, 1935.
Wen-t'i yü yen-chiu 問題與研究.
Wu K'un-wu 吳昆吾. *T'iao-yüeh lun* 條約論. Shanghai, Shang-wu yin-shu-kuan, 1933.

Yin-tu hua-ch'iao chih 印度華僑志.

GLOSSARY

Chung-Jih mao-i hsieh-ting 中日貿易協定.
Jih-pen fang-hua t'ung-shang shih-chieh t'uan 日本訪華通商使節團.
Nichu boeki kyotei 日中貿易協定.
tu-li ti-wei 獨立地位.

NOTES ON CONTRIBUTORS

Philippe Ardant, currently cultural counsellor at the French Embassy in Morocco, is professor at the University of Paris—Nanterre and author of *L'Administration Chinoise* (Berger-Levrault, Paris, 1968).

Hungdah Chiu, professor of international law (on leave) at National Chengchi University in the Republic of China and research associate at the Harvard Law School, is author of *The Capacity of International Organizations to Conclude Treaties* (Nijhoff, 1966), *The People's Republic of China and the Law of Treaties* (Harvard University Press, 1972), co-editor of *Agreements of the People's Republic of China, 1949–1967: A Calendar* (Harvard University Press, 1968), and *Law in Chinese Foreign Policy* (Oceana, 1972).

Jerome Alan Cohen is professor of law and director of East Asian legal studies at Harvard Law School. He is the author and editor of many books on China and served as chairman of the panel on China and World Order of the ASIL.

Colonel G. I. A. D. Draper, O. B. E., LL.B., LL.M., is reader in charge of law studies at the University of Sussex, barrister-at-law of the Honourable Society of the Inner Temple, consultant to the secretary-general of the United Nations and to the International Committee of the Red Cross, Geneva. He is author of *The Red Cross Conventions* (Stevens and Praeger, 1958), and *Civilians and the NATO Status of Forces Agreement* (Sijthoff, Leyden, 1966).

George Ginsburgs is professor and chairman of the Department of Political Science, Graduate Faculty, New School for Social Research, New York. He is the author of *Soviet Citizenship Law* (Sijthoff, Leyden, 1968) and co-author, with M. Mathos, of *Communist China and Tibet: The First Dozen Years* (Nijhoff, The Hague, 1964).

Gene T. Hsiao is professor of government and director of Asian Studies at Southern Illinois University, Edwardsville. He has written extensively on the foreign trade law of the People's Republic of China and is author of a forthcoming book on *Legal Aspects of China's Foreign Trade.*

James C. Hsiung, associate professor of politics at New York University, is author of *Ideology and Practice: The Evolution of Chinese Communism* (Praeger, 1970), and *Law and Policy in China's Foreign Relations* (Columbia University Press, 1972). He directs the Politics Department and the East Asian Studies Program at Washington Square College, New York University.

Ko Swan Sik is head of the Department of Public International Law, Inter-University Institute of International Law (T. M. C. Asser Instituut), The Hague, and general editor of the *Netherlands Yearbook of International Law*. He is a former reader in public international law at the University of Indonesia, Djakarta, and author of a standard work on multiple nationality (in Dutch, Sijthoff, 1957).

Shao-chuan Leng, Doherty Foundation Professor of Government and Foreign Affairs at the University of Virginia, is author of *Japan and Communist China* (Institute of Pacific Relations, 1959), *Sun Yat-sen and Communism* (with N. D. Palmer; Praeger, 1961), and *Justice in Communist China: A Survey of the Judicial System of the Chinese People's Republic* (Oceana, 1967), and editor of *Law in Chinese Foreign Policy* (with Hungdah Chiu; Oceana, 1972).

Carl Pinkele teaches political science at the University of Wisconsin, Oshkosh.

Gilbert P. Verbit is associate professor of law at the Faculty of Law, Boston University.

Byron S. J. Weng, assistant professor of political science, Wright State University, Dayton, Ohio, is the author of *Peking's UN Policy: Continuity and Change* (Praeger, 1972).

Index

Harvard Studies in East Asian Law

1. *Law in Imperial China: Exemplified by 190 Ch'ing Dynasty Cases (translated from the* Hsing-an hui-lan) *with Historical, Social, and Juridical Commentaries.* By Derk Bodde and Clarence Morris. 1967

2. *The Criminal Process in the People's Republic of China, 1949–1963: An Introduction.* By Jerome Alan Cohen. 1968

3. *Agreements of the People's Republic of China, 1949–1967: A Calendar.* By Douglas M. Johnston and Hungdah Chiu. 1968

4. *Contemporary Chinese Law: Research Problems and Perspectives.* Edited by Jerome Alan Cohen. 1970

5. *The People's Republic of China and the Law of Treaties.* By Hungdah Chiu. 1972

6. *China's Practice of International Law: Some Case Studies.* Edited by Jerome Alan Cohen. 1972

Bei Fragen zur Produktsicherheit wenden Sie sich bitte an:
If you have any questions regarding product safety,
please contact:

Walter de Gruyter GmbH
Genthiner Straße 13
10785 Berlin
productsafety@degruyterbrill.com